Performance

Performance: a critical introduction was the first textbook to provide an overview of the modern concept of performance and its development in various related fields. This comprehensively revised, illustrated edition discusses recent performance work and takes into consideration changes that have taken place in the study of performance since the book's original publication in 1996. Marvin Carlson guides the reader through the contested definition of performance as a theatrical activity and the myriad ways in which performance has been interpreted by ethnographers, anthropologists, linguists, and cultural theorists. Topics covered include:

- the evolution of performance art since the 1960s
- the relationship between performance, postmodernism, the politics of identity, and current cultural studies
- the recent theoretical developments in the study of performance in the fields of anthropology, psychoanalysis, linguistics, and technology.

With a fully updated bibliography and additional glossary of terms, students of performance studies, visual and performing arts or theatre history will welcome this new version of a classic text.

Marvin Carlson is the Sidney E. Cohn Professor of Theatre and Comparative Literature at the Graduate Center of the City University of New York. He has received the ATHE Career Achievement Award, the George Jean Nathan Award for Dramatic Criticism, the Calloway Prize and the ASTR Distinguished Scholarship Award. He has published widely in theatre history and theory, performance studies, and dramatic literature.

Performance

A critical introduction

Marvin Carlson

Second Edition

Routledge
Taylor & Francis Group

NEW YORK AND LONDON

First published 1996
This second edition published 2004
Simultaneously published in the UK, USA and Canada
by Routledge
270 Madison Ave, New York, NY 10016
and Routledge
2 Park Square, Milton Park, Abingdon, Oxon, OX14 4RN

Reprinted 2006, 2007 (twice), 2008, 2009 (twice), 2010

Routledge is an imprint of the Taylor & Francis Group, an informa business

Typeset in Palatino by Wearset Ltd, Boldon, Tyne and Wear,
England
Printed and bound in Great Britain by TJ International, Padstow,
Cornwall

Library of Congress Cataloging in Publication Data
Carlson, Marvin A., 1935–
    Performance: a critical introduction / Marvin Albert Carlson.—
2nd ed.
        p. cm.
Includes bibliographical references and index.
1. Performance art—United States. 2. Arts, American—20th
century. 3. Performance art. 4. Arts, Modern—20th century.
I. Title.
    NX504.C35 2003
    700'.973'09045—dc21   2003007508

British Library Cataloguing in Publication Data
A catalogue record for this book is available from the British
Library

ISBN10: 0–415–29926–8 (hbk)
ISBN10: 0–415–29927–6 (pbk)

ISBN13: 978–0–415–29926–8 (hbk)
ISBN13: 978–0–415–29927–5 (pbk)

Contents

Illustrations

Preface

When the first edition of this work was published seven years ago, performance had already emerged not only as a particular new orientation within the world of theatrical presentation, but also as a significant critical metaphor within contemporary culture at large. During the intervening years significant changes have taken place in both the microcosm of performance art and the macrocosm of social and cultural performance in general. The fairly clear division between traditional theatre and performance art that once existed has today largely disappeared, as techniques and concerns once primarily associated with one or the other have been developed and exchanged between them, in the inevitable continuing exploration of new means that has always characterized performative activity. A growing interest in and utilization of technology and modern media in both theatre and performance art has further blurred the boundaries between these performative activities.

On the larger cultural level, "performance" has continued to develop as a central metaphor and critical tool for a bewildering variety of studies, covering almost every aspect of human activity. Performance discourse and its close theoretical partner, "performativity," today dominate critical discourse not only in all manner of cultural studies, but also in business, economics, and technology. The rise of an interest in performance reflects a major shift in many cultural fields from the what of culture to the how, from the accumulation of social, cultural, psychological, political, or linguistic data to a consideration of how this material is created, valorized, and changed, to how it lives and operates within the culture, by its actions. Its real meaning is now sought in its praxis, its performance. Moreover, the fact that performance is associated not just with doing but also with re-doing is important—its embodiment of the tension between a given form or content from the past and the inevitable adjustments of an ever-changing present make it an operation of particular interest at a time of widespread interest in cultural negotiations—how human patterns of activity are reinforced or changed within a culture and how they are adjusted when various different cultures interact. Performance implies not just doing or even re-doing, but a self-consciousness about doing and re-doing on the part of both performers and spectators, an implication of great interest to our highly self-conscious society.

The present book seeks, as did its earlier version, to place these developments in a general artistic and cultural context, to suggest their historical development and their present and future implications. The rapid expansion of performance discourse, especially in the area of culture studies, has required an extensive reworking of sections of this book in order to provide as comprehensive and as clear a discussion as possible of the current state of performance studies.

Acknowledgments

The colleagues, friends, and artists who have provided information, suggestions, and inspiration for this book are far too numerous to list here, but my gratitude to them is nevertheless beyond measure. I must, however, single out for special thanks Jill Dolan, Joseph Roach, and Richard Schechner, whose own work in this field as well as whose friendship and suggestions have been a constant source of inspiration and pleasure. Particular thanks must also go to my editor at Routledge, Talia Rodgers, who encouraged me to undertake this complex project in the first place and who has been absolutely unflagging in her support and encouragement. Her support not only of this project, but also of the entire field of performance studies, will be suggested by the many titles from Routledge that I have drawn upon both in the first and second editions of this work. Finally, my warmest thanks to Joshua Abrams, whose aid in the preparation of this second edition was invaluable.

What is performance?

The term "performance" has become extremely popular in recent years in a wide range of activities in the arts, in literature, and in the social sciences. As its popularity and usage have grown so has a complex body of writing about performance, attempting to analyze and understand just what sort of human activity it is. For the person with an interest in studying performance, this body of analysis and commentary may at first seem more of an obstacle than an aid. So much has been written by experts in such a wide range of disciplines, and such a complex web of specialized critical vocabulary has been developed in the course of this analysis, that a newcomer seeking a way into the discussion may feel confused and overwhelmed. Yup.

In their very useful 1990 survey article "Research in Interpretation and Performance Studies: Trends, Issues, Priorities," Mary Strine, Beverly Long and Mary Hopkins begin with the extremely useful observation that performance is "an essentially contested concept." This phrase is taken from W.B. Gallie's *Philosophy and the Historical Understanding* (1964), in which Gallie suggested that certain concepts, such as art and democracy, had disagreement about their essence built into the concept itself. In Gallie's terms: "Recognition of a given concept as essentially contested implies recognition of rival uses of it (such as oneself repudiates) as not only logically possible and humanly 'likely,' but as of permanent potential critical value to one's own use or interpretation of the concept in question."[1] Strine, Long, and Hopkins argue that performance has become just such a concept, developed in an atmosphere of "sophisticated disagreement" by participants who "do not expect to defeat or silence opposing positions, but rather through continuing dialogue to attain a sharper articulation of all positions and therefore a fuller understanding of the conceptual richness of performance."[2] In his study of the "post-structured stage," Erik MacDonald suggests that "performance art has opened hitherto unnoticed spaces" within theatre's representational networks. It "problematizes its own categorization," and thus inevitably inserts theoretical speculation into the theatrical dynamic.[3]

The aims of this book

The present study, recognizing this essential contestedness of performance, will seek to provide an introduction to the continuing dialogue through which it has recently been articulated, providing a variety of mappings of the concept, some overlapping, others quite divergent. Recent manifestations of performance, in both theory and practice, are so many and so varied that a complete survey of them is hardly possible, but this book will attempt to offer enough of an overview and historical background to suggest the major approaches and sample significant manifestations in this complex field, to suggest what sort of issues are raised by the contested concept of performance and what sorts of theatrical and theoretical strategies have been developed to deal with these issues.

My own background is in theatre studies, and my emphasis will be on how ideas about performance and theories about performance have broadened and enriched those areas of human activity that lie closest to what has traditionally been thought of as theatrical, even though I will not be devoting a great deal of attention to traditional theatre as such, but rather to that variety of activities currently being presented for audiences under the general title of "performance" or "performance art." Nevertheless in these opening remarks it might be useful to step back at least briefly from this emphasis and consider the more general use of the term "performance" in our culture, to gain some idea of the general semantic overtones it may bear as it circulates through an enormous variety of specialized usages. I should perhaps also note that although I will include examples of performance art from other nations my emphasis will remain on the United States, partly of course because that is the center of my own experience with this activity, but more relevantly because, despite its international diffusion, performance art is both historically and theoretically a primarily American phenomenon, and a proper understanding of it must, I believe, be centered on how it has developed both practically and conceptually in the United States.

The display of skills

"Performing" and "performance" are terms so often encountered in such varied contexts that little if any common semantic ground seems to exist among them. Both the *New York Times* and the *Village Voice* now include a special category of "performance," separate from theatre, dance, or films, including events that are also often called "performance art" or even "performance theatre." For many this latter term seems tautological, since in simpler days all theatre was considered to be involved with performance, theatre being in fact one of the so-called "performing arts." This usage is still much with us, as indeed is the practice of calling any specific theatre events (or for that matter specific dance or musical events) "performances." If we mentally step back a moment from this common practice to ask what makes performing arts performative, I imagine the answer would somehow suggest that these arts require the physical presence of trained or skilled human beings whose demonstration of their skill is the performance.

I recently came across a striking illustration of how important the idea of the public display of technical skill is to this traditional concept of "performance." At a number of locations in the United States and abroad, people in period costume act out improvised or scripted events in historical buildings or villages for tourists, visiting schoolchildren, or other interested spectators—a kind of activity often called "living history." One site of such activity is Fort Ross in Northern California, where a husband and wife, dressed in costumes of the 1830s, greet visitors in the role of the last Russian commander of the fort and his wife. The wife, Diane Spencer Pritchard, in her role of "Elena Rotcheva," decided at one time to play period music on the piano to give visitors an impression of the cultural life of the period, but later she abandoned this, feeling (in her words) that it "removed the role from living-history and placed it in the category of performance."[4] Despite taking on a fictive personality, dressing in period clothes, and "living" in the 1830s, Ms Pritchard did not consider herself to be "performing" until she displayed the particular artistic skills needed to give a musical recital. Normally human agency is necessary for "performance" of this sort (even in the theatre we do not speak of how well the scenery or the costumes performed), but the public demonstration of particular skills is the important thing. These skills need not be human, as can be seen in such familiar expressions as performing dogs, elephants, horses, or bears.[5]

Patterned behavior

Despite the currency of this usage, most of her audience probably considers Ms Pritchard to be performing as soon as she greets them in the costume and character of a long-dead Russian pioneer. The pretending to be someone other than oneself is a common example of a particular kind of human behavior to which Richard Schechner has given the title "restored behavior," under which title he groups any behavior consciously separated from the person doing it—theatre and other role-playing, trances, shamanism, rituals.[6] Schechner's useful concept of "restored behavior" points to a quality of performance *not* involved with the display of skills but rather with a certain distance between "self" and behavior, analogous to that between an actor and the role this actor plays on stage. Even if an action on stage is identical to one in real life, on stage it is considered "performed" and off stage merely "done." In his well-known response to the Queen, Hamlet distinguishes between those inner feelings that resist performance and the "actions that a man might play" with a consciousness of their signifying potential. Although the common usage of the term "performance" in the theatre (Olivier's performance of Hamlet, or the performance of a play on some particular evening) might at first glance seem to be derived from the association with technical skill, I think in fact it is based more upon this doubled, repeated, or restored quality of the action. David Román, discussing the shades of meaning in a number of "keywords" in the theatre, makes a useful distinction between "performance" and production: "A performance stands in and of itself as an event; it is part of the process of production. A performance is not an entity that exists atemporally for the spectator; rather, the spectator intersects in a trajectory of continuous production. A production is generally composed of a series of performances."[7] Although, as Román notes, these performance are never the same, they are nevertheless consciously repeated copies, and even their deviations are part of the dynamic of "restored behavior."

Hamlet's response also indicates how a consciousness of "performance" can move from the stage, from ritual, or from other special and clearly defined cultural situations, into everyday life. Everyone at some time or another is conscious of "playing a role" socially, and recent sociological theory, which will be discussed in some detail in the second chapter of this book, has paid a good deal of attention to this sort of social performance. The recognition that our lives are structured according to repeated and socially sanctioned modes of behavior raises the possibility that all human activity could potentially be considered as performance, or at least all activity carried out with a consciousness of itself. The difference between doing and performing, according to this way of thinking, would seem to lie not in the frame of theatre versus real life but in an attitude—we may do actions unthinkingly, but when we think about them, this brings in a consciousness that gives them the quality of performance. This phenomenon has been perhaps most searchingly analyzed in various writings of Herbert Blau, to which also we will return later.

Keeping up the standard

So we have two rather different concepts of performance; one involving the display of skills, the other also involving display, but less of particular skills than of a recognized and culturally coded pattern of behavior. A third cluster of usages takes us in rather a different direction. When we speak of someone's sexual performance or linguistic performance, or when we ask how well a child is performing in school, the emphasis is not so much on display of skill (although that may be involved) or on the carrying out of a particular pattern of behavior, but rather on the general success of the activity in light of some standard of achievement which may not itself be precisely articulated. Perhaps even more significantly, the task of judging the success of the performance (or even judging whether it *is* a performance) is in these cases not the responsibility of the performer but of the observer. Ultimately Hamlet himself is the best judge of whether he is "performing" his melancholy actions or truly "living" them, but linguistic, scholastic, even sexual performance is really framed and judged by its observers. This is why performance in this sense (as opposed to performance in the normal theatrical sense) can be and is applied frequently to non-human activity—TV ads speak interminably of the performance of various brands of automobiles, scientists of the performance of chemicals or metals under certain conditions. I observed an amusing conflation of the theatrical and mechanical uses of this term in an advertisement on the New York subway in October of 1994, when the subway was celebrating ninety years of service. This was billed as "New York City's longest running performance."

Viewing performance as an essentially contested concept warns us against seeking some over-arching semantic field to cover such seemingly disparate usages as the performance of an actor, of a schoolchild, of an automobile. Nevertheless, I would like to credit one highly suggestive attempt at such an articulation. This occurs in the entry on performance by the ethnolinguist Richard Bauman in the *International Encyclopedia of Communications*. According to Bauman, all performance involves a consciousness of doubleness, according to which the actual execution of an action is placed in mental comparison with a potential, an ideal, or a remembered original model of that action. Normally this comparison is made by an observer of the action—the theatre public, the school's teacher, the scientist—but the double consciousness, not the external observation, is what is most central. An athlete, for example, may be aware of his own performance, placing it against a mental standard. Performance is always performance *for* someone, some audience that recognizes and validates it as performance even when, as is occasionally the case, that audience is the self.

When we consider the various kinds of activity that are referred to on the modern cultural scene as performance or performance art, these are much better understood in relation to this over-arching semantic field than to the more traditional orientation suggested by the piano-playing Ms Pritchard, who felt that so long as she was not displaying a virtuosic skill she could not be "performing." Some modern "performance" is centrally concerned with such skills (as in the acts of some of the clowns and jugglers included among the so-called "new vaudevillians"), but much more central to this phenomenon is the sense of an action carried out *for* someone, an action involved in the peculiar doubling that comes with consciousness and with the elusive other that performance is not but which it constantly struggles in vain to embody.

Theatre and performance art

Although traditional theatre has regarded this "other" as a character in a dramatic action, embodied (through performance) by an actor, modern performance art has, in general, not been centrally concerned with this dynamic. Its practitioners, almost by definition, do not base their work upon characters previously created by other artists, but upon their own bodies, their own autobiographies, their own specific experiences in a culture or in the world, made performative by their consciousness of them and the process of displaying them for audiences. Since the emphasis is upon the performance, and on how the body or self is articulated through performance, the individual body remains at the center of such presentations. Typical performance art is solo art, and the typical performance artist uses little of the elaborate scenic surroundings of the traditional stage, but at most a few props, a bit of furniture, and whatever costume (sometimes even nudity) is most suitable to the performance situation.

It is not surprising that such performance has become a highly visible, one might almost say emblematic, art form in the contemporary world—a world that is highly self-conscious, reflexive, obsessed with simulations and theatricalizations in every aspect of its social awareness. With performance as a kind of critical wedge, the metaphor of theatricality has moved out of the arts into almost every aspect of modern attempts to understand our condition and activities, into every branch of the human sciences—sociology, anthropology, ethnography, psychology, linguistics. And as performativity and theatricality have been developed in these fields, both as metaphors and as analytic tools, theorists and practitioners of performance art have in turn become aware of these developments and found in them new sources of stimulation, inspiration, and insight for their own creative work and the theoretical understanding of it.

Performance art, a complex and constantly shifting field in its own right, becomes much more so when one tries to take into account, as any thoughtful consideration of it must do, the dense web of interconnections that exist between it and ideas of performance developed in other fields and between it and the many intellectual, cultural, and social currents that condition any performance project today. These include what it means to be postmodern, the quest for a contemporary subjectivity and identity, the relation of art to structures of power, the varying challenges of gender, race, and ethnicity, to name only some of the most visible.

The plan of this book

This book attempts, in an admittedly brief way, to provide an introduction to this complex field of activity and thought. The three opening chapters seek to provide a general intellectual background and context for the modern idea of performance by tracing the interrelated development of this concept in the various modern human sciences—first in anthropology and ethnography, then in sociology and psychology, and finally in linguistics. As performance studies has developed as a particular field of scholarly work, especially in the United States, it has been very closely associated with the various social sciences, and a complex and interesting cross-fertilization has been the result. The study of traditional "artistic" performance such as theatre and dance has taken on new dimensions and begun to explore newly observed relationships between these and other cultural and social activities, while the various social sciences have found theatre and performance metaphors of great use in exploring particular kinds of human activities within their own fields of study. While the actual practice of modern performance art is most closely related to concerns in sociology and psychology, its theory and certain of its strategies relate importantly to anthropological and ethnographic interests. Linguistic theories of performance have to date proven of greater interest to theorists of traditional theatre than to those of performance art, but the implications of, for example, Derrida's critique of Searle offer intriguing possibilities for the analysis of performance art as well—especially, of course, in those examples of performance involved with linguistic strategies.

The middle section of this study consists of two chapters devoted to the background and recent history of what has come to be called performance art (or sometimes simply performance), with special emphasis upon its development in the contemporary United States. The first of these chapters looks backward to suggest some of the historical antecedents of this major contemporary cultural expression, and the second traces the historical development of modern performance from its appearance at the end of the 1960s to the most recent manifestations. While these two chapters contain some theoretical material they are primarily historical and descriptive, attempting to give some idea of just what sort of work has been associated with the idea of performance in the United States and elsewhere, and how it is related to and differs from more traditional theatrical forms.

An impressive body of theoretical writing has grown up around performance art, and the third section of the book examines, in different chapters, three of the major orientations of such writing. The first of these theoretical chapters deals with the relationships between performance and postmodernism, terms often rather casually linked in critical discourse, but in fact related to each other in very complex and occasionally quite contradictory ways. Postmodern dance, a particularly illuminating area for the study of the relationship of performance and postmodernism, is given particular attention in this chapter. The next chapter explores the relationship between performance and identity, a relationship that is in many ways central to how modern performance has developed and been theorized, particularly in the United States. These two chapters have certain dialectic implications, since the frequent associations of the postmodern with a loss of origins, a free play of signification, and an instability of truth claims seems to suggest that to the extent that performance is a significantly postmodern form it is very ill-suited to the grounding of subjectivity or identity, either for purposes of defining or exploring the self or for providing a position for political or social commentary or action. The final chapter explores this seeming contradiction in a more detailed manner, looking at the theory and practice of performance that seeks within the general assumptions of a postmodern orientation to find strategies of meaningful social, political, and cultural positioning—arguably the most critical challenge confronting performance today, and certainly the site where the most lively and interesting discussion of performance is now taking place.

Part I

Performance and the social sciences

Chapter 1

The performance of culture
Anthropological and ethnographic approaches

The term "performance," as it is encountered, for example, in departments or programs of "performance studies" in the United States today, is heavily indebted to terminology and theoretical strategies developed during the 1960s and 1970s in the social sciences, and particularly in anthropology and sociology. Especially important in making connections across the boundaries of traditional theatre studies, anthropology, and sociology have been the writings of Richard Schechner, coming from a theatre background, the anthropologists Victor Turner and Dwight Conquergood, and the sociologist Erving Goffman. For persons involved in theatre studies, a major statement of these converging interests appeared in the fall of 1973, in a special issue of *The Drama Review* devoted to "Theatre and the Social Sciences." In the introduction to that issue, guest editor Richard Schechner listed seven "areas where performance theory and the social sciences coincide." These were:[1]

1   Performance in everyday life, including gatherings of every kind.
2   The structure of sports, ritual, play, and public political behaviors.
3   Analysis of various modes of communication (other than the written word); semiotics.
4   Connections between human and animal behavior patterns with an emphasis on play and ritualized behavior.
5   Aspects of psychotherapy that emphasize person-to-person interaction, acting out, and body awareness.
6   Ethnography and prehistory—of both exotic and familiar cultures.
7   Constitution of unified theories of performance, which are, in fact, theories of behavior.

Schechner's listing is somewhat reminiscent of a similar attempt to suggest future areas of research between theatre and the social sciences published in 1956 by Georges Gurvitch to summarize the proceedings of a French conference on the subject. Anticipating the subsequent research of scholars like Goffman and Turner, Gurvitch called attention to the theatrical or performance elements in all social ceremonies, even in "a simple reception or a gathering of friends."[2]

Both of these lists outline a rather broader field than the main line of research has in fact followed, but each may be considered as a whole remarkably prescient about a significant part of modern performance study. Indeed, an understanding of contemporary usage of the term performance can probably most usefully begin with an overview of the most influential and relevant writings on the subject in anthropology and sociology. Accordingly, we shall consider in this chapter the issues and concerns surrounding performance in recent anthropological writing, and in the following chapter we will turn to sociology. The hope, in outlining developments in both fields, is by no means to provide a general introduction to recent anthropological or sociological theory, but rather to introduce the specific aspects of that theory that have contributed to current thinking about performance, both in theory and in practice.

Performance and anthropology

The field of anthropology has been a particularly rich source for the discussion of performance in recent years. Indeed, it has become so attractive a subject in that field that some anthropologists have expressed concern about its ubiquity. Dell Hymes, for example, has complained that: "If some grammarians have confused matters by lumping what does not interest them under 'performance,' cultural anthropologists and folklorists have not done much to clarify the situation. We have tended to lump what *does* interest us under 'performance.' "[3]

Hymes makes an attempt to confine the sprawling field of what is lumped under "performance" by contrasting it with two activity categories often confused with it: behavior and conduct. The first refers simply to "anything and everything that happens," the second to behavior "under the aegis of social norms, cultural rules, shared principles of interpretability." Clearly conduct is a certain subset of behavior, and performance Hymes defines as a further subset within conduct, in which one or more persons "assume a responsibility to an audience and to tradition as they understand it." Yet, in keeping with the essentially contested nature of performance, even this rather specific articulation raises as many problems as it solves, particularly in what is meant by "assuming responsibility." The audience certainly plays a key role in most attempts to define performance, especially in those attempts to separate performance from other behavior, but just how the performer is "responsible" to them has itself been the subject of much debate.

Even more problematic is the idea of responsibility to tradition. There is widespread agreement among performance theorists that all performance is based upon some pre-existing model, script, or pattern of action. Richard Schechner, in a happy and widely quoted phrase, calls performance "restored behavior."[4] John MacAloon has similarly asserted that "there is no performance without pre-formance."[5] On the other hand, much of the recent anthropological analysis of performance has laid special stress on how performance can work within a society precisely to undermine tradition, to provide a site for the exploration of fresh and alternative structures and patterns of behavior. Whether performance within a culture serves most importantly to reinforce the assumptions of that culture or to provide a possible site of alternative assumptions is an ongoing debate that provides a particularly clear example of the contested quality of performance analysis.

Precisely what performance accomplishes and how it accomplishes this can clearly be approached in a variety of ways, although there has been general agreement that within every culture there can be discovered a certain kind of activity, set apart from other activities by space, time, attitude, or all three, that can be spoken of and analyzed as performance. Folklore studies has been one of the areas of anthropology and cultural studies that has contributed most significantly to modern concepts of performance study, and one of the first anthropological theorists to utilize "performance" as a central critical term, William H. Jansen, employed it to deal with a major concern of the 1950s in folklore studies, that is, classification. Jansen suggested a classification model with performance and participation as two ends of a spectrum, based primarily upon the degree of involvement of the "audience" of the event.[6]

Theories of cultural performance

The term "cultural performance," now widely found in anthropological and ethnographic writing, was coined by Milton Singer in an introduction to a collection of essays on Indian culture that he edited in 1959. Here Singer suggested that the culture content of a tradition was transmitted by specific cultural media as well as by human carriers, and that a study of the operations of such media on particular occasions could provide anthropology with "a particularization of the structure of tradition complementary to the social organization."[7] South Asians, and perhaps all peoples, Singer argued, thought of their culture as encapsulated in discrete events, "cultural performances," which could be exhibited to themselves and others and which provided the "most concrete observable units of the cultural structure." Among these "performances" Singer listed traditional theatre and dance, but also concerts, recitations, religious festivals, weddings, and so on. All such performances possessed certain features: "a definitely limited time span, a beginning and an end, an organized program of activity, a set of performers, an audience, and a place and occasion of performance."[8] If one were to substitute "a script" for Singer's "organized program of activity," then these distinctive features of cultural performance could as easily be describing the traditional concept of theatre, and Singer's approach and his influence has unquestionably contributed significantly to the convergence of anthropological and theatrical theory in the area of performance from the early 1970s onward. His "features" of performance, especially their emphasis on performance as "set apart" in time, place, and occasion, find countless echoes in subsequent research, and his view of performance as a discrete concretization of cultural assumptions significantly contributed to what might be catagorized as the conservative interpretation of performance's role in culture.

During the next decade, the relationship between culture and performance became a matter of increasing concern in both folklore studies and general anthropology. Between his two surveys of the former field in 1963 and 1972 Richard M. Dorson noted the rise of a new orientation, which he called a "contextual approach" to folklore research.[9] The emphasis of such an approach shifts from the text to its function as a performative and communicative act in a particular cultural situation, and has looked to the field of sociolinguistics for much of its theory and methodology. Dell Hymes has characterized this blending of communication models and cultural placement as a new "ethnography of communication,"[10] and Dan Ben-Amos and Kenneth S. Goldstein, in their introduction to a 1975 collection of essays on folklore, suggest that the new emphasis falls not upon "the entire network of culturally defined communicative events, but upon these situations in which the relationship of performance obtains between speakers and listeners."[11]

Kenneth Burke

In their analysis of the component elements of this relationship, contextual folklorists began to converge with performance analysts in other fields. A common source for a number of these was the writings of Kenneth Burke, especially for those contextualists who began to consider the rhetorical function of folkloric performance. Roger Abrahams, for example, in advancing a "rhetorical theory of folklore," claimed that "performance is a way of persuading through the production of pleasure," and specifically recommended Burke as a source of analytic strategies.[12] Burke has perhaps been even more influential among performatively oriented sociologists than among anthropologists, but his interest in language and thought as "situated modes of action" and his pragmatic assertion that "every text is a strategy for encompassing a situation,"[13] were clearly extremely useful concepts for these contextual theorists. Burke's central utilization in his rhetorical analysis of a whole set of theatrical metaphors further emphasized for anthropological theory that aspect of the performative situation, but his model of action was even more influential in sociological theory, and it will be considered in more detail later when we turn to that tradition.

A shift in attention from the folkloric text to the performative context involved, as in Burke, a shift from traditional content to the more "rhetorical" study of means and techniques. In a 1986 study of oral narrative, Richard Bauman attempted to define the "essence" of performance in terms that clearly echoed the earlier formulations of Hymes, but equally clearly incorporated this new orientation. The definition began with a paraphrase of Hymes: "the assumption of responsibility to an audience for a display of communicative skill," but, significantly, continued "highlighting the way in which communication is carried out, *above and beyond its referential content*" (emphasis mine).[14] In an earlier study of verbal performance, Bauman suggested that performance was "marked as subject to evaluation for the way it is done, for the relative skill and effectiveness of the performer's display," and also "marked as available for the enhancement of experience, through the present enjoyment of the intrinsic qualities of the act of expression itself."[15]

Despite their apparent emphasis upon the "how" of performance, Hymes and Bauman remain firmly "contextual," giving much more attention to the total performance situation than to the specific activities of the performer. Yet another "essentially contested" aspect of performance involves the question of to what extent performance itself results from something the performer does and to what extent it results from a particular context in which it is done. When Bauman speaks of performance as being "marked" in order to be interpreted in a particular way, he is assuming, as most anthropological theorists have done, that it is this "marking" that permits a culture to experience performance *as* performance. The operations of this "marking" have been a particular concern of Gregory Bateson, whose writings, especially the 1954 essay "A Theory of Play and Fantasy", have provided several extremely important concepts and terms to performance theory. Bateson is concerned with how living organisms distinguish between "seriousness" and "play." In order for play to exist (and Bateson cites examples of it among animals and birds as well as humans) the "playing" organisms must be "capable of some degree of metacommunication," to signal to each other that their mutual interactions are not to be taken "seriously."[16] For the metacommunicative message "This is play" to operate, some mental operation must establish what is and is not included in "this." In Bateson's words, "every metacommunicative message is or defines a psychological frame" within which is contained the total subject of that message.[17] These closely related concerns of metacommunication and psychological framing have been of great importance in later thinking about performance, even though the conflation of "performance" and "play" raises problems of its own, to which we will later return. Anthropological and folklore theorists, as well as psychological and sociological theorists (in particular Erving Goffman) have built upon these ideas to develop a view of performance that owes more to context and to the dynamics of reception than to the specific activities of the performer.

Victor Turner

During the 1960s and 1970s, the developing interest among anthropologists in social context and play encouraged an interest in analytical models drawn from theatre and drama. Probably the most important contributor to this orientation was Victor Turner, beginning in the late 1950s with his *Schism and Continuity*. In this study of the Ndembu people, Turner first set forward the concept of "social drama" as a tool for social anthropologists.

Turner's "social drama," like Singer's "cultural performance," developed a model from the specific cultural form of theatre to apply to the analysis of a far larger body of cultural manifestations, though Singer's model drew more directly upon the performance situation of theatre and Turner's upon traditional structures of dramatic action. Thus Turner's concept is defined not by the situation of its enactment (its "frame" or marking), or by its particular physical dynamics (the focus of Barba), but by its organizational structure.

As Turner explains at some length in his *From Ritual to Theatre*, his concept of social drama was based upon the early twentieth-century work of Arnold van Gennep, especially on his 1908 classic *Rites de passage*. Van Gennep was interested in developing a model to analyze the organization of ritual as it governed the transition of individuals or whole societies from one social situation to another. He concentrated on ceremonies by which individuals passed from one role within their society to another, and the term "rites of passage" has become commonly associated with this process, especially with the puberty rites marking the change from child to adult. Turner points out, however, that van Gennep originally spoke of rites of passage as including any ceremony marking individual or social change—from peace to war, from plague to health, even regularly repeated calendrical or seasonal changes—and it is this more general type of transition that Turner seeks to analyze. Turner's intellectual debt to van Gennep has had major implications for subsequent performance theory. Despite their very different orientations, Singer, Hymes, Bauman, and Barba all generally view performance as an activity somehow "set apart" from that of everyday life, an orientation also of the "play" theorists we will consider presently. Turner, looking to van Gennep's rites of passage, emphasizes not so much the "set-apartness" of performance but its "in-betweenness," its function as transition between two states of more settled or more conventional cultural activity. This image of performance as a border, a margin, a site of negotiation has become extremely important in subsequent thinking about such activity; indeed, in the opening address to the first annual conference on Performance Studies, held in New York in the spring of 1995, Dwight Conquergood cited performance's location on the borders and margins as that which most clearly distinguished it from traditional disciplines and fields of study, concerned with establishing a center for their activity.[18]

Van Gennep suggested that rites of passage normally involved three steps, with particular types of rite involved in each: rites of separation from an established social role or order, threshold or liminal rites performed in the transitional space between roles or orders, and rites of reincorporation into an established order.[19] Van Gennep's terms are *rites de séparation, marge* or *limen*, and *agrégation*, translated by Turner as "separation, transition, and incorporation," but Turner also makes important and original use of M.B. Vizedon and G.L. Caffee's "preliminal, liminal, and postliminal."

The use of drama as a metaphor for non-theatrical cultural manifestations continued to mark Turner's work as he studied a wider variety of cultural manifestations. In his 1974 *Dramas, Fields, and Metaphors*, he explained how in his early attempts to analyze social activities among the Ndembu he combined the process-based structure of van Gennep with a metaphorical model derived from the cultural form of the stage drama,[20] and then subsequently expanded this analytic strategy from the village level of the Ndembu to complex sequences of events on the national level—such as the conflict between Henry II of England and Thomas à Becket, or the Hidalgo Insurrection in early nineteenth-century Mexico. In each of these "social dramas" Turner traced the same pattern: first a breach in an established and accepted norm (corresponding to van Gennep's separation), then a mounting crisis as factions are formed, followed by a process of redress, as formal and informal mechanisms of crisis resolution are employed (these two phases corresponding to van Gennep's transition), and finally a reintegration, very likely involving an adjustment of the original cultural situation (corresponding to van Gennep's reincorporation) or, alternatively, a recognition of the permanence of the schism.

Richard Schechner

No theatre theorist has been more instrumental in developing modern performance theory or for exploring the relationships between practical and theoretical work in theatre research and in social science research than Richard Schechner, and the interrelationship between Schechner and Turner was a particularly fruitful one. When Schechner in 1966 first called for approaches to theatre theory more informed by work in the social sciences, he suggested as possible sources cultural historians like Johann Huizenga or theorists of social psychology like Erving Goffman or Eric Berne. Later, however, he turned more toward anthropological work, and his investigations began to converge with those of Turner.[21] The two collaborated on a workshop exploring the relationship between "social and aesthetic drama," an experiment that, Turner reports, "persuaded me that cooperation between anthropological and theatrical people was not only possible but also could become a major teaching tool for both sets of partners," and that central to this cooperation were the concepts of "performance" and "drama."[22]

Schechner was especially interested in Turner's model of the "social drama," and drew upon it in a variety of ways as he was seeking to develop a theory and poetics of performance during the 1970s. He argued that Turner's four-phase plan was not only universally found in human social organization but also represented a form discoverable in all theatre. At the same time, Schechner sought to explore both the relationships and the differences between the performance and cultural placement of "social drama" and that of "aesthetic drama." In his essay "Selective Inattention" (1976), Schechner proposed a chart of this relationship which he and Turner both utilized in later writings. This chart represents aesthetic drama and

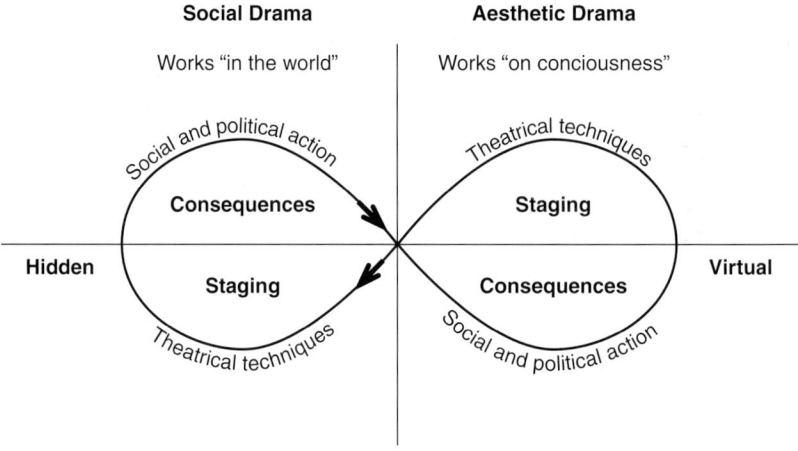

Figure 1.1 Richard Schechner's diagram of the flows between "social drama" and "aesthetic drama."

social drama as the two parts of a figure-of-eight lying on its side, with social energy flowing around this figure. The theatre person uses the consequential actions of social life as raw material for the production of aesthetic drama, while the social activist uses techniques derived from the theatre to support the activities of social drama, which in turn refuel the theatre.[23]

This diagram, and other insights from Schechner's work, were used extensively in Turner's 1982 book *From Ritual to Theatre*, in which Turner, while expressing great admiration for his work, diverges from Schechner in several ways. He does not agree that traditional drama normally echoes the four-stage pattern of his social drama; it tends rather to concentrate on the third phase, the ritualized action of redress. He also suggests that the figure-of-eight diagram is "somewhat equilibrist in its implications for my taste," since it suggests cyclical rather than linear movement. Nevertheless, he continued to cite Schechner's model in later essays as an important attempt to demonstrate the relationship between social drama and "expressive cultural genres" such as traditional theatre.[24]

Liminality and play

Liminal and liminoid

Turner also continued to develop his own complex elaboration of van Gennep's concept of the liminal and eventually opposed to it a related concept of his own, the liminoid, both of which terms have been widely used in subsequent writings about performance. In his 1969 book *The Ritual Process*, Turner called liminal activities "anti-structure," opposing the "structure" of normal cultural operations, a concept also indebted to van

Gennep. Such situations provide a space removed from daily activity for members of a culture to "think about how they think in propositions that are not *in* cultural codes but *about* them."[25] Although at this time Turner did not stress the subversive potential of the anti-structural, this aspect was subsequently emphasized by Brian Sutton-Smith in his studies of child and adult games. Sutton-Smith suggested that the "disorderly" quality of liminal activities sometimes merely involved "letting off steam" from an "overdose of order" (the conservative view), but could also be undertaken "because we have something to *learn* through being disorderly." What we have to learn is precisely the possibility of alternate orders. As Sutton-Smith argues:[26]

> The normative structure represents the working equilibrium, the "anti-structure" represents the latent system of potential alternatives from which novelty will arise when contingencies in the normative system require it. We might more correctly call this second system the *protocultural* system because it is the precursor of innovative normative forms. It is the source of new culture.

Turner dealt much more extensively with the social functions of this performative process in the essay "Liminal to Liminoid, in Play, Flow, and Ritual,"[27] which also showed Turner moving more toward the innovative possibilities of performance stressed by Sutton-Smith. Indeed, here Turner remarked that "what interests me about Sutton-Smith's formulations is that he sees liminal and liminoid situations as the settings in which new models, symbols, paradigms, etc. arise—as the seedbeds of cultural creativity in fact."[28] In fact Turner continued to accept the position of theorists like Singer that performance remained a culturally conservative activity of performance in tribal and agrarian societies. Although such performance, which Turner styled liminal, might seem to mark sites where conventional structure is challenged, this structure is ultimately reaffirmed. Liminal performance may invert the established order, but never subverts it. On the contrary, it normally suggests that a frightening chaos is the alternative to the established order.

In complex modern industrialized societies this sort of general cultural affirmation is no longer possible, and here we find instead what Turner called "liminoid" activities, much more limited and individualistic, devoted to play, sport, leisure, or art, all outside the "regular" cultural activity of work or business. Liminoid like liminal activities mark sites where conventional structure is no longer honored but, being more playful and more open to chance, they are also much more likely to be subversive, consciously or by accident introducing or exploring different structures that may develop into real alternatives to the *status quo*. This emphasis on the potential of liminoid activity to provide a site for social and cultural resistance and the exploration of alternative possibilities has naturally been of particular interest to theorists and practitioners of performance seeking a strategy of social engagement not offered by the more cultural-bound structures of the conventional theatre.

Turner's association of cultural self-reflexivity with cultural conservatism in traditional liminal situations and with the operations of cultural change in more recent liminoid activities continues to be much debated, as indeed does the whole question of the relationship between performance and cultural critique. Clifford Geertz has suggested a distinction between "deep play" and "shallow play" in performance, a distinction recalling Turner's liminal and liminoid, but seemingly reversing Turner's speculation about which sort of activity was radical and which conservative. According to Geertz, only those performances involving the participants in "deep play" are likely to raise real concerns about the fundamental ideas and codes of the culture.[29] Bruce Kapferer, on the other hand, seems closer to Turner, arguing that in "deep play" both performers and audience may be so involved in the activity that reflection does not occur and that, paradoxically, it may be in the more "distanced" experience of "shallow play" that cultural self-reflection is most likely to occur.[30] Clearly the question of the relationship between performance and its culture is another aspect of performance that demonstrates the essentially contested essence of this term, with some theorists viewing performance as reinforcing cultural givens, others seeing it as at least potentially subversive of these givens, and still others seeing it working under some circumstances in one way and in some the other, as in MacAloon's definition of cultural performances as "occasion in which as a culture or society we reflect upon and define ourselves, dramatize our collective myths and history, present ourselves with alternatives, and eventually change in some ways while remaining the same in others."[31] Even those who agree with MacAloon disagree on what stimulates some customs to change while others remain the same. Naturally these debates are of central concern to theorists and practitioners of socially and politically oriented performance, and we shall return to these concerns in that context.

Performance and play

In addition to the rite and ritual studies of van Gennep, Turner, as well as most other cultural anthropologists who have dealt with performance, has been much influenced by earlier research on human play. The two most widely known and most influential studies in this field are *Homo Ludens* by the Dutch cultural historian Johann Huizenga, and the closely related study *Man, Play, and Games* by Roger Caillois. The aim of both theorists was to analyze the function of play within human culture. Huizenga concentrated on culturally constructed and articulated forms of playful activity, such as performances, exhibitions, pageants, tournaments, and contests, while Caillois cast a broader net, including even the "playful" activities of children and animals. Caillois indeed proposes a continuum of playful activity extending from such spontaneous manifestations as an infant laughing at his rattle or a cat with a ball of yarn, to which he gave the term *"paidia,"* on through increasingly institutionalized and rule-bound play structures that Caillois called *"ludus."*[32]

This difference aside, the six essential "qualities" of play activity according to Caillois (it is not obligatory, it is circumscribed in time and space, undetermined, materially unproductive, rule-bound, and concerned with an alternate reality)[33] are basically identical with Huizenga's "characteristics" of play. The first quality of play, according to Huizenga, is that it is a voluntary activity, freely selected and capable of being suspended at any time. It is thus closely tied to "free time," or leisure. This connection is particularly important to Turner, who argues that the concept of leisure itself is one that arises with modern industrial society, which clearly divides human activity into periods of work and non-work. The activities of the non-working, leisure periods, play activities, are precisely those that Turner characterizes as liminoid. The association of liminoid with such circumscribed periods also recalls Huizenga's second characteristic, according to which play is set apart from ordinary life, occurring in a "temporary sphere of activity with a disposition all of its own."[34] Clearly this involves the process that theorists speak of as "framing."

Both Huizenga and Caillois see battles or contests as one central preoccupation of play. Caillois uses for this a term with a long history in theatre theory, *"agon,"* a concept which is also central to Turner's model of the "social drama." Another Caillois category, "mimicry," is perhaps even more central to traditional theatre, but both "conflict" and "mimesis," particularly the latter, have played a much less central and more problematic role in modern performance theory. Probably this is in part due to their close association with the theatre tradition, from which modern performance has often tried to distance itself. Caillois's other two categories, though seemingly more unfamiliar, in fact relate much more closely to common concerns of modern performance. The first of these is *"alea,"* or chance, a concern that entered the tradition of modern performance partly from the theatre experiments of dada and surrealism earlier in the century, partly from developments related to happenings and chance theatre in the 1960s, and partly from the writings and work of a key figure in modern performance, John Cage. All of these developments will be discussed more fully in the context of performance art itself, but here we might only note that Caillois himself sees *"alea"* as in a sense the opposite of *"agon."* In the latter, the emphasis is upon clever planning, logic, ingenuity, and control, all elements which Caillois sees in some measure as being opposed to the freedom and spontaneity of the play instinct. Performance theorists and practitioners have similarly looked to chance as a means of breaking free of the normally highly codified structures and expectations of the conventional theatrical experience.

Caillois' final category, *"ilinx"* or *"vertigo,"* performs a similar subversive function. Caillois describes this as "an attempt to destroy momentarily the stability of perception and inflict a kind of voluptuous panic upon an otherwise lucid mind."[35] The emphasis here is upon subversion, the destruction of "stability," the turning of "lucidity" to "panic," brought about by a foregrounding of physical sensation, an awareness of the body set free from the normal structures of control and meaning. In a sense, vertigo is to the body what chance is to the mind, a casting loose into free play, there of elements, here of sensations. Huizenga speaks, in distinctly more positive terms, of a similar freeing from normal structures and constraints, which he describes as a sense of "enchantment" or "captivation" that is felt in play.[36] Turner also speaks of this sense of "enchantment," though he favors the more familiar term "flow," derived from such psychological theorists as John MacAloon and Mihaly Csikszentmihalyi. During "flow," which these psychological theorists associate not only with play but also with creative and religious experience, reflexivity is swallowed up in a merging of action and awareness, a focus upon the pleasure of the present moment, and a loss of a sense of ego or of movement toward some goal.

Caillois does not specifically oppose vertigo to mimicry as he does chance to conflict, but it is striking that one of the major fault lines in modern theory runs down a divide that can be considered in precisely these terms—that is in the division Bert States makes between semiotics, based upon a model of mimesis, and phenomenology, based on one of physical sensation, or the model proposed by Jean Alter opposing semiosis to performance on essentially the same grounds (both the Alter and States models will be discussed in more detail later). To the extent that modern performance has defined itself in opposition to traditional theatre, it has largely followed these theoretical divisions, championing the operations of chance and the physical awareness of the performative situation against the control and the mimetic distance of conventional theatre.

Huizenga, in considering the cultural functions of play, sees them as primarily conservative, providing through the deepening of communal experience and the ludic display of communal values and beliefs an ultimate strengthening of cultural assumptions. Indeed, Huizenga considers the development or reinforcement of a community spirit or consciousness, "communitas," to be one of the basic features of play, and suggests that its effects often continue beyond the actual play experience. Thus cultural play, like Singer's cultural performance, provides a solidifying of the community, and the "actualization by representation" of the hidden values, assumptions, and beliefs of the culture.[37] This becomes particularly apparent as Huizenga explores the close relationships between play and ritual. Nevertheless, building upon the emphasis both he and Caillois give to the absolute freedom necessary for the functioning of play, there is clearly room for a much more subversive function, congruent with that suggested by Sutton-Smith and the later Turner, particularly when he notes that in "more advanced civilizations" the great cultural play periods of "savage societies" leave their traces in "saturnalia and carnival customs" characterized by disruptive and disorderly behavior.[38]

Subversive play

The theorist most associated with the concept of carnival and carnivaliza-tion in modern literary and performance theory is Mikhail Bakhtin, whose comments on this subject, particularly in his study of Rabelais,[39] bear a remarkable resemblance to Turner's discussion of liminal phenomena within a culture. During carnival, notes Bakhtin, "the laws, prohibitions, and restrictions that determine the structure and order of ordinary, that is noncarnival, life are suspended," making carnival "the place for working out, in a concretely sensuous, half-real and half-play-acted form, a *new mode of interrelationship between individuals,* counterposed to the all-powerful socio-hierarchical relationships of noncarnival life"(emphasis in original).[40] This vision of carnival as an unstructured testing ground for new social and cultural structures clearly marks it as an example of what Turner would classify as a liminal or liminoid activity. Bakhtin lists the categories of carni-val as free and familiar contact among people, the free expression of latent sides of human nature in eccentric conduct (recall the emphasis on freedom in Huizenga), profanations, and carnivalistic misalliances, allowing the combining and uniting of the most disparate and ill-assorted things. He stresses that these categories are not involved with abstract thought but with the sensuous playing out in the form of life itself, that is by cultural performance. This leads in turn to a consideration of specific carnivalistic acts, the most important of which is the mock crowning and decrowning of the carnival king, a ritual deeply imbricated with the pathos and emphasis on change, the concerns with death and renewal that lie at the base of the carnivalistic experience itself.

Like Turner, Bakhtin distinguishes between the carnivalization available to earlier cultures and its more mediated, truncated and scattered modern descendants, a shift that Bakhtin feels begins as early as the seventeenth century. Theatre and spectacle are of course one of the offshoots of this once mighty cultural force, and Bakhtin notes that "It is characteristic that the subculture of the theatre has even retained something of carnivalistic license, the carnivalistic sense of the world, the fascination of carnival."[41] The high point of carnival's interpenetration of the literary tradition, Bakhtin feels, occurred during the Renaissance, and his concept of the car-nivalization in Renaissance literature has been very influential among recent studies of Elizabethan drama,[42] but the concept of carnival as a site for the playful exploration and possible challenging of traditional cultural assumptions and roles has also attracted the interest of performance artists and theorists concerned with precisely these matters.[43]

An important critique of both Huizenga and Caillois was presented in 1968 by Jacques Ehrmann. In the theories of both of these authors, as well as those of the linguist Emile Benveniste, Ehrmann finds an assumed cleavage between play and seriousness, with play linked to dreams, imagination, gra-tuitousness, and such "free" phenomena, while seriousness is linked to such concepts as consciousness, utility and reality. In addition to creating what is in any case a highly suspect division, this strategy also simultaneously privileges the second term as the ground of the first, a neutral and objective referent needing no discussion.[44] In Huizenga's terms, "Play always represents something."[45] Ehrmann's argument suggests the common strategy of Derrida, who has similarly exposed the strategy of creating a false "grounding" of a binary by making one of its terms the axiomatic base of the other. Derrida's critique also has important implications for performance theory, to which we will return in exploring the relation between performance and postmodern thought. At this point, I wish only to emphasize that Ehrmann, like Derrida, resists the model that derives play from a fixed, stable reality that precedes and grounds it. In this more modern view, play, reality, and culture are all involved in a continually shifting pattern of concepts and practices that condition each other, and rather than attempt to separate or privilege any of these terms, the critic or theorist of human activity should have as a goal the explanation of "how this nature-culture manifests itself in different historical and cultural contexts."[46]

A closely related concern and analytic strategy has been offered by Marshall Sahlins, who suggests that anthropologists tend to think of cultures as being modeled by both "prescriptive" and "performative" structures, the former the relatively stable institutional forms of a society, the latter operations that evolve in response to contingent circumstances. Clearly there is a parallel here to the "play" and "reality" of Ehrmann, especially when play is associated with the cultural changes or adjustments opened by Turner and van Gennep's liminality. However, like Ehrmann, Sahlins cautions against so clear a dichotomy and, even more important, against the priority normally given in the social sciences to the prescriptive over the performative, clearly parallel to the priority Ehrmann finds given to the stable "reality" from which play derives. Certainly a cultural act can and often does arise from a social form, but all societies also continually improvise social form by means of acts, and the mixture of these strategies and the levels upon which they operate varies greatly from society to society.[47] The cautions of Ehrmann and Sahlins are extremely important in broadening the scope and the significance of liminal and performative activity. Indeed, in considerations of the social functioning of performance even Sahlin's flexible definition needs to be qualified, since it reinscribes the fixed/fluid dichotomy on another level, with "performative" acts associated, as always, with the fluid part of this familiar binary, dissolving (at least temporarily) the "prescriptive" already existing structures of the culture.

Performing anthropology

Turner's own explorations have been carried on by Colin Turnbull and others in directions that overlap in striking ways with performance theory of the 1990s, as Turner's did with performance theories of the 1970s and early 1980s. In a 1990 essay Turnbull specifically speculates on how his own theories seemed to be evolving in parallel directions with Turner's last work (he died in 1983). These new directions involved a shifting under-standing of the nature of cultural performance, and particularly of the per-formative nature of anthropological work itself. While the young Turner had applied a theatrical model to certain phenomena in a culture being ana-lyzed, Turnbull saw its potential relevance to the process of analysis itself.[48]

The anthropological process and performance, suggests Turnbull, have many points of correspondence, since the fieldworker is fulfilling the "role" of anthropologist expected by his society and also "performing" to achieve specific goals (these concerns echo those of Goffman, and will surface again in the next chapter). The fieldworker is also a spectator in a cultural performance, and in a more subtle sense within the specific context of a study this spectator is forced to modify normal behavior, giving it special significance for others. The next step in Turner's project, argues Turnbull, must be dealing with the recognition that liminal phenomena cannot simply be objectively studied, but must also be understood by participa-tion, informed by the sort of rigorous preparation and training that leads back to the disciplines of theatre. In short, the fieldworker can no longer rely upon the traditional methods of "objective" reporting of performance, not because objectivity is impossible (though it is at best extremely difficult) but because performance cannot really be understood in this way. Entering the liminal or performative situation requires, among other things, discip-line and concentration, a clearly defined goal, or perhaps the negation of all goals and a surrender of inner self to become something else. The first of these demands, says Turnbull, presents no problem to most anthropolo-gists, but the second, calling into question traditional academic objectives, inner beliefs, and the sense of identity, presents a far greater challenge.[49]

The shift in emphasis Turnbull suggests in fact represents a major shift in modern anthropology, from the model of the neutral objective reporter of cultural customs to that of a native from one culture observing natives from another, creating a complex interplay of influence and adjustment. Dwight Conquergood in 1985 suggested that five types of attitudes toward the ethnography of performance could now be charted out, four of them morally problematic. The suspect stances were that of the custodian, the enthusiast, the skeptic, and the curator. The custodian collects examples of performance, interested only in acquisition or exploitation. The skeptic, like many traditional ethnographers, stands aloof from and superior to the performance being studied. The enthusiast goes to the opposite extreme, seeking an easy identity in quick generalizations. The curator takes a tourist's stance, seeking exoticism or spectacle. Against all four of these, Conquergood champions a "dialogical" performance, which aims "to bring together different voices, world views, value systems, and beliefs so that they can have a conversation with one another." The result sought is an open-ended performance, resisting conclusions and seeking to keep interro-gation open.[50]

The "dialogical" performance of much anthropological work of the 1990s deeply affected not only the encounter with cultural material but also the reporting of it, as the hitherto presumably neutral and objective "reporting" of material was also revealed to be deeply involved with cultural presumptions and with performance. A number of anthropologists sought to write "performatively," attempting to introduce the evocative, dramatic, open-ended quality of the "dialogical" to their presentation of material. A striking example of this is Michael Taussig, a member of the Performance Studies faculty at New York University in the 1980s. A seminar in that program was reportedly the grounding for his 1997 book *The Magic of the State*, categorized by Routledge, its publisher, as "ficto-criticism." In this, as in earlier books, Taussig undertakes a neo-Marxist analysis of the modern imaginary, what he elsewhere calls "the poetics of the commodity,"[51] *The Magic of the State* explores the intersection between myth/ritual and power/money though the imaginations of a variety of probably fictional characters, like the sci-fi anthropologist Captain Mission, as they explore spirit possession on a magic mountain possibly located somewhere in South America. The work seeks "to state and restage" the "theatrics of spirit possession," a living reality "for most people for most of world history."[52]

Somewhat ironically, Taussig's bold experimentation with performativity and dialogism in his texts has taken him in quite the opposite direction to other postmodern ethnographers, who have manifested a performative consciousness by weaving their own bodies into their narratives as fully and consciously as Taussig has excluded his. Many of these, however, like Taussig, attempt to reintegrate with modern ethnographic discourse the previously rejected alternative discourses of magic and myth. Thus Stephanie Kane, in *The Phantom Gringo Boat* (1994), specifically aligns ethnography with the performative practice of shamanism "in its attempt to cross the gap between the known and unknown," and characterizes her own writing performance as an attempt "to write the magical real into the politics of the everyday,"[53] and Katherine Pratt Ewing, in *Arguing Sainthood* (1997) uses extensive fieldwork among Sufi mystics in Lahore to create a model of subjectivity constantly negotiated by construction out of shifting and competing realities.[54]

Corinne Dempsey, in a review article on recent ethnographic writing, likens Ewing's view of the performative interrelationship between interculturalism and subjectivity to that of Stefania Pandolfo in her writings on Morocco. Both writers, suggests Dempsey, see the subject as operating in a "gap between languages and cultures, between genders and categorizations," where "a certain kind of listening and intercultural dialogue becomes possible."[55] Pandolfo finds in Muslim sacred writing a figure that precisely expresses this concept as well as anticipating the play of representation and subjectivity in recent postmodern thought, *al-Finta*, which Pandolfo describes as "a polysemic concept at the limit of representation and thought, mark of an intractable difference, fracture, rift, schism, disjunction, or separation—separation from oneself—the figure of an exile that is constitutive of the position of subject, as both a possibility and a loss."[56]

The cultural experience of the body is central to the work of Kirsten Hastrup, who argues that one of the most important developments in anthropology between the 1980s and 1990s was a shift from "informative to performative ethnography." Hastrup quotes the distinction made earlier by Johannes Fabian: in the former "the ethnographer determines the questions and notes the answers," while in the latter "the ethnographer does not call the tune, but plays along."[57] Hastrup traces the concept of "performative ethnography" back to Turner, but suggests major changes in the concept since Turner proposed it. Turner's concern with "social dramas" remained external and observationist, continuing anthropology's traditional concern with expressions of experience rather than experience itself. However, Hastrup argues, most cultural knowledge "is stored in actions rather than in words," and so resists this sort of discursive analysis. The "clinical gaze" must therefore be abandoned in favor of an attempt to understand "embodied patterns of experience."[58]

Interestingly, Hastrup's search for methodological approaches to these "embodied patterns" led her to theatre, and specifically to the work of the performance theorist who has most closely associated himself with an anthropological approach, Eugenio Barba. In his various writings, but most extensively in the "Dictionary of Theatre Anthropology," *The Secret Art of the Performer*, co-edited with Nicola Savarese (1991), Barba focused upon the "socio-cultural and physiological behavior" of the performer across various cultures.[59] He divided potential bodily activity into three types: daily techniques, which are concerned primarily with communication of content, virtuosic techniques, such as those displayed by acrobats, which seek "amazement and transformation of the body;" and extra-daily techniques, which seek not to transform but to "in-form" the body, to place it in a position where it is "alive and present" without representing anything.[60] Barba places the foundations of performance not in the cultural frame or marking, but in a basic level of organization in the performer's body, at the "pre-expressive" level, the operations of which cause the spectator to recognize behavior as performance. The spectator (about whom Barba says relatively little) responds to performance not due to operations of some cultural "frame," but because of a pre-cultural set of universal "physiological responses" to such stimuli as balance and directed tensions.[61] Barba postulates that the pre-expressive level underlies all performance, Eastern and Western, providing a transcultural "physiology" independent of traditional culture and involving such matters as balance, opposition, and energy. The transcultural study of this physiology, seeking the general physical principles of pre-expressivity, Barba proposes as the mission of theatre anthropology.[62]

Hastrup agrees with Barba that much basic bodily experience is shared cross-culturally, and so provides a kind of grounding for anthropological analysis that can serve as a corrective to the intellectual, objective structures of cultural grammars. Just as theatre anthropology rejects the notion of the body as the performer's instrument in favor of the notion of "one person, combining bodily and mental images in a unified performance," so performative anthropology must develop a model that unites mind and body, culture and action.[63]

One of the most fascinating aspects of Hastrup's work is her reflections upon her own experience not as an ethnographer but as an informant. Their mutual interests, like those of Turner and Schechner a decade earlier, brought Hastrup and Barba together in the late 1980s, when Barba proposed creating a performance based on Hastrup's life and work. Hastrup's reflections upon this process, upon the relationship between behavior and restored behavior, between "me" and "not-me," between experience and reflexivity, make her reporting on the creation and the experience of Barba's production, *Talabot*, a unique and fascinating documentary of the convergence of self and other, and of theatre, performance, and anthropology at the close of the twentieth century.[64]

The role of the "reporter" is a less central concern when we move to

Figure 1.2 Odin Teatret's production of *Talabot*, 1988.

Source: Odin Teatret.

performance study outside the traditional area of anthropology (although it has stimulated some important theoretical speculation, which will be examined in a later chapter). In more general terms, however, performance, critical and theoretical, underwent a parallel and doubtless related development during the 1980s, moving from an almost exclusive preoccupation with the performer and the performative act to a consideration also of who is watching the performance, who is reporting on it, and what the social, political, and cognitive implications of these other transactions are upon the process. Moreover, a closely related concern proved one of the most stimulating areas of theoretical speculation in both ethnography and theatre studies in the late 1980s and 1990s. The move from a model of a fieldworker as a neutral observer to that of a fieldworker as a participant in performance, both in initial experience and in subsequent relaying of that experience to others, means moving into the complex field of intercultural performance. In the modern world of easy transportation and communication, not only anthropologists but also all sorts of cultural performances or parts of cultural performances can and do circulate with relative ease about the globe, weaving complex patterns of contact with other cultures or other cultural performances.

A number of European theatre theorists, most notably Patrice Pavis in France and Erika Fischer-Lichte in Germany, have provided important studies of interculturalism within the context of theatre studies. However, although this work is very much informed by anthropological models (Pavis, for example, bases his cultural analysis largely upon the work of French anthropologist Camille Camillieri), it has not been, at least so far, involved in the sort of direct ongoing mutual exploration and influence that characterized, for example, the work of Schechner and Turner in the 1970s. Nevertheless, an important element in recent anthropological studies shares with recent theatre studies of this sort a common interest in how cultural performance is affected by the increasing intercultural borrowings of the modern or postmodern world, and so quotations from current anthropological theories often show up in studies of a more traditionally theatrical nature. *The Predicament of Culture* (1988), by ethnographic historian James Clifford, is an important example of such theory, with its argument that modern world societies have become "too systemically interconnected to permit any easy isolation of separate or independently functioning systems" and that everywhere individuals and groups "improvise local performance from (re)collected pasts, drawing on foreign media, symbols, and languages." Clifford and others have spoken of this new interculturalism as "creolized,"[65] in reference to the mixed and layered culture of regions like the Caribbean.[66]

The function of performance within a culture, the establishment and use of particularly designated performative contexts, the relation of performer to audience and of the reporter of performance to performance, and the generation and operations of performance drawing upon or influenced by several different cultures—all of these cultural concerns have contributed importantly to contemporary thought about what performance is and how it operates. The emphasis of culture theories, however, remains focused primarily upon performance as an ethnographic or anthropological phenomenon. Equally important to modern performance theory has been consideration of performance from a social or psychological perspective, and to such theories we shall now turn.

Chapter 2

Performance in society
Sociological and psychological approaches

The recognition that all social behavior is to a certain extent "performed" and that different social relationships can be seen as "roles" is of course hardly a recent idea, and in certain periods of theatre history, such as the Renaissance and Baroque, this "theatrical" quality of regular social life appeared as a motif or a central subject in countless plays. It was not really until the twentieth century, however, that an exploration of the actual personal and social implications of this way of viewing human activity appeared, directed not toward the creation of an artistic product but toward the analysis and understanding of social behavior.

Researchers in both psychology and sociology became interested in the application of the theatrical concept of role playing to study in their own

Figure 2.1 A psychodrama scene on Moreno's therapeutic stage, New York, 1942.

fields during the 1940s and 1950s, and although there is a good deal of overlap in their analytic vocabulary, the two fields developed quite separate strategies, according to their own concerns. As performance studies was developing as a field of investigation during the 1970s and early 1980s, it was in general much more directly influenced by sociological models, particularly as represented in the work of Erving Goffman, whose writings in this area exerted an influence at least equal to, and perhaps even greater than Turner's in the anthropological study of performance. Psychological theories of performance were at that time less directly influential, but Schechner and others regularly referred to them, especially when they involved performance events more directly comparable to conventional "theatrical" performance than those dealt with by sociological theories. The leading name among the psychological theorists often evoked at that time was J.L. Moreno, who in 1946 presented the concept of psychodrama in a book with that title.[1] A variety of other competing role-playing approaches to psychotherapy followed, the most important being the behavior rehearsal of J. Wolpe and A.A. Lazarus. Eric Berne's transactional analysis was also often cited in *Tulane Drama Review* in the mid-1960s as the relationships between social science theory and the new idea of performance analysis were evolving.[2] Although performative images, metaphors, and strategies were extremely important in the writings of Freud, as well as of major Freudian revisionists like Jacques Lacan and Julia Kristeva, their work was rarely cited in the work of that first generation of modern performance theorists. In the later 1980s and during the 1990s, however, this situation was reversed, and while sociological performance analysis was by no means abandoned, most of the major new work in the field drew its inspiration from psychology and psychoanalysis—as was witnessed by one of the first major anthologies in the field as the new century opened, Patrick Campbell and Adrian Kear's *Psychoanalysis and Performance*.[3] We will consider the contributions of these various sociological and psychoanalytic theorists to performance theory presently, but first let us glance backward to two earlier theorists whose writings significantly anticipate some of the central features of later theorists of social performance. Both of these theorists, interestingly, are quite impossible to place in terms of conventional professions or academic areas, and there is little doubt that the scope and variety of their interests led to their interest in so ubiquitous a human phenomenon as performance.

Social performance

Nikolas Evreinoff and social roles

The first theorist considered here, Nikolas Evreinoff, is perhaps now best remembered as an experimental Russian playwright from the brilliant period at the turn of the century, and also for his organization of mass spectacles celebrating events of the Revolution. In addition to his varied theatre career, however, he was a successful musician and composer, novelist, historian, psychologist, biologist, archeologist, and philosopher; and his various books and articles, while nominally concerning theatre, draw upon all these interests. Between 1912 and 1924 he published a series of books and monographs, sections of which were woven together into the English collection *The Theatre in Life*, published in 1927.

The Theatre in Life begins with a discussion of the widespread phenomenon of play, an activity humanity shares with the animal kingdom, then proceeds to a concern with the specifically theatrical. Evreinoff rejects the general assumption of anthropological and theatrical theorists that theatre arose from ritual bases or evolved from an early interest in the aesthetic, expressed at first in images and dances. Instead he argues that the theatrical is itself a basic instinct, more fundamental than the aesthetic or even the organization of ritual. "The art of the theatre is pre-aesthetic, and not aesthetic," he argues, "for the simple reason that *transformation*, which is after all the essence of all theatrical art, is more primitive and more easily attainable than *formation*, which is the essence of aesthetic arts."[4] (This distinction is strikingly similar to that made by Eugenio Barba between expressivity and pre-expressivity.) Later Evreinoff observes that this ability to imagine something "different" from everyday reality and to "play" with this imagination, was also a pre-condition for religion, which required the ability to conceive of and personify "gods." "Man became first an actor, a player; and then came religion."[5]

In the opening chapters of *The Theatre in Life* Evreinoff's approach and examples are basically anthropological, but by the sixth chapter, "The Never Ending Show," he has moved to a much more distinctly sociological analysis. "We are constantly 'playing a part' when we are in society," Evreinoff avers, citing fashion, make-up and costume, the everyday operations of life and the social "roles" of such representative figures as politicians, bankers, businessmen, priests, and doctors. The life of each city, of each country, of each nation Evreinoff sees as articulated by the invisible "stage manager" of that culture, which dictates scenery, costume, and characters of public situations throughout the world. Each epoch has "its own wardrobe and scenery, its own 'mask.' "[6] Many of the concerns and metaphors of later role and performance theory in sociological literature are clearly already in place in Evreinoff's rather fanciful analysis, including not only the particular dynamic of the social self as defined internally and externally by culturally conditioned roles, but also the reinforcement of those roles by the costumes, properties and physical settings provided by the "stage management" of society. These same concerns can be found in the more influential writings of both Kenneth Burke and Erving Goffman.

Kenneth Burke and dramatism

Kenneth Burke, like Evreinoff, is difficult to categorize, though he has been referred to as a literary critic, a philosopher, a semanticist, and a social psychologist. Certainly his system of thought has had profound influence in all of those fields, and such leading performance theorists as Goffman, Turner, and Schechner have all followed his strategy of using the approach of "dramatism" to analyze a variety of social interactions and cultural behavior. The titles of Burke's two major statements on "dramatism," *A Grammar of Motives* (1945) and *A Rhetoric of Motives* (1950), indicate his central concern, which is the establishment of analytic terms and strategies for the discussion of human motivation and the devices by which people, consciously or unconsciously, try to influence the opinions or actions of each other.

Any complete statement about motives, argues Burke, must answer five questions, which lead to the "five key terms of dramatism:" "what was done (Act), when or where it was done (Scene), who did it (Agent), how he did it (Agency), and why (Purpose)."[7] The situation of human action within a "staged" context is what ties Burke most closely to subsequent performance theorists, and his particular interest in literary analysis has provided particular stimulation for critics who have sought to extend performance analysis into that area. Burke's central interest in motivation has proven for performance theory less important than his general approach, since those interested in the "theatrical" side of performance have tended to look more toward communication or the effect produced by performance than to the motivation of the artist. Theorists of social performance, on the other hand, have tended to place much more emphasis on the social constraints governing an act than upon its specific motivation.

Erving Goffman and role playing

Erving Goffman shares with these theorists a use of the metaphor of theatrical performance to discuss the importance and the operations of role playing in social situations, though his influence on performance theory outside the social sciences has been much greater. Barbara Kirshenblatt-Gimblett, for example, has pointed out the usefulness of some of Goffman's earliest analytic approaches to everyday behavior for the potential analysis of the more distinctly performative situation of storytelling.[8]

The essay to which Kirshenblatt-Gimblett primarily refers, Goffman's (1955) "On Facework," is striking in the similarity of the structure it imposes on "interpersonal ritual behavior" to Turner's "social drama."[9] Both describe an event structure in which the orderly flow of normal interaction, social or cultural, is disrupted by an incident, some breach of social or cultural norms. This precipitates a crisis, and sets in motion what Turner calls a "redressive stage" and Goffman a "corrective interchange." The normal phases of this crisis and redressive action are labelled by Goffman challenge, offering, acceptance, and thanks, and through their operations the equilibrium is re-established (though Goffman, like Turner, recognizes that the equilibrium may not mean a return to the old order; it may be an accommodation to a permanently changed new one).

The Presentation of Self in Everyday Life (1956) is Goffman's best known work, and is centrally concerned with performances, that indeed being the title of its opening chapter. Goffman defines performance as "all the activity of an individual which occurs during a period marked by his continuous presence before a particular set of observers and which has some influence on the observers."[10] This definition, though it raises a few problems, could serve very well for much of the artistic activity which has appeared in recent years under the title of "performance." It is important, however, to note that even this seemingly very general and calculatedly neutral definition reflects certain assumptions and biases. Perhaps most significant is where it locates what makes performance performance and not simply behavior. Goffman in this formulation does not emphasize, as for example Burke does, the conscious production of a certain type of behavior, as might be expected for a theory of "presentation" or of "role-playing." Both of these terms suggest the initiative of a subject, but Goffman stresses the fact that certain behavior has an audience and, moreover, has an effect on that audience. Indeed in terms of this definition, the individual might quite possibly be engaged in performance without being aware of it.

Goffman's definition nevertheless addresses what seems to be an essential quality of performance, that it is based upon a relationship between a performer and an audience. All theorists of performance recognize this in some measure but, as we have seen, theorists of cultural performance tend, not surprisingly, to place more emphasis upon the audience, or upon the community in which performance occurs. Theorists of social performance, if they are sociologists, naturally also tend in this direction, while ethical philosophers and psychologists equally naturally tend to emphasize the activities and operations of the performer. Although Goffman draws strongly upon both sorts of concern, his overall emphasis, as this definition suggests, is rather more toward the audience—how social performance is recognized by society, and how it functions within society.

Framing

This is even more clearly the case in another highly influential Goffman work, *Frame Analysis* (1974), which explores in considerable detail the concept and implications of "framing," a concept of central importance in performance theory. "Framing," like the concept of metacommunication already discussed in connection with the anthropological theories of Turner, comes from the influential 1954 essay by Gregory Bateson, "A Theory of Play and Fantasy." Central to Bateson's discussion of play (and to the closely related fields of histrionics, fantasy, and art) is the psychological notion of the "frame," which is the major enabling device allowing the fictive world of "play" to operate. Within the "play frame," all messages and signals are recognized as "in a certain sense not true," while "that which is denoted by these signals is nonexistent."[11] For Goffman the "frame" is an organizing principle for setting apart social events, especially those events that, like play or performance, take on a different relationship to normal life and normal responsibilities than the same or similar events would have as "untransformed reality" outside the confines of the frame.[12]

Goffman spends one chapter specifically on the peculiar and complex "keying" involved in the theatrical frame, closely related to his concept of performance. "Performance" Goffman defines as a framing arrangement which places a circumscribed sequence of activity before persons in an "audience" role, whose duty it is to observe at length the activities of the "performers" without directly participating in those activities.[13] Goffman particularly distinguishes his usage from that of certain linguists, who have called behavior "performance" when there is an assumption that this behavior is subject to evaluation. The concept of performance in linguistic theory, however, involves much more than this, and will be treated in detail in the next chapter.

Umberto Eco and ostentation

A concept very similar to framing that has become quite popular in semiotic analysis of performance is ostentation, introduced to this field by Umberto Eco in his 1977 article, "Semiotics of Theatrical Performance," one of the first articles in English to consider theatre from a semiotic perspective. The primary concern of semiotics is the operations of human communication, and it is from this perspective that semiotic theorists have considered both theatre and the construction or performance of social roles. Despite its title, much of Eco's article in fact deals not so much with theatre as with social performance, as may be seen in its central example. Eco selects for his analysis an imaginary figure from the writings of the pioneer semiotician Charles Peirce. Peirce imagines a drunkard exposed in a public place by the Salvation Army in order to serve as a sign communicating a message about the negative effects of drink. Like Peirce, Eco finds this example fascinating because it involves communication in an intriguingly indirect way. Normally signs are intentionally produced by human beings in order to communicate a message, and in this sense the various actions produced in social role-playing can be seen as signs of that social role or position. What then of the drunkard, whose red nose, slurred speech and so on are certainly recognizable as signs of his condition and whose appearance under the auspices of the Salvation Army permits him to stand as a sign for the evil effects of drink, but who is involved in all of this communication without necessarily being aware of it?

To approach this problem, Eco refers to another semiotician, Charles Morris, who allows consideration of the drunkard himself to be put aside by locating the central dynamic of the sign not in the intention of the sign producer, but in the interpretation of its receiver. According to Morris's formulation, something is a sign "only because it is interpreted as a sign of something by some interpreter."[14] The drunkard thus becomes a sign not because he has decided to do so, but because some person or group of persons, whom we may designate as his audience, recognize him as such. This still leaves us with the question of how they do this. Goffman's response would be that some conceptual frame has been established signalling to this audience that material within it is being presented for their observation and interpretation. Eco acknowledges that one may speak of this process in terms of frame analysis, but he suggests ostentation as an alternate, and in this situation, rather more accurate, term. Although it was Eco who brought this term into the modern theoretical vocabulary, it is by no means original to him. Eco himself notes its use in the writings of medieval logicians, in Wittgenstein, and among theatre theorists in the Eastern European Ivo Osolsobe. When something is ostended, it is picked up among existing items and displayed, as the Salvation Army has placed Peirce's drunkard in a public space. Although obviously related to framing, ostentation in fact characterizes a different operation. The former emphasizes special qualities that surround a phenomenon; the latter something about the phenomenon itself.

Different ways in which a physical phenomenon, be it an object or an action, is perceived, have also been the subject of analysis by phenomenological theorists, some of whom have a particular interest in theatre and performance. Bert States, dealing with the theatre's special relationship to the world of physical objects, discusses a process clearly related to Eco's ostentation which occurs when a living creature like a dog or an inanimate object like a piece of furniture is placed in an "intentional space" such as a stage. In the words of Shakespeare's Cleopatra, the object is thus "uplifted to the view," triggering a perceptual change during which, according to States, the consciousness slips "into another gear", allowing the viewer to regard the object so displayed as "a signifying, exemplary image."[15]

Performance and agency

The theories we have just been examining all place a major and in some cases an almost exclusive emphasis upon the audience and upon reception. This does not necessarily present a serious problem for semiotics insofar as it follows the general direction suggested by Morris, nor for phenomenology insofar as it focuses upon how the world is experienced. Performance analysis, however, must use reception study as only a part, if a necessary part, of its approach. Eco's drunken man suggests the problem. There is no question that he, his appearance, and even his behavior is a sign, but there is a very real question about whether he is involved in performance. Like the dog or item of furniture mentioned by States, the drunken man is essentially an object semiotized by ostentation or by placement within a theatrical frame. Even the frame is not of his own making, but is established by an external agent, the Salvation Army. Such a model does not really represent what we normally think of as theatre, where actors, even though they submit themselves to an external production apparatus to provide their "framing," are very much aware of the operations of their activity. Still less does the model represent modern performance, where performers often control much of the production apparatus that establishes their frame. Important as the audience function is, therefore, we must also necessarily consider the performer's conscious contributions to the performance process.

In fact, most theories of social performance also consider this a necessary concern. When Goffman, for example, proceeds to the specific analysis of social performance, he in fact turns his attention from the function of the "audience" to the activity of playing the social role, focusing upon the various ways that members of society, with greater or lesser degrees of success and with greater or lesser degrees of consciousness, pursue "the work of successfully staging a character."[16] The "interaction constraints" that transform "activities into performances" are essentially constraints not upon the audience but upon the role-playing individual: the selection of an appropriate "front" (setting, costume, gestures, voice, appearance, etc.) and the commitment to coherence and selective arrangement of material presented, both of these required by the direction of activity toward communication rather than toward work-tasks.[17] As he discusses the activities and choices involved in setting up this successful communication, Goffman is close to the definition of performance that sociolinguist Dell Hymes has derived from Goffman's theories: "cultural behavior for which a person assumes responsibility to an audience."[18] This reformulation does not deny the social aim of performance—"for" an audience—that Goffman stressed earlier, but nevertheless it places the responsibility of performance, and its agency, squarely back upon the performer.

Among the many theorists of social performance who have focused their attention more upon the activity of the performer than upon that of the audience or upon the reception process generally, the question of just what is meant by "assuming responsibility" often has been a central theoretical issue. Three general positions (with some inevitable overlap) may be distinguished among the theorists who have focused upon the implications of performance and role-playing in the construction of the social self. Each of these is involved with the relationship of the self being performed to the self performing. Goffman, in his consideration of social performance primarily in its communicative function, may be taken as representing what can be characterized as a position of neutrality. The "responsibility" taken by the performer is one of ease and clarity of communication, and the question of whether the "self" being represented is the "true" self or not is a relatively minor concern.

Perspectives on social performance

Negative views

Other theorists, however, have viewed social performance as much more value-inflected, positively or negatively. The negative arguments often recall Plato's ancient suspicion of mimesis, suggesting that the playing of social roles tends to deny or subvert the activities of a "true" self. Nietzsche offers a metaphor of performance as a kind of alien force that takes possession of the self:[19]

> If someone wants to *seem* to be something, stubbornly and for a long time, he eventually finds it hard to *be* anything else. The profession of almost every man, even the artist, begins with hypocrisy, as he imitates from the outside, copies what is effective. The man who always wears the mask of a friendly countenance eventually has to gain power over benevolent moods without which the expression of friendliness cannot be forced—and eventually then these moods gain power of him and he is benevolent.

Around the turn of the century, when the philosophy of Bergson and others had generated a widespread view of life as fluid and mutable, social roles were condemned by many writers and philosophers because of their rigidity. Thus Santayana:[20]

> Every one who is sure of his mind, or proud of his office, or anxious about his duty assumes a tragic mask. He deputes it to be himself and transfers to it almost all his vanity. While still alive and subject, like all existing things, to the undermining flux of his own substance, he has crystallized his soul into an idea, and more in pride than in sorrow he has offered up his life on the altar of the Muses. . . . Our animal habits are transmuted by conscience into loyalties and duties, and we become "persons" or masks.

More recent philosophers concerned with role-playing and social performance have focused less on flexibility and spontaneity and more on the taking of responsibility, especially in an ethical sense. Probably the best known example of this is Sartre, whose chapter on "Bad Faith" in *Being and Nothingness* (1943) is concerned primarily with the analysis of this phenomenon. In a striking passage (quoted in full by Goffman), Sartre analyzes the behavior of a waiter in a café, all of whose activity has a touch of the artificial, the imposed. He is, Sartre suggests, in fact "playing at *being* a waiter in a café." It is a kind of game, but a game with very serious implications, since it is through this "playing" that the waiter "realizes" his condition. Such performance is imposed, says Sartre, upon all tradesmen: "Their condition is wholly one of ceremony. The public demands of them that they realize it as a ceremony; there is the dance of the grocer, of the tailor, of the auctioneer, by which they endeavor to persuade their clientele that they are nothing but a grocer, an auctioneer, a tailor. A grocer who dreams is offensive to the buyer because he is not wholly a grocer." The characteristic of performance, that it is produced for an audience, Sartre sees as its greatest danger to the psyche. When we commit ourselves to become a "representation" for others or for ourselves, we exist "only in representation," a condition of what Sartre calls nothingness or bad faith. The social position substitutes attitudes and actions for being, substitutes the simple, predictable role desired by society for the complex consciousness that fulfills the needs of the self.[21]

Bruce Wilshire and ethical responsibility

A similarly negative view has been developed much more recently by phenomenologist Bruce Wilshire, who has attacked not the performance of a social role but even thinking of the social role in such a theatricalized metaphor, which he characterizes as false, alienating, and demoralizing. Wilshire argues that the use of this metaphor by such theorists as Goffman, who is a particular target for Wilshire's displeasure, blurs the distinction between "on-stage" and "off-stage" activity, with an attendant erosion of ethical responsibility. Wilshire does not deny the existence of social roles, but he argues that certain physical predispositions are "built into" the body before any social mimesis occurs and thus condition that mimesis—and, more importantly, creative or spontaneous acts, the realm of moral and ethical action, fall outside the realm of the "repeatable" or "enactable" patterns of social roles. Since Wilshire's "I" can become aware of "my" roles (even though this may be of the "meta-role" of evaluation of roles), "I" cannot be ever reduced to or entirely circumscribed by these roles.[22]

Wilshire's identification of ethical responsibility with the identity of the self and his conviction that the "aestheticizing" effect of performance or role-playing is inimical to such responsibility leads him to a spirited defense of the boundaries between "on-stage" and "off-stage" behavior, boundaries that many other modern theorists, and especially theorists of performance, find much more permeable. In his more recent "The Concept of the Paratheatrical" (1990), Wilshire insists with still greater force that even when activities are performance in one sense or another, "I as a person cannot be reduced to them." Whether performing or "performing," "I am the being who possesses potential for more than aesthetically evaluable acts." The difference again is that Wilshire insists that performance remains on the side of the aesthetic, and that to preserve an ethical and existential reality, indeed sanity itself, "in the end we must bound and limit the activities which count as paratheatrical."[23]

Positive views

Other theorists have given performance a much more positive and creative function, suggesting that performance, far from standing in the way of the development of the self, provides in fact the means by which, wholly or in large part, the self is actually constituted. Thus we find in Robert Park, a leading early twentieth-century sociologist of race relations, a recognition of the stability of such physical traits as racial markers, but an insistence nevertheless that social performance in fact really defines races as well as individuals:[24]

> It is probably no mere historical accident that the word person, in its first meaning, is a mask. It is rather a recognition of the fact that everyone is always and everywhere, more or less consciously, playing a rôle. We are parents and children, masters and servants, teachers and students, clients and professional men, Gentiles and Jews. It is in these rôles that we know each other; it is in these rôles that we know ourselves. Our very faces are living masks, which ... tend more and more to conform to the type we are seeking to impersonate.... In a sense, and in so far as this mask represents the conception we have formed of ourselves—the role we are striving to live up to—this mask is our truer self, the self we would like to be. In the end, our conception of our rôle becomes second nature and an integral part of our personality.

Perhaps the most uplifting vision of social performance as self creation is provided by William James, who divides the self into material, social, and spiritual constituents. His social self is very close to that of Goffman, especially in its emphasis upon the observers; a person "has as many social selves as there are individuals who recognize him and carry an image of him in their mind." Thus, practically speaking, one "has as many social selves as there are distinct *groups* of persons about whose opinion he cares."[25] James, unlike some theorists who regard the self as created by social performance, postulates a "self of all the other selves" which selects, adjusts, and can disown the rest. Nevertheless, he suggests that even this "self of selves" may ultimately seek its highest expression and fulfillment in an "ideal social self," recognized by the "highest *possible* judging companion, if such companion there be. This self is the true, the intimate, the ultimate, the permanent Me which I seek."[26]

Moreno and psychodrama

The potential positive effects of the performance in the construction and adaptation of social roles has been of particular concern to certain psychotherapists, who have made extensive use of theatrical models and even specifically theatrical techniques in their work. J.L. Moreno, the father of psychodrama, applies the dramatic model to human actions and motivations not simply for purposes of analysis, but also for therapy. He draws upon a large collection of theatrical examples as background for his theory, but suggests that the true precedent of psychodrama can be found in shamanistic rites or re-enactments undertaken for the purpose of catharsis and healing. The emphasis is not upon imitation itself but on "the opportunity of recapitulation of unsolved problems within a freer, broader and more flexible social setting."[27] Like many more recent theorists of social roles and social performance, Moreno argues that roles do not emerge from the self but that the self emerges from roles. A child is born into the world with a drive for spontaneity that allows it to maintain itself as a functioning organism, but it at once encounters auxiliary egos and objects that form its "first environment, the matrix of identity." The first such role assimilated is the mother role, itself a clustering of roles, and as the child develops, more roles are integrated as a "self" is built. The social roles, such as doctor and policeman, are added still later, in general on a more objective and conceptual level, which makes them generally more available for conscious enactment.[28]

Most of the specific examples discussed by Moreno are of individual persons enacting, in an improvisatory way, role aspects of their selves that seem to require therapeutic attention. From time to time, however, Moreno also suggests a more communal activity, where an "audience" of involved spectators share with the participants the insights gained by the enactment. The specifically therapeutic orientation of psychodrama may seem to set it apart from the emphasis upon simple play or aesthetic pleasure of theorists like Evreinoff or of the anthropological play theorists. This may be why Moreno and psychodrama, despite their very close ties to traditional theatre (with constant references to theatre practice in general as well as to such specific artists and phenomena as Stanislavsky, the Living Newspaper, and the *commedia dell'arte*), are cited from time to time by performance theorists, but have not really been extensively utilized in the way that Goffmann, Turner, and other sociological and anthropological theorists have. Nevertheless it should be noted that there are rather closer functional and structural similarities between Moreno's psychodrama and Turner's social drama than between the models of Turner and Goffman, who have been particularly popular with American performance theorists. Moreno's "recapitulation of unsolved problems within a freer, broader and more flexible social setting" as a strategy for the working out of personal crises might with equal ease be used to describe Turner's suggestion of the social operations in the "broader and more flexible" context of liminal or liminoid activity. The framing of psychodrama and of social drama is also typically more distinct and tightly controlled than that of Goffman's role-playing. The emphasis on replication of social activity also has close ties with Richard Schechner's concept of performance as "restored behavior," which will be considered presently.

Behavior therapy

The strategies and theories of the behavior therapists have attracted even less attention from theatre and performance theorists than has the work of Moreno, which is surprising since they also have drawn very specifically upon the theatrical model. This influence is stated with particular clarity in the article "Role Theory," contributed by behavior therapists T. Sarbin and V. Allen to the 1968 *Handbook of Social Psychology*. Here they recapitulate in some detail the conventional theatre process, in which the goal of the actor is to achieve a successful enactment of a role by means of practice. In this the actor may be aided by a coach whose function it is "to provide social reinforcement to the learner. Praise and criticism provide incentives for the learner, and at the same time furnish feedback which can be used to improve performance." In fact, behavior therapists have suggested, one need only substitute "client" for "actor" in this description and "therapist" for "coach" to obtain an accurate model of the clinical operations of behavior rehearsal.[29] In the early days of behavior therapy its role-playing techniques were called behaviorodrama or behavioristic psychodrama, but confusion with Moreno's approach caused its practitioners to seek another name. The term "replication therapy" had some vogue (and arouses intriguing associations with Schechner's concept of "restored behavior"), but gradually behavior rehearsal came to be the preferred term.[30] Although both behavior rehearsal and psychodrama share a strong interest in the theatrical model and utilize the performance of scripted behavior from the past for clinical purposes, their theoretical grounding and approaches are in fact quite distinct. Moreno focuses upon the theatrical concept of catharsis, and sees role playing as a method of freeing the client's spontaneity, allowing a breakthrough into a new social/psychological configuration. Behavior rehearsal focuses more on the theatre's rehearsal and learning process, with less emphasis upon new insight than upon gaining better social/psychological skills, under the guidance of a therapist who serves a function similar to the acting coach or director.

Eric Berne and Talcott Parsons

Although Eric Berne feels that the most rewarding moments of human experience are to be attained in what he calls intimacy or spontaneity, he also suggests that for most people such moments are rarely if ever achieved, and so "the bulk of the time in serious social life is taken up with playing games,"[31] a distinctly performative activity which involves the assuming of a role and the following of certain predictable actions with a concealed motivation. Berne's model becomes even more specifically theatrical when he moves up from the rather simple social interactions he calls games to larger, more complex sets of transactions, which he calls "scripts." Instead of dealing, as do games, with a simple reaction or situation, scripts are "an attempt to repeat in derivative form a whole transference drama," which indeed may even be split up into acts "exactly like the theatrical scripts which are intuitive artistic derivatives of the primal dramas of childhood." Berne specifically characterizes the script as a "performance" which is "by nature recurrent," even though the performance may be the work of a lifetime.[32]

Berne's model reflects one of the major orientations in modern sociology, owing much to a highly influential figure in establishing the field, Talcott Parsons. Although Parsons did not utilize as much specifically theatrical terminology as did Berne, his system for the analysis of human action, first extensively developed in his 1937 *The Structure of Social Action*, contains almost identical elements: an "actor," an "end" sought by the actor, a "current situation" which the actor seeks to transform by action, and a "mode of orientation," basically comparable to Berne's "script," drawn from a repertoire of normative patterns of activity provided by the society and repeated either directly or, as Berne suggests, "in derivative form" by individual social "actors."[33] Although this model, and variations of it, have been to date the most influential sociological concepts for performance theorists, other competing models offer provocative alternatives and relate, arguably more directly, to more recent work in performance itself.

Social constructionism

During the 1960s a competing orientation to the study of human action arose that came to be called "social constructionism," from P.L. Berger and T. Luckman's study, *The Social Construction of Reality* (1967). Although this new direction was prefigured by Karl Mannheim's study of the "sociology of knowledge," *Ideology and Utopia* (1936), the theorist generally credited with establishing it as a major direction was Alfred Schutz. Schutz argued that instead of following institutionalized, externally given, and essentially stable "scripts," the "actors" of the social world navigate this world by using a patchwork of "recipe knowledge," in which "clear and distinct experiences are intermingled with vague conjectures; suppositions and prejudices cross well-proven evidences; motives, means and ends, as well as causes and effects, are strung together without clear understanding of their real connections. There are everywhere gaps, intermissions, discontinuities." Schutz suggests that there is apparently "a kind of organization by habits, rules and principles," but the origins and operations of these have been scarcely studied and may be impossible to determine.[34]

"Social constructionism" thus hypothesizes that patterns of social performance are not "given in the world" or "pre-scripted" by the culture, but are constantly constructed, negotiated, reformed, fashioned and organized out of scraps of "recipe knowledge," a pragmatic piecing together of pre-existing scraps of material recalling the process French theorists have called *bricolage*. An important extension of Schutz's work has been developed by Harold Garfinkel, to which Garfinkel has given the name "ethnomethodology"—a study of these pragmatic methods by which "common-sense actors" constitute their social world.[35] The potential implications for this constructive orientation for performance are considerable, since it suggests how performance, while operating within the highly coded systems of a culture, may yet generate constantly new configurations of action.

A similar view of pragmatic human activity is advanced in Michel de Certeau's *The Practice of Everyday Life*, which, drawing upon sociological studies like those of Goffman and ethnomethodological work like that of Garfield, distinguishes between "strategies" (much like Schutz's "recipe knowledge"), the institutionalized frameworks, scripts, or patterns of action that serve as general guides to behavior, and "tactics," the specific instances of behavior improvised by individuals according to the perceived demands of the moment and unknowable in advance.[36] Even though de Certeau's tactics never directly oppose cultural strategies, their operations in improvising upon these strategies and combining elements of them in new ways provides a continual performative ground for change, since new strategies come into being through tactical improvisation. Contemporary performers seeking to resist, challenge, or even subvert the dominant codes and assumptions of their culture have found Certeau's "tactics" a useful theoretical and practical tool. A tactic, says de Certeau:[37]

> insinuates itself into the other's place, fragmentarily, without taking it over in its entirety, without being able to keep it at a distance. It has at its disposal no base where it can capitalize on its advantages, prepare its expansions, and secure independence with respect to circumstances ... because it does not have a place, a tactic depends on it—it is always on the watch for opportunities that must be seized "on the wing." Whatever it wins, it does not keep. It must constantly manipulate events in order to turn them into "opportunities."

This is the behavioral equivalent of the operations of Bakhtin's utterance, but even more oriented toward working for an expression "outside" an established "proper" system. As Wlad Godzich notes, in summarizing de Certeau's contributions to discourse theory, de Certeau "recovers an agential dimension for us in as much as it recognizes that discursive activity is a form of social activity, an activity in which we attempt to apply the roles of the discourses that we assume," thus placing us "squarely in front of our responsibility as historical actors."[38] This active operation from an "outside" position makes this concept of great importance for theorists interested in performance as resistant to social and cultural "givens." Alan Read, for example, whose *Theatre and Everyday Life* provides a fascinating application of the insights of de Certeau and other social constructionists into the phenomenon of theatre, asserts unequivocally that theatre "is worthwhile because it is antagonistic to official views of reality."[39]

Erving Goffman and keying

Of the many social theorists associated with social constructionism, only Erving Goffman has so far exerted widespread influence among performance theorists, partly because of Goffman's greater general visibility outside the field of sociology and partly because of the specifically performative metaphors he has often employed. On the whole, however, Goffman stresses the improvisatory, ad hoc nature of social performance much less than most social constructionists, and this makes him much less useful than others might be in the currently active area of socially or culturally resistant or transformative performance.

One concept of Goffman that does point in this direction is that of "keying," which does consider at least one sort of transformative performance. For purposes of analysis Goffman needs to be able to isolate sequences or happenings from the ongoing stream of human behavior, and these sequences he calls "strips of experience." A "strip of experience," he is careful to point out, is not necessarily a natural division for those involved, or even an analytical device for inquirers, but is simply a "raw batch of occurrences (of whatever status in reality) that one wants to draw attention to as a starting point in analysis."[40] Whenever such a sequence of activity is given coherence by some cultural frame, then it is subject to replication and transformation within the social world through two basic processes: fabrication and keying. In the case of fabrication, one or more individuals manage a strip of activity so that others will have a false idea of what is going on. Keying, much more directly connected with what is normally thought of as performance, involves a strip of activity already meaningful on some terms that is transformed by recontextualization into something with a different meaning. Among the basic "keys" in our society Goffman mentions such "playful" redoings as make-believe or contests, ceremonial redoings, and technical redoings (such as theatrical rehearsals). He might also have mentioned, though he does not, the more "serious" keys represented by the "scripts" of Eric Berne or the re-enacted behavior of psychodrama or behavior therapy.

Goffman's concepts of "keying" and the "strip of experience," while conceived for sociological analysis, have proven extremely useful also to ethnographic theorists with a performance orientation. Both Richard Bauman and Dell Hymes have explored the concept of "keying," though from somewhat different directions. Bauman, rather closer to Goffman, uses "keying" to refer to the metacommunication (in Bateson's sense) that establishes a performative "frame," seeking, in his terms, "to determine the culture-specific constellations of communicative means that serve to key performance in particular communities."[41] Hymes uses the term to suggest degrees of "authenticity"—distinguishing rote or perfunctory performances from those that successfully fulfill "the standards intrinsic to the tradition in which the performance occurs."[42]

Richard Schechner and restored behavior

Goffman's "strip of experience" is a major inspiration for Richard Schechner's closely related "strip of behavior," a central concept in his *Between Theater and Anthropology* (1985). Goffman, however, emphasized the function of the "strip" in the process of social analysis, while Schechner is concerned with the strip as a mechanism for performance. The process of strip transformation that interests Schechner is closely related to what Goffman calls "keying," but Schechner creates his own term for this phenomenon, "restored behavior," a term that has proven very useful for subsequent performance theorists. With this shift in terminology comes also a shift in focus. "Keying" emphasizes the transformations themselves, while "restored behavior" emphasizes the process of repetition and the continued awareness of some "original" behavior, however distant or corrupted by myth or memory, which serves as a kind of grounding for the restoration. Schechner compares a culture's use of restored behavior to a film director's use of a strip of film. The source of this strip may be apparently honored, but in practice the strip, removed from its conditions of origin, now becomes raw material available to make "a new process, a performance."[43] Human cultures offer a rich variety of restored behaviors—organized sequences of events that exist separately from the performers who "do" these events, thus creating a reality that exists on a different plane from "everyday" existence. Schechner lists shamanism, exorcism, trance, ritual, aesthetic dance and theatre, initiation rites, social dramas, psychoanalysis, psychodrama, and transactional analysis as among the performances that utilize restored behavior. The recent concern with citationality, which will be discussed in the following chapter, explores this same dynamic of restoration within the operations of language.

One might note that in all the cases cited by Schechner the operations of restored behavior are marked for both participants and spectators by various framing devices. From the point of view of the performer, restored behavior involves behaving as if one is someone else or even oneself in other states of feeling or being. The difference between such operations and Goffman's "presentations of self in everyday life" Schechner calls a difference in degree, not in kind,[44] though it seems important to note that for the operations of restoration to function, there must even in everyday life be at least some consciousness of performing a social "role." This double consciousness, on the part of both the performer and the audience, provides the subject for some of Schechner's most thoughtful analysis in this book. He speaks of a visitor to one of America's restored villages, such as the Plimoth Plantation, as operating with an awareness of "being in" the seventeenth and twentieth centuries at the same time. Two actually exclusive frames are allowed to coexist by an effort of the imagination, analagous to the famous "willing suspension of disbelief." In applying this paradoxical awareness to the performer, Schechner cites the research of the British psychoanalyst D.W. Winnicott on how babies learn to distinguish between self and other. Between the baby's growing awareness of self and of an exterior reality there exists a realm of "transitional phenomena,"[45] a realm that Schechner likens to Bateson's "play frame" and to the liminal transitional domains of Turner and van Gennep.

What these parallels seem to suggest is that it is extremely difficult, and ultimately perhaps not particularly useful, to try as Wilshire does to draw a clear distinction between the "real" world of "responsible" human action, and the "imaginary" realm of play or performance. On the contrary, an important tradition of modern anthropological and psychoanalytic theory suggests that the realm of play not only overlaps "reality" in important ways, but in fact often serves as the crucible in which the material that we

Figure 2.2 A guest and an "inhabitant" at Plimoth Plantation.
Source: Plimoth Plantation.

utilize in the "real" world of "responsible" action is found, developed, and cast into significant new forms. Indeed, social constructionism and ethnomethodology introduce into the most common of everyday activities the kind of openness, improvisation, and experimentation that more conventional social theory has normally associated with states of "play."

Binocular vision and the actual

Since the raw material of both traditional theatre and social performance is found in the everyday world of object and actions, its use in these activities inevitably carries with it associations from that world. In a 1994 essay "Invisible Presences: Performance Intertextuality," I have used the term "ghosting" to describe the external associations that the continually recycled material of theatre brings in from the external world as well as from previous performance.[46] For semiotic theorists interested in the representative function of this material in traditional theatre, such associations may seem largely disruptive or distracting. Thus Michael Quinn in "Celebrity and the Semiotics of Acting" (1990) discusses how associations from an actor's life and career outside the theatre may confuse the mimetic process by creating a link between actor and audience "quite apart from the dramatic character."[47] In performance art, unlike traditional theatre, the performer's personal contribution is very often foregrounded, and a certain measure of celebrity is often built into the reception assumptions, but both theatre and performance continually play with the boundary between the actual and the imaginary. Objects and actions in performance are neither totally "real" nor totally "illusory," but share aspects of each. As Bert States has observed, the perceptual change involved in the process of framing or ostentation never involves a simple change from viewing an object as a part of everyday reality to regarding it as a signifying image. Framing or ostentation adds this function but it does not completely remove the perceptual awareness of the object as an object in the real world. A major contribution of phenomenological theorists like States to theatre and performance theory is surely this attention to the fact that theatre to a large extent utilizes everyday objects, situations, and people as raw material—what States calls "the real in its most real forms"— to construct fictions that by employing this material have an unusual claim upon actuality. Not only the operation, but indeed the peculiar power of theatre, States argues, derives from the "binocular vision" or double relationship to the object of performance that its audiences must carry out. It is not, as a simple theory of make-believe or illusion would suggest, that the audience is involved in "joining its being" to the illusory, but rather in joining to "a certain kind of *actual*,"[48] which holds in continual tension the mimetic and the "real." Richard Schechner has memorably expressed this "binocular" situation in terms of a double negativity. Within the play frame a performer is not herself (because of the operations of illusion) but she is also not not herself (because of the operations of reality). Performer and audience alike operate in a world of double consciousness. This "not me ... not not me"[49] quality of performance has been found a useful formulation by a number of subsequent performance theorists.

Although States calls this peculiar in-between quality of material in the theatrical frame "a certain kind of actual," the "certain kind of actual" encountered in theatre and perhaps even more noticeably in performance art involves not only the material utilized but, even more importantly, the social, cultural, and psychological effects of this activity. In many cases, and especially when performance is viewed from a social science viewpoint, the entire performative situation becomes "a certain kind of actual," with real and lasting effects upon the community or individuals within it, as can be seen in the social dramas of Turner or the psychodramas of Moreno. Indeed, Schechner suggested in 1970 the use of the term "actual"[50] to characterize those cultural performances in both tribal and industrialized societies that make this claim. According to Schechner, an "actual" happens "here and now," makes any reference to past events present, involves consequential, irrevocable acts in a concrete space, and results in its participants experiencing some change in status and therefore recognizing that they have something important at stake in the event.[51] Having "something important at stake," like the "taking responsibility" of Morris and others mentioned earlier, emphasizes both the seriousness and the importance of agency in this process.

The operations of agency and of social or cultural negotiations will be involved to some extent in any performance. Even in the case of Eco's drunken man, when the performer may be quite unaware of the implications of his display, the agency of the production apparatus takes over these responsibilities. In conventional theatre such an apparatus is still an important part of the situation, though agency is dispersed throughout the organization and so is shared at least to some extent by the individual performers. When we turn to other sorts of cultural and social performance, even more responsibility can become available to these performers. In recent performance art, the personal agency of the performer is often of central concern. The performance artist may work as an individual who combines several traditional theatre positions—actor, director, designer, playwright. The performer is not, like Eco's drunken man, "uplifted to the view" by another authenticating agency; it is as a result of the performer's own decision that the presentation to an audience takes place.

Performance and psychoanalysis

Closely related to this dynamic of self-presentation is the normally very close relationship between the "self" of the performance artist and the "self" being presented. Indeed, as we shall discuss later, some theorists have considered this absence of traditional character impersonation as one of the most distinctive characteristics of this approach. Attention to the construction of a "self" also moves us from the social concerns of sociology and anthropology to the personal concerns of psychology and psychoanalysis, an area that attracted far more attention from performance theorists (and performers) in the 1990s than it had previously. Alan Read, in his 2001 article "The Placebo of Performance," argues that the continuing close relationship between performance and psychoanalysis, found everywhere in the images and metaphors of Freud's writing, was "first consummated on a fine evening in 1889 when Sigmund Freud took a night off from the 'Congress in Hypnotism' he was attending in Paris to see a performance artist [Yvette Guilbert]."[52] This is precisely the point in Freud's career, Read notes, when he moved away from hypnosis to "psycho-analysis proper."[53]

The Freudian patient's "revisiting" of past conflicts, with all of the mechanisms related to that process, bears so close a similarity to the "restored behavior" of performance theory that it is rather surprising that Freud and psychoanalytic theory did not figure more prominently in the early days of modern performance theory, but in fact performance theorists first became interested in psychoanalysis not primarily because of its central attention to restored behavior, but because of its attention to the process of identity formation, and especially the formation of gender roles. Although Freud's male-oriented system and his association of women with passivity, masochism, and hysteria was naturally troubling to feminist theorists studying the relationship between identity and performance during the 1980s, the cultural dominance of the Freudian system and the extent of its considerations of the subject of identity formation required a confrontation with this system, and accommodation of some sort with it.

Identification and psychosemiotics

The construction of social, cultural, and personal identity, and the significance of performance to this process, became one of the most important concerns of both theoretical writings on performance and in performance work itself (see Chapter 7) in the last decades of the twentieth century. Freud's writings provide some of the most extensive and provocative speculations on this subject. In one of the first major studies of feminism and theatre, Sue-Ellen Case's 1988 book of that name, Case proposed the development of a "new poetics" of theatre and performance.[54] Case grounded her theoretical project in semiotics, a theoretical approach derived from linguistics, which I will discuss more fully in the following chapter. This provided a method for analyzing the symbolic functions the figure of a woman fulfilled on stage, specifically her position as the object of the presumably male viewer's consumptive gaze. The cultural system that established the domination of the male viewer Case refers to as psychosemiotics, the male-oriented system of identity formation and identity performance first elaborated by Freud and continued, most importantly for Case, by Jacques Lacan. Case proposes a challenge to this system through the development of a "feminist psychosemiotics" that would expose the male-oriented assumptions of this dominant system and offer validation for alternate identity positions and performances.

Elin Diamond and psychoanalytic theory

By the time of the appearance of the collection *Performing Feminisms* in 1990, editor Sue-Ellen Case could speak of performance and feminism's growing "romance with psychoanalytic theory" despite its troublesome tendency toward transcendentalism or essentialism,[55] and devoted most of the opening section of this collection to essays dealing with identity, performance, and psychoanalytic theory. Each of these essays, interestingly, dealt with such theory primarily not directly from Freud but from neo-Freudian Jacques Lacan, who in the 1980s became a major influence within contemporary theory. Although Lacan shared Freud's masculine orientation, he offered to feminist theorists a highly useful model of identity formation—that is, one which denied a fixed identity but instead saw identity as socially constructed within the realm of language and social practice. Elin Diamond, summarizing this position at the opening of her article "Refusing the Romanticism of Identity," recognizes the importance of this insight, but points out that in the Lacanian system identity is still masculine, and she praises several feminist dramatists who, in her opinion, share Julia Kristeva's further modification of the Lacanian system, and seek to "dissolve identities, even sexual identities."[56]

Diamond established herself as a major figure in the recuperation of Freudian and psychoanalytic concepts for feminist and performative theory in a series of influential articles between 1989 and 1992, pursuing the feminist and performative implications of such key psychoanalytic terms as imitation, mimicry, identification, and hysteria.[57] Referring back to Freud's increasing interest throughout his career upon the process of identification, and its essential role in the shaping of the ego, as well as upon Lacan's model of social construction of identity,[58] Diamond theorizes the ego in essentially performative terms as "a theatrical fiction, permeable, transformable, a precipitate of the subject's psychic history with others."[59] Seeking in her 1992 "The Violence of 'We'" a feminist approach to identification (as she did earlier to mimesis in her 1989 "Mimesis and Mimicry"), Diamond seeks to dismantle "the phenomenological universals of transcendent subjects and objects" and place identity "in a more unstable and contingent relation to identification" than it had been in the classic Freudian tradition.[60]

Ann Pellegrini and racial identity

Ann Pellegrini, in *Performance Anxieties* (1997), extended the kind of psychoanalytic performance analysis that had previously been utilized by Diamond and others to study the construction of gender to race as well, with particular attention to Jewishness and blackness, both in the culture in general as well as in the work of particular performance artists such as Anna Deveare Smith and Sandra Bernhard. Despite Freud's shortcomings, Pelligrini notes, "his richly complicated understanding of the way unconscious identifications form and are continually transforming the character of the ego on the model of an other unhinges self-identity to open up the space between."[61] This project of "unhinging" of self-identity and "opening up" of a space between identity formations became, during the 1980s and 1990s, one of the major strategies in what has been often called "resistant" performance; performance which in a variety of ways sought to challenge the identity formations favored by the dominant surrounding culture and the value systems associated with these. I will consider some of the specific performance strategies employed, in Chapter 8.

Pathologies of identification

Hysteria

Perhaps no part of Freud's speculations on identification has stimulated more provocative and original work among performance theorists than the focus in his writings around 1900 on the pathology of identification, in cases of hysteria, homosexuality, and melancholia (though one might note that, as in much of Freud's work, his views later shifted, and this largely negative view of these processes was to some extent subsequently qualified). In the recuperation of psychoanalytic theory, especially by feminist theorists, each of these "pathologies" has been explored not only for its potential in opening up previously denied or hidden space in the field of identity formation, but also for a better understanding of the processes and potentials of performance itself. Freud himself gave particular attention to hysteria, connecting it with performance in his first speculations on both subjects in the 1900 *Interpretation of Dreams:*[62]

> Identification is a highly important factor in the mechanism of hysterical symptoms. It enables patients to express in their symptoms not only their own experiences, but those of a large number of other people. It enables them, as it were, to suffer on behalf of a whole crowd of people and to act all the parts in a play singlehanded.

Aside from the specific evocation of performance, this striking passage also stresses the threat the hysteric poses to Freud's stabilizing and regularizing system by its uncontrolled proliferation of identity. Such studies as *La Jeune Née* (1975) by Hélène Cixous and Catherine Clément[63] and Sarah Kofman's *L'Enigme de la femme: la femme dans les textes de Freud*[64] focused upon the hysteric as a key threat to the Freudian binary gender system (active/male versus passive/female), a "speaking body" that defies the grammar of the patriarchy and thus must be criminalized, suppressed, and "cured" to protect the operations of that system. Such studies in turn provided a grounding for feminist discussions of hysteria as a trope and as a strategy in both traditional theatre and modern performance art. One of the most important contributors to this discussion was Elin Diamond, whose influential writings on identity during the late 1980s and early 1990s have already been mentioned. These formed the basis of her 1997 book *Unmaking Mimesis*, which developed the close strategic ties between the modern realistic drama and the contemporary rise of psychoanalysis, both centrally concerned with the study of and "cure" of the hysteric woman.[65]

Homosexuality

Feminist interest in performance in general and in the performance of identity in particular was soon followed by performance work from representatives of other disadvantaged groups, among them a group less central to Freud's writings than the hysteric but one no less consistently regarded as a pathological threat to proper identity formation: the homosexual. Both male and female homosexual artists and theorists contributed significantly to the performance world of the late twentieth century, but in theory the more challenging work was provided by women, possibly because of the stronger theoretical base already provided by feminist work in general. The first two major feminist theorists of performance, Sue-Ellen Case and Jill Dolan, explored the potentials and implications of lesbian performance. Among the many theorists who followed them, the one most directly concerned with psychoanalytic analysis and one of the most highly regarded was Lynda Hart, particularly in her 1998 work *Between the Body and the Flesh: Performing Sadomasochism*. At several points in this book Hart confronts the tension that forces feminists who employ psychoanalytic paradigms continually to justify this work in view of that system's "host of offenses against women of all sexual persuasions."[66] Nevertheless, she insists that her work requires an engagement with psychoanalytic theory, "for I find if I don't use it, it uses me."[67] Drawing upon the work of Teresa de Lauretis and, through her, Anna Freud, Hart, in a widely used modern strategy of resistant reading, finds gaps and openings within the apparently monolithic, masculine, normative Freudian system. Just as Diamond and Irigaray challenged the Platonic stabilizing system of mimesis by foregrounding what it sought to silence and exclude in its search for stability, Hart finds lesbian sadomasochism a means of challenging psychoanalytic models of masochism "precisely because within them lesbian sadomasochism is theoretically impossible."[68] Hart's work is particularly significant in the intersection of modern performance theory and psychoanalytic theory not only because of the disruptive site that it opens within the latter, but also because she departs from most previous academic psychoanalytic analysis of sadomasochism by focusing not, as Freud did, upon the formation of identity, but upon the relationship between identity and performative practices—a central concern in performance theory at the end of the twentieth century.

Melancholia

Freud's first extended treatment of melancholia appears in the 1915 paper "Mourning and Melancholia," and deals with the challenges to identity formation posed by the loss of a loved object. Freud himself later took a more positive view of melancholia, writing in the 1923 *The Ego and the Id* that his earlier work "did not appreciate the full significance of this process, and did not know how common and typical it is." Now he suggested that melancholia was in fact essential to identity formation, since the ego itself seemed to be built upon a series of rejected "object-choices," such rejection being the source of melancholia.[69] Later psychoanalytic theory, for example that of Lacan, stressed this more complex view, seeing melancholia as the expression of the ambivalent gain of symbolic representation resulting from the loss that melancholia reflects.[70] During the late 1990s the close association between identity, melancholia, repetition and performance became a major theme in performance theory. A leader in such work was Peggy Phelan, whose book *Mourning Sex* (1997) put forward as its central concern "how we perform our mourning, how we recover from trauma and loss," utilizing the strategies of psychoanalytic theory, which "accounts for the affective force of the sexual and psychic remaking that surviving loss entails."[71] Building upon her earlier book *Unmarked* (1993), dealing with the importance of the process and concept of disappearance in performance,

Phelan here focuses upon trauma, the body and psyche's performative response to this dynamic of loss, tracing the operations of trauma through a variety of mimetic activities—theatre, dance, painting, film, courtroom trials, and writing itself. For her discussions on trauma Phelan draws primarily upon the work of Cathy Caruth, who edited a major anthology on this subject in 1994.[72] Here and in her 1995 article "Traumatic Awakenings," Caruth stresses the importance of an "unarticulated shift" by Freud in *Beyond the Pleasure Principle*, emphasized in turn by Lacan's reading, from the trauma associated with one's own death to that associated with the deaths (or potential deaths) of others. The ethical dimension of this shift Caruth also associates with the work of the philosophy of Emmanuel Levinas, who similarly stressed the ethical resonances of trauma.[73] This ethical dimension of trauma has led psychoanalytic theory back into the domain of anthropology, as performance theorists have studied how traumatized communities utilize performance "both as a symptom of distress and as part of the healing process."[74] This quotation is from Diana Taylor, whose various studies of performance practice in Latin America have provided important insights into the performative qualities of mourning, memorialization, and the operations of historical trauma.

Judith Butler and melancholia

Judith Butler, one of the most influential performance theorists of the late twentieth century, provided an important contribution to the study of the relationship between performance and melancholia in the final two chapters of her 1997 book, *The Psychic Life of Power*. The development of Butler's theories is probably best understood by tracing her development of John Austin's linguistic concept of performativity and the challenge mounted to that concept by Jacques Derrida. I will take up that part of her work in more detail in the next chapter, on linguistic theory, but *The Psychic Life of Power* shows Butler working in a somewhat different (though related) direction. Its central concern is with subjection, and with the role of social power in identity formation. Here Butler takes the unusual step of weaving together the psychoanalytic insights of Freud with theorists of social relationships like Foucault and Althusser, concerned, as she has been in most of her writings, with the dynamics of gender formation, and explores the role of melancholia in that process. Following Lacan's reading of Freud, Butler suggests that the division within the self that gives rise to melancholia also gives rise to representation and thus to performance, but performance itself is haunted by melancholia, since it is it doomed to repetition that recalls loss but never recuperates it.[75] Thus it is not enough to say (as some simplifications of Butler have done) that "gender is performed," unless performance is understood as akin to "acting out" in the psychoanalytic sense. Here the loss of melancholy is both refused and incorporated in the performed identification, paradoxically both present and absent. "Gender itself," Butler proposes, "might be understood in part as the 'acting out' of unresolved grief."[76]

Chapter 3

The performance of language
Linguistic approaches

Semiotics

Although the early work in modern performance theory was dominated by strategies and concerns derived in large part from sociology and anthropology—an orientation challenged during the late 1980s and 1990s, as we have seen, by a turn toward psychology and psychoanalysis—another field in the social sciences, linguistics, was also significant. While seemingly much less prominent in performance theory, linguistics has in fact provided not only some of the most fundamental analytical tools of that theoretical tradition but indeed some of the most basic concepts for understanding what performance is, including the development of the closely related, crucial, and complex concept of performativity.

Inevitably we must begin with the analytic system that forms the ground of all modern linguistics: semiotics. Semiotics was proposed as a new approach to the study of human social behavior by the father of modern linguistics, Ferdinand de Saussure. The 1916 *Course in General Linguistics*, compiled from notes by Saussure's students after his death, called for a "new science" of semiology within the general field of social psychology, which would study "the role of signs in social life."[1] The sign that Saussure proposed as the basic unit of human communication was a social construct which united a meaning (the "signified") with an abstract representation of that meaning (the "signifier"). Thus in the English language, the signified concept of a particular type of quadruped has been culturally bound to the written signifier "dog." Linguistic theorists throughout Europe built upon Saussure's work throughout the following century, but the strategies of his proposed new science also gradually came to be applied to the analysis of a very wide variety of cultural phenomena, including the arts.

An important part of the framework of modern semiotic theory was provided by Roman Jakobson, who proposed dividing any speech event into six constitutive elements: a sender must deliver a message to a receiver, the message, which is framed in a certain mutually understood code, delivered through a physical or psychological context, and referring to a particular context. Each of these constitutive elements provided an important area for subsequent semiotic analysis.

During the 1960s and 1970s a number of European theorists began applying semiotic analysis to theatre. This interest spread to England and America during the 1980s, where semiotics provided a grounding vocabulary, procedural model, and basic orientation for much future work, as suggested by the comment already cited in Sue-Ellen Case's groundbreaking 1988 book *Feminism and Theatre*: "an effective starting point for the intersection of new theory with performance and feminist poetics may be found in the field of semiotics."[2]

The poststructuralist challenge

Occasionally semiotic analysis was applied in the 1970s and 1980s to certain kinds of performance, especially social performance, most notably in Umberto Eco's work on ostentation discussed in the previous chapter. However, by the time semiotics was gaining critical interest in America and England it was being challenged by European poststructuralist theory, which in large part defined itself in opposition to semiotic theory. Jean-François Lyotard, for example, a leading poststructuralist, challenged the entire theory of signs as developed by classical linguistics, since it was based upon absence—the sign by definition standing in for a primary and grounding, but not present reality. Generally speaking, poststructuralist theorists found this absent ground of meaning philosophically unacceptable, insisting that all positions were relative, shifting, and negotiable. Thus a theatre which sought to reflect life and consciousness accurately should be built, as life and consciousness themselves were, not upon the "representative substitutions" of signs, but upon the "libidinal displacements" of flows of psychic energy.[3]

This opposition between absence and presence and between structuralist stability and poststructural flux was echoed in a variety of ways in theorists of the next decade, and became particularly important for those attempting to develop a theoretical grounding for the rapidly developing new field of performance. Josette Féral, for example, in a key 1982 essay in *Modern Drama* called "Performance and Theatricality," distinguished between these two fields of activity in terms extremely close to those of Lyotard. Theatre, Féral suggested, was based upon the semiotic, built of representation, of signs of an absent grounding reality, while performance deconstructed the semiotic codes of theatre, creating a dynamic of "flows of desire" operating in a living present.[4]

An important concern among performance theorists in the early days of that field's development was to show how performance differed from theatre, and for many, the association of theatre with discursivity, structure, absence and semiotics and of performance with libidinal flow, presence, and poststructuralism provided a convenient and useful means for doing this. Thus semiotic theory, while it remained an inescapable element in the intellectual background of modern performance theory became, consciously or unconsciously, more and more excluded from the further development of that theory.

The linguistic tradition

Noam Chomsky's competence and performance

Performance first emerged as an important term in linguistic theory in the writings of Noam Chomsky who, in his *Aspects of the Theory of Syntax* (1965), distinguished between "competence," the ideal general grammatical knowledge of a language possessed by a speaker of it, and "performance," the specific application of this knowledge in a speech situation. In fact this division strongly echoes the division made at the beginning of modern linguistic study by Ferdinand de Saussure between *la langue*, the basic organizing principles of a language, and *la parole*, specific speech acts. Chomsky's formulation had the advantage of stressing ability and action, but it still preserved the emphasis of traditional linguistics upon *la langue* or upon competence, the structuralist study of abstract principles, generalized from a variety of individual examples.

This grounding in some sort of transcendental system or set of givens has continued to dominate much subsequent work on the interrelationship of human action, language, and thought, even in the writings of some theorists who have specifically sought to emancipate themselves from the assumptions of traditional positivism. Jürgen Habermas, for example, developed a theory of communicative competence and performance that drew heavily upon Chomsky, though he sought to apply Chomsky's more narrowly linguistic concerns to such broader matters as truth, justice, and freedom. Like Chomsky, Habermas posits a tacit knowledge of these "universal" values which speakers recognize even though their communicative performances may be distorted by the ideologies of a particular social context.[5]

As early as the 1960s, however, many scholars interested in linguistic study began to regard performance not simply as a restricted, circumscribed, even corrupted derivative of competence, but also as a positive and enabling activity of its own. Traditional linguistic theory remained a strong inspiration for them, but so did the sort of parallel research and writings elsewhere in the humanities and social sciences discussed in the previous chapters—in the writings of Kenneth Burke and Erving Goffman, for example, or in anthropological or folklore studies. New terms stressing this interdisciplinary attitude became increasingly popular—"ethnography of communication," for example, and especially "sociolinguistics."[6]

Dell Hymes and functional linguistics

Dell Hymes, one of the leading developers of modern sociolinguistics, very much reflects these relationships and concerns, urging a more "functional" linguistics to supplement more traditional "structural" linguistics. The former would draw upon sociological and anthropological analysis and methods to look at performance and the contextualization of the speech event rather than the grammatic or linguistic rules that might inform it. Concern shifts from the structure of the *langue* to the event in which specific speech takes place, and the speech community and situation is looked to as the matrix and repository of codes and meanings rather than some general homogeneous cultural community.[7] In a 1982 article on "Linguistic Indeterminacy and Social Context," Dore and McDermott proposed that "Talk is not simply a set of propositions transmitted from encoder to decoder, in which context is occasionally useful as an added interpretive grid through which to pass strange utterances. Rather, people use talk reflexively to build the very contexts in terms of which they understand what they are doing and talking about with each other."[8] We have seen in the previous chapters how well this approach in general, and the writings of Hymes in particular, have fitted into the developing interest in approaching a wide variety of social and anthropological concerns through an emphasis on performance.

Mikhail Bakhtin and the utterance

Bakhtin, whose writings on carnival have entered performance theory along with analagous concerns in modern anthropology, has also importantly contributed to linguistic performance theory through his contextually-oriented work on the "utterance," a central concept in his writing. According to Bakhtin, the utterance is a strip of language that is "always individual and contextual in nature," an "inseparable link" in an ongoing chain of discourse, never reappearing in precisely the same context even if, as often occurs, a specific pattern of words is repeated.

All words, Bakhtin proposes, exist in three aspects: "as a neutral word of a language, belonging to nobody; as an *other's* word, which belongs to another person and is filled with echoes of the other's utterance; and, finally, as *my* word, for, since I am dealing with it in a particular situation, with a particular speech plan, it is already imbued with my expression." Like Derrida (whom we shall consider later in considering his disagreement with Searle), Bakhtin sees all speech as being involved with citation of previous speech, but he also stresses that no citation is ever entirely faithful because of the ever-varying context. We continually "assimilate, rework, and re-accentuate" the already existing words of others, even though they still carry with them something of "their own expression, their own evaluative tone."[9] This double orientation of speech, always involved both with reproduction and also with flux, looks to the same phenomenon as the concept of "restored behavior;" a creative tension between repetition and innovation that is deeply involved in modern views of performance, linguistic and non-linguistic. We shall see, when we turn to the strategies of resistant performance, that this tension is there of major significance.

For Bakhtin, utterances, in a naturally more elaborate manner than particular words, involve a complex layering of previous usages and current context, resulting in a plurality of "voices:"[10]

> Any utterance, when it is studied in greater depth under the concrete conditions of speech communication, reveals to us many half-concealed or completely concealed words of others with varying degrees of foreignness. Therefore, the utterance appears to be furrowed with distant and barely audible echoes of changes of speech subjects and dialogic overtones, greatly weakened utterance boundaries that are completely permeable to the author's expression.

Bakhtin speaks of three categories of words within narrative: direct (denotative), object-oriented (direct discourse of characters, also univocal) and ambivalent, when the writer appropriates another's words for a new use, but does not or cannot remove from them the marks of appropriation. This third process Bakhtin sees as the goal of narrative writing, a situation in which a variety of "voices" can be heard within a single "speech," giving rise to a variety of "meanings" as well as calling attention both to the open-endedness of the speech as well as to its performance within a context. Bakhtin uses the term "monologism" to refer to structures or texts that emphasize a singular message, unaffected by context, and "dialogism" to refer to more open texts and to an awareness of the way they are articulated within a specific milieu.

Julia Kristeva's first published work in France, "Le Mot, le dialogue, et le roman,"[11] dealt centrally with Bakhtin, and Kristeva has been extremely important in calling the attention of subsequent performance theorists to Bakhtin's work. Kristeva links together Bakhtin's concepts of carnival and dialogism under the operations of performance and dramatic action. She speaks of carnival as a mise-en-scène in which "language escapes linearity (law) to live as drama in three dimensions. At a deeper level, this also signifies the contrary: drama becomes located in language. A major principle thus emerges: all poetic discourse is dramatization, dramatic permutation (in a mathematical sense) of words." In the scene of carnival, discourse attains a "potential infinity," where "prohibitions (representation, 'monologism') and their transgression (dream, body, 'dialogism') coexist."[12] The "doubleness" of this operation should be emphasized. Carnival is not simply a parodic reversal, but a true transgression. It is not the other side of the law; it contains the law within itself, as Bakhtin's polyphonic utterance includes what would be excluded by the representation of a monologistic "meaning." Even on "the omnified stage of carnival," Kristeva notes, language "remains incapable of detaching itself from representation" even as it repudiates its role in representation by parodying and relativizing itself.[13] This process is strikingly similar to the operations of restored (or keyed) behavior in anthropological theory where an established form and a contextualized variation are experienced as somehow coexisting within the same action. It also bears strong similarities to the concept of the fluid libidinal "performance" theorized by Josette Féral and others in opposition to the semiotic, monologistic operations of "theatre."

Speech act theory

John Austin

One of the most influential contributions of linguistic theory to the wide range of writings about performance in modern society is, however, much less directly related to the social contextualization of the speech event. This is the concept of speech act theory, developed primarily by John Austin and John R. Searle. One might say that these theorists have provided a methodology for considering language as performance, as Turner, for example, has provided a methodology for considering culture as performance, or Goffman for considering social behavior as performance. But further, they have provided the grounding for the concept of performativity; a concept and term that has become almost as widely circulated, and perhaps even more contested, than that of performance itself.

The foundations of speech act theory were laid in the William James Lecture series delivered by Austin at Harvard in 1955, and published as *How to Do Things with Words*. In these lectures, Austin called attention to a particular type of utterance which he named a "performative." In speaking a "performative," someone does not simply make a statement (the traditional focus of linguistic analysis, which Austin labels the "constative") but also performs an action—as, for example, when one christens a ship or takes marriage vows.[14] Since the primary purpose of the performative is to do something rather than simply to assert something, Austin suggested that its success had to be judged not on the basis of truth or falsity, as was the case with an assertion, but on whether the intended act was in fact successfully achieved or not. To these alternatives, Austin gave the names "felicitous" or "infelicitous." Originally, Austin considered performative statements to be characterized by certain verbs ("performative verbs") spoken in the first person and the present tense, such as "I promise," or "I swear." Subsequently, however, he suggested that other expressions without this characteristic functioned in the same manner. "Go away," for example, operated the same as "I order you to go away," involving not truth or falsity but the success or failure of the command as an act. Such performatives Austin called implicit. This, however, created a new problem, for almost any utterance can be seen as an implicit performative; constatives could be "performatively" recast to begin with "I assert" or "I declare." Far from seeing this as a weakening of his theory, Austin suggested that we take such activities as stating, describing and reporting "a bit off their pedestal" and recognize "that they are speech-acts no less than all these other speech-acts that we have been mentioning and talking about as performative."[15]

Figure 3.1 Performative speech and action. Bette Davis christening a World War II battleship, 1943.

Source: Everett Collection.

The general term that Austin began to apply to his concerns was "illocution." In an attempt to separate out the various general ways in which "to say something was to do something," he distinguished three types of verbal "actions" and, since these are operating on different levels, all three are typically involved in a single utterance; they are the locutionary, the illocutionary, and the perlocutionary. Locutionary acts involve making an utterance with a certain sense and reference, roughly equivalent to "meaning" in the traditional sense. Illocutionary acts are utterances with a certain conventional "force" (as opposed to "meaning"); they call into being, order, and promise, but also inform, affirm, assert, remark, and so on. The focus here is on the force such utterances seek to apply to their discursive situation. In perlocutionary acts, analysis focuses not upon what the utterance is doing but on what it seeks to bring about in a hearer: convincing, persuading, deterring, even surprising or misleading.[16]

John R. Searle

Austin's student, John R. Searle, continued to develop the theory of speech acts, most notably in a 1969 book with that title. While the Austin lectures focused on the particular rather restricted type of utterance that he designated as the "performative," Searle stresses the performance aspect of all language: "The unit of linguistic communication is not, as has generally been supposed, the symbol, word or sentence, or even the token of the symbol, word or sentence, but rather the production or issuance of the symbol or word or sentence in the performance of a speech act."[17] Again, as with anthropological or social performance, we find Searle's performative approach to language looking to the particular context of the act, the intentionality of the producer of the act, and the presumed or actual effect of the act upon those who witness it. "A theory of language," says Searle, "is part of a theory of action," but action undertaken as "a rule-governed form of behavior."[18] Searle feels that Austin's strategy of setting off certain utterances as doings rather than sayings makes too sharp a distinction, since all language is also doing. Even the simple process of uttering words and sentences performs what Searle calls an "utterance act." This utterance act is made up of reference to objects and concepts, such reference constituting the performance of a "propositional act." Whenever a particular intention is involved in the utterance (as it almost invariably is), even if this intention is a simple assertion or statement, the performance of that intention Searle calls an "illocutionary act," while the effect on any hearer, following Austin, is designated as the "perlocutionary act."[19]

The effect of this sort of analysis is to shift the apparent focus of Austin from a few rather specialized speech situations to a recognition of the performative nature of language in general, and to shift from the traditional linguistic concerns with the structure and formal elements of language to a concern with the intentions of the speaker, the effects on the audience, and the analysis of the specific social context of each utterance. This orientation is now generally characterized by linguists as "pragmatics," although this term was not used by either Austin or Searle. It was coined by semiotician Charles Morris, who defined it as the "the science of the relation of signs to interpreters,"[20] a definition expanded by a subsequent scholar in this field, R.C. Stalnaker, to "the study of linguistic acts and the contexts in which they are performed."[21]

Julia Kristeva

A differently focused but equally important correction to Austin was provided by Kristeva. While Searle attacked Austin's neutral and descriptive "locutionary" on the grounds that illocution and perlocution was always involved, Kristeva attacked it on the related grounds that description itself was based upon symbolic convention, and thus involved already in illocution and perlocution and the performative "scene" of shifting and negotiated meanings.[22]

The approach of Austin and Searle seems to find within language itself a division that performance theorists have often sought to place between language and physical action (or in some cases between theatre and performance itself). On the one hand we have the semiotic, the linguistic, the symbolic, whose elements stand in for absent realities and whose utilization is governed by more or less fixed abstract structures. On the other hand we have the realm of physical presence, whose elements offer an accessible reality, which, however, can only be understood within a specific, never precisely repeated context (as we have seen, Bakhtin, and subsequently Kristeva, make a similar distinction within a model that suggests how these two opposing operations coexist within performance). Communication is still involved, but the emphasis is not on the traditional communication of an abstract and unitary thought content, but of an original movement, an effect, a force.

Emile Benveniste

The emphasis placed upon the changing social context of the utterance in speech act theory and the tendency to apply performative analysis to a very wide range of linguistic phenomena aroused strong reaction among linguistic theorists who preferred a more formal or structural approach. Particularly influential was Emile Benveniste, who in the essay "Analytical Philosophy and Language" supported Austin's constative/performative division but faulted Austin for not making the distinction between them absolutely clear. To correct this imprecision, Benveniste insisted that any performative "must conform to a specific model, that of the verb in the present and in the first person," and moreover, must be uttered by "someone in authority" who has the power to effect the act uttered. Anyone, says Benveniste, can shout "I decree a general mobilization" in a public square, but this is not an act, and thus not a performative statement, "because the requisite authority is lacking. Such an utterance is no more than *words*."[23]

Jerrold Katz

A quite different attempt to limit and control (if not marginalize) Austin's performative is represented by the work of Jerrold Katz, a psycholinguist who looks less to the structuralist approach represented by Benveniste than to its major rival in modern linguistic theory, the transformational grammar of Chomsky. Like Benveniste, Katz tries to give Austin's division a rigidity and specificity Austin avoided and, again like Benveniste, he does this by focusing not upon the slippery area of language use (what Chomsky called performance) but upon the more stable and abstract system that theoretically provided the foundations for this use (Chomsky's "competence"). In the preface to his *Propositional Structure and Illocutionary Force* (1977), Katz states frankly that in order to develop his own theory "the performance slant that

Austin gave speech act theory had to be eliminated, and the basic ideas of the theory had to be removed from the theory of acts and relocated in the theory of grammatical competence." In place of speech act theory Katz proposes two new related theories—one of competence, one of performance—both notably based on abstract operational principals rather than on speakers or speaking situations. The "competence" theory concerns "what the *ideal* speaker-hearer knows about the illocutionary information embodied in the *grammatical structure* of sentences," (emphases mine), while the "performance" theory concerns the "principles that determine how the information about illocutionary force *embodied in the structure of a sentence* and the information about a speech context *assign an utterance meaning* to the use of a sentence" (emphases mine).[24] Although Katz undertakes to "save Austin from Austin"[25] by removing the blurriness, ambiguities, and uncontrolled spread of performative concerns in Austin's work, he ends, like Benveniste, in developing a brilliant and highly influential theory which in fact turns radically away from Austin's orientation on language as a human activity toward a concern with language in the abstract, as structure or grammar.

The literary speech act

Shoshana Felman

What is at stake here is a conflict that in various forms is very widely manifested in modern thought, and in which "performance" and "language" are both deeply involved. A particularly articulate exploration of the struggle may be found in Shoshana Felman's *The Literary Speech Act: Don Juan with Austin, or Seduction in Two Languages* (1980), who uses Austin and Benveniste, along with Jacques Lacan and Molière's *Don Juan*, to pursue a project in literary, linguistic, and philosophic texts based on the tropes of promising and of truth. In each of these three domains Felman sees a struggle between a force of playfulness, of transgression of established boundaries, and a force which seeks to police and defend those boundaries. Don Juan, says Felman, "does nothing but *promise the constative*,[26] a promise, like Austin's performatives, enacted for its own sake, outside the real of truth or falsehood. Don Juan's opponents in the play, like Austin's, attempt to establish and protect the truth value of the constative, and reject the disruptive seductions of play or performance. It is the performative element of Austin's thought, Felman concludes, that most disturbs his critics, and ties him most closely to thinkers like Nietzsche, Lacan, or Kierkegaard. This can be seen not only in the humor of the approach (a quality most puzzling to "serious" theorists), but also in what Felman calls its "radical negativity." Ultimately, act and knowledge, the constative and performative, while they constantly interfere with each other, can never be made totally congruent. Radical negativity, recognizing this, commits the "scandal" of rejecting the demands of history and normalizing theory for a negative/positive alternative, for truth or falsity, to seek a position outside of the alternative which nevertheless and paradoxically is the ground of history.[27] Naturally such an approach makes impossible any orderly analysis of language, history, or any human activity, and it is for this reason, as Monique Schneider observed in an extended review of Felman's book, Katz and Benveniste insist that "the performative must remain one linguistic category among others. The linguistic domain must be protected against the scandal of a general invasion by the performative of the territory of language as a whole."[28] We have already seen how a similar fear of a "general invasion by the performative" has been manifested by defenders of other territories of social and cultural interaction, and John Lechte, in his study of Kristeva, remarks on the similarity of orientation in Kristeva and Felman, both interested in the tension between the communicative aspect of language, and its scandalous, disruptive aspect.[29]

Felman's study is not only a thought-provoking analysis of a major debate in contemporary cultural study; it is also a provocative approach to a major classic drama, which she sees as performing this same debate in theatrical terms. Her work thus provides an important example of how speech act theory can be utilized in dramatic criticism. It is also a particularly significant text in that its speculations on performance have equally important implications both for the application of speech act theory to literary texts and for its application to the study of performance in general. A central concern for Felman is the relation between speech and the body. Although these two elements cannot be separated in the speech act they can never be made fully congruent either, since the actions of the body are never entirely volitional or capable of linguistic articulation. The speaking body always creates an excess that subverts the very speech it produces.[30] This latter insight, which draws upon the insights of both psychoanalysis and performativity, is clearly more central to the specific concerns of this book, but before pursuing it a brief survey of the more "literary" side of modern speech act theory may be useful—not only for the light it sheds on the analysis of theatrical performance, but also for the strategies it has developed that have in turn enriched later work on performance in general.

The proliferation of studies applying speech act theory to literary or theatrical works is a bit surprising, since Austin himself specifically excluded literary language or language "spoken by an actor" from the processes of illocution or perlocution. Language in poetry he ranks among the "aetiolations, parasitic uses, etc., various 'not serious' and 'not fully normal' uses," where "the normal conditions of reference may be suspended, or no attempt made at a standard perlocutionary act, no attempt to make you do anything." Since such speech is not the speaker's own, the speaker does not take responsibility for it.[31] Despite Felman's in many ways accurate placement of Austin among the playful destabilizers of traditional dichotomies, on this point at least he remains quite conventional—accepting the traditional structural strategy of driving a wedge between "literary" and "actual" language, with the former characterized in such diminutive ways as "parasitic," "not serious," "not fully normal," and so on. Nevertheless, as Andrew Parker and

Eve Kosovsky Sedgwick have pointed out in the introduction to their 1995 collection *Performativity and Performance*, "Austin's parasite has, of course, gone on to enjoy a distinguished career in literary theory and criticism."[32] They call attention also to Austin's interesting characterization of literary and theatrical language as not only parasitic, but as "aetiolations" of language, a word denoting a decadent or diseased form. Thus Austin's performative, they note, "has been from its inception already associated with queerness," a situation which "has hardly changed substantially today."[33]

Literature as act

Somewhat surprisingly, when speech act theory began to be utilized in the early 1970s by scholars of literature, it was with a full acknowledgement that Austin himself had exempted literature from this theory. Richard Ohmann was an important leader in this approach, undertaking to view literature as a "quasi-speech-act." In "Speech Acts and the Definition of Literature" (1971), Ohmann proposed an "illocutionary" approach to literature based on a reader's activity and knowledge of speech acts.[34] The social self of the reader, as conditioned by such matters as gender, class, and race, is given particular attention in Ohmann's "Literature as Act,"[35] bringing his speech act interest very close to reader-response theory and to such reader-response concerns as Stanley Fish's "community of readers."

Stanley Fish's 1980 *Is There a Text in this Class?* was a pioneering work in what has come to be known as reader-response theory, which emphasizes the importance of interpretive communities of readers and how they control the meaning of literary speech acts. In a chapter suggestively entitled "How to Do Things with Austin and Searle," Fish uses Shakespeare's *Coriolanus* as a model of how speech acts operate with communities of interpretation. Fish, for example, calls attention to Coriolanus' error in thinking he can find a world where he can escape social obligations: "There are only other speech-act communities, and every one of them exacts as the price of membership acceptance of its values and meanings."[36]

Like other pioneers in the application of speech act theory to literature, Fish denied the clear distinction between literature and ordinary language found in Austin (and even more distinctly in Searle). In their constant oppositions between "real or serious" and "artificial or fictional" discourse, Fish argues:[37]

> the left-hand term stands for something that is available outside of language, something with which systems of discourse of whatever kind must touch base—Reality, the Real World, Objective Fact. What I am suggesting is that these left-hand terms are merely disguised forms of the terms on the right, that their content is not natural but made, that what we know is not the world but stories about the world, that no use of language matches reality but that all uses of language are interpretations of reality.

Mary Louise Pratt and the tellable

Essentially this same argument is developed in much greater detail by Mary Louise Pratt, whose *Toward a Speech Act Theory of Literary Discourse* (1977) identified the distinction between literature and ordinary language as a fallacy invented by the Russian formalists and maintained by subsequent structuralist theorists. She argued both that so-called ordinary language contains the same sort of features presumably characteristic of "poetic" discourse, and that literature like other language "cannot be understood apart from the context in which it occurs and the people who participate in it."[38] An important source for Pratt was the work of the American sociolinguist William Labov on the oral narrative of personal experience, a type of ordinary discourse that is consciously and aesthetically constructed. Labov analyzes the normal structure of such narratives and characterizes their content as, for example, in response to a question, "tellable" assertions are normally elaborated "stories" that "represent states of affairs that are held to be unusual, contrary to expectations, or otherwise problematic." Their speaker is:[39]

> not only reporting but also verbally *displaying* a state of affairs, inviting his addressee(s) to join him in contemplating it, evaluating it, and responding to it. His point is to produce in his hearers not only belief but also an imaginative and affective involvement in the state of affairs he is representing and an evaluative stance toward it.

The relationship between this common situation in everyday speech and written literary narratives is clear, as is Pratt's idea of how both illocution and perlocution operate in "tellable" assertions. The emphasis upon "display" recalls Umberto Eco's interest in "ostentation" as a strategy for signalling an "aesthetic" response. Pratt's other major source is the work of H.P. Grice, another speech act philosopher, who presented some highly influential correctives to Austin in his William James lectures of 1967, *Logic and Conversation*. Pratt derives from Grice two helpful analytic concepts: the Cooperative Principle and conversational implicature, which assume a tacit contract between speaker and hearer in a literary speech situation. They "have commitments to one another as they do everywhere else," and far from being "autonomous, self-contained, self-motivating, context-free objects which exist independently from the 'pragmatic' concerns of 'everyday' discourse, literary works take place in a context, and like any other utterance they cannot be described apart from that context."[40]

Julia Kristeva and the problem of the "author"

There is no question that Pratt's approach provides for literature an illocutionary dimension much closer to what Austin has in mind for regular discourse than Ohmann provides, and a number of subsequent literary analysts have followed Pratt in considering the "performative" qualities of various works of fiction as elaborate "speech acts" of their authors. This, however, requires the designation of the original author as the authoritative "speaker" of the text, and the assumption that the text guarantees a continuing more or less stable context of communication between that speaker and an audience—assumptions very much at variance with the postmodern concept of the "author" as a shifting "function" in the text. Kristeva, for example, develops this concept from Bakhtin, who observed that the "author" not only contained a variety of voices but also operated as a position, presenting itself as a speaking subject addressing an imagined reader. Similarly the actual reading process involves the projection back of a speaking "author," so that each new reading involves a new "perform-ance" by a new set of "voices."[41] Kristeva evokes both performance and car-nival in describing this process: "The scene of the carnival introduces the split speech act: the *actor* and the *crowd* are each in turn simultaneously subject and addressee of the discourse. The carnival is also the bridge between the two split occurrences as well as the place where each of the terms is acknowledged: the author (actor + spectator)."[42]

Intentions and effects

Sandy Petrey proposes a way around the problem of the author's "inten-tion" in *Speech Acts and Literary Theory* (1990), suggesting that what words do, inside and outside literature, "depends not on speakers but on (conven-tional) context,"[43] and that speech act theory should be involved not with intentions but with effects. This is a point stressed by Austin in his first lecture, which rejected as mistaken the view that "words are uttered as (merely) the outward and visible sign, for convenience or other record or for information, of an inward and spiritual act."[44] The intention *assumed* by the speech act must be distinguished from the normally quite inaccessible actual intention of the speaker. This concern is developed in some detail by Teun A. van Dijk in *Text and Context* (1977), which argues that "We under-stand what somebody does only if we are able to interpret a doing as a certain action. This implies that we reconstruct an assumed intention, purpose and possible further reasons of the agent." An action cannot really be defined or analyzed unless the analysis takes into account "the various mental structures *underlying* the actual doing and its consequences."[45] Van Dijk's "underlying mental structures," intentions and purposes correspond essentially to Austin's illocutionary and perlocutionary forces, but the pres-ence of the key qualifier "assumed" in van Dijk's formulation is an essential qualification, recalling (as do Bakhtin and Kristeva) that, from an audience point of view, the intentions of an author/speaker are necessarily a con-struct. Van Dijk also suggests that immediate purposes be distinguished from long-term global purposes, that the immediate effect of a single speech act can normally best be understood as a single operation in a whole series of actions directed toward a general goal.[46]

Drama as a literary speech act

Ross Chambers has specifically applied Austin's theories to analysis of theatre, but he begins by rejecting Austin's concept of the "parasitic" nature of fictive discourse. Also, like Kristeva, he emphasizes that the role of the "speaker" in such discourse cannot operate within the standard illocutionary model, which assumes a speaker is in contact with a specific, known hearer:[47]

> Very quickly cut loose from its ties with its "author," an artistic discourse keeps addressing constantly new hearers who must interpret it in continually varying contexts. The "performative" underlying aesthetic discourse would be then something like: "I offer myself for your interpretation" or "I invite you to interpret me"—always supposing that such an act could be attributed to the message itself (become its own sender) and that the receiver designated here as "you" could be conceived as a perfectly indeterminate "to whom it may concern."

Umberto Eco extends this strategy in an extremely important direction for theatre and performance theory, claiming a similar illocutionary operation for the activation of an interpretive relationship not only between a reader and a literary text, but also between an audience member and a performance. Within the fictive world of the play, says Eco, actors make speech act "pseudo-statements" to each other (understood by the audience through the operations of Ohmann's mimetic activation). But, Eco continues, the production also involves a necessary speech act presented by the performer corresponding to Chambers' aesthetic performative which establishes that fictional world: "I am now going to act." The establishment of the theatrical frame can be thus conceived as a speech act: "through the decision of the performer ... we enter the possible world of performance."[48]

Chambers makes a useful distinction, based on standard linguistic theory, at the beginning of his analysis, observing that:[49]

> like any discourse, the theatrical text can be thought of as énoncé and as énonciation. In the first case, it is considered, one might say, "grammatically," in its components and how they work together. In the second, it appears in the context of a communication situation, as an act destined to produce an effect on one or several spectators.

Chambers then proceeds to comment on both of these levels. On the level of the énoncé, illocution within the narrative world of the play, he notes:[50]

> It is easy to determine that the basic subject of dramatic narration is the illocutionary relationship, a communicative exchange between a sender and a receiver of a speech in a given context.... It is quite correct to think that the particular vocation of theatre is to explore the consequences of this intuition that "to say is to do," and "to do is to say."

On the level of énonciation, illocution between play and audience, he suggests a variety of social functions proposed for the drama, citing theatrical theorists like Brecht and anthropological theorists like Caillois.

One of the most comprehensive engagements with Austin's concepts in dramatic analysis has been Timothy Gould's 1995 "The Unhappy Performative," which challenges the widespread application of the performative to concerns developed out of feminist and deconstructive literary and performance theory. Like Felman, Gould suggests that the theatrical is more fully invested (as is Austin's philosophy) with the constative function of language than with the performative function. Gould reads *Antigone* as a struggle to maintain the constative control of discourse, made more difficult, if not impossible, by the demands of conflicting values and political reality.[51]

Speech acts within the drama

Chambers' attempt to apply speech act theory to both levels of theatre as a discourse is rather unusual. Generally speaking, those theorists who have applied speech act analysis to theatre have worked primarily or exclusively on the level of the énoncé, the operations of illocution within the fictive world of the play; a level which is more clearly compatible both with traditional literary analysis and also with the use of speech act analysis in ordinary speaking situations. Indeed Joseph A. Porter, who applied Austin's theories to Shakespeare's history plays in his 1979 *The Drama of Speech Acts*, argued that speech act theory could not in fact be applied to the drama as a whole because there was "no single speaker who is the doer of the action," but that it was ideal for analysis of the workings of the fictive world portrayed, since this world is based on speech acts. Porter even proposed that one might rephrase Aristotle in Austin's terms: "speech action is the soul of verbal drama."[52] Ohmann similarly argues that "in a play, the action rides on a train of illocutions," and that "movement of the characters and changes in their relations to one another within the social world of the play appear most clearly in their illocutionary acts."[53]

In view of Austin's specific exclusion of literature from his theory, it is perhaps not surprising that performative speech act theory has not been widely utilized in the analysis of drama. Occasional striking and successful analyses of this type do appear, however, such as Branislav Jakovljec's insightful performative analysis of Ibsen's *A Doll's House*, which appeared in 2002 in *Theatre Journal*.[54] Such analyses provide a model of how this theory might be productively applied to other works of dramatic literature.

Speech act theory and semiotics

Keir Elam

A particularly extensive example of the application of speech act analysis to drama is Keir Elam's *The Semiotics of Theatre and Drama* (1980), the first book-length application of semiotic theory to theatre studies in English. Indeed so central was speech act theory to Elam's approach that many readers assumed, until other works in the field began to appear, that semiotics and speech act theory were essentially identical. Nevertheless, despite its comprehensive analysis of various aspects of discourse, Elam's book really only directed its analysis to the fictive world of the play. In a typical passage, Elam asserted that:[55]

> Dramatic discourse is a network of complementary and conflicting illocutions and perlocutions: in a word, linguistic *interaction*, not so much descriptive as performative. Whatever its stylistic, poetic and general "aesthetic" function, the dialogue is in the first place a mode of *praxis* which sets in opposition the different personal, social and ethical forces of the dramatic world.

Eli Rozik

Application of speech act analysis to theatre in a more general manner has been most notably carried out in a number of articles by Eli Rozik.[56] Drawing upon the vocabulary not only of speech act theory but also of semiotics, Rozik has suggested that theatrical speech acts should be considered as verbal indexes of actions, an index being a sign which, according to Peirce, signifies "by virtue of contiguity, particularly, a part-whole relationship."[57] Given this "part-whole" relationship, speech acts should not be analyzed as if they were self-contained units (which speech act theory, despite its interest in context, has tended to do), but rather in terms of the complex actions of which they are a part.

This shift in focus from speech to act characterizes Rozik's approach, and moves him away from linguistic theorists like Austin and Searle and literary theorists like Fish and Rivers toward action theorists like Teun van Dijk, Geoffrey Leech and Stephen Levinson.[58] When speech acts are considered in terms of their force, Rozik argues, they become better understood, despite their use of language, as part of a different set of human phenomena. Functionally speaking, "they are not a part of language, but a part of action." By way of illustration, Rozik cites several possible speech acts along with non-verbal gestures all of which express the same action "force," such as making a threat or asking pardon.[59] As we move from the illocutionary interpretation of such acts (verbal and non-verbal) to the mental construction of the character they gradually illuminate and the fictive world of which that character is a part, a process is assumed which is the theatrical equivalent of the mimetic process outlined by Ohmann for the reader of fiction, similarly constructing a fictive world by the interpretation of illocutionary forces. Rozik again looks, however, not to literary or speech act theorists but to pragmatic or action theorists to suggest this broader reception concern. Van Dijk, for example, seems to Rozik to move speech act theory very close to a strategy for the analysis of the total dramatic action, where individual speech acts are calculatedly organized by playwright, director, and actor to serve as easily decoded indexes of actions, and where in conventional dramatic structure "every speech act in a play, whatever its location, indicates not only *immediate* purposes but also *global* ones."[60] Van Dijk's idea of global purpose seems to come very close to Stanislavky's concept of the super-objective.

Rozik, like other theorists applying speech act or action theory to drama or fiction, devotes most of his attention to what is happening within the fictive world, though he does provide a number of stimulating suggestions about the double operations of theatrical speech acts on their two receivers—the characters in the play and the audience. He gives particular emphasis, for example, to what he calls ironic conventions, a variety of theatrical devices such as the soliloquy, the aside, and functional characters such as the chorus, all of which "depart from the basic iconic nature of the theatrical text" but by that very departure "play a crucial role in the communication between author and audience, different from that played by the interaction among characters."[61] Elsewhere he provides brief but stimulating speculations about the dynamics of the invitation to interpretation mentioned by Eco and Chambers. These observations suggest how a perlocutionary analysis of theatre speech act's effect on its audience might be pursued.

Clark and Carlson's "Hearers and Speech Acts" (1982) similarly, and perhaps even more surprisingly, fails to extend its interesting analysis of a Shakespeare play (here *Othello*) to the operations of theatre itself. They suggest that in addition to the traditional "illocutionary" act directed at the addressee there is in all conversations involving more than two people a second illocutionary act directed at all "hearers" in the conversation, and serving to inform them jointly of the assertion being made. Although they take as their basic example Othello's "Come, Desdemona," with Iago and Roderigo as other "hearers," they do not explore the fact that in the theatre there is an even more important set of secondary "hearers" in the actual audience, who also are being "informed jointly of the assertion, promise, or apology being directed at the addressees."[62] If such a statement is illocutionary because "Othello not only intends to give an order to Desdemona but intends the other hearers to understand that he is giving this order," this same illocutionary argument clearly extends to the audience as well although the "intention" shifts to another level; that of the speaking actor, not the speaking character.

Another literary critic much interested in speech act analysis is Elias Rivers, who argued in his 1983 *Quixotic Scriptures* that "the theatre of Golden Age Spain, like that of Elizabethan England, provided a sociolinguistic laboratory within which to test old and new ideas about the authority of speech acts."[63] Rivers pursued this approach in a 1984 NEH seminar which resulted in a collection of essays, published in 1986, applying speech act theory to a range of classical and modern plays.[64] Since that time speech act theory has become a standard tool of literary analysis, still applied primarily to Shakespeare and Spanish Renaissance plays, but also a variety of other traditions, including the drama of Germany, France, and Ireland,[65] though most such work follows Fish, Clark and Carlson in keeping this analysis within the fictive world of the play.

Text and performance

Thus during the 1970s and 1980s speech act theory joined with the new performative interest in the social sciences in general to effect a major change, one might almost say a revolution in the areas of literary studies most associated with performance. During those decades, however, it had far less effect upon performance theory not so much tied to traditional dramatic literature. After 1990, however, this situation essentially reversed, with the literary use of speech act analysis distinctly declining while the Austinian concept of performativity moved to a central position in performance theory. A typical indication of this change may be traced in the shifting interests of the interdisciplinary journal *Literature in Performance*, established in 1980 by the Speech Communication Association of America. Its original editorial policy was stated in fairly conventional and traditional terms: to study "literature through performance" and to serve those "involved in the teaching oral interpretation."[66] Soon, however, the journal began to show a growing interest in a variety of performance, with articles from religion, folklore, anthropology, psychology, sociology, and cultural history along with the more predictable pieces on the teaching and practice of theatre and oral interpretation. By 1989 the concerns of the journal and the field had sufficiently shifted to call for a new title, *Text and Performance Quarterly*. In the opening editorial to this new version of the journal, James W. Chesebro suggested that the new title implied not only a shift in orientation from literature to a far more diverse set of communication forms, but also an interest in a variety of theoretical questions surrounding the term "text" in contemporary thought. Central to this new orientation, according to Chesebro, is a recognition that both text and performance are conditioned by their media, making an interest in the operations of media essential to both text and performance.[67] Subsequent issues have in fact continued to emphasize rather traditional performative analysis of drama, novels, and poetry, but this important and eclectic journal has also offered a wide variety of articles drawing upon Austin and Searle, Fish, Bakhtin, and Goffman and Turner, and concerned with performances by no means wholly literary in origin. Here, as elsewhere, the concept of performance seems to be serving as an impetus to dissolve traditional disciplinary and methodological boundaries in order to explore more general concerns.

Performativity and citation

Jacques Derrida

The introduction to the 1995 anthology *Performativity and Performance*, edited by Andrew Parker and Eve Kosofsky Sedgwick, speaks of a "theoretical convergence that has, of late, pushed performativity onto center stage." The editors attribute this emergence to the "renewal" of the "specifically Austinian valences" of the term "performance" by Jacques Derrida and Judith Butler,[68] two of the most influential theorists of the late twentieth century. Derrida was the first major practitioner of deconstruction, a central strategy of poststructuralist theory which defined itself largely in opposition to the Western metaphysical tradition in general and to the operations of modern linguistic theory, founded on the work of de Saussure, in particular. Semiotics, like European metaphysics in general, was based upon an assumption of stable, self-authenticating meanings or systems of meanings, and was built upon a model of primary grounding reality lying behind and stabilizing individual manifestations of speech, or the "derived speech" of writing. Derrida, on the contrary, sees this "primary reality" to be as "derived" as writing itself, already conditioned by prior structures and rejected material of which it bears only the traces. Indeed, poststructuralist theorists in general, whatever their individual differences, found the traditional absent ground of meaning philosophically unacceptable, insisting that all positions were relative, shifting, and negotiable. We have already noted how the influence of this approach, in the writings of theorists like Lyotard, Féral and others, provided a position for the development of a poststructuralist view of the unstable and flowing art of performance that opposed it to the traditional and more theoretically stable "semiotic" or "structuralist" art of theatre.

Students of contemporary theoretical speculation will recognize this privileging of spoken language over its "parasitic" derivative, written language, as a typical manifestation of the "metaphysics of presence" that Jacques Derrida has called into question in so much of his criticism. It is therefore not surprising that despite certain common assumptions Derrida challenged Austin on this matter, initiating a heated and well-known debate between proponents of speech act theory on the one hand and of deconstruction on the other that has tended to overshadow more positive relationships between speech act analysis and current literary and performance theory. Even in its broad outlines this debate goes far beyond our particular concern, which is the contribution of this approach to modern ways of thinking about performance, but one central concern in Derrida's first essay on the question, "Signature, Event, Context," concerning citation, has become so important to subsequent writings on performance by Judith Butler and others that it deserves some special attention.[69]

As a result of its interest in the "presence" and the specific context of linguistic performance, there is little suggestion within Austin's theory of performance of the performance concepts of restored or repeated behavior, although Searle's characterization of language as "rule-governed" behavior might be considered as opening this possibility. Speech acts are very closely tied to their creators and their context, and seem to be considered as essentially untainted by the sort of mimetic aura that Wilshire and others find ethically troubling in other theories of social performance. Derrida, however, has pointed out that this apparently clear and comfortable division between non-mimetic speech and mimetic writing is an illusion. Although Austin specifically excludes from his system citation (which, like literature, he considers to be a "non-serious" use of language), Derrida, like Bakhtin earlier, argues on the contrary that it is only by virtue of citation, or what he calls "iterability," that performative utterances can succeed. A performative could not open a meeting, launch a ship or seal a marriage if it were "not identifiable as *conforming* with an iterable model," if it were not identifiable in some way as a "citation."[70] It is important to note, however, that for Derrida citation is never exact because, like Bakhtin's utterance, it is always being adapted to new contexts. Any citation, indeed any sign, "can break with every given context, engendering an infinity of new contexts in a manner which is absolutely illimitable."[71] This argument moves the concept of linguistic performance back into the realm of repeated (or restored) and contextualized activity that is so basic to performance theory.

Pierre Bourdieu

A very different disagreement with Austin on the nature of the "force" or authority behind a performative utterance was developed by Pierre Bourdieu in his *Language and Symbolic Power* (1991). The implied formalism of Austin's position, in which performatives operate because over time they have become established by stable linguistic and social situations, seems to Bourdieu to ignore the shifting but undeniable power of social institutions. Austin's central error, argues Bourdieu, is that "he thinks that he has found in discourse itself—in the specifically linguistic substance of speech, as it were—the key to the efficacy of speech." This position, however, tempts one to forget "that authority comes to language from outside" and that language "at most *represents* this authority, manifests and symbolizes it."[72]

Although Bourdieu does not engage Derrida by name, Derrida seems to be the primary example of the "linguistic formalists" whom he accuses of attempting to correct Austin, but in fact repeating his error of confusing the linguistic and social dimensions of language and therefore continuing to privilege the former and thus undervaluing the central role played by the social context in determining whether an utterance will succeed as performance or not.[73]

Judith Butler

It is surely Judith Butler more than any other single theorist who has made performativity a central term in modern performance theory, and her work both incorporates and extends the writings on this subject by Austin, Derrida, Bourdieu, Felman, and many others. At the center of the writings of one of the most influential recent writers on gender, Judith Butler, is a view of gender not as a given social or cultural attribute but as a category constructed through performance, and thus characterized not by a pre-existing essence or unchanging social determination but by the always shifting dynamic of performativity. In Butler's first major study of this phenomenon, *Gender Trouble* (1990), she called gender "performative," a "doing." Equally important and equally revolutionary, she characterized it also as "not a doing by a subject who might be said to preexist the deed." On the contrary, the "subject" is itself "performatively constituted" by acts, including acts that signify a particular gender.[74] These acts in turn are not singular events, but "ritualized production, a ritual reiterated under and through constraint, under and through the force of prohibition and taboo, with the threat of ostracism and even death controlling and compelling the shape of the production."[75]

Somewhat surprisingly, in view of the subsequent development of the concept of performativity by Butler and others, there is no mention of Austin and Searle in *Gender Trouble*. The major theoretical grounding of the book, Butler later stated, was the work of a variety of recent French theorists, among them Foucault, Lacan, and Kristeva, especially upon the relationships between gender formation, language, and power. The concept of performativity itself Butler says she found in Derrida, interestingly not in his debate with Austin but in his commentary on Kafka's "The Law," where Derrida argues that the "anticipation of an authoritative disclosure of meaning installs and authorizes that meaning," a process she speculated might be similar to that of gender formation.[76]

The concept of gender performativity developed in *Gender Trouble* seemed to leave little room for altering performed categories, since agency itself arises not from choosing some subject existing before the performance of identity, but rather from the "self" constituted by performance. Therefore Butler's next book, *Bodies that Matter* (1993), addressed the possibility of the alteration and modification of gender performance. In developing the theoretical grounding for this strategy, Butler shifted her attention from Derrida's commentary on Kafka to his debate with Austin and Searle, Derrida's emphasis upon the citationality of performative utterances, and the inevitable slippage of such citationality. Applying this linguistic debate to the matter of gender performance, Butler argued that gender performance too was citational, thus never precisely repeating the absent original and opening a space for challenge and change. Gender she now posited as "a sedimented effect of a reiterative or ritual process which operates through the reiteration of norms," a reiteration which both "produces and destabilizes."[77]

Butler cited as the major sources for this new emphasis Lacan, for whom "every act is to be construed as a repetition, the repetition of what cannot be recollected, of the irrecoverable," and Derrida, for whom "every act is itself a recitation, the citing of a prior chain of acts which are implied in the present act and which perpetually drain any 'present' act of its present-ness."[78] Lacan's emphasis upon the compulsive attempted repetition of the irrecoverable looks back, as was discussed in Chapter 2, to Freud's concept of melancholia and to repetition that recalls loss but never recuperates it—a concern central to Butler's 1997 book *The Psychic Life of Power*.[79] Melan-choly's awareness of loss is both refused and incorporated in the performed identification, paradoxically (as the citation from Derrida suggests) both present and absent.

Austin and the tradition of speech act theory is again central to Butler's 1997 *Excitable Speech: A Politics of the Performative*, in which Butler studies the operations of hate speech, of what constitutes the power of speech to harm, dealing with highly charged modern speech act controversies such as cross-burning, pornography, gays in the military, and censorship, and the power the national legal system, and particularly the Supreme Court, exer-cises over such controversies by exerting the authority to decide what is a speech act (especially an injurious one) and what is not. As Butler argues, "the Court's speech exercises the power to injure precisely by virtue of being invested with the authority to adjudicate the injurious power of speech."[80] The critique Butler mounts of the Court's 1995 denial of the per-formative effects of cross-burning in the name of defending "free speech" has since, strikingly, resurfaced, when in 2002 the issue again came before

Figure 3.2 A cross burning with Ku Klux Klan members. Stone Mountain, Georgia, 1971.
Source: Everett Collection.

the Court and Justice Clarence Thomas, in a highly publicized session of the Court, reversed his previous position in terms that brought performativity to the center of the debate. While in 1995 Thomas had written that cross-burning was essentially communicative, conveying a "political and religious message of white supremacy" which, however reprehensible, was protected by the First Amendment, in 2002 Thomas argued that cross-burning was in fact performative, that it contained "no communication, no particular message," but was designed, in Austin's terms, to "do some-thing"—that is "to cause fear and to terrorize a population."[81]

In both of her publications from 1977, but particularly in *Excitable Speech*, Butler first explored the linkage between her own developing theories and the work of the cultural theorist Pierre Bourdieu. Although Bourdieu, as we have seen, took issue with both Austin and Derrida on the operations of the performative, Butler seeks a position that incorporates elements of each of these. Bourdieu provides a social grounding for the performative which is lacking in Derrida's decontextualized model, while Derrida's concept of iterability frees the performative from the rigid and essentially untrans-formable rituals of social custom.[82]

Butler finds particularly useful in this respect the idea of *habitus* developed in Bourdieu's *The Logic of Practice*,[83] since, again unlike Derrida, Bourdieu underscores the importance of the body as the site for the rituals of performativity. Butler calls the *habitus* "a tacit form of performativity, a citational claim lived and believed at the level of the body."[84] What Bour-dieu does not acknowledge, however, or suppresses, is the paradox that while the body operates in society by means of speech acts it remains uncontained by those speech acts, producing both an excess and an absence, the "scandal" of embodied speech analyzed by Felman, whose work on *Don Juan*, and on Austin, Butler cites approvingly in this context. Butler's weaving together of the work of such French poststructuralist and psychoanalytic theorists as Derrida, Lacan, and Kristeva, the speech act work of Austin and Searle, and the cultural theory of Althusser, Foucault, and Bourdieu has produced a discussion of performance and performabil-ity in both language and body of enormous richness and complexity, and one that holds a key position in current writing on these subjects.

Performance and the social sciences: a look backward

In the three chapters opening this book I have considered some of the most influential ways in which the concept of performance has been developed within the modern fields of psychology, anthropology, sociology, and lin-guistics. I have also discussed some of the ways in which the concept has been complicated and enriched as it has flowed from one of these fields to another and circulated back to them after development by yet other theo-rists whose primary interest lay elsewhere—in gender studies, in cultural studies, or in human performance in general. The various disciplinary uses of the term performance (and the more recently popular term performativity) have resulted in so rich a web or field of meanings, some of them quite contradictory, that, as I warned in the introduction, attempting to find a fairly stable connotation or even group of connotations for either of these ever-fluid terms is quite impossible. Nevertheless, before leaving the more theoretical section of this study to take a focused historical look at performance within the tradition of art and entertainment, a few general summary observations may perhaps be attempted. First, as already noted, performance and performativity are deeply involved both with the reinforcement and the dismantling of stable systems of meaning and representation, far more closely associated with the paradoxical world of poststructuralism and postmodernism (which I will consider in a later chapter) than with the ordered and stable systems sought by structuralism and high modernism. Secondly, and related to this, performance and performativity, in whatever field they are utilized, are always involved with a sense of doubleness, of the repetition of some pattern of action or mode of being in the world already in existence, even when, as Derrida has often argued, that authenticating "original" is illusory—an effect of the inevitable doubling and sense of distance resulting from consciousness itself. Although clearly this is most stressed in psychoanalytic theory, especially as it has been developed after Freud, the concept of performance in almost all disciplines is always associated with consciousness and reflection and thus with a sense of the "restored" even if, as in trauma, the "restored" is unrecoverable, or even perhaps, as deconstruction suggests, is in fact an illusion of language and consciousness.

When the field of performance studies began to appear in American universities, and subsequently in universities around the world, many of its grounding theories, strategies and terms came from the social sciences. However, the application of social science methodologies to a wide range of human activities was by no means the only thing that characterized performance studies, and nor was it necessarily the aspect of performance studies that most striking separated it from the field from which it took most care to distinguish itself—theatre studies. Another very important innovation of performance studies was its interest in a broad range, contemporary and historical, of quasi-theatrical performative activity which had for the most part been ignored by more conventional theatre scholars with their traditional interest in the literary text. Part II will briefly survey what new material and new perspectives this opened, first in the study of historical material, and then in contemporary material especially that sort of activity specifically called "performance" or "performance art."

The art of performance

Chapter 4

Performance in its historical context

Performance's new orientation

The new interest that developed in "performance studies" during the 1970s was much involved, as the previous chapters have noted, with exploring the concept of "performance" in the social sciences and considered the theoretical implications of that concept. Two other important aspects of performance studies were more closely related to traditional theatre studies, although in emphasizing physical activity and embodiment rather than the presentation of a literary text (the traditional concern of theatre studies) performance studies opened up different material for study as well as providing new critical tools for this work. Part II of this book will present an overview of these two more theatrically oriented aspects of performance studies, the first dealing with historical and the second with more contemporary work. Even though many of the avant-garde theatre artists of the past century looked (as did avant-garde experimenters in the other arts) to popular and folk forms for inspiration, theatre scholars for the most part continued to neglect such forms even while elevating the avant-garde tradition to a central place in histories of the art. With a few exceptions, most notably the *commedia dell'arte*, folk and popular forms were sacrificed to the literary and high culture bias of traditional theatre studies.

Performance studies, on the contrary, emphasized such folk and popular material, even (some critics of performance studies have asserted) to the neglect of traditional theatre. Thus an alternative historical theatre tradition was made available, based not upon the staging of literary texts, often not even upon mimesis, but on the display of the active body. This chapter will briefly outline the shape of that alternative tradition. In the contemporary world, the rise of performance studies in the academy was paralleled by the rise of a new genre in the art and theatre world called "performance" or "performance art," which, like the historical study of performance, placed its emphasis upon the present body instead of on the absent text of traditional theatre. The development of this new orientation in theatre and art will be the subject of Chapter 5.

When this modern "performance" or "performance art" began to be recognized during the 1970s as an artistic mode in its own right, it naturally began to stimulate an array of secondary material. First came reviews and studies of individual performances, then more general studies of the new approach and attempts to place it within contemporary culture and an historical tradition, even though the protean nature of performance, a characteristic of such work from the very beginning, made the task of chroniclers, commentators and source seekers a difficult one. RoseLee Goldberg, who wrote the first history of "performance" in 1979[1] and issued a revised and expanded history of "performance art" in 1988,[2] observed that this phenomenon "defies precise or easy definition beyond the simple declaration that it is live art by artists." Goldberg argues that the mutability of such art results from its iconoclastic focus: "The history of performance art in the twentieth century is the history of a permissive, open-ended medium with endless variables, executed by artists impatient with the limitations of more established art forms."[3]

The avant-garde tradition

In the course of her book Goldberg traces this history of revolt and experimentation, beginning with futurism, then proceeding to experimental theatre of the Russian Revolution, dada and surrealism, the Bauhaus, Cage and Cunningham, happenings, Anna Halprin and the new dance, Yves Klein, Piero Manzoni, and Joseph Beuys, and to body art and modern performance. Except for the more recent manifestations this history is essentially the history of twentieth-century avant-garde theatre, and historians and theorists of performance art have generally followed Goldberg in viewing it within that tradition. So the authors of *Performance: Texts and Contexts* (1993) remark that performance art "belongs in the traditions of the avant-garde," and trace its heritage from futurism through dada, surrealism, happenings and the poem-paintings of Norman Bluhm and Frank O'Hara.[4] This heritage clearly influences the authors' proposed "definition" of performance art. Though they admit that such works "vary widely," they rather boldly assert that "*all* share a number of common characteristics" (emphasis mine). These are:[5]

> (1) an antiestablishment, provocative, unconventional, often assaultive interventionist or performance stance; (2) opposition to culture's commodification of art; (3) a multimedia texture, drawing for its materials not only upon the live bodies of the performers but upon media images, television monitors, projected images, visual images, film, poetry, autobiographical material, narrative, dance, architecture, and music; (4) an interest in the principles of collage, assemblage, and simultaneity; (5) an interest in using "found" as well as "made" materials; (6) heavy reliance upon unusual juxtapositions of incongruous, seemingly unrelated images; (7) an interest in the theories of play that we discussed earlier [Huizenga and Caillois], including parody, joke, breaking of rules, and whimsical or strident disruption of surfaces; and (8) open-endedness or undecidability of form.

Although this is in fact a very useful categorization of a number of frequent characteristics of modern performance art, obviously not all performance art shares all these characteristics. Moreover, in Goldberg as well as in others who have followed her model these characteristics are so heavily weighted toward an avant-garde orientation that they are very likely to distort a reader's idea not only of what has been included in modern performance art, but also of how that art is related to performance history. When, for example, *Performance* discusses Whoopi Goldberg, one of four "performance artists" analyzed in some detail in this book, only passing mention is made of Whoopi Goldberg's similarity to Ruth Draper, the great monologue artist of the 1930s and 1940s,[6] and the monologue tradition in which Draper worked is not considered at all even though the futurist, dadaist "background" of modern performance art is carefully traced following the model established by RoseLee Goldberg.

It could surely be argued, however, that the now standard "experimental" genealogy leading from the futurists through dada and surrealism to the happenings and then to modern performance art is much less relevant to the work of a performer like Whoopi Goldberg than the great twentieth-century monologue tradition in America, including such great women artists as Beatrice Herford, Marjorie Moffett, and especially Draper. It is unquestionably correct to trace a relationship between much modern performance art and the avant-garde tradition in twentieth-century art and theatre, since much performance art has been created and continues to operate within that context. However, to concentrate largely or exclusively upon the avant-garde aspect of modern performance art, as most writers on the subject have done, can limit understanding both of the social functioning of such art today, and also of how it relates to other performance activity of the past. Therefore, before looking at the relationship of modern performance to the avant-garde tradition let us consider, at least briefly, some of its relationships to other and much older performance activities.

Despite her emphasis upon the close relationship between the avant-garde and performance art in the twentieth century, RoseLee Goldberg in her very brief remarks on performance in earlier periods does cite a few examples that might at first seem quite unrelated to performance as she subsequently chronicles it: medieval passion plays, a 1598 mock naval battle, royal entries, and elaborate court spectacles designed by da Vinci in 1490 and Bernini in 1638. Performance in these examples is clearly not based on a concern about "the limitations of existing artistic forms," and nor does it involve, as much modern performance does, the physical presence of the artist. What it does provide, argues Goldberg, is "a presence for the artist in society," a presence that can be variously "esoteric, shamanistic, instructive, provocative or entertaining."[7]

Jean Alter and the performant function

What seems to be involved in each of these cases is a manifestation of the artist's "presence" through a striking display of technical accomplishment and virtuosity, a theatrical and social phenomenon discussed insightfully by Jean Alter in his *A Socio-Semiotic Theory of Theatre* (1990). Here Alter suggests that the art of theatre is always based on the "dual appeal" of two coexisting functions. The traditional communicating of a story, carried out with "signs that aim at imparting information," Alter calls theatre's *referential function*. To this he adds a *performant function*, clearly closely related to Goldberg's idea of performance in earlier periods, which is shared by other such public events as sports or circus and which seeks to please or amaze an audience by a display of exceptional achievement. Such performances are most often associated with acting, but they are achievable by any of the arts of the theatre—lighting, design, directing, costuming. According to Alter, these performances are not primarily concerned with communicating by "signs;" they stress instead the direct physical experience of the event.[8] Hence the importance of physical presence; the technical skill and achievement of the performer, the visual display of dazzling costumes or scenic effects are dependent for a certain part of their power upon the fact that they are actually generated in our presence.

As Alter notes, theatre inevitably involves both performant and referential functions, as most writers on the subject have in one way or another acknowledged. Nevertheless, most such writers in the West, from Aristotle onward, have devoted comparatively little attention to the performant function and a number of very influential ones, among them Goethe, Charles Lamb, and most of the symbolists, have considered the performant a troubling distraction, if not an aesthetic flaw. Plays have been traditionally regarded as stable written objects, their various manifestations in different productions a more or less accidental part of their history, not really essential to their understanding, and when plays have been placed in a broader context of human activity that context has been until quite recently only a literary one. From Aristotle to Hegel theorists spoke of the three forms of poetry—epic, lyric, and dramatic—a division continued into more modern times as prose, poetry, and drama. Not until the rise of the modern interest in performance was there much thought that a play might be presented in a different contextualization—not as a cousin of such literary forms as the poem or the novel, but of such performance forms as the circus, the sideshow, the parade, or even the wrestling match or the political convention. Thus even if we separate performance from the broader social and anthropological usages discussed in previous chapters and consider it only within the much more limited confines of an artistic or entertainment activity consciously produced for an audience, and thus seek its historical context in earlier artistic and entertainment activities, our investigation will be more useful and productive if we acknowledge this new contextualization, moving outside the traditional "referential" orientation of theatre studies to the more "performative" activities that often surround this tradition but which have tended to be marginalized or ignored completely.

Folk and popular performance

The popular tradition

There has always been, surrounding and doubtless long predating the more formally structured social activity that has been called theatre, a vast array of other sorts of entertainment activity that could be designated as performance. The classic period had its musicians, its mimes, its jugglers, even its rope-dancers, mentioned by Terence in the prologue to *Hecyra*. In the Middle Ages there were the troubadours, the scalds and bards, the minstrels, the mountebanks, and that miscellaneous group of entertainers that

Figure 4.1 Medieval performer depicted in a late thirteenth-century Bible.

Source: Bibliothèque Municipale, Saint-Omer, France.

in England were designated as the glee-men, "a term which included dancers, posturers,[9] jugglers, tumblers, and exhibitors of trained performing monkeys and quadrupeds."[10]

The range and variety of such activity was much greater than is often assumed today. The word "jester" today, for example, very likely calls up the mental image of a court clown, perhaps a bit unstable mentally, but possessed of a certain wit or at least verbal dexterity and daring. Yet there were in fact many types of jestours (or gesters); some literally recited the medieval gestes, tales of famous persons and heroic deeds, but others told popular tales, comic tales, anecdotes, verses and ballads or gave moral speeches. They used every sort of verbal material, some learned, some patched together from a variety of sources, and some original with the teller.[11]

Many a modern performance artist, monologuist, or stand-up comedian would likely, in terms of technique and approach, fit very easily into this versatile company. The natural gathering places for such performers were the great medieval and renaissance fairs, but like the strolling players of the period (and often in league with them) they traveled about the countryside, performing in marketplaces, in great houses, in taverns—wherever an audience could be assembled. Elizabeth I grouped jugglers and minstrels along with itinerant thieves, beggars, and gypsies in her Vagrancy Act, designed to discourage such activity,[12] but in fact, contrary to the impression left by literary studies of the period, even the most "respectable" theatre was deeply involved with such performance. As M.C. Bradbrook observes:[13]

> The theatre of the Elizabethans, in its social atmosphere, was less like the modern theatre than it was like a funfair.... Merriment, jigs and toys followed the performance: songs, dumb shows, fights, clowns' acts were interlaced. When Leicester's Men visited the court of Denmark in 1586 they were described as singers and dancers; Robert Browne of Worcester's Men, who toured the continent for thirty years with other English actors, jumped and performed activities.

In 1647 popular entertainments were outlawed in England along with the theatres, but such official discouragements never lasted very long, and nor were they very widely effective. Traveling performers, like traveling actors, could normally find audiences for their offerings somewhere or other. The ever-curious John Evelyn witnessed in London during the summer of 1654 a variety of popular entertainments, including a "famous rope-dancer, called The Turk."[14]

Rope-dancing (performance on a tightrope) was one of the most popular types of performance in England and on the continent during the next century—so much so that when fairground entertainers began to establish permanent theatres in Paris in the late eighteenth century and the authorities wished to draw a clear legal line between them and "legitimate" theatre, one of the common distinctions was that tumbling and rope-

Figure 4.2 The "celebrated performer on the rope" Madame Saqui, London, 1820.
Source: Harvard Theatre Collection.

dancing was to be found in the minor houses. Not infrequently, in defer-
ence to such distinctions, actors wishing to present a more conventional
play would enter the stage with a somersault or walking on a rope before
continuing with a more conventional presentation.

Fairs and circuses

The late seventeenth century also saw the establishment in London and
Paris of what were then called music-booths, the ancestors of the later
music halls, cabarets, vaudevilles, and café-concerts, which offered a
variety of performance in a series of "acts"—vocal and instrumental music
alternating with rope-dancing and tumbling. The fair nevertheless
remained the favored center of such entertainment, as John Gay's ballad
singer (himself one such performer) notes in "The Shepherd's Week:"[15]

The mountebank now treads the stage, and sells
His pills, his balsams, and his ague-spells;
Now o'er and o'er the nimble tumbler springs
And on the rope the venturous maiden swings;
Jack Pudding, in his party-coloured jacket,
Tosses the glove, and jokes at every packet.

Although the performative elements of the greatest of the London fairs, Bartholomew Fair, were banned in 1840,[16] many of the types of performance that it sheltered and encouraged, as well as new entertainments in a similar vein, were found much more frequently from the late eighteenth century onward in the new center for such entertainment, the circus. The circus was developed in London and Paris by Phillip Astley, but soon gained enormous popularity in Europe and then around the world. Circus historian John Clarke dates the origin of the modern circus to 1780, when Astley offered in London a variety of horse acts, his own speciality, along with tumbling, rope-vaulting, a human pyramid, and even a clown.[17]

Within thirty years innumerable circuses had been formed in Europe and America, where it achieved a kind of apogee under the leadership of some of the greatest showmen of the era. Phineas T. Barnum's search for spectacular entertainment led him to sponsor almost every type of performance

Figure 4.3 The Forepaugh Circus (1880s), showing the variety of performance acts offered.

Source: Harvard Theatre Collection.

available in the mid-nineteenth century, and his collaboration with James Anthony Bailey produced the largest and most famous circus of the century, assumed after Barnum's death by America's other great circus entrepreneurs, the Ringling Brothers. Probably the biggest rival in popular entertainment to the great circuses of the later nineteenth century was the spectacular Wild West Show of William Cody. This featured many of the traditional performance exhibits of the circus such as clowns, acrobatics, and equestrian acts from around the world, but added other performance activities of its own, such as historical re-enactments of famous battles, anticipating the living history movement of the next century. Entrepreneurs like Barnum and Cody were perhaps the best known of the purveyors of performative spectacle in the late nineteenth century, but behind them lay innumerable shows and performative events, some frankly presented for entertainment and others under the guise of scientific demonstration or ethnographic display, that operated in countless venues in Europe and America from humble traveling freak shows to huge international fairs and expositions.[18]

The growth of alternative forms of entertainment, and particularly the coming of films and television, surely contributed to the steady decline in the fortunes of the theatre in the early twentieth century, and on 16 July 1956 the Ringling Brothers and Barnum and Bailey Circus, the "greatest show on earth," ended its performance with a playing of "Auld Lang Syne" and folded its tents for the last time (although it continues to perform in a variety of indoor venues). In the 1970s, however, the circus experienced a rebirth in both Europe and America, in a movement that both looked backward to the historic roots of this form of entertainment and around it to the growing interest in performance as an activity. The so-called "new circus" was thus closely related both historically and artistically to the rise of "performance art," and so will be discussed as a part of that phenomenon in Chapter 5.

Solo performances

The marketplace, the fairground, the circus—gathering places for a large general public—have traditionally been the favored sites of performance, but solitary performers or small group of performers displaying their skills before a small gathering, even a single family in a medieval great hall, offered a more intimate performance model that has not disappeared in more recent times. Private court entertainments, aristocratic salons and soirées, and private parties today offer a continuing tradition of such activity, some of which might be called avant-garde but much of which is quite traditional. A well-known example from the late eighteenth century is the "attitudes" of Lady Emma Hamilton; poses and movements suggesting to entranced observers a great variety of emotions as well as evocations of classical art.[19]

Lady Hamilton's attitudes inspired several popular women performers of the next generation, such as Ida Brun in Denmark and Henriette Hendel-Schütz in Germany, as well as the enormously popular *tableaux vivants* that swept Europe during the next century. Her tarantella and her shawl dance drew new attention to these forms not only in the theatre but in private society, where such dances became a favored choice as "a party entertainment for the ladies of the bourgeoisie."[20] It will be remembered that a century later, Ibsen's Nora offers a performance of the tarantella at her fateful Christmas Party. These lively dances, with their emphasis upon emotional expressiveness and freedom from traditional dance movement, anticipated in important ways modern experimental dance, with its own close relationship to performance art. Indeed one of Lady Hamilton's biographers notes that "The modern-day spectacle which resembles the Attitudes is, of course, Isadora Duncan's Greek dance."[21] Duncan herself, as we shall see, contributed importantly to the development of modern experimental performance.

American minstrelsy

Blackface minstrelsy, America's first popular mass entertainment and its first original contribution to world theatre, began as solo street entertainment, banjo-playing Negro performers being a well-established part of the street life of major urban centers in the Eastern United States by the beginning of the nineteenth century, and with white imitators of this street entertainment performing in black make-up in theatres, summer garden entertainments and circuses.[22] The most famous of the minstrel solo performers was Thomas Dartmouth Rice, whose blackface creation "Jim Crow" became an international sensation during the 1830s. The next decade saw the rise of the more elaborate minstrel shows, consisting of several performers playing different instruments and mixing song, dance, and comic routines. By 1850 minstrelsy had become the most popular public entertainment in America, with hundreds of companies regularly performing. Like the circus, with which it maintained close ties, a minstrel company would announce its arrival in town with a spectacular parade, with the performers appearing in colorful traditional costume. Although the shows became increasingly elaborate in the later nineteenth century, the basic form remained much the same: a first part with the costumed blackface performers seated in a semi-circle providing a program of ballads, comic songs, instrumental numbers, and comic dialogue; and a second part, the olio, which consisted of a wide range of variety acts, dances, short farces, and burlesques, very similar to the standard and equally popular burlesque and vaudeville bills in other theatres.

Vaudevilles and reviews

Although its use of blackface and its ethnic parody gave the minstrel show a particular niche in nineteenth-century entertainment, the structure and often even individual elements in it had very close ties, as we have noted, to other popular forms of the period—the circus, vaudeville and variety shows, and the music hall—all providing a fertile ground for performance activities presented in review form. Peter Jelavich's summary of the offerings in the German vaudevilles (known as *Variétés* or *Singspielhallen*) at the turn of the century suggests the range: "juggling, wrestling, tightrope-walking, trapeze-artistry, clowning, pantomime, folk songs and folk dances, skits, restrained striptease, and costume ballet."[23]

The American theatrical tradition, developed during this period, was strongly oriented in this performative direction, so much so that Richard Kostelanetz has suggested that the almost universal attempt by theatre scholars to develop a European-style history of literary theatre for America has been misguided. Rather, Kostelanetz proposes, "what theatrical genius we have had in America gravitates not to formal theater or literary drama, but to informal theater, where the performer is the dominant figure," and that just as America created its own indigenous "opera" in musical comedies and vaudevilles, so it developed "its own kind of theater—not of literature, but of performance."[24] One important strand of this was the one-person show, a significant part not only of the minstrel tradition, but of much nineteenth-century entertainment. Tony Pastor, who has been called "the father of American vaudeville," began as a circus clown, and in a career stretching from the 1840s to the close of the century created one-man comic songs and skits on almost every political and social concern and fad of the day.[25] Its story has been engagingly traced in a recent book by John Gentile,[26] who follows its development from the platform readings of authors like Dickens and Twain, through the lectures and performances organized by the Lyceum and Chautauqua circuits on to the early twentieth-century solo monologuists like Ruth Draper and Cornelia Otis Skinner and to modern impersonations of earlier performers, such as Willym Williams as Dickens and Hal Holbrook as Twain, and a variety of other historical impersonations, and individual readings of such classics as selections from Shakespeare or the Bible. This tradition is continued in contemporary performance in the autobiographical work of Spalding Gray and Quentin Crisp, and in the character creations of Whoopi Goldberg, Lily Tomlin, and Eric Bogosian.

The cabaret

Near the end of the nineteenth century a new form in the music hall tradition, the cabaret, drew upon the public love of such physical and visual theatricality to develop another center for performance activity that would in turn inspire major innovators in the modern drama like Wedekind and Brecht, as well as a wide range of avant-garde performance activity. Laurence Senelick, a leading contemporary chronicler of cabaret material, places in the variety-oriented European cabaret the roots of the avant-garde tradition that Goldberg and others trace from the futurists onward into

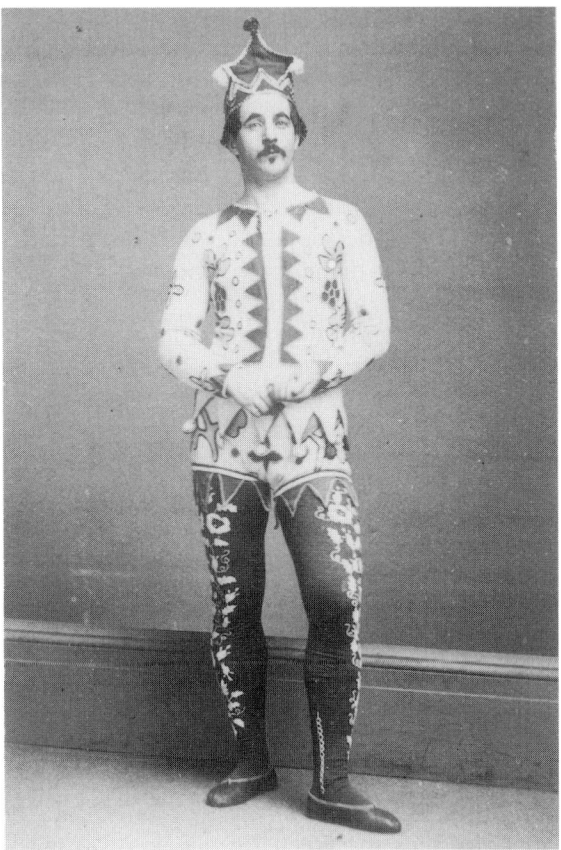

Figure 4.4 Tony Pastor.
Source: Harvard Theatre Collection.

modern performance. One must look to the cabaret, argues Senelick, for the beginnings of "many of the most exciting innovations in twentieth-century performance art."[27]

> Emerging from bohemian haunts, the cabaret was the earliest podium for the expressionists, the DADAists, the futurists; it was a congenial forum for experiments in shadowgraphy, puppetry, free-form skits, jazz rhythms, literary parody, "naturalistic" songs, "bruitistic" litanies, agitprop, dance-pantomime, and political satire.

Because of this extremely eclectic range, and probably because it sought from the outset to utilize popular forms in new ways, the cabaret enjoyed a far longer career and attracted a far larger and more diverse public than the various rather specialized and esoteric artistic avant-gardes that in part emerged from it. In both the eclecticism and the spread of appeal from its original bohemian creators to a much more general public, the cabaret more closely prefigures the dynamic of modern performance than any of the more specialized avant-garde movements. Nevertheless, individually and collectively these movements have unquestionably provided influences and models for such performance, and certainly for individual performers. Therefore let us briefly examine this probably more familiar terrain, stressing those aspects of it most closely related to recent performance art.

Experimental performance

Russian innovations

The brilliant innovative Russian theatre at the beginning of this century provided models of performance unparalleled in their richness and diversity. In the utopian early years of the Revolution, before the stifling uniformity of socialist realism was imposed by Stalin, this innovation was not, in the frequent pattern of Western European experimentation, considered to be primarily by artists for artists, but a spirited search for new approaches to art that could speak to a new and much more broadly based public. With this goal in mind, leading theatre innovators emphasized physicality and spectacle (what Alter calls the performative side of theatre) and also sought inspiration in such previously scorned popular forms as the fairground and the circus. Cabaret-type theatres enjoyed a tremendous popularity in Russia beginning in 1908, headed by the famous Bat, which was frequented by Moscow Art Theatre performers, and Nikolas Evreinoff's Crooked Mirror, specializing in parody and the grotesque. Meyerhold in his famous 1912 essay "The Fairground Booth" approvingly quotes Ernst von Wolzogen, founder of Germany's first literary cabaret, in arguing that the spirit of cabaret, variety, and fairground performance can provide a conciseness and profundity, clarity and vigor denied to the traditional drama, "where the play takes up a whole evening with its ponderous bombastic exposition of depressing events."[28]

Other innovators sought even more literally and specifically to merge theatre with varieties of popular performance. Meyerhold's student Sergei Radlov rejected the actor's bond to "someone else's words" and invited clowns, acrobats and jugglers into his "Popular Comedy" theatre in 1920 to develop improvisatory work,[29] inspiring in turn the circus and variety oriented "Factory of the Eccentric Actor" (FEKS) in Petrograd in 1922–3 and Sergei Eisenstein's influential concept, the montage of attractions, applied by him to the revival of an Ostrovsky play in 1923. Nikolai Foregger experimented with music hall routines and with, elaborate and spectacular scenic effects, and called for a closer alliance between the theatre and the circus, claiming that in the golden ages of Elizabethan England and Renaissance Spain the theatre and the circus had operated as inseparable "Siamese

Twins." The arts of the future, said Foregger, are the cinema and the music hall, the obvious appeal of the latter being the living body as an expressive instrument.[30]

Isadora Duncan

The appearance of Isadora Duncan in St Petersburg in 1904 had a profound effect on both dance and theatre in Russia, focusing attention on the individual performer and upon the natural movement of the body. Evreinoff credited Duncan with revealing to him the simplicity and inevitability of "real, honest art,"[31] and Tairov looked to Duncan as well as to masters of the traditional ballet such as Mikhail Fokine and Anna Pavlova as models for restoring a lost sense of the corporeal to theatre.[32]

The subjective approach championed by Duncan was soon challenged by the more objective eurythmics of Emile Jaques-Dalcroze and the biomechanics developed by Meyerhold, but all three contributed to a powerful

Figure 4.5 Isadora Duncan in Athens, 1903.

Source: Raymond Duncan Fine Arts and the Isadora Duncan Foundation.

new interest in the expressive qualities of the body and to the convergence of dance and theatre, both central to the development of modern performance. In a 1914 class in stage movement Meyerhold remarked that "the new actor's view of the stage" was "as an area for the presentation of unprecedented events," very much the view of a modern performance artist, and among possible models and inspirations for such work he cited Jaques-Dalcroze, Isadora Duncan, Loie Fuller (another American pioneer of the modern dance), the circus, the variety theatre, and Chinese and Japanese theatres.[33]

Pageants and spectacles

Alongside the intimate experimental work of the Russian Revolution, the inspiration for much subsequent avant-garde theatre, there developed a very different approach to experimental performance which also could be seen reflected in the performance art work of the late twentieth century. This was the production of mass spectacles, involving hundreds or even thousands of participants, often regular citizens rather than actors. The writings of Rousseau, condemning the conventional theatre as the plaything of a decadent aristocratic minority, and calling instead for vast civic pageants in the open air, open to and involving all, was a major inspiration for the development of the great pageant/performances of the French Revolution, and both that theory and practice in turn inspired an interest in such performances after the Russian Revolution.

A vogue for large outdoor civic pageant/performances spread to many countries in the late nineteenth century. In Germany from the 1870s onward, in the aftermath of the Franco-Prussian War, huge outdoor spectacles were given in many locations, recreating historical and legendary events and mixing historical figures with mythic and allegorical representations. These spectacles anticipated and may have served as the models for the very similar civic pageants presented to hundreds of thousands of spectators in locations across England and America between 1905 and 1925. This movement contributed strongly both to the idea of theatre as an outgrowth of community activity and of dance as a modern creative expression. Among its leaders were the sister and brother Hazel and Percy MacKaye, he stressing pageantry as a populist form, she as a powerful tool for the suffrage movement. The role of women in American pageantry as writers, directors, and producers was especially significant.[34]

One fascinated spectator at a number of such spectacles in America was Platon Kerzhentsez, a leading theoretician for the development of proletarian culture in Revolutionary Russia. His 1918 book *Creative Theatre* provided the intellectual basis for the great Russian mass spectacles of subsequent years, the most famous of them being Nikolai Evreinoff's *The Storming of the Winter Palace* in 1920, involving more than 8000 participants, army units, armored cars and trucks, even a battleship, and played before an audience of more than 100,000.[35]

Futurism

In terms of the number of people involved, both as performers and as public, Russia's Revolutionary spectacles far surpassed the modest evenings of the Western European futurists, dadaists, and surrealists. Nevertheless, these latter exerted then (and still exert) an influence on the popular imagination and on subsequent artistic experiments far out of proportion to their numbers. They were highly visible, taking place in traditional centers of artistic activity and supported by a strong and well established publicity organization. The launching of futurism in 1909 was a typical example, with a manifesto by Filippo Marinetti in the widely-circulated Parisian paper, *Le Figaro*. Futurism is in fact rather better known for its manifestos than for its actual artistic achievements, but both contributed importantly to the performance tradition of this century. The interest of the futurists in movement and change drew them away from the static work of art and provided an important impetus for the general shift in modern artistic interest from product to process, turning even painters and sculptors into performance artists. Far from seeking to stimulate positively a mass audience, the futurists were often frankly and proudly confrontational, arousing public outrage that anticipated the scandals of later performance art. One of Marinetti's manifestos spoke proudly of "The Pleasure of Being Booed," a likely consequence of challenging the anticipations of complacent audiences by demanding from artists "an absolute innovative originality" and by renouncing conventional "historical reconstruction" and "psychological photography" in favor of "a synthesis of life in its most typical and significant lines."[36] The "Variety Theater" manifesto of 1913 praised that form of entertainment over traditional theatre because of its healthy "dynamism of form and color," including jugglers, ballerinas, gymnasts, and clowns, because, in short, it rejected conventional psychology in favor of what Marinetti called *fisicofollia*, "body-madness."[37]

Despite a strong interest in the physical body in such manifestos as these, futurist productions very often emphasized the mechanical, surrounding (and even hiding) the actor's body in the trappings of modern technology—for which futurism had an inexhaustible passion. Turning bodies into machines or replacing bodies by machines can certainly be found in modern performance, but the tendency of futurism to move toward theatres of puppets, machinery, even colored clouds of gas, on the whole ran counter to later more determinedly body-oriented performance. Most futurist performances also followed a variety format, with a sequence (or a simultaneous presentation) of bits of short performance material—skits, acrobatics, mechanical, lighting, and sound effects, rapid display of movements or objects. This dazzling and quickly moving variety was essential to the futurist aesthetic of speed, surprise, and novelty, but it resulted in a presentation format that on the whole looked backward to the performances of the cabaret, the vaudeville, the circus, and the variety stage rather than forward to the performance art of recent times, which has been largely devoted to the display of individual acts, even if only of very short duration.

Dada and surrealism

Dada had an even more direct connection to cabaret culture than futurism, developing out of performances in the Cabaret Voltaire in Geneva, Switzerland. Musical performances and poetry readings formed the basis of activities here, from which Tristan Tzara and others developed the approach they christened dada. Futurism's influence was strong in the antiestablishment and antitraditional attitudes, the bizarre activities, and even in the style of Tzara's manifestos. His report on the first dada evening might as readily have come from Marinetti, as these excerpts suggest:[38]

> ...the people protest shout smash windowpanes kill each each demolish fight here come the police interruption. Boxing resumed: Cubist dance, costumes by Janco, each man his own big drum on his head, noise, Negro music/trbatgea bonoooooo oo ooooo...

The final section of this excerpt recalls one of the most important interests of the futurists, as well as of the dadaists—in bruitism or "noise music," an exploration of the expressive qualities of non-musical sound. As dadaist Richard Huelsenbeck explained: "Music of whatever nature is harmonious, artistic, and activity of reason—but bruitism is life itself."[39] This interest in non-musical sound of course prepares the way for the pivotal experiments of John Cage, himself a major influence on subsequent experimental theatre and performance.

As a pioneer in experimental performance, Cage is perhaps even more widely known for his utilization of chance techniques in composition, and here too his innovations were to some extent anticipated by the dadaists. Both dada and surrealism were interested in spontaneous creative activity. Some of this involved pure chance, such as Hans Arp creating collages by allowing scraps of paper to fall randomly on the floor, Tzara creating poems by pulling words from a hat, or, more theatrically, dada performance's attempt to stimulate and incorporate audience reaction. There was also, however, an interest in tapping and expressing the unconscious— what André Breton called "pure psychic automatism" in his First Surrealist Manifesto of 1924. Breton described this as an attempt "to express either verbally, in writing, or in some other fashion what really goes on in the mind. Dictation by the mind, unhampered by conscious control and having no aesthetic or moral goals."[40]

Picabia's ballet *Relâche* in 1924 featured interaction with the audience, various "performances" interspersed with the main action (such as a chain-smoking fireman pouring water from one bucket to another and a stage-hand chugging across the stage in a small automobile trailing balloons), a tableau vivant of Cranach's *Adam and Eve*, film clips, and blinding lights in the eyes of the audience.[41] In his review of the production, Fernand Léger praised the work for surmounting the boundaries of ballet and music hall: "author, dancer, acrobat, screen, stage, all the means of 'presenting a performance' are integrated and organized to achieve a total effect."[42]

Perhaps the most important contribution of the surrealist movement to subsequent experimental theatre and performance was the theoretical writing of Antonin Artaud, which exerted an enormous influence in the 1960s and 1970s. In his visionary *The Theater and Its Double*, Artaud advanced his own powerful version of the argument found throughout the early twentieth-century avant-garde that the traditional theatre had lost contact with the deeper and more significant realms of human life by its emphasis on plot, language, and intellectual and psychological concerns. The subjugation of the theatre to the written text must be ended, to be replaced by a spectacle of direct "physical and objective" action:[43]

> Cries, groans, apparitions, surprises, theatricalities of all kinds, magic beauty of costumes taken from certain ritual models; resplendent lighting, incantational beauty of voices, the charms of harmony, rare notes of music, colors of objects, physical rhythm of movements whose crescendo and decrescendo will accord exactly with the pulsation of movements familiar to everyone, concrete appearances of new and surprising objects, masks, effigies yards high, sudden changes of light, the physical action of light which arouses sensations of heat and cold, etc."[43]

The Bauhaus

In addition to the continuing and by no means insignificant influence of its cabaret, Germany during the 1920s contributed importantly to the development of both the theory and the practice of modern performance through the work of the influential art school, the Bauhaus. This was the first school to undertake a serious study of performance as an art form. Oskar Schlemmer was the leader of this enterprise, and his writings and abstract dance compositions (most notably the *Triadic Ballet* of 1922) attracted European-wide attention to the compositional possibilities of the human body in space. Laszlo Moholy-Nagy, another major Bauhaus figure, stressed the importance but not the centrality of the performing figure as one contributing element to a work of "total theatre." Instead of this figure's traditional role as the "interpreter of a literarily conceived individual or type, in the new THEATRE OF TOTALITY he will use the spiritual and physical means at his disposal PRODUCTIVELY and from his own INITIATIVE submit to the over-all action process."[44]

The observations by Moholy-Nagy on Bauhaus performance and by Léger on the surrealist *Relâche* make similar points, and both suggest not only the importance of the various avant-gardes of the 1920s for later performance work but also certain ways in which it had quite different emphases. Moholy-Nagy notes one of the key contributions of this experimental tradition, the rejection of the traditional concept of the performer as an interpreter of an already existing literary text in favor of the performer as creator of an act or an action. Closely related to this is the shift, already seen in futurism, from product to process, from the created object to the act of creation. Of almost equally great importance was the breaking down of traditional boundaries—between the plastic and performing arts, between the high arts of theatre, ballet, music, and painting, and popular forms such as circus, vaudeville, and variety, indeed even between art and life itself, as in the concept of bruitism. On the other hand, as both of these observations suggest, much of the avant-garde tradition we have been tracing placed little emphasis on the individual performer, a central concern of more recent performance. The futurists and dadaists favored loose, revue formats, often overlaid with simultaneous actions. The surrealists and Bauhaus artists also regarded the individual performer essentially as one element in a larger picture—the abstract performance as a whole. A very similar orientation can be found in the *Merzbühne* theories of dadaist Karl Schwitters, who is often cited as one of the forerunners of modern happenings and performances. Schwitters followed in his own career the trajectory later suggested by Kaprow, from painting through collages and assemblages to the sort of activity involved in happenings, mixing objects and human actions in a free-wheeling phantasmagoria, uniting sound and lighting effects with sewing machines, shoes, bicycle tires, dentist's drills, and people walking on their hands and wearing hats on their feet.[45]

Modern mime and dance

The tradition of mime

Mimes, as we have seen, have appeared among the standard creators of popular entertainment since classic times and have occasionally (as in the case of the great French mime of the romantic period, Debureau) been considered among the leading performing artists of their time. After Debureau, mime gradually declined in France, until it experienced a remarkable renaissance in the early twentieth century that again brought it to international importance. The widespread interest in gymnastics and the study of the human body in motion that was involved in such varied performative experiments as Dalcroze's eurythmics, Meyerhold's biomechanics, the dance work of Fuller and Duncan, and the mechanical ballets of the Bauhaus also inspired Jacques Copeau to make "corporeal mime" the center of his work at the École du Vieux Colombier in Paris in the early 1900s. Work with Copeau in turn inspired Etienne Decroux to devote his life to this study, and to become the most influential theorist and teacher of mime of the century. Among his pupils were Jean-Louis Barrault and Marcel Marceau, whose work spread a fascination with mime around the world. Marceau became one of the best-known performers of the twentieth century—perhaps the best known solo performer of his generation—and the fact that the white-faced mime with his distinctive costume and activity remains one of the most familiar types of street performer in urban centers around the world is a testimony to his continuing influence.

Many experimental companies and individual performers of the late 1960s and 1960s, especially in Canada, were based upon training with Decroux. Montreal in particular has become a world center of what has come to be called postmodern mime, with two internationally known companies—Carbonne 14, founded in 1975 by Gilles Maheu, and Omnibus, founded in 1977 by Jean Asselin and Denise Boulanger all three students of Decroux.[46]

Another line of descent from Copeau leads through Copeau's son-in-law, Jean Dasté, who trained the leading teacher of mime for the post-Decroux era, combining features of Copeau's work with studies of the Italian *commedia* and clowns. The best-known representative of Lecoq's training is the still popular Mummenschanz Company, originally two Swiss mime and mask performers and one Italian (Andres Bossard, Bernie Schurch, and Floriana Frassetto), who made their first European tour in 1973. Their abstract combinations of masks and unconventional and disorienting arrangements of bodies suggest a relationship both to traditional mime and to the experiments of the futurists, the dadaists, and the Bauhaus, but with a far greater popular appeal than any of those experiments achieved.

Paris-based mime also entered the modern American experimental theatre through the work of R.G. Davis, founder of the San Francisco Mime Theatre, who applied the mime techniques he had learned in France to political action during the 1970s. Davis's own summary of the evolution of the Mime troupe indicates how deeply it was involved with various aspects of the performative tradition we have been tracing, moving "from elite theatre (mime) into an avant-garde period (happenings) to outdoor popular theatre (commedia dell'arte) and then on to radical politics."[47]

St Denis and the tradition of dance

The individual performer was much more favored in the dance, the major contribution of America to the varied performance experimentation in the early twentieth century. The influence of Isadora Duncan and Loie Fuller on Russian experimental theatre of the Revolutionary period has already been mentioned, but their impact, along with that of Ruth St Denis, was equally great in Germany and France, where all three American dancers appeared before the First World War, pioneering revolutionary individual approaches to the art form. Of the three, only St Denis, with her partner Ted Shawn, produced a major line of successors, headed by Martha Graham, Doris Humphrey, and Charles Weidman, who during the 1930s essentially defined "modern dance." In these dancers the rather romantic and personal style of the Duncan generation was replaced by a more consciously theatrical approach, but also one rather more concerned with abstract allegorical or mythic subjects. The next generation, headed by such dancers as Erick Hawkins, Katherine Litz, Midi Garth, and Jack Moore, was diverse in its experimentation, from the cool abstractions of Hawkins to the sprightly dada and surrealist playfulness of Litz, but had in common a rejection of the general and mythic themes of the previous generation in favor of individual clarity and independence. This new emphasis was seen most clearly, and has exerted the most influence on performance, in the work of Merce Cunningham, a leading dancer with Graham before pursuing his own direction.

John Cage and Merce Cunningham

Closely linked with Cunningham is his frequent collaborator, John Cage, whose revolutionary ideas on music and aesthetics have profoundly influenced modern experimentation in all the arts. Indeed, Natalie Crohn Schmitt argues in her 1990 *Actors and Onlookers* that in the contemporary theatre the traditional aesthetics and world-view represented by Aristotle have been replaced by that of Cage, itself a reflection of the altered view of nature under the influence of modern scientific theory. Central to this shift is a recognition that "events do not possess discrete facts and discrete perceivers; rather the two are joined in an observation,"[48] a recognition placing new emphasis upon the phenomenal experience of performer, performance event, and audience, and a fresh interest in their complex interrelationship. Cage's 1937 manifesto, *The Future of Music*, opens with a call for the utilization of everyday material in performance that distinctly recalls the bruitism of the futurists:[49]

> Wherever we are, what we hear is mostly noise. When we ignore it, it disturbs us. When we listen to it, we find it fascinating. The sound of a truck at 50 m.p.h. Static between the stations. Rain. We want to capture and control these sounds, to use them, not as sound effects, but as musical instruments.

Later, Cage qualified even the "capture and control" aspects of this concern, turning control over to various chance operations and capture over to the creation of specific frames around material not subject to the decisions of the artist. Perhaps his most famous work, *4' 33"* (1952), clearly illustrates this latter strategy, placing a pianist who does not play before an audience for four minutes and thirty-three seconds, during which time whatever the audience hears is "music."

An important parallel in dance to Cage's experiments was taking place concurrently on the West Coast in the San Francisco Dancers' Workshop Company, formed in 1955 by Anna Halprin. Halprin carried on the interest of early experimenters like Fuller and Duncan in the performance of everyday activities. Her utilization of walking, eating, bathing, and touching in dance compositions has clear affinities to Cage's use of natural and artificial noises in musical ones, and her interest in "task-oriented movement" which was "unrestricted by music or interpretive ideas"[50] helped prepare the way for happenings and other performance activities of the 1960s. Halprin also shared Cage's interest in improvisation and free association as a way of breaking free of conventional artistic organizational strategies.

Cage and Cunningham met in 1938, and they began to collaborate regularly in the mid-1940s. In 1948 they taught and performed at Black Mountain College, a center for experimental artists from all fields that been established in 1933 and that had particularly close ties with the Bauhaus movement. Back at Black Mountain in 1952, Cage and Cunningham, along with Robert Rauschenberg and others, produced an untitled event that has been often cited as the model for the wave of happenings and related performance events that swept the art world in the late 1950s and early 1960s. In many respects this event recapitulated many of the motifs and practices of earlier avant-gardes. Performances took place in and around an arena audience, each timed to the second. Cage read a dadaist lecture, films were projected on the ceiling, Cunningham danced in the aisles, followed by an unplanned excited dog who was enthusiastically incorporated into the performance. David Tudor, Cage's earlier silent pianist, poured water from one bucket into another, perhaps quoting one of the actions in *Relâche*.

This event was taken as an experimental model by Cage in the course on experimental music that he began to teach at New York's New School for Social Research in 1956. Pioneers of the avant-garde art of the 1960s, painters, musicians, poets, and film makers, found inspiration in these classes, which helped to create an art scene much oriented toward performance. Jim Dine appeared at his Reuben Gallery opening in New York in costume, Red Grooms painted for an audience in Provincetown in 1958 and a 1959 article in *Art News* proclaimed that "what counts is no longer the painting but the process of creation" and that the latter should be the object of the audience's attention.[51] Such activity prepared the way for the body art of the 1960s, which will be considered in Chapter 5.

Non-dramatic events

Happenings

A key event in the history of modern performance was the presentation in 1959 of Allan Kaprow's *18 Happenings in 6 Parts* at the Reuben Gallery. This first public demonstration established the "happening" for public and press as a major new avant-garde activity, so much so that a wide range of performance work during the following years was characterized as "happenings" even when many creators of such events specifically denied the term. Audiences at Kaprow's happenings were seated in three different rooms where they witnessed six fragmented events, performed simultaneously in all three spaces. The events included slides, playing of musical instruments, posed scenes, the reading of fragmentary notes from placards, and artists painting on canvas walls. During the following months Kaprow and others created a large number of such works, some entirely technological (such as Claes Oldenburg's *Snapshots from the City* (1960), a collaged city landscape with built-in street and immobile figures on a stage against a textured wall, flickering lights and found objects on the floor), others involving the actions of a single artist, much more in the style of what would later be thought of as performance art (such as Jim Dine's *The Smiling Workman* (1960), in which Dine, dressed in a red smock with hands and face painted red drank from jars of paint while painting "I love what I'm..." on a large canvas, before pouring the remaining paint over his head and leaping through the canvas).[52] A similar and much more notorious converging of painting and the body was offered in Paris this same year, when Yves Klein's *Anthropometries of the Blue Period* presented nude models covered with blue paint pressing against a canvas like living brushes. In Milan the following year Piero Manzoni went further still, converting living bodies into "authentic works of art " by signing them as if they were paintings.

Kaprow chose the title "happening" in preference to something like theatre piece or performance because he wanted this activity to be regarded as a spontaneous event; something that "just happens to happen."[53] Nevertheless, *18 Happenings*, like many such events, was scripted, rehearsed, and carefully controlled. Its real departure from traditional art was not in its spontaneity, but in the sort of material it used and its manner of presentation. In his definition of a happening, Michael Kirby notes that it is a "purposefully composed form of theatre," but one in which "diverse alogical elements, including non-matrixed performing, are organized in a compartmental structure."[54] "Non-matrixed" contrasts such activity to traditional theatre, where actors perform in a "matrix" provided by a fictional character and surroundings. An act in a happening, like Halprin's "task-oriented" movement, is done without this imaginary setting. In Alter's terms, it seeks the purely performative, removed from the referential. The "compartmental structure" relates to this concept; each individual act within a happening exists for itself, is compartmentalized, and does not contribute to any overall meaning.

Theatre scholars and historians naturally tend to place happenings and later performance art in the tradition of the theatrical avant-garde, looking back, as we have just been doing, to futurism, dada, and surrealism. It is important to remember, however, that these movements were really movements in other arts, organized by non-theatre artists, that expanded into performance. The same is true of the happenings, and indeed Kaprow traces their historical evolution not back through these performance avant-gardes but through modern painting. The Cubist collages, he suggests, attacked classical harmonies by introducing "irrational" or non-harmonic juxtapositions, and "tacitly opened up a path to infinity" by introducing foreign matter into the painting. "Simplifying the history of the ensuing evolution into a flashback, this is what happened; the pieces of paper curled up off the canvas, were removed from the surface to exist on their own,

Figure 4.6 Car Wash, a happening created at Cornell University by Allan Kaprow, May, 1964. Participants are licking strawberry jam off Volkswagens.

Source: Cornell University Archives.

became more solid as they grew into other materials and, reaching out further into the room, filled it entirely."[55] Thus canvas evolves through collage to assemblage and environments. As environments become more complex, and the activities of participants in them, both spectators and performers, become more regulated and structured, environments become happenings.

In fact, Kaprow deplored the "theatrical" aura which began to surround the happenings as soon as an audience appeared, an aura which suggested either a "crude" avant-garde or else the popular performance world of "night club acts, side shows, cock fights and bunkhouse skits," instead of "art or even purposive activity."[56] To combat this Kaprow suggested a number of guidelines, among them keeping the line between art and life fluid and perhaps indistinct, seeking themes entirely outside the theatre or other arts, using several different locales and discontinuous time to avoid a sense of a theatrical "occasion," performing happenings only once, and eliminating entirely the traditional passive audience.[57]

Kostelanetz and the Theatre of Mixed Means

Recognizing Kaprow's desire to restrict the burgeoning application of the term "happenings" to all sorts of experimental performance, Richard Kostelanetz proposed a more embracing term, the "Theatre of Mixed Means," in a 1968 book with that title. Performances of this type, said Kostelanetz in a subsequent summary, "differ from conventional drama in de-emphasizing verbal language, if not avoiding words completely, in order to stress such presentational means as sound and light, objects and scenery, and/or the movement of people and props, often in addition to the newer technologies of films, recorded tape, amplification systems, radio, and closed-circuit television."[58] Kostelanetz divides such activity into four genres: pure happenings, staged happenings, kinetic environments, and staged performances. Pure happenings are very loosely structured, encourage improvisation, tend to envelop audiences, and are rarely if ever done in traditional theatrical spaces. Included in this category are the private "events," a genre particularly favored by the dadaist movement Fluxus (its founder, George Maciunas, described it as "Neo-Dada"), which gained the most attention in Germany and the United States. Fluxus was a loosely associated group of artists, writers, and performers, many of whom studied with John Cage. In 1963 they produced one of the first collections of performance art, conceptual art, event structures and similar material, simply called *An Anthology*, and contributed importantly to performance, installation, and video art for the rest of the century through the work of such artists as Joseph Beuys, Yoko Ono, Charlotte Moorman, and Nam June Paik.

Kostelanetz's "staged happenings" are more controlled events, occurring within a fixed space, often a theatrical stage—for example, the Cage/Cunningham *Variations V* (1965), with a stage filled with vertical poles that generated an electronic sound as dancers approached them. The development of the "new dance" during the 1960s, drawing upon such sources as Halprin, Cage and Cunningham, Kaprow and Fluxus, produced some of the most memorable work of this sort. Central to such activity were the concerts of the Judson Dance Group, where such emerging artists as Yvonne Rainer, Simone Forti, Deborah Hay, Meredith Monk and Carolee Schneemann experimented with chance composition, non-dance movement, and multi-media spectacles. Often these mixed live performers with films and slides, preparing the way for the much more elaborate mixed media work of the 1980s and 1990s.[59] "Kinetic environments," according to Kostelanetz, created "a constant, intrinsically interminable, enclosed field of multisensory activity through which spectators may proceed at their own pace." Finally, "stage performances" resembled traditional theatre, but with less emphasis on speech and more on mixed media.[60] Examples of this would include much recent avant-garde theatre: the Living Theatre, Robert Wilson, Richard Foreman, the Wooster Group, and modern dance-theatre— Meredith Monk, Pina Bausch, Maguy Marin. Timothy Wiles, seeking a descriptive term to characterize this latter non-traditional activity, has suggested "performance theatre," recognizing, like Kostelanetz, that this sort of theatre event "finds its meaning and being in performance, not in literary encapsulation."[61]

Thus in the course of the 1960s various strands from the visual arts, especially painting and sculpture, from experimental music and dance, from the traditions of avant-garde theatre, as well as from the evolving world of the media and modern technology, combined to offer an extremely varied mixture of artistic activity, much of it centered in New York, that stressed physical presence, events, and actions, constantly tested the boundaries of art and life, and rejected the unity and coherence of much traditional art as well as the narrativity, psychologism, and referentiality of traditional theatre. Although some such activities were spoken of as performances, that was not commonly used as a term to describe them; indeed some experimenters, such as Kaprow, specifically rejected the term as too closely associated with traditional theatre. The terms performance and performance art only began to be widely utilized after 1970 to describe much of the experimental work of that new decade, which, although it expressed new concerns and took new directions, drew much of its inspiration and methods from the complex experimental mix of the 1960s. The following chapter will trace the development of this tradition after 1970.

Living history

The path I have just been tracing, through various experiments in the various arts, visual and performing, clearly provided the direct line of genealogy for the sort of work that began to be called performance or performance art in the 1970s, and which will be the subject of the next chapter. Nevertheless, certain developments outside this tradition also contributed significantly to the public image of and growing interest in performance as a human activity in the late twentieth century. One of the most important of these was the cultural phenomenon known in America as "Living History," which became during the twentieth century a major tourist activity, source of recreation, and, for many, primary mode of both performative experience and cultural memory.

I have already mentioned the American and English pageant movements as well as the spectacles of the Russian Revolution, many of which involved the re-enactment of historical events, especially military ones, often on the actual sites of those events. Such performances anticipated the Civil War re-enactments of the 1960s in America, which in turn inspired countless battle re-enactments all across America, and then in many other parts of the world during the rest of the century. Battle re-enactments in America have covered almost the entire scope of the nation's history, and have ranged in size from the annual re-enactment of the opening skirmish of the Second Seminole War in Tampa, Florida, involving many more persons than the original event, to a re-enactment in Texas of the Japanese attack on Pearl Harbor, with Japanese and American aircraft, simulated bombings of the American fleet, and huge numbers of American ground forces, surpassing in scope even Evreinoff's memorable *Storming of the Winter Palace*.[62]

Less spectacular, but today even more widespread in many parts of the world, was a different type of historical performance, dealing with domestic life. The first major manifestation of this sort appeared in Stockholm in 1881 with the creation of Skansen, an outdoor museum where historic structures were gathered from all over Sweden and surrounded by appropriate flora and fauna and housing performing "natives" (Lapp reindeer-herders, country fiddle-players, Darcalian peasants), much in the tradition of the living ethnographic displays that had become a popular feature of the great nineteenth-century international expositions. The Skansen idea spread all over Europe, but the idea of a museum village with living costumed "inhabitants" proved particularly attractive in the United States, where it inspired countless imitations, the most famous of them being two entire restored communities: Colonial Williamsburg in Virginia, and Plimoth Plantation in Massachusetts. At first the costumed inhabitants, as at Skansen, were simply generic representatives, often demonstrating some trade, like a blacksmith or carpenter, but in the late 1960s and early 1970s James Deetz, the assistant director of Plimoth Plantation, introduced the practice of making each inhabitant a specific person, with a complete biography, period accent, and ability to converse with visitors in detail about their imaginary life. In a striking instance of the converging performative consciousness of social science, tourism, and the living museum, Deetz in 1981 compared visitors to Plimoth Plantation to "anthropology fieldworkers going in to experience a community and elicit from it what they could."[63]

By the mid 1980s there were over 650 living history homes and communities in the United States. Visitors can now meet a huge variety of historically documented and wholly imaginary persons in their homes or workplaces across America. They can have tea at the Vanderbilt mansion in upstage New York with actresses playing society leaders Madeline Astor and Rosmond Vanderbilt, or, at the other end of the social scale, may meet, at the Tenement Museum on New York's Lower East Side, actors playing members of the Confino family, Italian immigrants who arrived in this country in 1916. Whatever the suspension of disbelief visitors bring to these encounters, they are obviously aware of their performative nature. In this way a large public unfamiliar with the importance of the concept of role-playing in modern social science or performance studies have encountered first hand a memorable example of the performative nature of human society.

Chapter 5

Performance art

The beginnings of performance art

Performance and performance art emerged during the 1970s and 1980s as major cultural activities in the United States as well as in Western Europe and Japan. So complex and varied has been such activity and so popular has it proven with the public and the media that, like postmodernism (a product of the same historical culture), its very ubiquity and popularity have made it very difficult to define. What will be attempted in this chapter, therefore, is a discussion of the general parameters of this diffuse field and of some of the most prominent of its features and practitioners. Perhaps it would be best to begin in the early 1970s, when the terms "performance" and "performance art" were just coming into vogue in the American artistic community, and to see what concerns in the art world encouraged such activity and what interests and felt needs among theatre theorists encouraged critical speculation upon this activity.

As performance art developed during the 1970s and 1980s, becoming always more varied in its manifestations, and moving if not into the mainstream of contemporary culture at least into the general public consciousness, its relationship to many of the traditional entertainers in popular culture, such as the clown, the manipulator of physical objects, the monologuist and the stand-up comedian, became clearer. In its earlier days, however, performance art was, like the earliest cabaret performances, futurist evenings, or dada exhibitions, created by and for a very limited artistic community. What it had most in common with these and other experimental movements in both theatre and dance of the early twentieth century was an interest in developing the expressive qualities of the body, especially in opposition to logical and discursive thought and speech, and in seeking the celebration of form and process over content and product.

Although the primarily European avant-garde of the early twentieth century provided a background and lineage for early performance art, and in certain cases even provided direct inspiration through individual European artists who brought such experimental concerns to the United States during the 1930s and 1940s, the major foundations for the performance work in New York and California in the 1970s came not out of experimental theatre work but out of new approaches to the visual arts such as environments, happenings, live and conceptual art and to dance by such innovators as Anna Halprin, Simone Forti, and Yvonne Rainer.

Conceptual art

When performance appeared as an artistic phenomenon around 1970, it had a close but ambiguous relationship to the then popular experimental form, conceptual art. The term derives from a 1913 definition by Marcel Duchamp of the artist as one who selects material or experience for aesthetic consideration rather than forming something from the traditional raw materials of art—an approach that led first to his exhibition of already existing objects, the "ready-mades," and eventually to a consideration of real-life activities as art. Even those concept artists who worked on something close to traditional painted surfaces, such as Jasper Johns with his collages or David Hockney with his photomontages, nevertheless called attention in their works to the process of creation and perception. Works like the tableaux of Edward Kienholz, the mixed media abstractions of Judy Pfaff, or the disturbing assemblages of icons of racial stereotyping discovered and presented by Bettye Saar move off their surfaces to claim significant physical and psychic space in the external world. Earth and site artists like Robert Smithson or Christo have extended concept art to large natural and human environments to make social and political statements, or to alter conventional perceptions of the sites targeted by their work.

Finally, certain artists like Kaprow in the United States, Gilbert and George in England, and Joseph Beuys in Germany began to follow Duchamp in extending this interest in process, in perception, and in the revelation of already existing material to the activities of the human body as a part of the found or constructed environment. The body, often the artist's own body, was manipulated and worked as an artistic material. By the middle of the 1960s such work had begun to be regarded not simply as a type of concept art but as an approach of its own, to which the terms body art and performance art began to be given.

Body art

In its first manifestations, performance art was largely and often very specifically concerned with the operations of the body. In 1960 Yves Klein in Paris presented his "Monotone Symphony," in which he, dressed as a conductor, directed a group of musicians playing a single note while three nude women coated each other with paint and then rubbed themselves against large sheets of paper. Soon after in Italy, Piero Manzoni began signing human bodies instead of paintings, while the British team Gilbert and George presented "living statues," and in Vienna Hermann Nitsch and the Aktionists presented "Dionysian" rituals prominently featuring nudity and blood.

Interest in such work developed in both New York and California in the mid-1960s, although still without a commonly accepted name for it. The California magazine *Avalanche*, in its opening issue (1970), offered a survey of recent "Body Works:" "Variously called actions, events, performances, pieces, things, the works present physical activities, ordinary bodily functions and other usual and unusual manifestions of physicality. The artist's body becomes both the subject and the object of the work."[1] In such work, the "verb and subject became one," and "the equipment for *feeling* is automatically the same equipment as for *doing*."[2] By around 1970, however, the term "body art" was that most generally applied to such work, and the early 1970s saw the best-known of the body art pieces.

Bruce Naumann was one of the first of the body artists, taking his cue, several chroniclers of the movement have suggested, from Marcel Duchamp's act of having a star shaved on the back of his head in 1921.[3] In the mid-1960s Naumann began making videotapes of parts of his body and audiotapes of its sounds, by making casts of parts of his body and by manipulating it or moving through a series of repeated gestures. Later he created performance environments requiring the participants to follow a carefully controlled set of actions.

Almost any sort of physical activity was explored by the body artists of the 1970s. Some, taking their clue from Kaprow, simply offered examples of "real-time activity"—walking, sleeping, eating and drinking, cooking—presented straightforwardly or with a distinctly playful edge, as in Tom Marioni's first major event, a beer party at the Oakland Museum in 1969 with the dada-flavored title "The Act of Drinking Beer with Friends is the Highest Form of Art." The following year Marioni founded the Museum of Conceptual Art in San Francisco, an important center for such experimentation. The Bay Area became for a time the center of "life art," involved with framing, intensifying, or ostending everyday activities. Bonnie Sherk performed such actions as "Sitting Still" (1970) and having a "Public Lunch" (1971) in unlikely places, and placed a performative frame around certain of her activities as a short order cook at Andy's Donuts, as in "Cleaning the Griddle" (1973). Howard Fried, trained as a sculptor, placed framing devices around a wrestling match, a baseball game, and a golf lesson. In 1973 Linda Montano and Marioni spent three days handcuffed together in order "to achieve a heightened awareness of habitual behavior patterns."[4] This served as a kind of trial run for her most famous performance piece, "One-year Performance," for which she spent the entire year 1983–4 chained to fellow artist Tehching Hsieh.

Chris Burden and Vito Acconci

An important part of early 1970s performance, however, and certainly the part that attracted the most attention from the media and the general public, were those pieces that went beyond everyday activity to push the body to extremes or even to subject it to considerable risk or pain. The artists most associated with work of this sort were Chris Burden and Vito Acconci. Chris Burden's first major performance piece, "Five-Day Locker Piece" (1971), confined him to a small locker ($2 \times 2 \times 3$ feet) in a campus art gallery, recalling a similar box confinement Beuys did with Fluxus in 1965. For his "Shoot" (1971) a friend shot him in the arm, fascinating the national media. During the next several years he toyed with electrocution, hanging, fire, and a variety of sharp objects piercing his flesh. Two themes run through his many interviews about his pieces. One is that he was trying to use extreme body situations to induce certain mental states. "The violent part wasn't really that important," he said in 1978, "it was just a crux to make all the mental stuff happen."[5] The other is that such acts partook of reality instead of the "more mushy" illusory world of theatre. "It seems that bad art is theatre," Burden posited in 1973. "Getting shot is for real ... there's no element of pretense or make-believe in it."[6] After 1975 Burden turned away from works dealing with his own body, but a concern with violence and structures of power continues to inform his later work, as in "Samson" (1985) at the Seattle Art Gallery, where the entry turnstile was

Figure 5.1 Chris Burden in his performance piece *Trans-fixed*, Venice, California, April 1974.

Source: Chris Burden.

attached by rigging to two massive timbers so that if enough patrons passed through, the front of the building would collapse.

Acconci's body works, which were given in New York while Burden was working primarily in California, were strongly influenced by the idea of "power-fields," described in *The Principle of Topological Psychology* by Kurt Lewin. Each of Acconci's works was thus involved with "setting up a field in which the audience was, so that they became a part of what I was doing ... they became part of the physical space in which I moved."[7] Like Burden, Acconci performed a number of dangerous pieces that violently rejected the traditional illusion of theatre, but most were less spectacular and in a number he was not physically visible at all—as in the notorious "Seedbed" (1971), in which he reportedly masturbated under a ramp over which his gallery audience walked. Acconci worked in video, installation art, and performance, explaining in a 1979 essay that his primary concern was not with the medium (the "ground"), but with the "instrument," his own body. He sought to focus "on myself as the instrument that acted on whatever ground was available."[8]

Performance art and theatre

As artists and critics struggled to define the emerging new genre of performance (and to draw boundaries through which individual artists, predictably, were always slipping), theatre was probably the most common "other" against which the new art could be defined. In Washington in 1975 Kaprow headed a panel on Performance and the Arts which included Acconci, Yvonne Rainer, and Joan Jonas, whose performance works incorporated elements from Zuni and Hopi ceremonies of her native Pacific Coast. Attempting to define performance, this panel noted that the space utilized in performance "is more often like a work space than a formal theatrical setting," and that performance artists initially avoid "the dramatic structure and psychological dynamics of traditional theater or dance" to focus upon "bodily presence and movement activities."[9] The opportunities offered by multi-media performance for a more open-ended structure clearly also had an appeal. Looking back on her career in the 1995 interview, Jonas suggested: " What attracted me to performance was the possibility of mixing sound, movement, image, all the different elements to make a complex statement. What I wasn't good at was making a single, simple statement."[10]

This orientation certainly was widespread in the performance work of the early 1970s, especially due to the influence of Kaprow and the happenings and the visual art background of most of the leading practitioners. Theatre was not, however, so easily denied. The very presence of an audience watching an action, however neutral or non-matrixed, and presented in whatever unconventional space, inevitably called up associations with theatre. Moreover, even as performance emerged as a distinct genre in the early 1970s, many of its practitioners utilized distinctly theatrical approaches. Despite the great range of experimental practice at this period, it is possible to group these more "theatrical" performances into two general types which remained fairly distinct through the 1970s, until they joined together in what was widely regarded as the emergence of performance art into mainstream cultural consciousness—Laurie Anderson's *United States* in 1980. On the one hand there was performance as it was for the most part developed in California and New York—the work of a single artist, often using material from everyday life and rarely playing a conventional "character," emphasizing the activities of the body in space and time, sometimes by the framing of natural behavior, sometimes by the display of virtuosic physical skills or extremely taxing physical demands, and turning gradually toward autobiographical explorations. On the other hand there was a tradition, not often designated as performance until after 1980 but subsequently generally included in such work, of more elaborate spectacles not based on the body or the psyche of the individual artist but devoted to the display of non-literary aural and visual images, often involving spectacle, technology, and mixed media. Both approaches were usually undertaken outside traditional theatre spaces, but one-person performance tended to favor "artistic" venues such as galleries, while the larger spectacles sought a wide range of performance spaces, both indoors and out. An important part of this latter activity came to be known as "site-specific" or "environmental."

The theatre of mixed means

During the late 1960s and early 1970s these image-oriented spectacles came to be recognized as representing an important area of avant-garde experimentation and they were given various labels, but performance was not among them.[11] In 1968 Richard Kostelanetz gave the label "the theatre of mixed means" to new works which rejected the verbal and narratological emphasis of traditional theatre "in order to stress such presentational means as sound and light, objects and scenery, and/or the movement of people and props, often in addition to the newer technologies of films, recorded tape, amplification systems, radio, and closed-circuit television."[12] In 1977 Bonnie Marranca coined the term "Theatre of Images" to describe this same tradition: works that rejected traditional plot, character, setting, and especially language, to emphasize process, perception, the manipulation of time and space, and the tableau to create "a new stage language, a visual grammar 'written' in sophisticated perceptual codes."[13]

Both Kostelanetz and Marranca traced the tradition of this new visual and aural theatre back to a mixed heritage of artistic and theatrical avant-gardes—the new dance, the cinema, Cagean aesthetics, popular culture, experimental painting, the happenings, the artistic "isms" of the early twentieth century. To this eclectic list one could add early performance art itself, since several of the most influential practitioners of such spectacle, such as Laurie Anderson and Robert Wilson, began as performance artists working with very simple means.

Early British performance art

Contemporaneously with the development of happenings and of early performance art in the United States, a number of groups in Europe were experimenting with performance work emphasizing visual images rather than the body, much of it presented out of doors and often with a particular interest in odd, Rube Goldberg-type mechanical contraptions. British performance artists took the lead in such work in the mid-1960s under the combined influence of the American happenings, a renewed interest in Dada and other avant-garde theatre experiments, and the anarchic British comedy tradition. The People Show, founded by Jeff Nuttall in 1965 and characterized by alternative theatre historian Sandy Craig not only as Britain's "oldest and still [1980] most influential performance art group" but also as the "post-Dadaists of British theatre,"[14] introduced to its audiences a new kind of open and free-wheeling experience, offering collages of atmospheres, moods and striking images clustered around some central theme.

Despite its title and its formation in the revolutionary year 1968, The Welfare State, at least in its early years, was not overtly political, but operated in a spirit much closer to the carnivalesque People Show. The 1972 "Welfare State Manifesto" stated among its goals to:[15]

> make images, invent rituals, devise ceremonies, objectify the unpredictable, establish and enhance atmospheres for particular places, times, situations and people. In current terminology we fuse art, theatre and life style, but we aim to make such categories and role definition in itself obsolete.

Rather more formalistic was The Theatre of Mistakes, founded in 1974 by Anthony Howell, a former member of the Royal Ballet, who, under the influence of Artaud, Noh drama, and recent experiments in painting and sculpture, set up a workshop of "performance art" in order to explore the neglected "art of action, the art of what people do."[16]

In the United States and, generally speaking, on the European continent, the first modern performance artists tended to emphasize their artistic backgrounds and to reject any connection with popular performance. However, many British performance artists from the beginning consciously incorporated into their experiments material from street mime, clown acts, and traditional vaudeville and burlesque, certain artists even specializing in such material, albeit with a theoretical or avant-garde consciousness that gave it a new context and orientation. The British willingness to mix popular entertainment with artistic experimentation could be seen in the popularity of such groups as the "world's first pose band," founded in London in 1972, which revived the nineteenth-century popular tradition of the tableau vivant to present extremely funny evenings of tableaux, most of them mocking the pretensions of the current art and society world.

Jérôme Savary

During this same period the British gave a warm welcome to a related experimental performance group from Paris, Jérôme Savary's Grand Magique Circus. Savary was an important international pioneer in the mixing of variety entertainment with physical spectacle, and in utilizing the sort of unconventional locations that would come to be associated with "site-specific" theatre. In a 1970 interview in *Tulane Drama Review*, Savary noted: "I am a firm believer in magic, in the creation of atmosphere. To liven things up we use real fires, smoke of all types and colors, fireworks, animals in the theatre. Sometimes we use a little tree or a chair, but derisively." The current avant-garde Savary condemned as too intellectual (and indeed the intellectual French avant-garde has never had much respect for Savary). He sought instead a broad general public, reared on television and the movies and open to "visual forms of entertainment."[17]

After Savary's troupe visited Britain in the early 1970s, suggesting the avant-garde possibilities of such entertainment, circus skills, live music, and variety turns were developed by a number of younger British performance collectives such as Incubus and Kaboodle and by such feminist groups as Beryl and the Perils and Cunning Stunts. Such groups became known collectively as "Performance Art Vaudevillians." A similar interest developed somewhat later in America, where the quite eclectic group of mostly solo performers sometimes referred to as the "New Vaudevillians" became during the 1980s some of the most publicized experimental performers in the country.

Spectacle performance

Outdoor and site-specific performance

Large-scale outdoor spectacle, often utilizing fireworks, elaborate costuming and properties, and produced in an almost infinite variety of natural and constructed environments, became a specialty during the 1970s of the British company Welfare State, and during the following decade was a major sort of experimental performance in both Europe and America. Warner von Wely, who worked with Welfare State for three years, drew upon this inspiration to found Dogtroep, the leading outdoor theatre company in Holland, which has presented innovative performance at home, across Europe, and in America, involving elaborate visual images, bizarre mechanical constructions, and fireworks. The aim, says von Wely, is to "create ambiguous, hermetic images which you can hang meaning on, but which don't have any meaning themselves ... the dramaturgical structure is a pretext to show the images."[18] Another image-oriented company that has performed in a wide variety of non-theatrical spaces in England also descended from Welfare State. This was the International Outlaw University (IOU), established in 1976.

The 1980s also saw the development of certain artists and groups in the United States specializing in site-specific multimedia spectacles with huge casts and crews. In California Lin Hixson put together enormous environments like movie sets, with motorcades and musical-comedy-style choruses. Her 1984 "Hey John, Did You Take the Camino Far?" occupied the loading dock of an industrial building in downtown Los Angeles, but its song and dance numbers and the movements of its teenager gangs and their cars spilled out into the adjacent public streets with no clear division between the performance and the city beyond. Jacki Apple characterized her work as "the cultural autobiography of a white American of the TV generation."[19] In 1985 Anne Hamburger founded En Garde Arts in New York, which has produced an impressive range of site-specific events at locations all over the city. Among the most ambitious was the 1990 *Father was a Peculiar Man* by Reza Abdoh, who had recently emerged in Los Angeles as a major visionary director of large cultural epics in untraditional spaces, somewhat akin to the work of Hixson but with a much darker and more sexual dimension. *Father* was a series of visual and aural meditations on Dostoevsky's *The Brothers Karamazov* and on American popular culture of the 1950s and 1960s, performed by sixty actors and musicians throughout a four-block area of streets and warehouses in New York's meat-packing district. Its success placed Abdoh in the forefront of experimental American performance artists, but he created only four additional works before his untimely death from AIDS in 1995.[20]

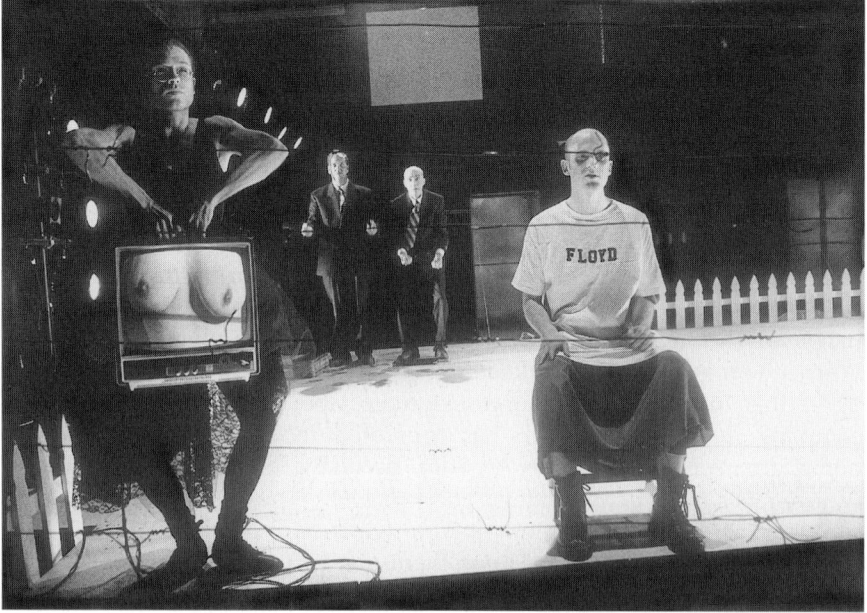

Figure 5.2 Reza Abdoh's *Quotations from a Ruined City*, New York, 1994.

Source: Paula Court.

Much so-called "site-specific" performance has only involved the use of unconventional performance spaces, indoors and out, with particular attention to the physical characteristics of the space and, at times, to its social or historical associations. However, in 1993 the British artistic team of Ewan Forster and Christopher Heighes, began creating site-specific performances designed particularly to reveal the "language" of certain historically, socially, and architecturally significant buildings and locations, such as an art deco London settlement house in the 1997 piece *Preliminary Hearing* or the layering of architecture, landscape, and social history at Froebel College, Roehampton, in the 1999 *The Curriculum*. This culturally-oriented turn in site-specific work tied their activities closely to a general shift in much performance work toward cultural concerns at the turn of the century—a shift that will be the focus of my final chapter.

In a special section devoted to Performance Art in *Artweek* in 1990, Jacki Apple suggested how the orientation of performance had shifted over its first decade:[21]

In the '70's performance art was primarily a time-based visual art form in which text was at the service of image; by the early '80's performance art had shifted to movement-based work, with the performance artist as choreographer. Interdisciplinary collaboration and "spectacle," influenced by TV and other popular entertainment modes, as in the new work of Lin Hixon, set the tone for the new decade.

Figure 5.3 Forster and Heighes' *Preliminary Hearing*, London, 1997.
Source: Fiona Colquhon.

Many of these new "spectacles," as we have seen, continued the anti-theatre orientation of early performance by seeking out non-theatrical spaces for their development, but despite the visibility and popularity of elaborate site-specific performances, especially in Europe, the technical demands of such work encouraged some of the best-known image and mixed-media performers to present most of their work in more conventional theatre spaces. This has been true of all three of the artists discussed in Marranca's book as the leading practitioners of the "theatre of images"—Richard Foreman, Lee Breuer, and Robert Wilson. Foreman's Ontological-Hysteric Theatre has, of these three, been most consistently developed in small, experimental performance spaces, offering approximately one elaborate production a year since *Angelface* in 1968. These productions are packed full of the elaborate visual and aural material that characterizes Foreman's work—posed tableaux; a welter of odd objects; sketches and fragments of words and sentences; all sorts of framing and pointing devices, such as boxes, windows, frames, and strings; recordings; odd sound effects; repeated movements—all contributing to a rich overlay that continually calls attention to the constructedness of Foreman's work and to the process of reception itself. Breuer and the Mabou Mines have worked with more conventional narrative, though presented in a colorful style stressing poses, movement, visual puns, and the incorporation of visual and aural echoes from a wide range of popular culture. Most of Breuer's work, like Foreman's, has been presented in modest experimental venues, but one section of his ongoing epic *The Warrior Ant* was offered in 1988 at the Brooklyn Academy of Music, a center of large-scale performance work, and he took full advantage of the facilities available there, with a number of bands and ethnic dancing companies, street parades, and huge and small scale puppets.

Robert Wilson

The Brooklyn Academy has also been the usual American venue for the best-known of the image-spectacle makers, Robert Wilson, whose first major work, *The Life and Times of Sigmund Freud*, premiered here in late 1969. Wilson began as a performance artist, dancer and designer in the 1960s, strongly influenced by the happenings and early performance work of that period. His *Sigmund Freud* was immediately recognized as a significant new approach in experimental performance, especially by such sympathetic viewers as Richard Foreman, who wrote in the *Village Voice*:[22]

> Wilson is one of a small number of artists who seem to have applied a very different aesthetic to theatre—one current among advanced painters, musicians, dancers and filmmakers—a non-manipulative aesthetic which would see art create a "field" situation within which the spectator can examine himself (as perceptor) in relation to the "discoveries" the artist has made within his medium.... Bodies and persons

emerged as the impenetrable (holy) objects they really are, rather than the usual virtuoso tools used to project some play's predetermined energies and meanings."

Wilson's visual operas of the 1970s, especially *Deafman Glance* (1970), the 168-hour *KA MOUNTAIN AND GUARDenia TERRACE* at the 1972 Shiraz Festival in Iran, *A Letter for Queen Victoria* (1974), and *Einstein on the Beach* (1976), established him as one of the leading experimental theatre artists of his generation—a position he still maintains. His manipulation of space and time, his fusion of visual, aural, and performing arts, his utilization of chance and collage techniques in construction, his use of language for sound and evocation rather than discursive meaning, all show his close relationship to earlier experimental work in theatre, music, visual arts, and dance. Speaking of *Einstein on the Beach*, Wilson advised: "You don't have to think about the story, because there isn't any. You don't have to listen to words, because the words don't mean anything. You just enjoy the scenery, the architectural arrangements in time and space, the music, the feelings they all evoke. Listen to the pictures."[23] Between 1973 and 1980 Wilson created at least one project a year with Christopher Knowles, a brain-damaged teenager whose unconventional approaches to perception, language and performance provided an important source of inspiration for Wilson and his theatre, reflected especially in the structure and use of language in *A Letter for Queen Victoria* and *The $ Value of Man* (1975).

Theatre-based mixed media and performance spectacle appeared as a highly visible part of the experimental performance scene in many theatre centers outside the United States during this period as well. Wilson himself began premiering the majority of his large-scale works abroad, particularly in Germany, and his work inspired many young European and Japanese artists (parts of Wilson's monumental international project, *the CIVIL warS* (1984) were developed in the United States, the Netherlands, Germany, Italy, and Japan). Robert Wilson type works became so important a part of the Italian experimental scene as to be considered a new genre, the "Nuova Spettacolarita (new spectacularity)" or "Media Theatre." The visual spectacles of Jan Fabre in Belgium, such as *The Power of Theatrical Madness* (1986), of the visceral Fura dels Baus in Spain, who terrorized international audiences with their *Suz/o/Suz* (1990), or of French-Canadian Robert Lepage in such performances as *Needles and Opium* (1992) extended this sort of performance imaginatively and internationally. In 1994 LePage founded in Quebec the multidisciplinary company Ex Machina, with which he created that same year one of the best-known multimedia spectacles of the decade, *The Seven Streams of the River Ota*. The Italian company Societas Raffelle Sanzio, directed by Romeo Castellucci, developed a major international reputation with experimental visual spectacles in this same general tradition in the late 1990s with their *Giulio Cesare* (1997), *Genesi* (1999), and *Il Combattimento* (2000).

Certain leading choreographers of the 1970s and 1980s worked in similar directions. Wilson himself worked with leading dancers and choreographers (with Lucinda Childs and Andrew deGroat in *Einstein on the Beach*, for example). Other contemporary choreographers have developed various combinations of dance, theatre, and performance art. Among these are Martha Clarke in America, whose painterly *Garden of Earthly Delights* and *Vienna: Lusthaus* (1986) were major dance and performance events of this period, and Maguy Marin in France, who has often drawn upon Spanish and surrealist sources as well as the work of Samuel Beckett in such pieces as *May B* (1981). Modern dance-theatre (*Tanztheater*) became particularly important in Germany, led by the work of Pina Bausch, whose use of shock and sexual violence (as in her 1984 *Bluebeard*) contribute to her association with German expressionism. She also has much in common visually with Robert Wilson's cooler and more abstract visual operas in her love of large-scale works with hypnotic sequences and monumental physical surroundings, such as the flooded stage and its wandering hippopotamus in *Arien* (1984).

The new circus

An important element of performance art since the 1980s has involved activity of this sort, set off from the traditions that inspired it by a modern ironic and reflexive consciousness of the performing act and closely and consciously related to the traditions of circus and clowning. A key figure in this revival was Hovey Burgess, an American who began his career as a street entertainer juggling on the streets of European cities in the mid-1960s. Back in New York in 1966 he taught circus skills at New York University and founded the Circo dell'Arte, which did commedia and circus inspired shows for two years in the city's parks.[24] When the Circo disbanded in 1970 some of its leading members, fascinated by the work of the San Francisco Mime Troupe which they had seen in Central Park, joined that company in California, where Larry Pisoni in particular was responsible for adding circus skills to the commedia and mime work the company was already doing. Burgess went on to teach juggling at Ringling Bros and Barnum and Bailey's Clown College (still thriving, although the organization by now performed only in large indoor spaces). His best-known student was Bill Irwin, who in 1975 went on from the Clown College to join Larry Pisoni and others who left the Mime Troupe to form the first of the "new American circuses," the Pickle Family Circus. The Pickles were most noted for their elaborate juggling routines and for their clown acts, based on the work of three men who soon established themselves as among the greatest modern clowns: Bill Irwin, Geoff Hoyle, and Larry Pisoni.[25]

The Pickle Family Circus, which continued until 1993, was the first of a group of new circuses that appeared in a number of countries during the 1970s to revolutionize and reinvigorate this traditional performance organization. In 1975 Silvia Monfort, director of the Paris Cultural Center, and Alexis Gruss Jr, scion of an ancient circus family, created the Cirque Gruss, removing all the subsequent elaborations of the form to return to the model of the first Parisian circus of Philip Astley 200 years before.[26] It was an enormous success, sparking a new interest in circus in Europe and inspiring a number of young Americans, among them Paul Binder, another juggler and graduate from the San Francisco Mime Troupe, who returned to New York to establish the second major American "new circus," the Big Apple Circus, in the summer of 1977. Yet another major "new circus," the Circus Flora, was formed in 1986 by a European cycling performer, Alexandre Pavlata, and Ivor David Balding, who served in the early 1980s as producer for the Big Apple Circus. Balding had also served as general manager for one of the surviving old-style circuses, the indoor Shrine circus, with which he became increasingly dissatisfied. In a 1992 interview with Ernest Albrecht he observed that the Shrine circus was all "about spectacle," while he had become committed to the Big Apple style, "which was about performance." Reporting this conversation, Albrecht tellingly observes: "In that observation Balding has identified the central and unifying theme of the New American Circus. Performance takes precedence over spectacle."[27]

Surely the best known internationally of the "new circuses," however, comes not from the United States but from Quebec: the Cirque du Soleil. Its genealogy is not intertwined with the other similar ventures in America, but the biography of its founder, Guy Laliberté, is very similar. At the age of eighteen he traveled through Europe as a street entertainer, much like Hovey Burgess or Paul Binder, and he returned to Quebec to pursue the same precarious existence and to evolve the idea of a new form of circus. He teamed up with Guy Caron, who had studied at the Hungarian State Circus School and had an extensive knowledge of the European circus scene. Together they developed the Cirque du Soleil, convinced the government of Quebec to provide a substantial subsidy, and gained almost at once an enormous critical and popular success, which became international when they dazzled American audiences in 1987 at the Los Angeles Arts Festival. Caron put his own stamp on the "new circus," derived from his experience in Europe. This was to unite each entire production with a specially pre-pared score, a theme, and a loose unified story line to which all perfor-mances in some way contribute. There is never a linear plot, but a series of often overlapping and interconnected acts, with inspiration drawn not only from traditional theatre and circus (clowns, jugglers, acrobats) but also from the modern world of MTV video, with its series of dreamlike, abstract, surre-alistic images that provide a mesmerizing if undefined continuity.[28]

Solo work

The new vaudevillians

The term "new vaudevillians" began to be used in the mid-1980s to describe a group of performers "who descend, either directly or in spirit, from the San Francisco Mime Troupe."[29] Not all of the so-called new vaude-villians accept this term, however, and nor does the leading chronicler of the group, Ron Jenkins, who studied with several members of this group at the Ringling Clown College. Possibly reflecting that background, Jenkins expresses in his 1988 survey study, *Acrobats of the Soul*, a preference for the terms "modern clowns" or "comic performers."[30]

Jenkins includes among these "modern clowns" ventriloquist Paul Zaloom, a former member of Bread and Puppet, who manipulates society's detritis—toys, utensils, milk cartons, boxes, and automobile parts—into a socially satiric "theatre of trash;" banjo performer Stephen Wade; the clown acts of leading contemporary circuses—the Big Apple, the Cirque du Soleil, and the Pickle Family Circus; magician clowns Penn and Teller (Penn Jillette being another graduate of the Clown College); monologuist Spalding Gray; The Flying Kara-mazov Brothers, whose speciality is juggling almost any conceivable objects; and two solo clowns, Bill Irwin and Avner the Eccentric. Putting aside Gray, whose presence in this company is a bit odd, Bill Irwin is probably the best known of this group, and he is for many the central example of the "new vaudeville" or of modern clown performance. Irwin's background includes training in modern dance, in clown performance with both the traditional Ringling Brothers and the contemporary Pickle Family, and in avant-garde theatre with Herbert Blau's KRAKEN ensemble, and this diverse blend informs his multi-layered performances. Irwin's *The Regard of Flight* (1982) mixed traditional clown routines with continually foiled attempts to establish a new avant-garde approach to theatre and with the running accompaniment of a critic from the audience commenting on the work.

By the late 1980s the most prominent "new vaudevillians" were taking their performance work back into the mainstream theatre. In the summer of 1987 Avner the Eccentric, the Flying Karamazov Brothers and other experimental performers presented a circus-like production of Shakespeare's *A Comedy of Errors* at the Lincoln Center, and Bill Irwin has appeared in a number of Broadway productions, among the most successful of which was a two-man clown show, *Fool's Moon*, in 1993, with David Shiner, formerly the leading clown of the Cirque du Soleil.

An even more conscious return to traditional vaudeville performance, though with the same ironic and self-conscious relationship to modern performance art, could be seen in a group of acrobats, jugglers, magicians, and variety acts that emerged in New York at the beginning of the new century. The Bindlestiff Family Circus, the newest "new circus," brought vaudeville to 42nd Street for the first time in almost half a century, while similar variety entertainments appeared in SoHo and Tribeca. Todd Robbins, director of the SoHo "Sideshow Saturday Night," consciously connected such activity to the modern performance tradition by suggesting that it should be called the "Newer Vaudeville."[31]

Persona performance and walkabouts

While some of the British and American "vaudevillians," especially those closest to the clown tradition, perform in recognizable costumes, the primary concern of their display has not been the presentation of a particular "character" in the theatrical sense, but physical activity and achievement—mime, physical dexterity, juggling, and so on. Other performance of the late 1970s and early 1980s displayed the body in costume, but without the vaudevillians' emphasis upon physical achievement. Generally speaking, these costumed performances did not seek to establish a coherent narrative character in the traditional sense, but to create a powerful visual image or to embody some historical or contemporary individual or type upon which the artist wished to comment—often in order to make some social or satirical point. Paul Best created a female alternate persona, Octavia, who appeared in make-up and costume in social situations that Best felt would reveal stereotyped gender expectations.[32] Other improvised public performances sought to reveal aspects of the artist's own personality or dreams. Eleanor Antin developed a whole series of "personae" built up in a series of performances, the best known being her black ballerina Eleanora Antinova, and her King of Solona Beach who appeared from time to time in make-up and costume to chat with his "subjects."[33]

Antin's roving King and Best's Octavia bear a close relationship to a type of European performance activity the British have called the "walkabout," in which costumed performers improvise interactions with the general public. Some attempt to blend in with their surroundings, often consciously seeking to stimulate amused confusion. The trio La Compagnie Extrêmement Prétentieuse pretends to be obsequious but incompetent waiters in

Figure 5.4 Eleanora Antin's "King of Solana Beach" chatting with his subjects, 1975.
Source: Ronald Feldman Fine Arts.

French street cafés. Théâtre Décale is made up of Inspector Clouseau-type detectives who look into people's luggage, inspect displays in shops, stop passing bicyclists, and then walk off with various items. One of the best known and most consciously subversive groups is Natural Theatre, which greeted Margaret Thatcher as pram-pushing nannies at Expo, appeared as pot-smoking policemen at the Glastonbury Festival, and has parodied protest demonstrations by demonstrating in normal if rather outdated clothes against bicycles. Other groups attract attention by assuming interesting public roles. The German Scharlatan Theater has pretended to be a film crew setting up for a shoot. The actors of Spain's Trapu Zaharra Teatro Trapero appear as seemingly harmless, bewildered mental patients with bandaged heads, who appeal for comfort to passersby until they are picked up and carried off by what appears to be a real ambulance. Other walkabout performers are more eccentric still. Natural Theatre has appeared as egg-headed aliens from space, and the German trio The Crazy Idiots roam city streets in penguin costumes, confronting and even attacking passersby.[34] Most walkabout work is performed by one, two, or three performers, but Natural normally works with more, as does the Amsterdam company Tender, which has become so familiar a part of the local intellectual landscape that Amsterdam citizens will often assume, correctly or not, that any odd occurrence that they note in the streets is a Tender performance.

Autobiographical performance

American "walkabouts" have tended to be more interested than parallel European performances in the exploration of alternate "selves," indeed the use of performance to explore alternate "selves" or to reveal fantasies or psychic autobiography had by the mid-1970s become a major approach to performance in the United States. For much of the general public this still remains the most familiar and accessible manifestation of this movement. The work of Antin suggests two quite different directions such work could take. One direction presents alternate "selves," one per performance or several in sequence, exploring concerns vital to the performer's psyche. An example would be Whoopi Goldberg's dramatic monologues, which enjoyed a successful Broadway run in 1985, drawing upon her marginalized position as a performing black woman to depict a range of "outsider" personae, yet harkening back also to the mainline entertainment monologue tradition of Ruth Draper and Beatrice Herford. Such popular and important contemporary monologue artists as Eric Bogosian and Anna Deveare Smith can also be viewed as working in this tradition, but both also draw very consciously upon the material and attitudes surrounding modern performance art. Bogosian's background includes performance art work, and he has been characterized as "less a writer or actor than a mixture of stand-up comic and performance artist."[35] Bogosian himself has commented on his ambiguous position:[36]

> People from theater came and said, "That's not theater".... Perform-
> ance artists came and said "That's not performance art." But I don't
> really care what you call it. That's not important. What's important is
> effect.

It is doubtless the depiction of created "characters" that makes many
persons who are interested in performance art unwilling to apply this label
to performers like Whoopi Goldberg and Eric Bogosian. Much more clearly
in the performance tradition is another type of contemporary monologue
work. This utilizes a distinctly more individualized autobiographical
narrative that avoids the alternate "selves" which have a tendency to crys-
tallize into new "characters" with a distinctly "theatrical" feel. Despite its
privileging of language uncharacteristic of early performance art, this sort
of work still focuses on the specific persona of the performer, displaying
now both body and psyche. A well-known example of this approach is
Spalding Gray, who has spun his dreams, memories, and reflections into a
fascinating series of oral histories, delivered simply sitting at a table with
notes and a glass of water. Solo performance art and monologue has been
particularly associated in the late 1980s and early 1990s with feminist and
gay performers such as Holly Hughes, Karen Finley, and Tim Miller, and
will be considered in more detail in later chapters.

Laurie Anderson

Autobiographical material is also the foundation of the work of Laurie
Anderson, whose *United States* is in many respects a pivotal event in
modern performance. It brought the concept of performance art to a wide
general public for the first time, as was witnessed by such mass circulation
periodicals as *Time*, which called it "the biggest, most ambitious and most
successful example to date of the avant-garde hybrid known as performance art,"[37] and *People*, which observed that Anderson was "the only practitioner of that quirky, free-form genre called 'performance art' to have
catapulted into pop culture."[38]

In addition to the public attention *United States* brought to performance
art, however, it was a key work in bringing together the two hitherto quite
disparate approaches to performance represented by individual performers
stressing the body, and the mixed media "theatre of images." Anderson's
own career was distinctly influenced by leading practitioners in both
approaches. In the early 1970s she became interested in the body work of
Vito Acconci, who in 1974 sponsored an early concept work by Anderson,
O-Range. After this she explored autobiographical subject matter presented
in mixed media and with the aid of such gadgets as a self-playing violin,
suggesting the dadaist devices of such contemporary British performance
groups as The People Show. In 1976 she attended Philip Glass and Robert
Wilson's *Einstein on the Beach*, which inspired her to develop her small-scale
pieces into large and complex multi-media productions, these leading in

turn to *United States*, a seven-hour "performance portrait of the country" which combined stories, songs, slide projections, film, and, in a kind of tribute to the performance art tradition, a percussion solo played on Anderson's amplified skull. *People Weekly*, alert to Anderson's populist appeal, characterized it as a "whizbang techno-vaudeville." The songs and stories grew out of Anderson's dreams and experiences, including even the experience of creating this production, but, like the more minimalist work of Spalding Gray (for whom Anderson has also provided soundtracks), these personal musings reverberated through a cultural moment. Anderson is well aware of this, and has remarked:[39]

> If I were really just expressing myself, I wouldn't think that people would be that interested. I try to pick things that would make people say, "I was just thinking that a couple of days ago; I didn't say it exactly like that but I had that idea."

This sense of providing a voice and body to common (and generally unarticulated) experience is very important to much modern performance, especially that created by and for marginalized or oppressed communities. Performance artist Barbara Smith, for example, has explained: "I turn to question the audience to see if their experiences might enlighten mine and break the isolation of my experience, to see if performance art puts them into the same dilemma."[40]

The turn to language

Despite the enormous variety of performance activities during the 1970s and 1980s, it is possible to trace two overall and related trends. First, the initial widespread opposition of performance to theatre has steadily eroded, and second, the initial emphasis on body and movement, with a general rejection of discursive language, has given way gradually to image-centered performance and a return of language. In her brief survey of modern performance art in *Artweek*, Jacki Apple proposes precisely these three phases, arguing that by 1990 word had become "the dominant factor—the performance artist as poet, storyteller, preacher, rapper, with image at the service of text."[41]

This shift is clear almost everywhere one looks in recent performance. Solo performance, though still built upon the physical presence of the performer, relies heavily upon the word, and very often upon the word as revelation of the performer, through the use of autobiographical material. This is true whether one considers the work of a visual minimalist like Spalding Gray or the elaborate mixed media productions of Laurie Anderson. Even the physically oriented "new vaudevillians" such as Bill Irwin, Paul Zaloom, Avner the Eccentric, or the Flying Karamazov Brothers rely heavily upon language to provide an intellectual and often political or artistically self-reflexive depth to the physical display. Henry Louis Gates Jr, in a

Spring 1995 issue of *The New Yorker*, chronicles the recent appearance at two downtown New York performance spaces (especially at the Nuyorican Café, founded in 1989) of a new "scene" or "movement" in language performance called "rap meets poetry." Gates' description emphasizes the performative nature of this work, work that is "captivating in performance" even though it "just doesn't survive on the page." Gates' description of the performative space of this work is strikingly similar to Turner's limoid space of performance, a "hybrid space where cultural styles jostle and collide; where culture wars spawn not new resentment but new cultures."[42]

This new style of spoken performance, drawing upon the rhymes and rhythms of hip-hop, gained national attention during the 1990s through the circulation of hip-hop albums and of the physical bodies of performers appearing in spoken poetry competitions called "poetry slams" in cafés, colleges, and experimental spaces across America. This work came to be called Def Poetry, thanks in large part to the prominence of the Def Jam recording label and the growing popularity from the mid-1990s onwards of Russell Simmons's "Def Comedy Jam" on HBO. Def Poetry performance entered mainstream live entertainment in 2002 with a six-week performance in San Francisco, *Def Poetry Jam*, featuring nine young leading Def poet-performers. In November of that year this show opened in New York as *Def Poetry Jam on Broadway*. A lead article in the *New York Times* Sunday "Arts and Leisure" section pointed out the performance roots of the production, suggesting that it "brings to Broadway both the ancient traditions of bards and griots and the more recent resurgence of spoken-word performance."[43]

Word and image

The so-called "theatre of images," especially in the United States, has also accepted the word as an important part of its activity. This has always been true of Richard Foreman and Lee Breuer, for example, but even Robert Wilson, after a kind of transition in which words were employed rather as chance elements, has since the late 1980s turned increasingly toward the staging of plays from the verbal tradition—Chekhov, Ibsen, Euripides, Büchner, Shakespeare. Wilson even moved from the huge multi-media spectacles that established his reputation to offer in the summer of 1995 his own solo adaptation of *Hamlet* for the Lincoln Center's Serious Fun Festival.

The majority of the most prominent new experimental groups that emerged in England and America during the 1990s demonstrated variations of this new blending of word and image. The return of Lin Hixson from Los Angeles to her native Chicago in the early 1990s to form the company Goat Island is emblematic of this shift. With Goat Island Hixson turned from the spectacular, visual, site-specific work she had done in Los Angeles to a more intimate, concentrated collective creations with the five other members of that group. In a 2002 "Letter to a Young Practitioner," they described their work thus:[44]

> Friends unfamiliar with Goat Island's performances ask me what they do, and I tell them: they use text, but not to tell a standard theatrical narrative or story; and they use movement, though it's not what you would expect by the term "dance." And combining those texts and movements creates something beyond those individual components of text and movement, and the best word we have for this is "performance."

A "performance" composed, like those of Goat Island, of alternating sequences of "found" textual material, from literary sources, the media, historical records, or popular culture, with non-dance movement sequences, became so familiar during the 1990s as to become almost a distinct sub-genre of American and English performance. The use of found material, textual, physical, and frequently not primarily theatrical or dramatic, its group discovery and its collective development during the rehearsal process can be found in much experimental work of the late twentieth century. The most likely specific inspiration for the practice and performance structure of 1990s groups like Goat Island, however, is the Wooster Group, the most prominent American experimental company of the late twentieth century, whose rehearsal and production practice strongly suggests this same pattern. In her introduction to the book on the leading British performance group Forced Entertainment, compiled by its director and writer Tim Etchells,[45] Peggy Phelan suggests such an influence, but notes that while The Wooster Group "has been intent on deconstructing" dramatic classics, more recently formed companies, like Forced Entertainment, "have been interested in creating new texts and movement performances that obscure the distinction between fact and fiction, truth and dream."[46] Etchells describes the creative process for Forced Entertainment in terms that could apply to a number of Europe and America's leading young performance ensembles organized near the end of the twentieth century. Each member brings raw material to the process—"a few scraps or fragments of text, an idea or two for action, a costume, an idea about space, a sketched-out piece of music—everything unfinished, distinctly incomplete"—from which the completed pattern of text and movement gradually evolves.[47]

Politics and performance

One of the trends that encouraged a greater use of language in both solo and group performance from the mid-1980s onward, especially in the United States, was that political and social concerns became one of the main lines of performance activity, especially in work involving individuals or groups with little or no voice or active role in the current system. The importance of political and social content, closely tied to the importance of language in more recent performance art, has not only altered the landscape of current performance but has also changed views of its historical development. Performance historians now recognize that during the mid- to late 1960s many types of political demonstrations included consciously performative elements but were not associated with performance art when it developed because of its original emphasis upon non-discursive activity. Richard Schechner called attention to the performance art qualities of the political actions carried out by such groups and individuals as the Provos, Abbie Hoffman and, later, Jerry Rubin: "dropping dollar bills on the floor of the Stock Exchange; dumping a truck of soot and garbage on the brass of Con Ed; showing up at HUAC meetings dressed as a revolutionary war patriot."[48]

At the same time, more formal companies, such as America's Bread and Puppet Theatre, San Francisco Mime Troop, and Teatro Campesino or England's Cartoon Archetypical Slogan Theatre (CAST), also applied many of the strategies of modern performance to political and social concerns, stressing visual display, reviving folk and popular performance elements from vaudeville, clown acts and puppet shows, and presenting their work out of doors or in unconventional non-theatrical spaces. Indeed Françoise Kourilsky, in her book on Bread and Puppet, has suggested that American experimental theatre of this era could be generally divided into two types, those groups who looked for inspiration to "oriental rituals and primitive ceremonies" like the Living Theatre, the Open Theatre and the Performing Group, and those politically-oriented theatres like the Mime Troop, the Bread and Puppet, or the Campesino, who looked to "early forms of popular Western spectacle, the commedia, marionettes, parades."[49]

Another inspiration for political performance art in the 1970s and 1980s was Situationist International, a group of artists and intellectuals inspired by the writings of Guy Debord in France—especially his 1967 *Society of the Spectacle*. Central to Situationist thought was the performance of politically charged public "aesthetic actions," as in the multimedia explorations of public space and public perception of Dan Graham (Performer/ Audience/Mirror, 1977) or the live action/video political satires of Doug Hall (The Eternal Frame, 1975).

Now that "performance" had entered the cultural vocabulary, such actions as Greenpeace's plugging of chemical effluent pipes or hanging ecological banners on the Statue of Liberty (1984) or on Mount Rushmore (1987) were duly reviewed in the journal *High Performance*.[50] Certainly it is true that the Greenpeace ecological actions, consciously or not, were converging with ongoing performance experimentation much more clearly rooted in the art world. Earth artists like Smithson and Christo had since the 1960s been utilizing environmental themes, as did current performance work such as Joseph Beuys's "7000 Oaks" (1982–7), which gathered support to plant trees throughout Kassel, Germany,[51] or Brazilian artist Bené Fonteles, whose garbage delivery performances in 1984, 1986, and 1987 piled truckloads of litter on a city's main square to "bring back to the people of Cuiabá the garbage and litter they left behind in the forest, creeks and waterfalls during weekend picnics."[52]

Certain ecological "performances" suggested a return to the installations and other object-oriented aspects of early performance art, but, on the whole, performance, both personal and political, has remained particularly associated with the actions of a human body or bodies. How bodily performance has continued to engage questions of identity on the one hand and of social, cultural, and political issues on the other, will be the focus of my final two chapters.

Live art, liveliness, and the media

Live art

The Arts Council of Great Britain established a new division of "live art" in 1994, and Helen Spackman, a London-based performance artist and theorist, has argued that the emergence of this new official terminology in fact marks a major transition in the perception and practice of modern performance art from the "publicly perceived self-indulgence and frequent technical inadequacy of early performance art" to the "visual/performative hybridity" of more recent "installation, site-specific and body art." More generally, she sees this transition as one from the high modernist, essentialist and reductive orientation of early "performance art," which viewed the body as "the privileged site of authentic presence," to the more complex, fragmentary, ambiguous, technologically innovative operations of the "live art" of the 1990s, which she relates to a shift from modernism to postmodernism in the performative consciousness.[53]

The relationship between performance and postmodernism is a complex one, and will be explored in more detail in the following chapter, although certainly a general change in much performance art can be traced from the 1970s through the 1990s toward the more "fragmentary, ambiguous, and technologically oriented work Spackman characterizes as "postmodern." The use of the term "live art" to characterize this later work raises questions of its own, however, because the very quality of liveness has become one of the areas of postmodern destabilization. As Spackman suggests, the essentialist privileging of the body as a source of authenticity or cultural resistance, widespread in the 1960s and 1970s, was widely challenged by later theorists such as Johannes Birringer, who accused such work of a general failure "to disrupt the conditions of its own specularity," thus leaving it subject to the "cultural hegemonic of the spectacle."[54] This challenge to the resistant performing body and the responses to it will be dealt with in more detail in later chapters. A subsequent and quite different challenge to "live art" was posed by Philip Auslander in his 1999 book *Liveness*, which argued that in contemporary mediatized culture the quality of liveness is losing or has already lost whatever primacy it may have held in cultural consciousness, and that so-called live performances are increasingly becoming "second-hand recreations of themselves as refracted through mediazation."[55]

Live art and the media

Auslander's *Liveness* has been controversial. Few would dispute the importance of "mediazation" on contemporary consciousness, but the contemporary consciousness has also, in such diverse matters as sexual politics, dietary fads, and the cloning controversy, taken an almost obsessive interest in the body. In a special program for British Channel 4 in February 1994 called *Bodyism*, Erica Jong argued that an interest in the body permeated the art, thought and culture of late-capitalist, Western society.[56] In fact the arguments of both Auslander and Jong are to some extent reflected in the increasing importance of performance work in the 1990s that in one way or another mixes bodies and technology. Spackman's distinction between earlier "essentialist" performance art which "privileged the body" and the "more complex, technologically innovative" performance art of the 1990s is overly simplistic, since such groups as Fluxus, the Judson Church choreographers, the Situationists, experimental film artists of the 1960s and 1970s— even such leading "body artists" as Burden and Acconci—were deeply involved in complex and technologically innovative work. Nevertheless, the increasing sophistication of available technology, especially digital technology, did mean that the importance and variety of such work steadily increased during the final years of the twentieth century, and multimedia techniques became central to the work of small experimental companies like the Wooster Group or the Builder's Project, to major avant-garde productions like those of Robert Wilson or Robert Lepage, to mainstream theatre and stadium productions like the Broadway musical *Tommy* (1995), featuring multiple video projections around the proscenium and to the common use of video projection in rock concerts, a central example for Auslander of contemporary "mediazation" of live art.

An even closer relationship between the body and technology was being explored during this same period by cyber-oriented artists such as France's Orlan or Australia's Stelarc, who did not simply submit their bodies passively to technology, but actively engaged it, creating an ongoing performative dialogue between corporeality and cybernetics. Orlan and Stelarc were featured, along with other recent body art performers such as Bruce Gilchrist, Franko B. and Ron Athey, at the spring 1996 performance festival at London's Institute of Contemporary Arts, entitled *Totally Wired: Science, Technology, and the Human Form*, which explored ethical, political, and social ramifications of this intersection by means of performance. The work of these recent body artists will be considered in more detail in Chapter 7.

Performance and new technology

These experiments at mixing the body and current technology, although an important and striking part of late twentieth-century performance art, are only a part of a change in the concept and practice of performance during the 1990s that was sufficiently significant and embracing as to be characterized by some theorists as a Kuhnian "paradigm change." This is the position taken, for example, by Johannis Birringer in his book *Media and Performance* and in the opening essay in a special issue of *Theatre Journal* in December 1999 devoted to "Theatre and Technology." "Since the 1960s" Birringer observes:[57]

> movements in happening, body art, Fluxus, conceptual art and pop art, the entire paradigm of high art has shifted, and the blurring of boundaries and of the confluences between art, technology, and popular media have widened the spectrum of "performance art" to a point where actions, events, concerts and installations could include any combination of media or (in)formal means of presentation.

Even more important than this expansion of the concept of performance art, Birringer argues, has been the "new paradigm change" that occurred near the end of the century, "namely the shift from the analog spectrum to the digital era of recording, transmission and global communications (computer, ISDN and Internet networks)." Since the history of performance in the twentieth century was "marked by the advent of new technologies of representation," the digital revolution of the 1990s suggests "a new futurism of virtual performance possibilities."[58]

Looking ahead

Although the specific term "performance art" faded in importance toward the end of the twentieth century, the term performance itself retained its prominence in much cultural theory of the 1990s, and continued to develop in directions often far removed from the rather abstract art world origins of the movement. Part III will trace some of the operations and implications of that development. Chapter 6 will consider the complex inter-relationships between performance and postmodernism, two widely employed terms in modern cultural practice, whose relationships with each other have been the subject of much theoretical discussion. This chapter will conclude with a further exploration of the impact upon both postmodernism and performance of the new technologies of representation. Chapters 7 and 8 return to the material of this book's first two chapters: performance and the social sciences, anthropology and psychology, the study of the individual human psyche and that of the human being as the member of a society. The perspective, however, will now be reversed. While the first two chapters dealt with the development and use of the concept of performance in these two human sciences, the last two will consider how performance has recently been used to explore and illuminate the concerns of these disciplines: "performance and identity" considers the shaping and social action of the individual, the traditional domain of psychology, while "cultural performance" studies performance as an instrument for the actions of social and cultural groups, the traditional domain of anthropology.

Part III

Performance and contemporary theory

Chapter 6

Performance and the postmodern

The contemporary terms "performance" and "postmodernism" are products of the same cultural environment and both have been widely and variously employed to characterize a broad spectrum of activities, especially in the arts. The relationship between them is thus a highly complex one. Critics and reviewers have found "postmodern" a useful tag to apply to much contemporary performance work. Thus Bill Irwin has been tagged a "postmodern choreographer" by the dance critic of the *New York Times*[1] and as a "postmodern clown" by its theatre critic.[2] Performers themselves have claimed the term, sometimes to give their experiments a fashionable contemporary cachet and perhaps rather more often (given the ironic and self-reflexive nature of much contemporary performance) to poke a bit of fun at the whole process of genre names and critical fashion. Thus we find New York performance artist Annie Sprinkle offering a 1991 show with the title "Post-Porn Modernism," while a popular San Francisco performance group styles itself Pomo Afro Homos (Postmodern Africa-American Homosexuals).

Yet there is clearly a much closer relationship between performance and postmodernism than the former's occasional amused appropriation of a currently fashionable critical term as a way of poking fun at such fashion. Nick Kaye, in his thoughtful and stimulating recent study of the relationship of these two terms, suggests that "the condition of 'performance' may be read, in itself, as tending to foster or look towards postmodern contingencies and instabilities," and that performance "may be thought of as a primary postmodern mode."[3] Michel Benamou introduces the major anthology *Performance in Postmodern Culture* (1977), which he co-edited with Charles Caramello, with the similar observation that performance is "the unifying mode of the postmodern."[4]

Theorists of the modern and postmodern

Ihab Hassan

One of the first attempts to articulate a postmodern aesthetic was Ihab Hassan's *The Dismemberment of Orpheus: Towards a Postmodern Literature*, in

1971. In tracing the development of this aesthetic in literature Hassan selects as a key figure Marcel Duchamp, who, as we have seen, also occupies a key position in the development of the aesthetic of modern performance. Even more strikingly, in a 1982 essay on "The Question of Postmodernism," Hassan offers a rather surprising binary table opposing features of modernism and postmodernism (surprising in that such binary organization would seem itself a strategy quite opposed to the postmodern project). The first opposition in this table pits two art movements with strong "performative" orientation—Pataphysics and Dadaism—as representatives of postmodernism, in contrast to romanticism and symbolism, representing modernism. Somewhat further in the list, we find "process/performance/happening" offered as the postmodern opposition to modernism's "art object/finished work." This distinction between the work-in-itself (finished, complete, and unchanging) and the work-in-progress (incomplete, contingent, and fluid) is widely found in systems like Hassan's that seek to oppose modern to postmodern attitudes, and we will later consider the background and some of the implications of such a distinction. When Hassan summarizes postmodernism "as an artistic and philosophical, erotic and social phenomenon," his list of characteristics closely resembles what one might draw up to characterize "performative" activity. According to Hassan, "postmodernism veers towards open, playful, optative, disjunctive, displaced, or indeterminate forms, a discourse of fragments, an ideology of fracture, a will to unmaking, an invocation of silence—veers toward all these and yet implies their very opposition, their antithetical realities."[5]

Thomas Leabheart

Thomas Leabhart, in his book *Modern and Post-Modern Mime*, offers a very similar view of postmodernism. Speaking of Leonard Pitt, a mime "who began as a pure modernist and who discovered his own postmodernism," Leabhart discusses Pitt's "post-modern synthesis of theatrical elements" in the 1985 work *2019 Blake*, a solo piece directed by San Francisco performance artist George Coates with music by composer Paul Dresher. In the program note to this production Dresher spoke of his music as defying:

> a single stylistic definition, drawing as it does from such seemingly disparate sources as non-western (particularly West African, Indonesian, and North Indian) traditions, European classical and renaissance musics, the experimental tradition of the twentieth century, jazz, and rock and roll. From these Dresher is able to create a hybrid music that acknowledges the universal musical ideas and techniques at the core of the various traditions and styles but transcends the exotic surfaces of each.

Approvingly quoting this passage, Leabhart comments: "That is as good a definition as one could hope to find of post-modernism, in its multiplicity, its eclecticism, its non-linearity and its juxtaposition of disparate elements to form a resonant whole."[6]

Clement Greenberg, Michael Fried, and modernism

The historical relationship between performance and postmodernism is, however, much more troubled than the current theoretical coziness between them would suggest. When performance began to be viewed as a particular new kind of art activity around 1970, its theoreticians and practitioners were almost entirely associated with the art world, then still dominated by the theoretical interests of minimalism and high modernism. These interests were much concerned with separating out the arts in order to find and develop the "essence" of each. Two statements of the goals of modernist art, both extremely influential and widely cited, may be taken as central examples of this attitude: Clement Greenberg's "After Abstract Expressionism" (1962) and Michael Fried's "Art and Objecthood" (1967). Greenberg interpreted the history of art as a progressive, empirical search for "the irreducible working essence of art and the separate arts." In this project each separate art rejects the "dispensable, unessential" conventions of its own tradition as well as elements of other arts to seek its own formal essence, which Greenberg saw in pictorial art as "flatness and the delimitation of flatness."[7] Students of theatre history may be reminded of modernist attempts in that field also, such as those of Gordon Craig and Adolphe Appia at the turn of the century and, subsequently, Artaud, to strip away accumulated conventions and the borrowings from other arts to discover the "essence" of theatre. In early performance theory and practice this modernist or minimalist attitude can be clearly seen—in body art works, for example, that consisted only of simple actions, devoid of narrative, mimesis, or aesthetic shaping.

An essay bridging between "After Abstract Expressionism" and "Art and Objecthood" was Greenberg's "Recentness of Sculpture," discussed at length by Fried, which introduced the concept of *presence* to the analysis of modern minimalist art. Presence, Fried noted, involved not the obtrusiveness or often even aggressiveness of the work but:

> the special complicity that that work extorts from the beholder. Something is said to have presence when it demands that the beholder take it into account, that he take it *seriously*—and when the fulfillment of that demand consists simply in being *aware* of it and, so to speak, in acting accordingly.

Such presence, Fried remarks, might in fact be called a kind of *stage* presence, and as such is antithetical to the essential minimalist project, which rejects the situation or the interaction with a viewer to be wholly manifest

Figure 6.1 Trisha Brown and members of her company in *Line Up*, 1977.
Source: Lois Greenfield.

within itself.[8] Similarly, Fried denies any effect of duration in the art experience, presence being available in the perceptual instant and duration of experience being "paradigmatically theatrical." The attention to situation and to the participation of the spectator, introducing in turn irrelevant questions of value, the consciousness of an experience in time, and a rejection of the search of the essence of each art in favor of a blurring of boundaries, all of these Fried characterizes as theatrical tendencies in art, leading to his often-quoted pronouncement: "The success, even the survival, of the arts has come increasingly to depend on their ability to defeat theatre."[9]

The heritage of Antonin Artaud

Given Fried's rejection of both duration and reception it is difficult to imagine how performance of any kind could qualify as a modernist or minimalist expression, but a number of theorists and practitioners involved with performance during the 1970s attempted to create something of this sort. Significantly, like Fried, they all saw performance's separation from and rejection of theatre as central to their vision. An important precursor in this project was Antonin Artaud, who offered a particularly influential example of an attempt to restore the art of performance to its essence, which he felt had been corrupted by speech and words, logic and narrative. His interest in a variety of media—light, sound, color, space, gesture—seems far removed from the essentialism of Fried, but there are also strong points of similarity. Artaud too sought an art complete within itself, in which both the passage of time and the split between observer and observed ceased to exist. Early performance, such as body art, conceived under the influence of minimalist theory, shared certain of Artaud's concerns, and came closer than most subsequent performance to addressing them. Such performance sought what might be characterized as a physical rather than a psychic essentialism. Like Artaud, this performance rejected the "theatrical" trappings of discursive language, narration, and character, but in the name of minimalism and anti-theatre it also rejected Artaud's interest in non-verbal spectacle, seeking the "essence" of performance in the operations of the body in space.

Closely associated with the rejection of theatre in both Artaud and early performance artists and theorists was a rejection of the "pretense" of theatre, of its attempted evocation of another, "absent" reality through mimesis. Happenings and similar experiments were based upon pure "presence;" they were, in Michael Kirby's term, "non-matrixed." The traditional semiotic orientation of theatre gave way in the new experimental work to a phenomenological orientation, specifically characterized as "non-semiotic" by Kirby, who attempted to find structures that would "work against sending a message about something."[10] This idea is strongly felt in Marranca's *Theatre of Images*, which she sees as focused upon "process—the producedness, or seams-showing quality of a work," in an attempt:[11]

> to make the audience more conscious of events in the theatre than they are accustomed to. It is the idea of *being there* in the theatre that is the impulse behind Foreman's emphasis on immediacy in the relationship of the audience to the theatrical event.

The work of Richard Foreman is often cited by phenomenological theorists, and quite appropriately, since Foreman in both his practice and his writing rejected traditional theatre's interest in attempting to infuse the audience with some imaginary idea or emotion. He sought instead to call attention to the audience's moment-by-moment existence in the theatre, to seeing what is there, to seeing themselves seeing, and thus aiming to "ground us in what-it-is-to-be-living."[12]

Thus Fried's rejection of "theatricality," interpreted in the case of performance as a rejection of the narrative, discursive, mimetic quality of traditional theatre, fitted in well with a growing interest in non-narrative, non-discursive, non-mimetic performance, concerned with the immediate

Figure 6.2 Richard Foreman's *Bad Boy Nietzsche*, 2000.
Source: Paula Court.

experience of an event. Indeed, despite a tendency by the early 1980s to characterize performance art as a postmodern phenomenon, its roots and much of its early development were really more distinctly modernist, as Xerxes Mehta pointed out in a review of current performance art in the early 1980s. Far from being a "postmodern" phenomenon, Mehta concluded, this work was "in its insistence on flatness and abstraction, and in its profound indebtedness to every major modern art movement since Cubism, firmly in this century's great tradition of modernist formalism."[13]

Postmodern dance

Sally Banes

The contradictory pulls of modernism and postmodernism on performance have been articulated most clearly in dance theory, where the two terms have gained almost universal currency, even while their precise meanings have been hotly debated. There has also been a kind of evolution in the associations of the term postmodernism that can be seen, for example, in the writings of Sally Banes, the theorist most associated with applying this term to dance. Banes locates the development of "postmodern dance" in the 1960s, centered on the Judson Church in New York, but soon spreading out through galleries, lofts, other churches, and various largely non-proscenium spaces. Among the avant-garde modern dancers who prepared the way for postmodern dance, Banes cites Merce Cunningham, James Waring, and Anna Halprin, all of whom had students who were leaders in the postmodern generation. The Cage/Cunningham multimedia event at Black Mountain College in 1952 and the subsequent development of happenings and of various experiments with blending art forms, utilizing real-world and chance material, unconventional spaces and variable time (including simultaneity), all contributed to the dance experiments.

Despite these innovations, Banes suggests that throughout the 1950s, even in the work of Cunningham, the traditional modern dance aesthetic still ruled, an aesthetic regarding dance in terms of a particular expressive function, carried out in certain patterns composed of particular styles and materials. The break from this expressive tradition that launched postmodern dance Banes locates at the Judson Dance Theatre between 1962 and 1964, growing out of Robert Dunn's classes in choreography at the Cunningham Studio. Dunn specifically challenged the approach of influential teachers of modern dance, such as Louis Horst and Doris Humphrey, who viewed dance as expressing feelings through the natural languages of the bodies and rhythms of life echoed in the essentials of choreographic form.[14] Dunn saw as one of his goals liberating dancers "from Louis and Doris," and the tradition they represented of "appropriate" and even "essential" dance forms and functions. Dunn looked instead to "various sources of contemporary action: dance, music, painting, sculpture, happenings, literature."[15] This eclecticism naturally led to a wide range of experimentation, though one might still argue (as Banes does not) that Judson Dance had not so much broken from modernism as from the traditional idea of what constituted dance. What was really rejected was the expressionist aesthetic that anchored conventionalized movement to a literary idea or musical form.

Reactions to Banes

Other theorists and commentators on the contemporary dance scene have objected to Banes's line of argument, not because she categorizes the Judson work and related manifestations as postmodern—that categorization is now widely accepted in the dance world—but rather because she argues that this "postmodern" work has its closest parallels to "modernist" work in the other arts. "Often it has been precisely in the arena of post-modern dance that issues of modernism in the other arts have arisen," Banes suggests. "Thus in many respects it is post-modern dance that functions as *modernist* art."[16] In opposition to this, Nick Kaye, in his study of postmodern performance, argues that postmodern dance is far too varied and complex a phenomenon to be characterized in this manner, and that in any case a performative art like dance, whether modern or postmodern, could never achieve a really "modernist" form. The "reduction" of dance to a modernist "legitimating essence" of movement is a highly problematic maneuver, and the rejection of duration and situation by modernist theorists like Fried would exclude from the modernist project not only what Fried calls "theatre" but also dance and indeed any performance.[17]

Susan Manning, in the course of an extended debate with Banes carried on in the pages of *The Drama Review* in the late 1980s, argued somewhat similarly that Banes's approach misrepresented both modern and postmodern dance by conflating their aesthetic concerns. If, as Banes states, postmodernism is based on "acknowledgment of the medium's materials, the revealing of dance's essential qualities as an art form, the separation of formal elements, the abstraction of forms, and the elimination of external references as subjects,"[18] then it not only corresponds closely to the modernist project in other arts (as Banes herself points out) but also, Manning argues, in fact corresponds closely to the project of modern dance itself as it was described by such dance historians as Lincoln Kirstein and John Martin in the 1930s.[19]

Unquestionably many theorists and performers in the dance world agreed, at least in general, with the concept of postmodern dance articulated in *Terpsichore in Sneakers*. As early as 1975 *The Drama Review* offered a special issue on "Post-modern Dance," in the Introduction to which Michael Kirby defined such dance in the same minimalist terms that were then highly fashionable in the art world—and, for that matter, in the world of performance art, in which Kirby also had a very strong interest. Postmodern dance, suggested Kirby, "ceases to think of movement in terms of music," is not involved with "such things as meaning, characterization, mood or atmosphere," and uses lighting and costume "only in formal and functional ways."[20] Six representatives of this new orientation described their recent work for this special issue: Joan Jonas, Laurie Dean, Trisha Brown, Lucina Childs, Simone Forti, Steven Paxton, and David Gordon. Clearly this approach informs, for example, a 1981 review of Bill Irwin by Anne Kisselgoff, the dance critic of the *New York Times*, who comments that "Like a good post-modern choreographer, Mr. Irwin uses repetition, changes in speed and dynamics, and breaks in pattern to achieve his effect. Pure movement is all."[21] The power of the essentialist paradigm is clear when one considers how astonishingly inappropriate it is to suggest that "pure movement is all" in this or indeed in any of Irwin's productions, which are full of ironic content. More to the immediate point, however, is the question of what makes this "good postmodern" work, when such a concept as "pure movement" is so obviously modernist? Clearly the assumptions here are in line with Banes's argument in *Terpsichore in Sneakers* that postmodernism in dance would be called modernism anywhere else. When this criticism was written, at the beginning of the 1980s, there seems to have developed a general consensus that "postmodern dance," though it referred to a distinct body of experimentation, was something of a misnomer since this work was really more modernist—essentially the same point that Mehta made at this same time about so-called "postmodern" performance art.

More recently, however, responding to the increasing complexity of dance experimentation and perhaps also to such criticisms as those of Manning and Kaye, Banes has put forward a more complex model of post-modern dance. In the concluding essay of a *The Drama Review* forum in 1992 asking "What Has Become of Postmodern Dance?" Banes suggested that the modernist "analytic postmodern dance" that was the focus of her 1987 book was really framed by periods of quite different experimentation. Early 1960s experimental dance, she suggests, was created in a spirit of "democratic pluralism," ranging from minimalism to "a welter of multimedia," with minimalism becoming dominant later as this generation "increasingly allied itself with the art world."[22] By the late 1980s and 1990s, however, a second generation of postmodern choreographers as well as international and media influences once again encouraged stylistic diversity and work which, Banes argued, had much closer affinities to postmodernism as it had been defined in other artistic fields.

Strategies of postmodernism

Charles Jencks and Linda Hutcheon

Not surprisingly, when Banes looked for models of usage in other fields her attention turned to architecture, since even though the term "postmodern" was occasionally to be encountered in art criticism as early as the 1930s it did not gain much currency or much specificity until it was popularized by Charles Jencks, who began in 1975 to apply it to the field of architecture. Central to Jencks's formulation was the concept of "double coding." Post-modern architecture, according to Jencks, calculatedly appeals to a double audience of experts and the general public by combining elements of mod-ernism and of classicism in a playful, decorative, and self-conscious blend.

Probably the most fully developed theoretical statement of this approach to postmodernism is Linda Hutcheon's *A Poetics of Postmodernism* (1988), devoted primarily to literature, although suggesting that analogous work can be found in painting, sculpture, film, video, dance, television, and music (she does not, unhappily, mention either theatre or performance art). Hutcheon traces a phenomenon similar to Jencks's double-coding in recent "paradoxical" fiction, which ironically and self-consciously "uses and abuses, installs and then subverts, the very concepts it challenges."[23] Umberto Eco suggested a similar double coding in postmodern literature, which mixed contemporary experiment with an ironic and self-conscious utilization of traditional forms, allowing (as Eco's considerable popular success with *The Name of the Rose* demonstrated) an appeal to both popular and specialized audiences. John Barth also emphasized the potential appeal of postmodernism both "to a more general public and to devotees of high art" and stressed the "performative" quality of postmodern work, work "that is more and more about itself and its processes, less and less about objective reality and life in the world."[24] This approach to postmodernism focused upon the tendency of the modernist project in all of the arts to become increasingly an art for artists and critics, highly abstract and technical, and saw postmodernism, at least in part, as a reaction, restoring art to a broader public without sacrificing its aesthetic richness or complexity.

The "second generation" of postmodern choreographers, Banes now argued, was producing works that could be considered part of the "canon of postmodernism" as defined by Jencks. Such work had clear parallels to postmodern architecture through its "references to classicism and to other dance cultures, its plenitude of theatrical means, and its increased accessibility." In short, Banes now suggests that postmodern dance "began as a *postmodernist* movement, underwent a *modernist* interlude, and has now embarked on a second *postmodernist* project."[25] Thus at least for this new generation (and for much recent work of the older generation) the concepts of postmodernism in dance, as articulated by Banes, and those in architecture, as articulated by Jencks, seem to be converging. This convergence had already been argued as early as 1983 by Roger Copeland, whose essay "Postmodern Dance/Postmodern Architecture/Postmodernism" suggested that much current work in dance, and in particular that of Twyla Tharp and Laura Dean, had the same "essential characteristics" as postmodern architecture, these being "a retreat from the doctrines of purity and unity, a learned and eclectic historicism, and perhaps a new determination to heal the century-old rift between the modernist avant-garde and the middle class mainstream."[26]

Double-coding and parody

The general popularity of postmodernism as a critical term has guaranteed its wide appearance in recent writings in the fields of theatre and of performance art but, for good or ill, neither of those fields has produced a specific theorist like Jencks in architecture or Banes in dance, who has provided a kind of focal point, however disputed, for usage of the term. Thus postmodernism has never really been established as defining a particular approach or even a group of artists within the theatre (as, for example, such earlier art terms as naturalism or expressionism did). Certain works may be characterized by one writer or another as postmodern,[27] but the term is most frequently encountered as describing certain tendencies or strategies that recall or seem to relate to postmodern work as it has been described and analyzed in other fields, particularly in architecture, dance, and literary studies.

Thus the concept of double-coding, associated by both Banes and Jencks with postmodern expression, has clearly influenced certain critical appraisals of both performance art and recent experimental theatre. It is most likely by analogy with Jencks's model, and not at all because of their use of "pure movement," that the term postmodernist has been so often applied to Bill Irwin and to other representatives of the so-called new vaudevillians. Similarly, one could argue that the simultaneous installation and subversion of already familiar codes and material that Hutcheon characterizes as a postmodern practice has become virtually a trademark of the Wooster Group, with its reworkings of material from Eliot, O'Neill, Wilder, Miller, Flaubert, Chekhov, and others.

Parody, pastiche, and ironic citation are certainly involved in the work of these and many other performers who have been characterized as postmodern, but the operations of double-coding surely provide only a partial perspective. It is clear that even performers like the Wooster Group, who are much involved with cultural citation, cannot be primarily characterized as experimenting with double-coding and, even more seriously, many so-called postmodern performers cannot be said to be involved with double-coding at all.

Hal Foster and "neoconservative" postmodernism

The inadequacy of an attempt to associate postmodernism narrowly or exclusively with Jencks's approach is specifically challenged by the art theorist Hal Foster in his 1984 essay "(Post) Modern Polemics," which suggested that in current American cultural politics there were "at least two positions on postmodernism;" one that he considered "aligned with neoconservative politics," the other "related to poststructuralist theory."[28] Although Foster does not mention Jencks by name (at least not in this particular essay), it is clearly his approach to postmodernism that Foster characterizes as "neoconservative," a program designed "to recoup the ruptures of modernism and restore continuity with historical forms."[29] Thus, at least rhetorically, neoconservative postmodernism seeks to move beyond the abstract sterility of modernism by balancing against this abstraction a return to representation, to the images and meanings of earlier periods. Poststructuralist postmodernism, on the other hand, is based on a critique of representation: "it questions the truth content of visual representation, whether realist, symbolic or abstract, and explores the regimes of meaning and order that these different codes support."[30] Having made this distinction, however, Foster proceeds to problematize it, suggesting that the neoconservative's apparent return to history and to style is in fact a celebration of pastiche, which erodes both style and history in a "hysterical, historical representation in which history is fragmented and the subject dispersed in its own representations."[31] In short, the two positions with which Foster began collapse epistemologically into one, in which the subject is decentered, representation is denied, and the sense of history and of the referent rejected.

In this formulation Foster seems clearly influenced by cultural critic Fredric Jameson, who he approvingly quotes in defining the "modernist paradigm" as involving a "valorization of myth and symbol, temporality, organic form and the concrete universal, the identity of the subject and the continuity of linguistic expression" and in opposition to the postmodernist paradigm, which stresses "discontinuity, allegory, the mechanical, the gap between the signifier and signified, the lapse in meaning, the syncope in the experience of the subject."[32] The alleged playful pluralism of postmodern art Jameson condemned as being often little more than a fondness for pastiche and a "flat" multiplication of style, in contrast to the "deep" expression of modernism. In postmodern expression, the traditional unified work of art expressing a unified personality gives way to a "schizophrenic" art, reflecting a shattered and fragmented culture. Neither Foster nor Jameson are ultimately concerned with a mere description of the phenomenon of postmodernism, however. Both are deeply interested in whether and where a strategy for political expression can be found within this new mode of thinking. Neither Jencks's double-coded "pastiche" postmodernism, which Foster specifically characterizes as allied to neoconservatism, nor a poststructuralist dispersal of the subject, meaning, and discursive language would seem to provide any grounding for an engaged, critical art. This problem has been a central one in postmodernism, and we will return to it in the final chapter of this study.

Postmodernism, poststructuralism, and theatricality

Postmodernism and poststructuralism

We have traced, through Jencks's concept of double-coding and related theoretical expressions, something of the background of what Foster characterizes as "neoconservative" postmodernism. Let us now turn to his second current, which has recently become the more important one in writings on theatre and performance. This is postmodern expression as it is related to poststructuralism. The phenomenological approach to performance, with its emphasis (despite Fried's warnings) upon presence, became much more problematic with the arrival of poststructuralist theory, since this brought into question both the sense of plenitude and the freedom from external values and assumptions claimed by the phenomenological approach. The challenge posed to the aesthetics of presence by poststructuralism challenged also performance's modernist and essentialist claim of distinction from the other arts in general and theatre in particular—a claim based upon the presence of the performing body. Yet as this modernist view of performance was fading it was gradually replaced by a postmodernist view of performance, one which did not give up the vocabulary of presence and absence, or of theatre and performance, but which treated these terms and their relationships in a radically different way.

Henry Sayre has suggested that performance, under the influence of poststructuralism, has moved from an "immanentist aesthetics of presence," which seeks to transcend history and escape temporality, to an "aesthetics of absence," which accepts contingency and the impingement of the quotidian upon art.[33] According to Sayre, the modern vocabulary of absence derives primarily from the writings of one of the central figures of poststructuralism, Jacques Derrida, who in an important sense "is to the literary establishment what performance and conceptual art are to the museum: he exposes the weaknesses of the System, points out its strategic ellipses, and undermines its authority—to borrow his word, he *deconstructs* it."[34] To simply replace an aesthetics of presence with one of absence, however, would merely reverse the traditional structure, not reject it, and Derrida constantly warns against the temptation of merely reinscribing a binary system by reversing its terms. Derrida's project is rather to suggest a constant field of interplay between these terms, of presence impregnated with absence, a field perpetually in process, always in-between as it is in-between absence and presence. Such art "rejects form, which is immobility, and opts, instead, for discontinuity and slippage."[35]

Much of Derrida's writing addresses the concerns mentioned by Sayre, but two 1968 essays are of central importance to the related concerns of theatre, performance, presence and absence. "The Theater of Cruelty and the Closure of Representation" and "La Parole Soufflée" both explore questions raised by Antonin Artaud's modernist Theatre of Cruelty project. Derrida rejects the possibility of Artaud's visionary theatre in an argument that could be extended to reject not only Fried's attempt to purge art of the "theatrical," but also much of the phenomenological privileging of presence in happenings and early performance art and theory. All through this tradition runs the themes of language, discursive thought, and indeed traditional symbolic systems in general as structures of repetition deriving their power and authority ultimately from some originary essence or event, but removed from the power of that origin. Modern art, performance, or the Theatre of Cruelty have sought by various strategies to bring about an occurrence uncontaminated by this derivative, secondary quality. Derrida, however, argues that escape from repetition (and thus theatre) is impossible, that consciousness itself is always already involved in repetition.[36] This removal of a center, a fixed locus of original meaning, brings all discourse, all action, and all performance into a continuing play of signification, where signs differ from one another but a final, authenticating meaning of any sign is always deferred (combining differing and deferring, Derrida creates one of his best-known neologisms, speaking of the play of "*différance*").

After Derrida, theorists and performers acquainted with his (or with related) poststructuralist thought could no longer comfortably embrace the goal of pure presence so attractive to modernism. Very much in the spirit of Derrida, Herbert Blau in "Universals of Performance" (1983) specifically rejects the attempt of the modernists to create an experience of unmediated presence by removing "theatre" from "performance." In fact, asserts Blau, theatre, which involves both mediation and repetition, "haunts *all* performance," forcing the recognition that there is something in the nature of *both* theatre and performance that "implies no first time, no origin, but only recurrence and reproduction."[37]

Josette Féral: performance and theatricality

The poststructuralist rejection of the "pure" presence of modernism (and of early performance art) did not, however, inspire a postmodern rejection in toto of either presence or performance, but rather a reinterpretation of both concepts. Two key essays in this reinterpretation appeared together in a special issue of *Modern Drama* in 1982 devoted to the theory of drama and performance. These were Josette Féral's "Performance and Theatricality: The Subject Demystified" and Chantal Pontbriand's "The eye finds no fixed point on which to rest..." Pontbriand devotes much of her essay to the concept of presence, but distinguishes between "classical presence" and "postmodern presence." Both utilize performance, but the former is deeply involved in mediation and repetition. Its goal is to bring forth in present time previously established truths, to restore and reactualize the presence of such material.[38] Pontbriand does not place "modern presence" in a special category, since its assumptions parallel those of "classical presence"—performance is used to actualize in the present hidden and universal truths that in fact lie outside of time and space. Despite the more phenomenological cast of the "modern" attitude, however, it shares with the "classical" this assumption of a primary, authenticating truth elsewhere, and thus it is necessarily involved with representing rather than presenting. While the minimalist work still sought to embody, to codify some sort of meaning, postmodern performance offers an "inchoative breaking-up," a "continual movement, displacement, or repositioning."[39] Nick Kaye has utilized very similar terms, suggesting that the postmodern "might be best conceived of as something that *happens*," and that this happening involves "breaking free of specific forms and figures. The reason that performance is particularly suited to postmodern experience is that it shares with postmodernism a refusal to be placed, vacillating between presence and absence, between displacement and reinstatement."[40] In this vacillation, this refusal to be placed, we can again see operating Derrida's "play of *différance*."

Féral utilized Fried's rejection of theatre as a starting point in her discussion of the differences between theatre and performance, but she took this discussion in a quite different direction, away from the context of modernist and minimalist art theory and much more toward the work of the French postmodernists and poststructuralists, drawing concepts and lines of argument not only from Derrida but also from such poststructuralist psychoanalytic theorists as Jacques Lacan and Julia Kristeva. She is thus much less concerned with such matters as presence and duration (at least as Fried approaches them) than with representation, the Lacanian imaginary, and the construction of the subject. She begins not with the minimalist goal of reducing arts to their "essences" (a goal incompatible in any case with postmodern relativism and dissolving of boundaries) but with the poststructuralist strategy of problematizing structuralist assumptions and seeking the seams and margins where structures are negotiated. Theatricality she sees as devoted to representation, narrativity, closure, and the construction of subjects in physical and psychological space, the realm of codified structures and of what Kristeva calls the symbolic.

Féral directly opposes performance to activity of this kind; it undoes or deconstructs the competencies, codes, and structures of the theatrical. Although it begins with the materials of theatre—codes, bodies seen as subjects, actions and objects involved in meaning and in representation—it breaks down these meanings and representational relationships to allow a free flow of experience and desire. Narrativity is denied, except for ironic quoting with a certain remove, so as to reveal a narrative's inner workings or its margins. There is "nothing to grasp, project, introject, except for flows, networks, and system. Everything appears and disappears like a galaxy of 'transitional objects' representing only the failures of representation." Performance "attempts not to tell (like theatre), but rather to provoke synaesthetic relationships between subjects."[41]

Performance as experience

In such writings, the attention given by critics like Fried to the art object shifts to an attention to the art experience, a shift implied in the very concept of performance but, like the concept of presence, approached in a quite different way by poststructuralist and postmodernist theorists. Jean-François Lyotard's highly influential *The Postmodern Condition* (1984) was purportedly concerned with contemporary science and the problem of knowledge but, as Fredric Jameson observed in his Foreword to the English edition, Lyotard's speculations also had profound implications "in the directions of aesthetics and economics."[42] In aesthetics, Lyotard's focus upon the event and upon "performativity" as a working principle of knowledge both profoundly affected postmodern thought about performance. The postmodern condition, argues Lyotard, arises from a contemporary erosion of belief in those forms which he calls "metanarratives" that formerly provided legitimacy for a wide variety of cultural norms, procedures, and beliefs. The "modern" period he characterizes as dedicated to knowledge that legitimated itself "with reference to a metadiscourse ... making an explicit appeal to some grand narrative, such as the dialectics of the Spirit, the hermeneutics of meaning, the emancipation of the rational or working subject, or the creation of Wealth." "Simplifying to the extreme," Lyotard defined postmodernism "as incredulity toward metanarratives."[43] Having lost the support of the metanarratives that tied scientific discovery to absolute freedom and knowledge, modern science has split into a host of specialties, each following its own procedures or language-game, incapable of harmonization with the rest through any appeal to an overall truth or authority. The language-games that support what we call knowledge are composed, says Lyotard, of two aspects, *discourse* and *figure* (roughly analogous to the *parole* and *langue* of classical linguistics). *Discourse* is the general process and structure through which a narrative gives meaning, while *figure* is the specific event of narration. The modern emphasizes *discourse* as controlling and limiting the contingency of *figure*, subjecting it to some assumed universality. The postmodern asserts the power of *figure* to claim its own disruptive space, no more and no less "universal" than others. Says Lyotard: "no single instance of narrative can exert a claim to dominate narratives by standing beyond it."[44] This orientation, like that of Bakhtin's performative "utterance" or de Certeau's "tactics," shifts attention from general intellectual or cultural structures to individual events, and from the determination of a general truth or general operating strategy to an interest in "performativity," activity that allows the operation of improvisatory experimentation based on the perceived needs and felt desires of the unique situation. The test of reality within this new orientation is not what can be demonstrated to be generally "true," but more simply what can be demonstrated. Through Lyotard "performativity" and the privileging of the event becomes tied to "postmodernism" and, like postmodernism, begins to be applied to a broad range of contemporary cultural phenomena. An excellent summary of these relationships is provided by David George in his 1989 "On Ambiguity: Towards a post-Modern Performance Theory." George argues that the postmodern emphasis on such terms as play, game, contradiction, process and performance suggests that:

> we may be entering an age in which there *are only* media (semiosis, assumptions, paradigms, models) and no ontology, only experiences (and no Self except the one like and actor's career made up of the parts we enact and rewrite), a world in which difference is primordial (no Ur-whole), and time endless.

In such an age, George concludes, "performance is the ideal medium and model."[45]

The role of the audience

Among the effects of this new orientation is a shift outward from the early performance focus upon the performing body to the more general performance situation, including of course the audience, the audience that Fried attempted to exclude precisely because it introduced into the art experience a sense of contingency, time, and situation. When theorists speak of the performative quality of art as being its most postmodern aspect, they are frequently concerned precisely with the contingency the work must undergo when it becomes involved in the process of reception. Joel Weinsheimer, commenting upon the work of reception theorist Hans Georg Gadamer, stresses the importance and the implications of performance in undermining the idea of an essential play text:[46]

> Performance is not something ancillary, accidental, or superfluous that can be distinguished from the play proper. The play proper exists first and only when it is played. Performance brings the play into existence, and the playing of the play is the play itself.... It comes to be in representation and in all the contingency and particularity of the occasions of its appearance.

For Gadamer, however, theatre was a particularly clear but by no means unique example of this phenomenon. All arts (not only the so-called performing arts) "perform" in this way, existing only in the moments of their reception in different contexts, and thus change as they move through time and space. Only by denying the dynamics of reception and the performativity of all art can Fried and the minimalists seek to establish unchanging "essential" works. Even the earliest experiments with performance art moved in this direction, and by the end of its first decade the change in orientation was generally accepted and acknowledged. The analysis and theory of reception subsequently played an important role as attention shifted from the work of art to the art event. This change is clearly reflected in the responses of a group of performance artists surveyed at the beginning of 1980 by *Artforum*, which asked: "What shifts in emphasis, esthetic or otherwise, have impermanence and specificity of project and performance art brought about?" Vito Acconci observed that by choosing to use the gallery "as the place where the 'art' actually occurred" he shifted attention from "art-doing" to "art-experiencing." This involved, as most of the artists noted, a new attitude toward the audience and to their active collaboration. As Eve Sonneman observed, the audience was given "a multiplicity of choices" and encouraged "to build its own syntax of esthetic pleasure or intellectual work."[47]

The building of this syntax, however, necessarily remains a provisional, partial, and ongoing process, the event, as Féral and Pontbriand argued, a continuing flow of energies and negotiations. Postmodernism, notes Barbara Freedman in her psychoanalytic study of Shakespearian comedy, utilizes the metaphor of theatre for the same reason that modern psychoanalysis has used it (and for the same reason that Fried rejected it): because it denies "the possibility of an objective observer, a static object, or a stable process of viewing." Both postmodernism and psychoanalysis "employ theatrical devices to subvert the observer's stable position, and so result in a continuous play of partial viewpoints—none of them stable, secure, or complete."[48]

Jon Erickson has pointed out how a sensitivity to the audience's role problematizes many traditional assumptions of how political theatre works. Too often theorists of such theatre "assume that the audience is simply a projection of themselves, and that, since they desire a certain theatrical strategy to work (usually to illustrate an already assumed theory), it does indeed work for everyone." In fact, suggests Erickson, for audiences who do not share the agenda of a particular theorist or performer, a work of presumed subversion or resistance may not be experienced in that way at all. "In fact, the more sophisticated these strategies become in their use of irony, for instance, the more likely the opposite meaning will be assumed and reinforced, not undermined."[49] We will return to this concern in our discussion of feminist performance and masquerade.

Postmodern performance and politics

The emphasis upon the unique event, the power of the observer, and the test of performativity at the expense of general truth all might seem to remove postmodern performance from a meaningful engagement with any political, social, or cultural concerns. With no metanarratives, no authenticating knowledge and thus no apparent base for action or even meaningful social observation, does postmodernism provide for performance only a play of energies and relative positionings? Certainly this is a charge that some politically-oriented theorists have made against it. From the late 1980s onward, however, a number of theorists have specifically addressed the question of locating a serious critical function in at least certain aspects of postmodern performance.

Randy Martin's *Performance as Political Act* (1990) argues that the performing body is by its nature involved in resistance to what he calls the "symbolic," the attempt of authority in art or in politics to enforce a unified and monolithic structure opposed to the "overflowing" quality of the moving, acting, and desiring body. On both the personal and public levels the symbolic attempts to limit the meanings of action and the body, to channel the flows of desire, but such limitation is inevitably in conflict with the symbolic-defying carnivalesque potential of the performing body. The tension, emotionality, flows of desire, and kinetic circulation of performance can, says Martin, "instigate a tension in the social body" that disrupts the smooth structure of authority, and individual performances create "interventions, ruptures in the conditions of reproduction of dominance." In performance, subject and object are realigned to replace the "solitary authority" of the symbolic with the "polyphonous circulation of human feeling."[50]

Philip Auslander, in a series of essays and in his 1994 book *Presence and Resistance*, has drawn together the writings of a range of postmodern theorists with an analysis of such contemporary artists as Laurie Anderson, the Wooster Group, and contemporary stand-up comedy to seek a potential for political work. He notes in both Jameson and Foster a suggestion that it might be possible within the terms of postmodernism to develop resistant and critical operations; indeed Foster styles his more liberal postmodernism that of "resistance." However, Auslander continues, postmodernist art's resistance is not to any specific political practices (the type of resistance represented by much of the political performance of the 1960s), but rather resistance to representation in general, a more abstract and difficult strategy. In this regard, he quotes Lyotard:[51]

To hang the meaning of the work of art upon its subsequent political effect is once again not to take it seriously, to take it for an instrument, useful for something else, to take it as a *representation* of something to come; this is to remain within the order of representation, within a theological or teleological perspective. This is to place the work of art, even when one is dealing with non- or anti-representational works, within a (social, political) space of representation. This leaves politics as representation uncriticized.

The final sentence points the way toward a politically engaged postmodern performance. Instead of providing resistant political "messages" or representations, as did the political performances of the 1960s, postmodern performance provides resistance precisely not by offering "messages," positive or negative, that fit comfortably into popular representations of political thought, but by challenging the processes of representation itself, even though it must carry out this project by means of representation. It is of necessity, says Auslander, "an elusive and fragile discourse that is always forced to walk a tightrope between complicity and critique."[52]

Similarly, Alan Read has suggested that theatre is not ultimately committed to representation, "the reflection of an 'existing' proposition as though it were fact," but rather to the presentation of "exemplary and radical" alternatives and possibilities. Postmodernism has called attention to this ethically engaged, performative side of theatre because of a common interest in "the destabilisation of norms, the dissolution of certainties." Read aligns the operations of performance with those of ethics, always involved not only with normative conduct, but with the negation and defiance of norms. De Certeau's description of ethics, he suggests, applies also to the possible worlds of theatre and performance: "Ethics is articulated through effective operations and it defines a distance between what is and what ought to be. This distance designates a space where we have something to do."[53]

After postmodernism

In the course of the next two chapters we will examine a range of performances and performance practices in the age of postmodernism; first those involved with individual identity and then those involved with more general cultural practice. The majority of these might be classified as political, challenging various gender, ethnic, and other cultural assumptions and practices of the surrounding society. Together they form a considerable body of evidence for the proposition that, at least in the domain of performance art, the postmodern consciousness has not been guilty of the charge often made against it: that it is a largely political conservative theoretical system, uninterested in and not engaged in specific social problems. Nevertheless, as the twentieth century drew toward its close many prominent cultural theorists complained that while postmodernism had indeed prepared the way for a new more politically enlightened and efficacious cultural practice, it had not in fact realized its potential. Barbara Adam and Stuart Allen effectively summarized this concern in the introduction to their 1995 collection *Theorizing Culture*, which began with the question "Are we currently witnessing the 'twilight' of postmodern cultural theory?" to which the editors (and their contributors) responded with a "cautiously hopeful 'yes.'"[54]

The reason that this "yes" is hopeful is that these social theorists feel that the "radical potential" of postmodernism's attack on "the imperialism of unifying conceptual schemes embodied in 'master' narratives," and the consequent foregrounding of "the fluid ambiguities and uncertainties of tentative, "local" stories and accounts" resulted for the most part only in celebrations of pluralism and textual play. The "rich diversity of cultural forms, practices, and identities," however, was celebrated:[55]

> at the expense of a critical analysis of their implication in the daily renewal of the pernicious logics or class, sexism, racism, homophobia, ageism and nationalism, amongst others, that are all too indicative of "postmodern" societies.

With this concern in mind, the editors of and contributors to this volume have sought to move beyond the oppositional logic that still haunts the modernism/postmodernism (and foundationalism/relativism) discourse, and to seek a politically aware and responsible cultural theorizing "after postmodernism." This involves a more complex and nuanced view of such matters as relations of power, whose regulations of bodies, institutions and communities, almost invariably regarded negatively in postmodern thought, are seen as both repressive and productive, and the replacement of the "view from no-where" so typical of postmodern cultural theorizing with a view from "now-here," which is "inescapably local, partial and fragmentary, and yet contextual, interconnected and globalizing."[56] The new globalized culture, Adam argues in her own contribution to this volume, requires a more extended and open theoretical strategy than the binary opposition at the heart of postmodernism:[57]

> Instead of the "implicit binary code inherent in the prefix "post," we need code combinations, code syntheses and neither–nor approaches, we need to embrace the future—contingent, ambiguous, uncertain, multiple—and use temporally open concepts that do not re-embed us in the conceptual mode of "either-or" choices.[57]

The shift in cultural theorizing "after postmodernism" that forms the focus of Adam and Allen's important collection we will also see reflected in much cultural performance of this same period, which will be addressed in Chapter 8.

Chapter 7

Performance and identity

The previous chapters have sought to demonstrate how modern concepts of performance and performance art developed, first in association with the modernist and minimalist movements in the arts and then in relationship to postmodernism. Looking back on the development of performance from the early years of the new century, one of the most striking features of modern performance activity and performance theory has been the steadily growing interest in performance's social or political function, this despite the tendency in both modernism and postmodernism to de-emphasize or even to reject such specific social or political activity. An earlier chapter, on modern performance art, provided a brief overview of this recent development, particularly marked beginning in the late 1980s. One aspect of socially engaged performance was so central to performance theory and practice in the late 1980s and early 1990s that for many it became emblematic for modern performance art in general. This was performance particularly associated with the construction or exploration of personal identity, and such work will be the focus of this chapter.

Early feminist performance

The most elaborately developed area of identity performance, both in theory and in practice, has involved performance by women, although during the later years of the twentieth century many of the concerns explored by women performers and theorists of performance during the 1970s and 1980s have been further developed in relation to performance concerned with gay men and with members of various ethnic minorities.

The rapid development of feminist thought and activity in the 1970s and 1980s brought into being a great variety of different approaches to both feminist performance and feminist theory (and eventually, in the late 1980s, to the interplay of theory and performance). Already by the middle of the 1980s a variety of "feminisms" had developed, but most theorists, while utilizing slightly different terms and characteristics, tended to catagorize them under three general groupings. Jill Dolan, one of the first theorists of feminist performance, adapted in her *The Feminist Spectator as Critic* (1988) the categories from Alison Jaggar's *Feminist Politics and Human Nature* (1983)—

liberal, cultural (or radical), and materialist feminism.[1] These divisions can be roughly compared with those in Michelene Wandor's studies of British feminist performance, *Carry On, Understudies* (1986)—bourgeois feminism, radical feminism, and socialist feminism.[2]

Liberal and cultural feminism

Liberal feminism had close ties to various types of political action performance in the 1960s—performances that tended to call attention to unfairness and sexual inequality in various areas of contemporary society, and sought to foster equal consideration, rights, and protection regardless of sex. Cultural or radical feminists, concerned that the so-called "universality" of liberal feminism too readily accepted the male-created standards for such "universality," sought instead to define and support the idea of a woman's culture, separate and different from the culture of men. Linda Walsh Jenkins, writing in 1984 in the recently founded journal *Women and Performance*, for example, called for an "authentically female" performance "replete with female signs" and based on a "biogrammar" derived from "experiences the body has known on the basis of gender."[3] Similarly, Rosemary K. Curb called for a "theatrical language capable of communicating female perceptions which have been erased by the fathers and thus appear non-existent to the dominant culture."[4]

Materialist feminism

Although materialist feminism shares common concerns with both liberal and cultural feminism, it attempts to avoid the tendency of liberal feminism to "absorb women into the male universal" as well as that of cultural feminism to "overturn the balance of power in favor of female supremacy."[5] Instead of liberal universalism or cultural essentialism, materialist feminism views gender as culturally constructed within a set of power relationships. In the words of Sue-Ellen Case, one of the leading theorists of feminist performance, the materialist position "underscores the role of class and history in creating the oppression of women" rather than assuming "that the experiences of women are induced by gender oppression from men or that liberation can be brought about by virtue of women's unique gender strengths."[6]

These various types of feminist theory, each of which could be closely related to particular feminist performance, provided much of the impetus for innovative performance work—especially in America during the 1980s. By the end of that decade, however, many leading performance theorists felt that a kind of critical impasse had been reached; what Case characterized as a "crucial stall" resulting from the difficulty of negotiating a workable relationship between the materialist and essentialist positions, particularly in the face of an ongoing and arguably increasing conservatism and reinforcement of traditional positions in society as a whole. While distrusting the exclusionary assumptions of the essentialists, the materialists envied these assumptions as providing a grounding for effective political resistance to the power of a dominant culture. A major political and theoretical project of feminist theory and performance in more recent years has been the seeking of strategies to move forward from this "stall"—a project given greater urgency by the concurrent development of modern gay and ethnic performances, which, in attempting to give voice and agency to other oppressed groups, has encountered similar practical and theoretical difficulties.

Women's performance in the 1960s

As we have seen, women artists were from the beginning of the 1960s centrally involved with modern performance. On the east coast were Yvonne Rainer, Simone Forti, Carolee Schneemann, performers associated with Judson Dance (such as Deborah Hay, Elaine Summers, Trisha Brown, and Lucinda Childs), and others associated with Fluxus (such as Alison Knowles, Yoko Ono and Charlotte Moorman). On the west coast, Anna Halprin in dance and Pauline Oliveros in music were major performance pioneers, soon followed by Barbara Smith, Bonnie Sherk, and others. Very little of this performance work, however, directly raised social or gender issues. Certain artists, among them Yvonne Rainer, Carolee Schneemann and Yoko Ono, produced pieces that clearly moved in this direction, but against considerable resistance. In a 1972 interview Yvonne Rainer recalled that she was criticized by her peers at the Judson in the early 1960s for exploring the idea of "female projections:"[7]

> I imitated women in the subway. I had screaming fits. I was sexy. I was always being someone else on stage.... What I was doing was taking things from life and transposing them in a dramatic form.

In the minimalist-oriented atmosphere of the Judson Dance, this interest in the female persona seemed both too personal and too close to the theatrical to gain much support.

Early interest in gender matters aroused much the same opposition in the world of performance art. Women artists, suggests Lucy Lippard, found little appeal in the main line of body art through the late 1960s, "when Bruce Naumann was 'Thighing,' Vito Acconci was masturbating, Dennis Oppenheim was sunbathing and burning, and Barry Le Va was slamming into walls."[8] Yoko Ono perhaps came closest to such work in pieces like her *Wall Piece for Orchestra* (1962), in which she knelt on stage and pounded her head against the floor, but this and the subsequent *Cut Piece* (1964), in which she sat passively while audience members cut away her clothing, looked at personal violation and violence in a very different and distinctly more feminist way than did the male body artists. Indeed these pieces from the early 1960s could be seen as preparing the way for Ono's cinematic study of victimization, *Rape*, in 1969.

Carolee Schneemann describes herself and Yoko Ono as working essentially alone against a predominantly male idea of performance in the early 1960s:

> In 1963, to use my body as an extension of my painting-constructions was to challenge and threaten the psychic territorial power lines by which women were admitted to the Art Stud Club, so long as they behaved *enough* like the men, did work clearly in the traditions and pathways hacked out by the men. (The only artist I know of making body art before this time was Yoko Ono).[9]

The pioneers of women's performance

In the early 1970s, however, the rise of the women's movement provided a much more favorable climate for performance work created by women and concerned with their private and public experience as women. Feminist art programs in Southern California schools were the leaders in such work, and during the 1970s a major part of performance work in California was related to feminist concerns. "I believe absolutely that the feminist movement in Southern California has affected the rest of the Southern California art world," said Eleanor Antin in a 1978 interview. "I really think that women practically invented performance in Southern California."[10]

Certainly there was a close tie between this work and the development of modern performance art in general. Jacki Apple has argued that "Unlike New York, with its geographically concentrated art community in downtown Manhattan, southern California's sprawling network of universities and art schools was the breeding ground for the performance art activities of the 1970s."[11]

A pioneer in such activity was Judy Chicago, who began such a program at Fresno State in 1970. Then she and several of her students, including Faith Wilding and Suzanne Lacy, moved to Cal Arts to set up a similar program there in 1971, where Chicago, Wilding, and Lacy all made important contributions as practitioners and theorists of women's performance. Performance was seen as central to both programs. As Chicago explained: "Performance can be fueled by rage in a way painting and sculpture can't. The women at Fresno did performances with almost no skills, but they were powerful performances because they came out of authentic feelings."[12] Women were also attracted to performance because it allowed them personal control. Unlike traditional actors, they created their own projects— serving as writer, producer, director, designer, cast, and often carpenter and costumier as well.[13]

In early feminist performance personal and psychological statements were often wedded to specific and repeated physical actions, as in Faith Wilding's well-known *Waiting* (1971), in which Wilding rocked back and forth monotonously, reciting a litany of the waiting women experience from birth to death. At "Womanhouse," a large decaying house transformed by the Cal Arts Feminist Art Program in 1972 into a center for feminist environments and performance, Sandra Orgel and Chris Rush repeatedly and obsessively carried out such conventional female activities as ironing and scrubbing—activities which, according to performance artist Martha Rosler, were designed to demonstrate "the preoccupations imposed on women" and to externalize "the highly negative inner response they provoke."[14]

Other performances sought not so much to display the burdens of imposed and unfulfilling activities imposed on women but to give new attention to their activities as women, fulfilling or unfulfilling. Linda Montano's *Home Endurance* (1973) "framed" sections of her everyday life. During a week she remained at home, asked friends to visit, and carefully documented all thoughts, food eaten, visits, and phone calls.[15] Most such performance, directly or indirectly, sought an emotional identification with the experience of women spectators. During her *Ordinary Life* (1977), Barbara Smith would turn to question her audience "to see if their experiences might enlighten mine and break the isolation of my experience," using performance to reveal common dilemmas.[16]

Mythic explorations

In her study of women's performance art in the 1970s, *The Amazing Decade*, Moira Roth distinguished, despite a good deal of overlapping, three major orientations in such work—performance related to women's personal experience, to women's collective past, and to exploring the strategies of specific feminist activism. The first two of these clearly relate more closely to the concerns of this chapter, as, under the impetus of the women's movement performance began to be utilized to understand better women's situation in society and in history. Cultural feminism had its greatest impact on performance during the 1970s, as performance artists drew upon a growing body of research into medieval witchcraft, prehistoric and non-Western goddesses and fertility figures, and ancient matriarchal cultures. Donna Henes has been involved since the 1970s in performance concerning American Indian myths, and particularly the Southwest Spiderwoman, whom Henes sees as the American Indian embodiment of the European Great Goddess. Mary Beth Edelson has drawn directly upon European Goddess worship, offering "images of my body as a stand-in for the Goddess," and traveling to a neolithic Goddess Cave in Yugoslavia in 1977 to perform a private ritual there.[17]

Other performers sought to relate mythic material to personal experience, as in Meredith Monk's *Education of the Girlchild* (1972), of which Sally Banes observed: "Its strange tribe of women could be goddesses, heroines, ordinary people or different aspects of one person."[18] Powerful pieces were also created in the late 1970s by performers who placed autobiographical material in a ritualized form that suggested general or universal almost mythic concerns. Two of the best known of these were Linda Montano's

Mitchell's Death (1978), using performance as an exorcism of her personal grief at the loss of her ex-husband and friend Mitchell Payne, and a major piece created the following year by Barbara T. Smith's *The Vigil* (1978) exploring her feelings and observations upon the death of her mother.[19]

Autobiographical performance

Ritualized and myth-related performance has been less common since the 1970s, while that related to autobiography and other personal experience has remained the most common and, for many, the most typical orientation of feminist performance. Moira Roth has given to such performance the title "personal clutter and the persistence of feelings," quoting from a memorable moment in modern performance art. In *Interior Scroll* (1975), a nude Carolee Schneemann extracted a text from her vagina which she read aloud. It recounted how a male "structuralist filmmaker" explained why despite his fondness for Schneemann he could not look at her films, citing their "personal clutter ... persistence of feelings ... hand-touch sensibility ... diaristic indulgence ... [and] primitive techniques."[20] Concerns with self, self-image, and the social self clearly gained little sympathy from the structuralists and modernists whose voices dominated experimental performance as well as experimental film in the early 1970s, but these were concerns central to the emerging women's movement of the same period, and this movement found in performance an important field for its expression. As Eleanor Antin described it, feminist performance "has been more a social, political and psychological thing about what it means to be a woman in this society, a particular woman, an artist ... very real political questions are often considered."[21]

One of the first manifestations of feminist performance, and still an important approach, utilized specifically autobiographical material, almost invariably, as Antin suggests, with a consciousness of the political and social dimensions of such material. In *The Story of My Life* (1973), Linda Montano walked uphill on a treadmill for three hours while reciting her autobiography into an amplification system.[22] Yvonne Rainer wove together autobiographical and fiction material in her *This is the Story of a Woman Who...* (1973), later made into a major feminist film.[23]

Autobiographical performance and formalist theory

It is important to stress the popularity and ubiquity of performance utilizing autobiography and other "personal clutter" from the beginning of modern performance art, since it is not only structuralist filmmakers like Schneemann's friend but also structuralist and modernist theorists and historians of performance who have attempted to write such work out of the historical record. Given the close relationship between early performance and the art of high modernism one can perhaps understand a continuing association between the two in the public mind, but even sophisticated theorists of performance art have sometimes favored a monolithic view of such activity based on formal and modernist principles. Josette Féral, for example, in looking back on the development of modern performance in a 1992 article, argued that although the term performance "endures and is becoming institutionalized," performance as it was practiced in the 1970s was quite different, being occupied with "one and the same function: to contest the aesthetic order of the time, to explore the artist's relation to art." Such formalist concerns, Féral contends, characterized performance until the mid-1980s, and with the fading of such concerns "true" performance art disappeared. It was replaced by another idea of performance, not as an activity involved only with the experience of art, but as a genre that can be turned to any concerns, marking a return to "message and signification." Féral argues that these more semiotic concerns are inimical to the original, aesthetically oriented aims of performance.[24]

Certainly it is true that during the 1980s more and more performance work became involved with social and political concerns (this will be discussed in my final chapter) and it is also true that, not unrelated to this development, language became an increasingly important part of the performance scene. Nevertheless, "message and signification" were an important part of performance art from its very beginnings, and nowhere more strikingly than in feminist performance art, in which both autobiographical and social performance clearly were anything but purely formalist in their orientation.

Persona performance

Seemingly even less compatible with the approach of formalist theorists like Féral, who have sought to separate "performance" from "theatre" by the absence of mimesis or role-playing in the former, is another sort of self-exploratory performance, also well established during the 1970s. This, sometimes called character or persona performance art, did not deal with autobiography or "real-life" experience, but with the exploration through performance of alternative, imaginary, even mythic selves. Martha Wilson's photographic *Posturing: Drag* explored making images as making identity, and she began to work with Jacki Apple, creating a composite fantasy self, Claudia, a self subsequently "played" by others as well. Apple, trained as a fashion designer, has concentrated on changing roles with others and the multiple roles as defined by others' perceptions. Even more detailed and elaborated was the fantasy persona "Roberta Breitmore," played between 1975 and 1978 by Lynn Hershman. Roberta, with her own driver's license, bank account, therapist, and fictional background, lived through many of the problems and personal conflicts of a woman of the mid-1970s before being ceremonially put to rest in a grave in Italy.[25]

One of the best-known persona artists is Eleanor Antin, who has called herself a "post-conceptual artist" concerned "with the nature of human reality, specifically with the transformational nature of the self." Her work on the self in the early 1970s, though related to contemporary male body art, was also distinctly feminist in its orientation and its concerns. In 1972 she offered an exhibit which claimed to "redefine the old terms" of art history and methodology, primarily by using her own body and experience as raw material. Her first video, called *Representational Painting*, showed herself making-up with the camera as a mirror, while a companion work, called *Sculpture*, displayed daily nude photographs of herself taken over a period of a month during which she lost eight pounds, changing her body to present a different "self" to the world.[26]

After the specific transformations of her body through the traditional women's strategies of cosmetics and weight loss, Antin became interested in the more complex question of "defining the limits of myself, meaning moving out to, in to, up to and down to the frontiers of myself. The usual aids to self-definition—sex, age, talent, time, and space—are merely tyrannical limitations upon my freedom of choice."[27] The exotic and imaginative alternative versions of her self that Antin explored included a King, a Ballerina, a Movie Star, and a Nurse, each developed over a number of years through a variety of performances. Each of these "personae" developed a complex fantasy life of its own; the Nurse, for example, has appeared as Florence Nightingale and has played out a complex series of relationships with characters in her own fantasy life, represented by paper dolls. The King has developed his "character" by moving about in make-up and costume among his "subjects" in Solana Beach and asking how things were going in the realm.[28]

It is important to remember, however, that the personae performed by Antin, Apple, or Wilson are not "characters" in the traditional stage sense— roles removed from themselves and "scripted" by others. A 1976 Los Angeles exhibition featuring the work of Antin and seven other "self-transformational" artists was aptly entitled "Autobiographical Fantasies."[29] It is precisely this insistence upon the personal and specific that unites much feminist performance art but also provides it with its major claim to social and political efficacy. Catherine Elwes, herself a performance artist, has stated that "When a woman speaks within the performance tradition, she is understood to be conveying her own perceptions, her own fantasies, and her own analyses." She "combines active authorship and an elusive medium to assert her irrefutable presence (an act of feminism) with an hostile environment (patriarchy)."[30]

Male performance

This political dimension of the relationship between performance art and identity is quite different when we consider male performers. Because the theatre has traditionally served as a podium for the expression of male concerns, the performance of personal perceptions or autobiographical fantasies by a male performance artist such as Spaulding Gray does not by its very nature involve this sociopolitical dimension. Gray can and does take up social and political concerns, but the simple asserting of his "active authorship" and "irrefutable presence" cannot carry with it the challenge to a patriarchal tradition posed by any female performance artist, whether her work speaks directly of political matters or not.

Matters become more complicated when we turn to male homosexual performance and its relationship to the expression or exploration of identity. Male homosexual identity is perhaps even more firmly excluded from the patriarchal system than female identity (a striking recent example is the assertion of Roy Cohn in Tony Kushner's *Angels in America* that even though he has sex with other men he does not have a homosexual *identity*). Erving Goffman's *Stigma* (1963) reviews then-current psychological and sociological work on the situation of the individual who, like the homosexual, is for one reason or another placed outside the realm of "full social acceptance." Goffman discusses the range of "management" alternatives available to those who fall within this realm of "spoiled identities," and two of these alternatives have particular relevance to identity and performance. Those attempting to divert attention from their stigma may "present the signs of their stigmatized failing as the signs of another attribute, one that is less significantly a stigma," or a stigmatized individual "can come to feel that he should be above passing, that if he accepts himself and respects himself he will feel no need to conceal his failing."[31]

The first strategy may be employed by shifting the performance of identity from the stigma itself (homosexuality) to what Esther Newton, in a recent book on female impersonation, calls the "halo effect"—the violation of culturally standarized canons and gender-coded canons of taste, behavior, and speech that normally signal sexual orientation. For men, such violations might include "effeminate" or overly "delicate" speech or behavior, an "aesthetic" orientation, an interest in fanciful or decorative costume, unseemly concern with personal appearance, and so on.[32]

Performance of this kind avoids claiming the stigma of homosexuality, but "manages" it by claiming an identity built upon these secondary signs. The late nineteenth-century dandy provided an important model for such performance, most notably in the figure of Oscar Wilde, who can be said to have used solo performance as a means of self display and self definition as well as a Goffmanesque "management" of the stigma of homosexuality.[33] In current performance, a parallel merging of management and identity formation can be seen in such performance as *An Evening with Quentin Crisp*, consisting of an autobiographical monologue and a question and answer session. Crisp's blatant femininity and high style call up certain echoes of Wilde, and one can easily hear a Wildean echo in Crisp's carefully coded observation: "I am someone who had been forced by life to be self-conscious and has now tried to make that self-consciousness into a way of life."[34]

Camp performance

Closely associated with the male strategies of social management is the concept of camp, a term that Susan Sontag brought into modern cultural discussion with her "Notes on 'Camp'" in 1964. Among the features of camp Sontag noted was its close relationship to nineteenth-century dandyism as well as its view of "Being-as-Playing-a-Role, the farthest extension, in sensibility, of the metaphor of life as theatre," where "Character is understood as a state of continual incandescence—a person being one, very intense thing."[35] In her 1972 book on female impersonators, Esther Newton elaborated on Sontag to suggest that camp was theatrical not only in emphasizing role playing but also in emphasizing performance and style, how something (including the self) looks and how it is *done*.[36]

The relationship between camp and the subversion of traditional gender roles has stimulated much interest among theorists and performers exploring the resistant possibilities of performance, and will therefore be considered in our next chapter, dealing with those concerns. Here, however, our concern is not with subversive performance but with enabling performance, providing a ground for identity construction or expression. For Wilde or Crisp, performance clearly provided a strategy for the social construction of an identity that permitted the integration of a normally troubling amount of "female" characteristics into a "male" persona. More commonly, however, camp performance is associated in the public mind with the actual performance of a "female" persona by a male, in the tradition of "drag."

Cross-dressing

The long and complex history of men playing women and women playing men within conventional theatre lies outside the scope of our concerns here, and is in any case rather less problematic than the traditional cross-dressed performance, since the line between actor and character in the conventional theatre is historically more clearly drawn.[37] Within the tradition of popular performance such as vaudeville, burlesque, circus, and minstrelsy the man dressed as a woman for comic or grotesque effect is a common phenomenon, but more "sympathetic" cross-dressings have also long been a part of this tradition, and there is no question that many cross-dressing performers have created alternate personae which operated for them precisely as does Eleanor Antin's "King" for the exploration and expression of a differently gendered part of their identity.[38] Perhaps the most elaborate and best known contemporary creation of a cross-gendered identity is Barry Humphries' Dame Edna, a beloved cult figure in England, who has filled Drury Lane with her solo performances, hosted a popular TV talk show in prime time, sung in the Royal Albert Hall, opened the annual Harrods Sale and turned on the Regent Street Christmas Lights, appeared in cameo roles in soap operas, and become one of the four Australians represented by waxworks at Madame Tussaud's. The "reality" of Dame Edna has become so overwhelming as to quite eclipse her male originator.[39]

As in much performance involved with identity and with social display, the operations of this sort of expression are always strongly conditioned by the performance circumstances. In his 1990 study of current gay performance, Mark Gevisser suggests that drag performances at downtown New York dance clubs are often less involved with social display than with "staged representation of often misogynistic ideas of who women are."[40] Although Laurence Senelick has traced the appearance of modern drag performance and female impersonation to a newly conspicuous homosexual subculture and to an interest in gender exploration in society at large in the later nineteenth century,[41] within the mass cultural context of traditional burlesque or vaudeville, drag performance often became little more than a gimmick (removing a wig after misleading the audience) or a source for crude caricatures of female types outside society's normal standards (such as the traditional comic "wench" of the minstrel show). Far from using their impersonations to suggest negotiability of gender roles or to express an alternative personality, most of the great female impersonators of the classic vaudeville and burlesque stage made a point of separating their "real selves" from these "roles" by stressing the masculinity of the former. According to vaudeville historian Joe Laurie Jr, Julian Eltinge, the most admired of such impersonators, emphasized his skill as a boxer (then considered a mark of a "real man") and even staged a saloon brawl in which he ejected some tough characters who made remarks about female impersonators being "nances," all of which seemingly increased his popularity.[42] The apparently more sympathetic treatment accorded camp and drag performance in such Broadway successes as *La Cage aux folles* and *M. Butterfly* still operates, predictably, according to the demands of mainstream entertainment and cultural assumptions. "Just as black culture has been presented to mainstream white America as a minstrel show," observes Gevisser in respect to such spectacles, "gay culture is presented to mainstream heterosexual America as a drag show."[43] Nevertheless, there is no question that as performance has been more and more utilized in recent years to gain political and social visibility, drag for some performers and some audiences can be seen as personally and politically enabling. The essay title "Gay Activist or Beauty Queen?" (1991) by performer David Drake expresses this tension. "Wearing a dress onstage is part of a gay aesthetic," argues Drake. "It's how one expresses oneself theatrically through a heterosexual society."[44]

Paul Best's appearances as "Octavia," in women's make-up and costume, in social situations are designed to make what Best has called "radical feminist" points. Best argues that Octavia's performative appearances work to reveal "the social and political implications of male vs. female clothing and how people are oppressed, confined, stereotyped and sometimes granted social approval according to what they wear."[45] However, Alisa Soloman and others (particularly women) have expressed some scepticism about male drag's ability to destabilize gender assumptions: "Precisely because 'man' is the present universal, and 'women' the gussied up other, drag changes meaning depending on who's wearing it." Since in this sense "femininity is *always* drag," men dressed as women almost invariably are involved in the parody of gender, women in the performance of it."[46] This view of "femininity as drag" is central to masquerade theory and performance, and we will return to it in Chapter 8.[47]

Controversies of the 1990s

The NEA Four

Much less easy to assimilate into the burlesque "drag show" tradition, and therefore much more disturbing to the conservative critics of contemporary performance, have been performances by gay artists that address the real-life experience of homosexuals in today's society. In 1990 the National Endowment for the Arts touched off a major controversy by taking back funding already awarded to four performance artists, three of them homosexual (Tim Miller, Holly Hughes and John Fleck), the other a confrontational feminist (Karen Finley). The artists, claiming censorship, protested this action in the courts, but after two lower courts supported them and restored the withheld grant money, the United States Supreme Court in 1998 rejected their arguments. The decade-long controversy made the "NEA Four" one of the most visible examples of the rise of conservative thought and political power in the United States, especially as this impacted upon the arts. At the same time, somewhat paradoxically, it gave to the artists under attack a national prominence and visibility far beyond what any of them had previously experienced. It also brought "performance art" to national attention, although with a distinct coloring of scandal.[48]

Inevitably, the NEA controversy has affected the subsequent work of all four of these artists as well as the public perception of that work. While all four have continued to work with autobiographical material, the use of that material in their pieces before 1990 was on the whole distinctly more private and personal, often dealing with their family relationships, their sexual awakenings, or their closest personal friendships, as can be seen even in the somewhat sensationalized summary of the four works refused funding provided in the notes to the opinion by Justice Scalia:[49]

> Finley's controversial show, 'We Keep Our Victims Ready,' contains three segments. In the second segment, Finley visually recounts a sexual assault by stripping to the waist and smearing chocolate on her breasts and by using profanity to describe the assault. Holly Hughes' monologue, 'World Without End,' is a somewhat graphic recollection of the artist's realization of her lesbianism and reminiscence of her mother's sexuality. John Fleck, in his stage performance 'Blessed Are All the Little Fishes,' confronts alcoholism and Catholicism.... Tim

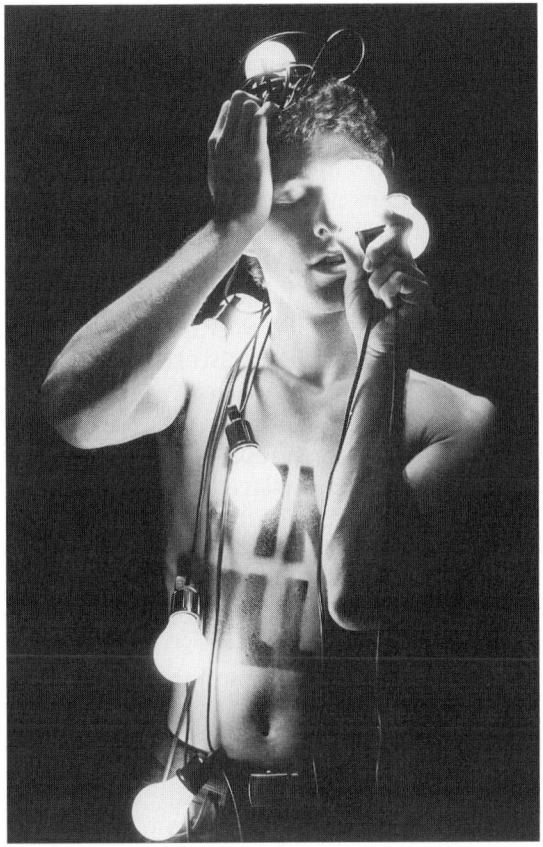

Figure 7.1 Tim Miller in *Postwar*, 1982.
Source: Paula Court.

> Miller derives his performance 'Some Golden States' from childhood experiences, from his life as a homosexual, and from the constant threat of AIDS.

The work of these artists from 1990 onward has inevitably been marked by the NEA controversy, both because of their own experience and because the public now primarily associated them with this controversy. The later work of Hughes and Miller in particular is distinctly more political in its concerns, although this change in some measure reflects a changing orientation in performance art itself during the closing years of the century. I will return to that later work in the following chapter, which focuses upon social and cultural concerns in recent performance.

John Fleck produced very little performance work after 1990, turning instead to film and video work, though he returned to the performance stage in 2001, after more than a decade, with a new piece, *Mud in Your Eye*. This returned to his old themes of sexual confusion and his confrontations with conservative religion—now, however, given new relevance by the rise of the religious right. A red, white, and blue background covered with stars provided a distinct political edge to the production.

The relative obscurity of Fleck for the general public after 1990 was balanced by the high visibility of Karen Finley, the most vilified and best known of the NEA Four. This is perhaps not surprising, since her work has little of the warmth and charm of Miller, Hughes or Fleck, but is much more directly confrontational and physically disturbing. Elinor Fuchs has suggested that the ritualized, even sacred bodies of female performers like Carolee Schneeman during the previous decade were replaced by performers like Finley with "the obscene body—aggressive, scatalogical, and sometimes pornographic."[50] In her earlier performances, such as *I'm an Assman* (1982), Finley gained an international reputation for her use of obscenity and abuse of her own body in performance, a reputation solidified among followers of avant-garde theatre by a controversial cover story on her career by C. Carr in the *Village Voice* in June of 1986[51] and among the more general public by the NEA controversy four years later. Although Fleck turned to films and Hughes and Miller, despite their new notoriety, still performed primarily for audiences interested in the kind of work they were doing, Finley became a much more public figure in the 1990s, gaining major awards (a Guggenheim in 1995, an Obie in 1998) and the continued attention of the scandal-loving media. A year after being named "Woman of the Year" by *MS Magazine* (in 1998), she created a new uproar by appearing in the nude in a six-page article in *Playboy* (July, 1999). She has continued, however, to create performance work based on personal experience, as in her 2002 *The Distribution of Empathy*, one of the first performance works to deal with the terrorist attacks upon New York the previous September.

Body art of the 1990s

Performance art again caused problems for the NEA in 1995, when conservative senators protested the funding of the Walker Art Center in Minneapolis because it had provided a modest grant to Ron Athey for his *Four Scenes from a Harsh Life*, a work containing bloody mutilations (the fact that Athey was HIV-positive gave reports on this activity a particularly scandalous force). The performance of such ordeals, even more than the early work of Karen Finley, recalls some of the extreme spectacles of body art twenty years before by performance artists like Vito Acconci and Chris Burden. Athey's work, however, comes from a quite different base and reflects the performance world of the 1990s just as Acconci and Burden reflected theirs. Body art was calculatedly decontextualized and physical mutilation used to emphasize the power and presentness of the moment, the experience of pain removing the body from the abstractions of representation. Athey, on the other hand, has used the performance of pain and mutilation to express and control autobiographical demons—his impoverished childhood, his severe upbringing in a Pentecostal family, his former heroin addiction, his several suicide attempts, his experiments with consensual sadomasochistic sex, his HIV-positive status. The imagery of martyrdom haunts Athey's work, as in the 1994 piece *Deliverance*, where as St Sebastian he wears a crown of thorns that causes blood to run down his face and body. Like the NEA Four, Athey's visibility was significantly increased after conservative attacks on his work, and during the late 1990s he toured throughout the world. He was also the subject of a powerful documentary film in 1998.[52]

An even closer connection between the suffering body, performance, and identity construction was offered by Bob Flanagan, who died in 1996 at the age of 43, one of the oldest survivors of cystic fibrosis (a degenerative illness of the lungs and digestive system that is normally fatal by early adolescence). Flanagan first gained wide notoriety for his 1989 performance piece in Los Angeles in which he nailed his penis to a wooden plank while making jokes. In his widely toured *Visiting Hours* (1992) he welcomed audience members to a hospital room constructed in a gallery, where he was hooked up to the oxygen tank necessary for his breathing and surrounded by various monitoring devices and pictures of his sadomasochistic experiments. He and his partner/collaborator Sheree Rose shared with others the connections they had discovered between sexuality, sickness and pain. Flanagan's work, like Athey's, has inspired a rather sensationalized documentary film, *Sick: The Life and Death of Bob Flanagan, Supermasochist*, which appeared in 1997.[53]

The French performance artist Orlan's ongoing surgical project bears an interesting relationship to both the suffering bodies of Athey and Flanagan and the early body work of Eleanor Antin, and became probably the best known example of performance through body modification in the late twentieth century. In a series of performance works in the 1970s and 1980s in France, Orlan explored social and cultural images of women, especially prostitutes and saints—works that led in 1990 to a series of cosmetic operations, not, like Athey and Flanagan, as expressions of pain, but as commentaries on the social shaping of women's bodies. A 1993 article by Barbara Rose in *Art in America* brought Orlan to American attention,[54] after which she became a favored subject in performance conferences.[55] As her series of operations, performed before a camera and without anaesthetic, has continued, Orlan is purportedly changing her face to resemble a composite of idealized types of feminine beauty represented by classic paintings such as the *Mona Lisa*. In some of the film sequences, one may notice a phrase printed on the sleeve of one of Orlan's assistants, "The body is but a costume."

Victim art

While for the general public the highly publicized NEA controversies were the most visible cultural attacks on performance of the 1990s, for those in

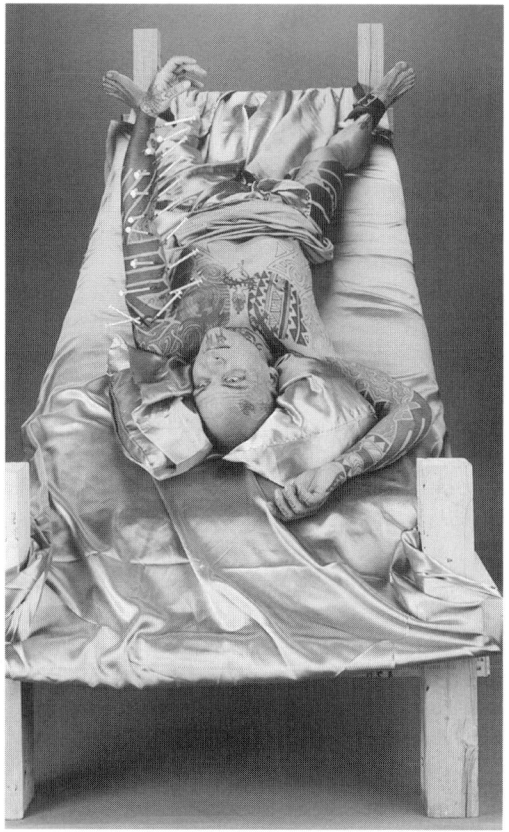

Figure 7.2 Ron Athey in *Four Scenes from a Harsh Life*, 1993.

Source: Ron Athey.

the art world another attack of almost equal concern was that mounted in early 1995 by Arlene Croce, the dance critic of the *New Yorker*, against what she characterized as "victim art."[56] Refusing either to see or to review the production *Still/Here* by Bill T. Jones, one of the leading experimental and politically engaged dancers of the decade, Croce charged that as a black man and a victim of AIDS, Jones's use of autobiographical material made objective criticism impossible. Echoes of the previous NEA controversies permeate Croce's article. Robert Mapplethorpe, an NEA-funded artist whose sexually explicit photographs were among the reasons for attacks on the Endowment in the late 1980s, Croce cites as another case of "pathology in art." This leads to a rhetorical question that suggests neither Mapplethorpe nor Jones, but rather Ron Athey: "If an artist paints a picture in his own blood, what does it matter if I think it's not a good picture?"[57] Croce, not a conservative Southern Senator but the most powerful dance critic in America, inevitably created a firestorm of controversy, and focused attention once again upon the conservative suspicion of contemporary autobiographically based performance, especially that created by members of racial or sexual minorities. Critic Dale Harris, in the *Wall Street Journal*, though more openly conservative than Croce, was no less severe in his condemnation and even more specific on the source of it: "Mr. Jones is black. He is also homosexual ... Mr. Jones himself is HIV-positive.... I mention all this because Mr. Jones's alienated persona is impossible to separate from his choreography. He himself is more often than not the main subject of his work—embittered, hypersensitive, utterly self-bemused."[58]

Performance and ethnicity

Performance that is involved with identity and autobiography has been most elaborately developed in respect to gender and sexuality, and the aura of scandal and taboo that has surrounded much of this work in such public controversies as the NEA funding disputes or the Victim Art discussions has also made it the most publicized. By the middle of the 1980s, however, other aspects of personal history had begun to be increasingly explored by performance. Class and race then began to receive the kind of attention previously given to gender, providing a very different and much wider range of identity performance. While this is still very much a project in process, one of the most distinctive features of American performance work at the close of the century was the appearance of performers and spectatorial communities dedicated to extending the sort of gender and self exploration into new areas. The performance artists of the 1970s and early 1980s were almost entirely well-educated, white, and middle-class, while during the 1980s there emerged a much more significant number of performers of color and performers of a lower social class, bringing their different experiences and concerns onto the stage. This changing orientation was accompanied by a certain degree of tension and controversy within the world of performance itself, involving some of the best-known performance artists of the period.

Eleanor Antin, for example, began to be criticized for creations like her black ballerina. Antin always dissociated such figures from social commentary, claiming them only as alternative versions of herself, created primarily to explore that self. "They help me to get out of my own skin to explore other realities," Antin commented in 1989,[59] while C. Carr, in the *Village Voice*, accused this position of "presumptuousness and naïveté," of repeating, without sensitivity or cultural awareness, the white artist's traditional "blackface" playing of others."[60] Suzanne Lacy also aroused criticism for her conscious use of the performance of others, even though this was done to advance positive social goals. In several of her pieces, such as *Prostitution Notes* or *The Life and Times of Donaldina Cameron* (1977), Lacy had sought "to loosen the physical boundaries of the flesh, hence of the identity," explaining:

In these pieces I consciously moved into the realm of another experience, another social setting, and became one with that. That obviously does not mean that I become black or Chinese, but that I integrate myself as closely as possible into that experience to understand the correlations of our shared experience, to expand my identity and become the other. It is a self-educating process.[61]

Lacy encountered much resistance, however, from Chinese artists, who felt that a white feminist with her own agenda could neither understand nor represent their concerns, and saw this attempt to speak "for" them little different from male dramatists speaking for women. Similar reservations were expressed in the late 1980s by black feminists about the domination of feminist theory by educated, upper-class white women.[62]

The evolution of one major performance group, Spiderwoman, during this period provides a particularly clear example of this new tension. The first work of this company, *Women and Violence*, in 1976, was built upon autobiographical and historical material. The announced aim of the seven-woman company was the bringing together of the "diverse experiences as women" of American Indian women, lesbians, Scorpios, women over fifty and under twenty-five, sisters, mothers, and grandmothers.[63] During the 1980s, however, as women and men of color began to use performance art to seek self-definition and to explore and express their more specific social, cultural, and ethnic concerns, the non-white members in Spiderwoman felt that the claimed diversity of the group was repeating the familiar social dynamic of becoming a mask for white control. So in 1981 the company separated, with the native American members retaining the name Spiderwoman, under which name they began to explore their particular ethnic memories, legends, and experiences.

Another important example of the change in identity performance in the final decades of the century is provided by the African-American performer Robbie McCauley. During the late 1960s McCauley experimented with a form called "jazz theatre" at the New Lafayette Theatre, while her future collaborator Jessica Hagedorn was developing in a similar direction with her "Gangster Choir," a form that mixed music and poetic autobiography. "I didn't know about performance art," she observes, "I just called it a poet's band." During the 1980s these two artists, together with a multimedia artist, Laurie Carlos, developed a series of performances called "Thought Music." "We were beginning to find our own voices," recalls Carlos, but could not readily do so in any of the conventional venues in either black or white theatre. "Performance art was the one place where there were so few definitions."[64]

In the late 1980s McCauley developed a series of performances, *Confessions of a Black Working Class Woman*, whose title suggests the developing class and ethnic concerns of feminist performance of that time. In this series of works, McCauley used personal material and the physicality of her body (perhaps most shockingly as a nude slave on the auction block in *Sally's*

Rape, 1989) to explore the effects of racism upon her own life history and that of her ancestors.[65]

The 1990s took McCauley's interest in storytelling, memory, and performance in another direction, into the domain of community oral history as a basis for her work. She began with American material (*Buffalo Project*, 1990, and *Mississippi Project*, 1992) and then undertook an international project with the 1995 *Stories Exchange Project*. Here she worked with five Czech Gypsies to develop a performance based on the sufferings of the Romany people under the Nazis.

During the 1980s and 1990s, performance by men and women of different ethnic groups became one of the most important areas of identity performance. A major center for such work, and indeed for performance art in general during the 1990s, was the Highways Performance Space, co-founded in Los Angeles in 1989 by Tim Miller and Linda Burnham, the founding editor of *High Performance*—America's major chronicle of performance art during its years of publication (1978–97).[66] Both Miller and Burnham saw the multiculturalism of Los Angeles as central to the orientation and the mission of Highways. In the early 1990s, Burnham contrasted the current Highways scene with the gallery performance of the 1970s and the club performance of the 1980s:[67]

> Now the majority of people we show here are doing solo work, and they're not coming out of visual art. They're mostly writers and theater people and a few dancers who want to push the envelope. More than half of what we see at Highways is about individual identity. It's about people from so many different cultures being pushed together in L.A. and introducing themselves to each other.

Similarly, Tim Miller in 1991 contrasted the work at Highways with current performance trends in New York, seeing the latter as remaining oriented toward the avant-garde art world and thus favoring technical virtuosity and formalist elegance, while the former existed in a more social context: "coming from cultural communities: Asian or Latino or lesbian or gay or whatever."[68] It was this multicultural focus, Miller suggested that made Los Angeles "the capital of performance art in North America" as the 1990s opened.[69] This combination of the study of individual identity and different cultures, with particular attention to disadvantaged, excluded or oppressed groups—gays and lesbians, the handicapped, the elderly, the poor, along with racial and ethnic minorities—characterized much of the most imaginative and provocative performance work in America in the early 1990s, and was a particular focus at Highways. Here Dan Kwong presented his *Secrets of a Samurai Centerfielder* (1989) and *Monkhood in 3 Easy Lessons* (1995), exploring the tensions of a gay son of Japanese/Chinese parentage struggling against dominant culture and sex-role expectations. Here Paulina Sahagun began in 1994 to perform works dealing with her Mexican/American background. Her *Local Loca* was presented at Highways

Figure 7.3 Dan Kwong in *Monkhood in 3 Easy Lessons*, 1995.

Source: Aaron Rapoport.

in 2002, but premiered the year before at the Los Angeles Women's Theater Festival, founded in 1994 as a venue for solo women's performance, and becoming an international festival in the new century.

Identity and the Def poet performers

Perhaps the most important new development of identity performance in the United States during the 1990s was the rise of Def poetry, which places autobiographical explorations at the heart of its subject matter. "I want to write *solely* about my personal feelings and perceptions," says Beau Sia, a leading Def performer and five-time member of a National Slam Team. "I also want to write them so that everyone can understand them. I want people to know what I'm going through."[70] Most of the prominent Def poet performers, like Sia, privilege personal expression and, not surprisingly, come from minority backgrounds, so there is a close social and cultural tie between this sort of performance and the more traditional performance art featured at such venues as Highways. In 2002 the production *Def Poetry Jam* brought to major stages in San Francisco and New York nine important young Def performers who may be taken as representative of the art. In addition to Beau Sia, a Chinese-American from Oklahoma City, these included Suheir Hammad, a Palestinian-American from Brooklyn, Black Ice, an African-American from Philadelphia, Staceyann Chin, a New Yorker born in Jamaica; and Mayda Del Valle, a Latina from Chicago's South Side. The four segments into which their show is divided suggest their ongoing concerns: "identity, memories, love, and a final message."[71]

From identity performance to cultural performance

In a 1990 report on current performance in Los Angeles, Jacki Apple observed that the majority of such work was now being produced by "a coalition of women, gay men, African-American, Hispanic and young Asian-American artists whose aesthetics and politics challenge both the art world's and the media's version of our socio-cultural reality."[72] Certainly the growing interest in multiculturalism and minority expression was one of the most important features of performance work in America at the end of the century, providing a stimulating diversity of approaches to the performance of identity.

Alongside this type of autobiographical performance, however, a similarly based but differently focused type of performance developed, concerned primarily not with the experience of a member of a specific ethic, gender, or sexual background within an over-arching culture, but with the experience of members of that background in general, or even with the processes of cultural and ethnic negotiations themselves. Individual performers, the best known of whom is probably Guillermo Gómez-Peña, developed new orientations in performance, neither specifically autobiographical nor attempting to construct abstract imaginative alternative identities like those of Eleanora Antin. Such performances were concerned less directly with personal experience than with general cultural dynamics, and were created to illuminate those dynamics. Such culturally oriented work, along with the attention of performance theorists generally toward performative activity outside the theatre or gallery, also encouraged attention toward the end of the century to the use of performance in more general cultural contexts to express the tensions and dynamics of the surrounding culture.

At the beginning of the 1990s, Gómez-Peña argued that the field of performance had significantly changed since the period when artists like Karen Finley talked about "mainstreaming radical ideas" as the goal of performance art. That goal, Gómez-Peña asserts, has been sufficiently attained, and now the goal should be to attack "the European myth of the artist as a marginal bohemian," still very prevalent in North America:[73]

I aspire to speak from the center, to be active in the making of culture. The same is true for gays, women, and artists of color, who can't afford to be marginalized anymore. Performance art is the one place where this can happen—where ritual can be reinvented, and where boundaries can be crossed.

Not individual expression or formal concerns but the "making of culture" indeed moved to the center of the interests of performance at the end of the twentieth century, and performance with that orientation will be the subject of the following chapter.

Chapter 8

Cultural performance

The performance of identity, often with the use of autobiographical material, became one of the most common forms of performance art from the early 1970s onward. Its frequent concern with providing a voice to previously silenced individuals or groups often involved such work in social and cultural issues as well. Other sorts of politically engaged performance, however, were also developing at the same time, even though, at least at the beginning, they were less associated with the specific term "performance." Such activities were less concerned with the exploration and expression of the identity of the individual and more with the social and cultural context within which that individual must operate. As cross-cultural concerns gained increasing importance near the century's end, with growing interest in the tensions and the dynamics of multiculturalism and post-coloniality, this cultural context became more and more a central concern of performance. Indeed, performance came to be recognized as a central operation in the ongoing construction of a culture and of its relationship with other cultures. As Phillip Zarilli observed: "performance as a mode of cultural action is not a simple reflection of some essentialized, fixed attributes of a static, monolithic culture but an arena for the constant process of renegotiating experiences and meanings that constitute culture."[1]

As the previous chapter was dedicated to the performance oriented toward personal experience, this chapter, without entirely excluding the personal, will consider performance and theory more oriented toward general cultural practices and tensions. It is important, however, to stress that this distinction is in large measure a matter of emphasis. Like most distinctions one might make in speaking of performance, it is very porous, since individual identity is of course developed within and operates within specific cultural contexts. Indeed, one of the questions taken up in this chapter (and an important part of contemporary performance theory) is whether it is even proper to speak of individual identity as distinct from cultural givens.

Guerrilla and street performance

While an important part of the lineage of modern performance art can be traced back, as we have noted, through the experiments of concept and body artists in studios and galleries (and sometimes in non-conventional spaces) during the 1960s, when we focus upon modern performance with a more distinctly social and political orientation a quite different genealogy suggests itself—one which lies not only outside the world of modern art, but which also in a number of prominent cases defines itself against it, as certain early performance defined itself in opposition to theatre. For the most part chroniclers of the early history of modern performance did not include the widespread and often highly theatrical street demonstrations of the 1960s in their considerations because performance was then primarily associated with the artistic community and with non-discursive activity. As early as 1970, however, Richard Schechner argued that much of what was at that time called "guerrilla theatre" could also be characterized as "performance."[2]

The term "guerrilla theatre" was coined in the late 1960s by R.G. Davis, a member of the San Francisco Mime Troupe, to describe the widespread popular performances of that time which used performance in non-theatrical public spaces to bring political messages to a broader audience.[3] While the majority of such theatre was devoted at that time to protests against the Vietnam War, social inequities suffered by various minorities were also addressed by such performance. In the case of two groups with particularly close relationships to subsequent political performance, these inequities involved not governmental or general social practice, but the ongoing discriminatory practices of the art world itself. The institutional bias toward white male artists inspired the first performative actions of both the Guerrilla Girls in New York and the Chicano ASCO group in Los Angeles.

Feminist guerrilla theatre and the Guerrilla Girls

When the modern woman's movement began in the late 1960s it existed in quite a different world from the apolitical, formalist, gallery-oriented "performance" work of the same period. Yet at the same time many radical feminists were much attracted to the symbolic values and performance strategies of the radical guerrilla and street theatre of the period. Feminist guerrilla theatre began to appear in a number of striking and well-publicized demonstrations such as the 1968 disruption of the Miss America pageant in Atlantic City, which included the crowning of a live sheep, the auctioning off of a Miss America dummy and the flinging of dishcloths, steno pads, girdles and bras into a Freedom Trash Can. Later the same year women in New York organized WITCH (Women's International Terrorist Conspiracy from Hell) and on All Hallows' Eve appeared costumed and masked as "Shamans, Faerie Queens, Matriarchal Old Sorceresses, and

Figure 8.1 The Guerrilla Girls in a demonstration.

Source: Guerrilla Girls.

Guerrilla Witches" to confront and cast spells upon the denizens of the Wall Street area. WITCH covens soon appeared all over America to engage in similar guerrilla theatre activity, hexing Pat Nixon and the Boston Transit Authority and holding a "spell-in" at the United Fruit Company. Robin Morgan, one of the pioneers in such activity, later observed that the participants in these demonstrations "identified politically with the confrontational tactics of the male Left and stylistically with the clownish proto-anarchism of such groups as the Yippies," but that "not having raised our own consciousness very far out of our combat boots, we didn't know what we were doing, or why."[4,5]

Later on the raising of consciousness redirected much of this "proto-anarchic" energy into more directly political and social activity, but the tradition of the feminist guerrilla theatre lives on, for example in the ongoing and highly visible activities of the Guerrilla Girls, whose posters and performance demonstrations (in gorilla masks) call attention to the continuing dominance of men in New York's art world.[6] Originally organized in New York, the Guerrilla Girls have carried their activities across America and into Europe. In 2001 they created a stir at the Academy Awards ceremony by distributing stickers with statistics about the dearth of Oscar-nominated women directors, a project that has now become an annual undertaking.

ASCO

Like the New York Guerrilla Girls, the Los Angeles-based Chicano group ASCO (the word means "nausea" in Spanish) grew out of political street theatre of the late 1960s, in this case student demonstrations against inferior segregated education. Four artists involved in these activities, Harry Gamboa Jr, Patssi Valdez, Willie Heron and GRONK joined together to protest the lack of Chicano representation in local cultural institutions, just as the Guerrilla Girls united to protest the under-representation of women artists. ASCO's first "action" was painting the names of its members across the front of the Los Angeles County Museum of Art in 1972. At a period when Chicano political art was primarily associated with the visual arts, posters and murals, ASCO specialized in street performance, perhaps most notably their "No-movies" in which ASCO members, much in the style of later European "walkabout" companies like the German Scharlatan Theater, set up street actions disguised as shootings of imaginary films.[7] ASCO steadily grew in size during the 1970s, and in 1979 gained one of its most prominent members, Daniel J. Martinez. Martinez says of his first meeting with Harry Gamboa: "We started to talk about identity, politics, and we talked about a new, reinterpreted version of conceptual art."[8] Gamboa and Martinez together led the group until its dissolution in 1989. Under the influence of Martincz, who had a particular interest in the media, the "No-movies" evolved into conceptual non-events for which the group would create simulated coverage, seeking to entice real reviewers who would in turn report on the events and give them a kind of virtual reality.[9] Among the interested observers of the ASCO performances was one of the most significant performance artists of the 1990s, Guillermo Gómez-Peña. ASCO also served as a model for other Latin artists seeking to challenge rigid and exclusionary systems elsewhere, such as the Cuban ARTECALLE group, formed in 1987, which staged unexpected guerrilla actions at public events to protest artistic censorship.[10]

Although D.J. Martinez was primarily known during the 1990s for a number of major and often controversial public arts projects, he continued to create occasional street performances as well—such as *How to Con a Capitalist* (1995), where, in a clown suit, he offered Mexican potatoes and Zapatista-inspired wooden guns for sale on the streets of Belfast, Northern Ireland. His works, Coco Fusco has suggested, "are best understood as interventions that push the boundaries of permissible public activity," transforming public spaces "into sites on confrontation."[11]

Social concerns in early feminist performance

Guerrilla or street theatre in both Europe and America has been on the whole less employed for consciousness-raising in particular groups than for calling the attention of all potential spectators to unresolved and often ignored problems in the surrounding society. This was also true when the concerns of feminist guerrilla theatre began to be explored later in the 1970s by women in the performance art scene. Suzanne Lacy and her collaborator Leslie Labowitz, for example, offered a powerful series of works in California seeking to raise community consciousness about rape (*Three Weeks in May*, 1977), commercial images of violence against women (*Record Companies Drag Their Feet*, 1977), and demeaning sexist images generally.

The years between the WITCH demonstrations of the late 1968s and the social activist performances of a decade later were of course also those of the emergence of the modern women's movement and of a rapidly developing theoretical as well as political discourse within this movement. As a result, later performances tended to be more concerned not only with making a specific political statement, but also with exposing the underlying social, cultural, and aesthetic practices and assumptions that supported and validated the specific phenomenon being displayed. Lacy and Labowitz' *Three Weeks in May*, after a series of events drawing on specific material related to recent rapes, ended more abstractly or theoretically with a scene in a gallery where four nude women, painted red, crouched mutely on a ledge. Jeanie Forte suggests that they "bore striking resemblance to the countless nude women hung on the walls of Western museums," thus providing a critique of the "cultural practice that has made of woman an object, a category, a 'sign,'" and suggesting "how such transposition of women into signs (or representations of femininity), endangers the lives of actual women."[12]

Clearly, in terms of the various subdivisions applied to modern feminism this latter concern (like cultural performance in general) accords most closely with the materialist, looking beyond the sort of individual case studies discussed in the previous chapter to the particular social apparatus or cultural practice that has produced them and to how this apparatus favors certain social interests rather than others. By the end of the 1980s there was widespread interest among feminist performers and theorists internationally in the questioning, the exposing, and perhaps even the dismantling of those cultural and social constructions and assumptions that governed traditional gender roles, stagings of the body, and gender performance, both on the stage and in everyday life.

German and English perspectives

During the 1970s German theorists and performers Ulrike Rosenbach (who has worked primarily with video and installation art) and Valie Export (more oriented toward the live body) developed an approach to performance which, echoing the earlier Vienna Aktionists, they called "feminist actionism." It pursued a similar disruptive agenda, seeking "to replace the equation material=body=nature by that of body=social construction= transfigured nature." According to Export:

> The representation of woman's body, as imprinted by history in the images of our phallocentric culture, demanded that these stagings of the body that had been defined by an alien ideology be brought into question and dismantled as occupations of the body by the forces of alien signs.

This questioning, involved an emphasis on "the social construction of the body, the body as a carrier of signs, and with it the social construction of the subject in performance."[13] In a striking use of body art to foreground cultural concerns rather than the personal or even visceral orientation of most American body art, Export had tattooed on her left leg a rendering of a garter belt clip, which she has suggested acts as a "historical antique" reminding her of "obsolete" definitions of women.[14]

A similar trajectory in political performance from guerrilla theatre through a more liberal theatre of political debate to a materialist examination of the politics of representation itself also occurred in modern feminist performance in England, according to Michelene Wandor's history of that movement, *Carry On, Understudies*. Wandor traces three general stages of such performance. The "vivid visual imagery of the early street theatre, with its spontaneity and its attack on stereotypical 'feminine' imagery" gave way in the mid-1970s to a "theatre of argument," attempting to "reclaim the experience of women and gays" from the "conventional prior ities of male heterosexual experience," including its class perspective. Finally, in a third phase, some of the early spontaneity returned but in a different context: "instead of using dressing-up and visual imagery to challenge the audience's assumptions about real-life oppression, the new spontaneity revolved around an examination of the way the theatrical forms themselves work to represent sexuality."[15]

The search for subjectivity

This growing interest in the cultural dynamics embedded in performance and theatrical representation itself was primarily stimulated by a materialist concern for exposing the operations of power and oppression in society, but theoretical writing on the subject was at least as much influenced by recent psychoanalytical theories as by political, social, or economic ones. The model of the psychological self developed by Freud and extended by his French follower, Jacques Lacan, exerted a particularly strong influence in modern cultural studies, and feminist theorists in particular found in Freud and Lacan the most fully developed model for the establishment of the dominant male subject in the patriarchal cultural system. The second chapter of this study considered the importance of this tradition in identity formation as well as in the development of psychoanalysis itself and its treatment of such psychic manifestations as hysteria and melancholy. Perhaps even more central to modern performance theory and practice was this system's discussion of the dynamics of representation. Lacan, following

Freud and indeed the traditional Western system of representation, places the male in the subject position. This subject enters self-consciousness and language with a sense of separation and incompleteness, an ongoing "desire" for an objectified Other that both threatens and promises a lost unity. Traditional theatre and visual art is based on this system, assuming a male spectator and offering the female as Other, the object of the male's desiring gaze. As Sue-Ellen Case has observed, within the patriarchal system of signs and of representation, "women do not have the cultural mechanisms of meaning to construct themselves as the subject rather than as the object of performance." The traditional audience is assumed to be the male subject, and the woman on stage "a kind of cultural courtesan," an objectified site for the fulfillment of desire. A wedge is thus driven between this courtesan sign, "woman," and real women that "insinuates alienation into the very participation of women in the system of theatrical representation."[16]

The female performer, subjectivity, and the gaze

Confronting this long-established system of representation, a central concern of women's performance art of the 1980s and early 1990s was the establishment of the women performer as a speaking subject—a phenomenon that this system denies. The British performance artist Catherine Elwes has argued that live performance, in which the traditional male gaze of the spectator can be returned or at least challenged or made problematic, offers possibilities for disruption of the conventional system of spectatorship which are impossible in representations offering permanently fixed and objectified images of women, such as the cinema, painting, or sculpture. The living woman performer, she suggests, can expose the (male) spectator "to the fearful proximity of the performer and the dangerous consequences of his own desires. His cloak of invisibility has been stripped away and his spectatorship becomes an issue within the work."[17]

The importance of at least calling attention to, if not successfully subverting, the power relationships involved in traditional spectatorship has led many performers in one way or another to "turn the spotlight" on the (male) spectator and challenge his invisibility. Some have done this literally, like Sonia Knox, who floods herself and her audience with the same uncompromising light.[18] Among the many performers who have challenged the voyeurism of performance in various ways a particularly striking case is Karen Finley, who has combined shifting gender positions, scatology, and perverse sexuality in her monologues, mocking the visual "consumption" of her nude or nearly nude body by coating it with a variety of mostly edible materials. Rather than offer herself as a passive object, Finley, in Dolan's words: "forces men to be passive in the face of her rage, and she desecrates herself as the object of their desire, thereby mocking their sexuality. Her refusal to play the game leaves the male spectator nowhere to place himself in relation to her performance. He can no longer maintain the position of the sexual subject who views the performance."[19] A similar direct challenge to the male gaze has been associated with the work of the pornographic star Annie Sprinkle, who was "discovered" as a performance artist by Richard Schechner. Schechner has reported that he was first attracted to Sprinkle's work by "her own sophisticated play with the gazing male."[20] Sprinkle has regularly challenged spectators to carry their interest in her naked body onto the stage itself, examining her genitals with a flashlight, even peering into her opened cervix.[21] However, even performances so disruptive and confrontational as those of Finley and Sprinkle risk, at least with some audiences, being neutralized by the power of the reception process they seek to challenge. Sprinkle continues consciously to blur the line between pornography and parody, while Finley, appearing in more conventional and commercial venues as a result of her increased visibility after the NEA scandals, has found, as Forte reports, that even her most shocking work has tended to become "re-inscribed in the fetishistic process associated with strip-tease or live sex, and not at all the feminist or subversive strategy that theory might endorse."[22]

The female body in performance

Some feminist theorists and performers, especially those interested in seeking a more essentially feminist mode of expressivity, have followed the lead of French theorists Luce Irigaray and Julia Kristeva in regarding traditional language as itself a male construction, dominated by the operations of logic and abstraction and reflecting the interests of the patriarchy. From this point of view, physical performance has been suggested as offering a possibility for women to escape what Kristeva has called the "symbolic" logical and discursive language of the father for the "semiotic" poetic and physical language of the mother.[23] The utilization of the body in performance may thus provide an alternative to the symbolic order of language itself, which many feminist theorists have claimed provides no opening for the representation of women within it.

Marcia Moen, working with Charles Peirce's modes of knowing, has suggested how the exploration of cognition based upon feeling and a bodily-felt sense of "rightness" can "engage the body in an *active* role, making possible, for example, resistance to the influences of power-knowledge discourses."[24] Others have gone further, arguing that the body in performance can provide not merely an alternative way of knowing but also an actual subversion of the dominant symbolic order of language. Jeanie Forte, for example, has pointed out that this potential disruption is much greater in physical performance than in the field of writing since the female body in performance involves not only the discourse of language, but "physical presence, real time, and real women in dissonance with their representations, threatening the patriarchal structure with the revolutionary text of their actual bodies."[25]

Sally Potter develops a similar argument in a 1980 catalogue devoted to women's performance in London. She posits that live performance always possesses a subversive and threatening quality, even when that performance involves the most traditional and highly codified roles—such as the graceful ballerina or the raucous comedienne—which seemed designed only to "reinforce stereotypes and gratify male desire." Real physical presence, says Potter, exerts a counter-power even here: "The ballerina's physical strength and energy is communicated despite the scenario; the burlesque queen's apposite and witty interjection transforms the meaning of what she is doing and reveals it for the 'act' it is."[26] Yet even some theorists who have supported this strategy have also expressed some misgivings about it. Rachel Bowlby, for example, has warned against too ready an acceptance of bodily "discourse" as the most effective way for women to "speak." "It remains to be shown,' cautions Bowlby, "that the female body is itself productive of a distinctive mode of subjectivity."[27]

Visibility and representation

Even more serious is the problem faced by both the graceful ballerina and the confrontational performer like Finley or Sprinkle, and that is that the female body itself is already so deeply inscribed as an object within the representational system that new performances, whatever their intention, tend to be re-inscribed within the same system. The performance space itself is already genderized, critics like Jill Dolan point out, and in this space women's bodies "become accountable to male-defined standards for acceptable display."[28] As Derrida warned: "by repeating what is implicit in the founding concepts . . . by using against the edifice the instruments or stones available in the house . . . one risks ceaselessly confirming, consolidating . . . that which one allegedly deconstructs,"[29] a warning summed up succinctly (and thus more memorably) in Audre Lorde's often-quoted "the master's tools will never dismantle the master's house."[30]

A variety of performative and theoretical responses have been developed to address this dilemma. Peggy Phelan, in *Unmarked* (1993), cautioned that the operations of visibility itself need to be subjected to more critical inquiry. In stressing performance's ability to make visible, she suggested, feminists have not considered the power of the invisible, nor the unmarked quality of live performance, which "becomes itself through disappearance." Without seeking to preserve itself through a stabilized copy, it "plunges into visibility—in a maniacally charged present—and disappears into memory, into the realm of invisibility and the unconscious where it eludes regulation and control."[31] Phelan cites the performance work of Angelika Festa as work "in which she appears in order to disappear"—appearing as a motionless figure wearing a mirror as a mask (*You Are Obsessive, Eat Something*, 1984) or hanging for hours from a slanted pole, her eyes covered and her body wrapped in cocoon-like sheets (*Untitled Dance (with fish and others)*, 1987).[32] Traditional representation, committed to resemblance and repetition, attempts to establish and control the Other as Same. This is the strategy of voyeurism, fetishism, and fixity, the ideology of the visible. If performance can be conceived as representation without reproduction, it can disrupt the attempted totalizing of the gaze and thus open a more diverse and inclusive representational landscape. As Elwes has noted, women performers should "never stay the same long enough to be named, fetishized."[33]

Resistant performance

Judith Butler and citation

Another approach to this problem was provided by the enormously influential work of Judith Butler. Her view of gender not as a given social or cultural attribute but as a category constructed through performance, scripted and enforced by society (see Chapter 3), clearly articulated the difficulties of challenging the pre-determined "roles" society provides. Yet Butler has also suggested a opening for change in such roles by drawing upon Derrida's concept of citation and the "slippage" involved in repetition. Within the very "taking up" of the master's tools, she sees potential, if qualified, agency: "There is no self that is prior to the convergence or who maintains 'integrity' prior to its entrance into this conflicted cultural field. There is only a taking up of the tools where they lie, where the very 'taking up' is enabled by the tool lying there."[34] There is a distinct similarity in this to De Certeau's suggestion that "The weak must continually turn to their own ends forces alien to them."[35] Such images suggest the operations of much modern resistant performance, the taking up of whatever tools the culture offers and employing them to work in a different direction. Philip Auslander nicely characterizes the precariousness of such postmodern political performance as "forced to walk a tightrope between complicity and critique."[36]

Although Butler more than any other theorist has been associated with the importance of performativity to resisting dominant cultural models of behavior, the concept of slippage in repetition, and even of the importance of this to cultural change, may be widely observed in postmodern theory. We have already noted a convergence upon this matter of Derrida's idea of citation, Bakhtin's of the utterance and de Certeau on the tactics of everyday action. To these one might also add Adorno, who recommended a "negative dialectic" in thinking, on the grounds that no pattern or concept is ever "totally congruent and isomorphic with the experience it purports to denote."[37] Human activity, he suggested "is characterized above all by the fact that the qualitatively new appears in it . . . it is a movement which does not run its course in pure identity, the pure reproduction of such as already was there."[38] In a passage strongly suggestive of Butler's description of gender constraints within a culture, Adorno speaks of an "enormous social effort of constraint and prohibition," based on what he calls "identity-thinking." This effort is continually exerted to deny or limit slippage, to maintain a total congruity between concept and experience, pure identity and repetition, but it can never be totally successful. The possibility of innovative agency is always present, not based upon a pre-existing subject constrained by regulatory laws but, as in Butler, in the inevitable slippage arising from the enforced repetition and citation of social performance.[39]

Masquerade and mimicry

Relying upon and indeed emphasizing the instability of repetition has provided a particularly important part of modern resistant political performance, especially by women and ethnic performance artists. Far from avoiding highly coded traditional representations of ethnic types, they have often sought out precisely such material in order to subject it to various types of ironic quotation—a kind of political double-coding. Performers working in this direction introduce into the playing of a role a subversive and parodic self-consciousness which is very widespread in contemporary engaged performance, by feminists and others, both in Europe and America.

Elin Diamond has suggested the use of the term "mimicry" to characterize these various forms of the sort of "ironic disturbance."[40] The modern concept of mimicry, itself a mimic distortion of Plato's conventional doctrine of "mimesis," is derived from French theorist Luce Irigaray, who saw in Plato's condemnation of mimesis an attempt to control the proliferation of alternatives to a stable and monolithic patriarchal Truth. Instead of the shadowy "mere copy" of mimesis, Irigaray proposes a multiple and excessive "mimicry" that undermines rather than reinforces the unique claim of patriarchal Truth. Women, she suggests, must "play with mimesis," must "assume the feminine role deliberately. Which means already to convert a form of subordination into an affirmation, and thus to begin to thwart it."[41]

In an analysis of Laurie Anderson, Herman Rapaport has suggested that she is utilizing a similar process, which he calls "miming." Recalling Jencks' characterization of postmodern as double-coded expression, Rapaport suggests that the postmodern artist may turn representation to critical or even subversive ends by stressing the disharmony of codes:

> in performing the hegemony Anderson is also miming it, and in doing so she is releasing or activating resonances within the collision of vernacular and elitist cultural expressions, resonances which undermine that hegemony's efficacy as a stable equilibrium in which the power of the elite culture seems natural.

In *United States* (1983), according to this view, Anderson, in "performing" the postmodern "hybridization of the elite and the vernacular," also performs:[42]

the hegemony's illusory unifications and subtly reveals its dissonanaces and discrepancies, but without necessarily enacting a critical stance of her own, a stance which would be recovered merely as another ideological or theoretical formation intended to dominate a field of relationships.

Other theorists have considered that the primary disruptive power of mimicry lies less in its conflict of codes, an emphasis that stresses its relationship to Jencks and postmodernism, than in its excess and exaggeration, an emphasis closer to Irigaray and her concern with the subversion of patriarchic unity and order. This is the direction taken by masquerade theory, which developed within the analysis of performance in film but which has more recently become important in live performance as well. In "Film and the Masquerade" (1982), Mary Ann Doane suggested that a woman film performer could subvert traditional roles and masks if she could "flaunt her femininity, produce herself as an excess of femininity—foreground the masquerade."[43] A slightly different perspective on this same performance strategy is offered by Mary Russo, who draws upon Bakhtin to postulate a carnivalesque performing body, consciously "making a spectacle of itself" in order to call attention to the spectacle as process and construction.[44] When Lois Weaver in *Upwardly Mobile Home* (1985) through "subtle exaggeration ... defuses the obvious fetishization" in the carefully choreographed artificiality of the country movie star, when Franca Rame in *Female Parts* (1977) exploits "the gender signs of heterosexual femininity" by the use of dyed blond hair and exaggerated make-up, when Rachel Rosenthal in *Rachel's Brain* (1987) appears as an "exaggerated parody of a salon aristocrat" whose speech on rational discourse disintegrates into whines, grunts, and stifled hysterical cries, different sorts of masquerade strategies are being employed.

The problem of re-inscription

Of course masquerade performances always run the danger Derrida cited in any deconstructive operation that seeks to turn established structures back on themselves—that this process may also, especially for a conventional audience, simply re-inscribe or reinforce those structures. This is a common problem in all postmodern political performances, which, as Auslander warns: "can turn into their own opposites by reifying the very representations they supposedly deconstruct." A striking and by no means unique example of this was encountered by the British feminist performance group Monstrous Regiment when they attempted, in *Time Gentlemen Please* (1978), to foreground the degrading sexual self-representation of women in traditional cabaret and stand-up comedy. A letter from a woman in the Communist Party *Morning Star* apparently understood the strategy, but nevertheless complained that "Far from creating a Dietrich image in order to subvert it, Monstrous Regiment appears to indulge itself in the creation, to revel in the fantasy." Director Susan Todd was forced to justify the performance in another letter, arguing that the women in the show "deconstruct their traditional mode of stage presence and abandon coyness, terror and self-doubt for a direct expression of sexuality." This, she insisted, "represented a victory for each women over self-denigration."[45] "Only the most cunning of female *masquerades*," suggests British performance artist Catherine Elwes, "can turn the spotlight on the mask and those for whom it is worn."[46]

Jon Erickson, in a 1990 article "Appropriation and Transgression in Contemporary American Performance," argued that such re-inscription or re-appropriation is almost inevitable so long as minority or marginalized performance allows itself, even through ironic subversion, "to be solely defined by what we are transgressing, resisting, or deconstructing." The more sophisticated ironic strategies become and the more attention is given to the appropriation and attempted devaluation of the dominant culture, the more likely it is, for audiences who subscribe to that culture, that traditional meaning "will be assumed and be reinforced, not undermined." Resistance only from within the terms "given us," Erickson argues, can at best merely be reformist, not revolutionary, and he urges that resistance be developed on the basis of "an alternative mode of perception or action" that can provide a clear dialectic alternative to the existing system.[47]

Lesbian performance

Rather than attempting in performance to resist conventional reception by various types of exaggeration, any of which run this danger of re-inscription, an important area of feminist theory and performance has followed the more radical strategy of placing woman in the position of the desiring subject of the performance "in contrast to the passive role traditionally granted women as the object of male desire."[48] Elwes suggests that the sexual aspects of women's physical presence in performance should be constantly explored and exploited precisely because "the unknown territory of women's desire can intensify her threat."[49] Lesbian performance has provided one of the most important areas for experimentation of this sort. In a 1986 article, Kate Davy argued that lesbian performance could undercut conventional reception "by implying a spectator that is not the generic, universal male, not the cultural construction 'woman,' but lesbian—a subject ... whose desire lies outside the fundamental model or underpinnings of sexual difference."[50] Similarly, in "Toward a Butch-Femme Aesthetic" (1988), Sue-Ellen Case suggests that the search for a heterosexual female subject "remains entrapped insofar as this subject "is still perceived in terms of men." Building upon masquerade and carnival theory, but rejecting their heterosexual assumptions, Case sees in the on- and off-stage butch-femme performance of a couple like Peggy Shaw and Lois Weaver of Split Britches a camp fulfillment of masquerade's project against essentializing social and theatrical roles and narratives. The point of

Figure 8.2 Peggy Shaw and Lois Weaver in *Killing Time*, 1991.
Source: Franklin Furnace and Split Britches.

lesbian camp performance, says Case, "is not to conflict reality with another reality, but to abandon the notion of reality through roles and their seductive atmosphere and lightly manipulate appearances."[51]

This strategy, Case suggests, can also be found in gay camp performance, at least in its more politically conscious manifestations. In a 1968 article on the recently organized Theatre of the Ridiculous, Stefan Brecht suggested that the work there represented the attitudes of the "free person [f.p.]" as distinct from the "authoritarian phony," the normal "civilized adult." Ridiculous performers "adopt and act roles as the f.p. playfully assumes his identity—without identifying and only for the sake of playing them." Through "farcical and ironic performance" it seeks the "corrosion of make-believe identity" as it is found in the "institutionalized society" of the authoritarian phony.[52] A similar point is made by Butler, who suggests that the replication of heterosexual relationships in non-heterosexual frames "brings into relief the utterly constructed status of the so-called heterosexual original." Therefore gay is to straight "*not* as copy is to original, but, rather, as copy is to copy."[53]

It is this corrosion of identity and foregrounding of constructedness in gay performance that Case relates to lesbian masquerade performance. However, other theorists such as Dolan and Davy, while praising Case's expansion of the sexual and performance terrain, have questioned her association of lesbian with gay camp performance. Davy approvingly quotes Earl Jackson, writing on male cross-dressing in Eastern and Western performance:[54]

> Throughout history, for various reasons, male homoerotic practices have been supportive of, rather than subversive to, hegemonic conceptions of masculinity. Even in the postmodern, late capitalist societies of the twentieth century, male homoerotic discourses are often reinscribed within the very patriarchy they would seem to countermand.

The tools of camp performance—artifice, wit, irony, exaggeration—are of major importance to lesbian performance, Davy concedes, but she also argues that these tools are employed toward an end that is central to lesbian performance and peripheral, at best, to gay camp. The former "dismantles the construction 'woman' and challenges male sexuality as the universal norm," and thus far more radically subverts the social relations of gender and gender ideology in everyday life.[55]

Teresa de Lauretis, in her 1988 "Sexual Indifference and Lesbian Representation", discussed other problems confronting lesbian theory and performance that she felt had so far been inadequately addressed by such theorists as Davy, Case, and Dolan. One was the difficulty of defining an autonomous form of female sexuality and desire free of the Platonic tradition and of the tendency to posit a unified viewer. The other was the attempt to alter the frame of visibility, of *what can be seen*.[56] Each of these areas of concern in fact received increasing attention in performance and theory of the 1990s.

The process of changing what can be seen, of giving visibility as well as voice to such hitherto excluded phenomena as female desire or female subjectivity, has in fact been a central concern of much feminist performance and performance theory, and of lesbian theory and performance in particular. The playful destabilizing of sexual roles performed by Split Britches or the exposure of the passive (male) spectator and the return of his gaze by Knox or Finley provide two quite different strategies for this, and tie modern feminist performance to the familiar concerns of "visibility politics," which have often involved various forms of what might be called social or public performance.

Strategic essentialism and the politics of representation

Each of the performers and spectatorial communities representing positions other than the dominant ones in the culture has been forced in some way to negotiate the same tension between a desire to provide a grounding for effective political action by affirming a specific identity and subject position and a desire to undermine the essentialist assumptions of all cultural constructions. This is the dilemma at the heart of Butler's work, the problem that the acting self comes into being only through pre-existing and oppressive cultural constructions. Intervention in the operations of the dominant symbolic systems—linguistic, theatrical, political, psychological, performative—seems to require, in Elin Diamond's words: "assuming a subject position, however provisional, and making truth claims, however flexible, concerning one's own representations." This operation has been appropriately termed "strategic essentialism."

It is important to bear in mind, however, particularly when speaking of recent performance, that clear-cut examples of neither an essentialist performance of identity nor a materialist performance dealing with the process of identity construction is as common as some sort of negotiated space between these positions. Most modern politically oriented performance is flexible very much in the manner that Diamond suggests, slipping back and forth between claiming an identity position and ironically questioning the cultural assumptions that legitimate it. The goal is not to deny identity but on the contrary to provide, through performance, alternate possibilities for identity positions outside those authenticated by conventional performance and representation.

Many of the performance artists discussed in the previous chapter as operating with identity, especially those working in the late 1980s and 1990s, are in fact best understood in the terms Diamond proposes: as simultaneously engaged in the claiming of and the ironic commentary upon identity positions. This complex and ambiguous performance strategy is particularly marked in the work of performance artists exploring their identity as members of culturally, ethnically, or sexually marginalized communities. Tim Miller's gay identity is central to his work, but so is a constant attention to making the audience aware of how this "identity" is being constructed through performance—a strategy David Román calls reminiscent of Brechtian distancing.[57] In a strategy very similar to Diamond's "mimicry" or to lesbian masquerade, the live performances of artists like Miller seek to produce "a chaotic multiplicity of representations, representations that displace, by the very process of proliferation, the authority of a conservative ideology of sexual hegemony, AIDS myths, and sexual practices."[58] This playing with performativity and excess of representation has been especially marked in the case of performers like Gómez-Peña, who consciously position themselves on representative "borders," and whose work will be discussed presently.

Recent political performance

Performance and the community

With the end of the Vietnam War the flourishing political street theatre of the 1960s and early 1970s diminished, but never entirely disappeared. In the 1980s political performance became more common again, fueled in the United States and in England by the materialism, the apparent indifference to the underprivileged and to the environment, and the suspicion of leftist or decadent elements in the arts that were features of Reagan-era America and Thatcher-era England. Solo performance, much of it engaging these themes, continued to appear, but the 1980s also saw a strong development of community-based engaged drama as performance artists took the interests and skills developed in the previous decade out to respond to the concerns of particular, usually disadvantaged, communities and not infrequently to bring members of those communities into the performances themselves. The way had been prepared for such activity by a number of politically engaged directors in Europe and Latin America during the 1960s and 1970s, such as Joan Littlewood and her Theatre Workshop in England,[59] Armand Gatti's interest in theatre for French workers and his colleague Gino Zampieri's Workers' Collective Theatre in Zurich,[60] and especially Augusto Boal's Form Theatre and Theatre of the Oppressed, developed in Argentina during the 1970s and subsequently a model for politically engaged performance around the world.[61]

During the 1980s, as public awareness of the concept of performance grew, these sorts of politically oriented public actions, which would probably have been called guerrilla theatre or street theatre in the 1960s and were given such names as workers' theatres, theatre workshops, or populist theatres in the 1970s, came much more to be associated with the world of performance. Performance, now widely associated with social and political concerns, with a close and constantly renegotiated relationship with its audience, and with the manipulation of a wide variety of media, accommodated such activity very readily. This can be seen in a 1982 statement of "Intentions" issued by Welfare State, a leading politically oriented performance group in England in the early 1980s inspired in part by the concerns of the communities where it performed and in part by a belief that art should resist the over-production and consumerism of the developed countries. The goals of this group were both artistic and social:

1 To fuse boundaries between painting, sculpture, theatre, music and events.
2 To analyse the relationship between aesthetic input and its social context.
3 To explore non-naturalistic and visual performance styles.[62]

The company's best-known work, repeated several times in the late 1970s and early 1980s, was "The Burning of the Houses of Parliament," which punctuated current social concerns with a series of spectacular fire sculptures and featured giant figures representing Margaret Thatcher and Guy Fawkes, a Hell Mouth, and a huge conflagration finale.[63]

In 1985 John Malpede organized the Los Angeles Poverty Department (its acronym, LAPD, an ironic quotation of the initials of the well-known Los Angeles Police Department). Malpede was himself a performance artist, but LAPD was established as a performance collective composed of members of the downtown Los Angeles skid row population, addressing the needs and concerns of that community and utilizing performance to help that population understand, cope with and, it is hoped, improve their conditions.[64] This sort of collective performance as a kind of social therapy and empowerment, hearkening back to certain aspects of 1960s activism and influenced by the philosophy and practice of politically engaged practitioners of the 1970s, especially Augusto Boal, gained new importance from the mid-1980s onward. In San Francisco, for example, Rhodessa Jones created The Medea Project in 1992 as a "performance workshop" designed to increase the self-awareness and self-esteem of women in prisons by creating performance pieces based on their personal histories.[65]

Political performance at the end of the century

In a 1992 article in *Discourse*, Josette Féral, as part of an analysis of Rachel Rosenthal's 1991 performance piece *Pangea*, suggests a distinct difference between performance art in the early 1990s and that of two decades before:[66]

> In place of the image of an essentially instinctual subject—that of performance art of the seventies—performance art of the nineties substitutes the image of a subject who refuses to eliminate tensions between the self and history and between politics and aesthetics, and who reestablishes the complexities of enunciation. Where performance art in the seventies was simply refusing the representation of a real it tried to attain in its immediacy ... performance art in the nineties has renounced the play of illusion. It has chosen to return to the real as a construction of the political, and to show the real as necessarily bound to the individual.

This model is surely reductive, even in the specific case of the performer that Féral is discussing. Rosenthal's powerful and admittedly often autobiographical performance works of the 1970s, dealing with her childhood in Paris (*Charm*, 1977), her relationships with her half-sister, still living in Africa (*The Head of Olga K.*, 1977), and personal fears and obsessions (*The Death Show*, 1978) were by no means simply presentations of an abstract "instinctual" body, but very much explorations of a specific self in an historical context. As Una Chaudhuri has noted, Rosenthal's "presentation of self is always more ironic than nostalgic, always more interested in moving beyond the self than in simply expressing it."[67]

Nevertheless, Féral is correct in drawing attention to an increasing interest in the political dimensions of performance from the late 1980s onward. Many elements within the culture contributed to this. The cultural confrontations surrounding the NEA and conservative attacks on the arts in general brought the attention of both public and artists to the potentially close connections between performance and politics. This can be clearly seen in the post-1990 works of both Tim Miller and Holly Hughes. Miller himself has characterized his 1989 piece *Stretch Marks* as pulling him to "the

Figure 8.3 Rachel Rosenthal in *Traps*.

Source: Franklin Furnace and Rachel Rosenthal.

beginning of a personal-meets-political ACT UP worldview."[68] His six productions of the 1990s, from *Sex/Love/Stories* (1991) to *Glory Box* (1999),
contain, as always, personal and family memories, but invariably Miller has
built upon his experiences as a gay man in the age of AIDS, and of the political and cultural struggles of that era. The personal and the political come
particularly close together in *Glory Box*, dealing with the immigration laws
in the United States that will not allow Miller's Australian partner American citizenship. Early in the new century Miller announced his decision, on
these grounds, to leave the United States. Holly Hughes has addressed
even more directly the effects of the NEA controversy upon her career and
her performance, by developing a performance based on that experience,
her amusing and rueful *Preaching to the Perverted* (1999).

The growing awareness during the 1980s (of both performance artists
and theorists) of the social and cultural dynamics of performance led many

of them to move from the more straightforward performance of identity that, as Féral observes, marked much work of the 1970s, to an exploration of the process of representation itself. This emphasis had distinct cultural and political implications, since it raised the question of what is at stake both socially and politically in the performance of ethnicity, gender, or sexuality—for whom, by whom, and to what end the representation is taking place. Judith Butler tellingly articulated this position by recommending a move away from an attempt "to solve this crisis of identity politics," by concentrating on who and what wields the power to define identity, "to proliferate and intensify this crisis" and "to affirm identity categories as a site of inevitable rifting."[69] This concern, perhaps most fully articulated by theorists of feminist and gay performance, took on new urgency and new importance as more and more performance work appeared during the 1980s representing the concerns of various ethnic minorities and of less advantaged socio-economic groups.

Post-colonial perspectives

The rise of post-colonial theory opened other perspectives on the cultural and political dimensions of performance, as the performance came to be recognized not only in the operations of hegemonic political powers but, perhaps even more important, in resistance to those powers. Highly influential in the development of these perspectives were the essays published by Homi Bhabha in the late 1980s and early 1990s, and collected in his 1994 work *The Location of Culture*. His discussions of the colonialist use of stereotype and mimicry, especially the latter, has strong affinities with the term as it has been developed by such performance theorists as Diamond.[70] In the essay "Of Mimicry and Man," first published in 1984, Bhabha posits mimicry as a colonialist strategy, requiring the colonized to imitate the colonial's cultural articulations and modes of behavior. Their inevitable failure fully to embody this alien perspective in turn provides evidence of their lack and inferiority. However, Bhabha locates a "comic turn" within this colonialist use of representation, since the representing of the Other as an incomplete or undeveloped Same may also work against the process of domination. This opening is offered by the destabilizing carnival of mimicry, and the menace of its "double vision, which in disclosing the ambivalence of colonial discourse also disrupts its authority."[71] Mimicry's ability to subvert the operations of colonialism "from within" has been questioned in post-colonial theory as it has in feminist theory,[72] but it remains an important and influential concept and strategy.

Other post-colonial theory sought to find strategies of resistance to hegemonic discourses that were not so deeply implicated in those discourses themselves. An influential example of this approach has been the work of Frank Gilroy, who suggests that the model of "embodied subjectivity" found in Black musical culture might provide a kind of alternative to the generally textual-based models of colonial domination. He therefore proposed an attention to the production and reception of "neglected modes of signifying practices like mimesis, gesture, kinesis and costume" and such cultural expressions as "antiphony, montage, and dramaturgy."[73] This approach to performance as "embodied subjectivity" within cultural studies has striking similarities to the idea of performance as "embodied subjectivity" developed earlier in feminist theory by such writers as Irigaray and Kristeva.

Spiderwoman: mimicry and countermimicry

Echoes of both Diamond and Bhabha are clear in Rebecca Schneider's illuminating 1993 analysis of several productions by the Native American performers who have taken the name Spiderwoman. Spiderwoman productions such as *Reverb-ber-ber-ations* (1990), Schneider argues, have consistently used the disruptive critical power of mimicry for both feminist and post-colonial ends. She discusses Spiderwoman's restaging of "Snake Oil sideshows" (*Winnetou's Snake Oil Show from Wigwam City*, 1989) and similar "exotic" material as comic, subversive mimicry that:[74]

> adroitly played in the painful space between the need to claim an authentic native identity and their awareness of the historical commodification of the signs of that authenticity. Their material falls in the interstices where their autobiographies meet popular constructions of the American Indian.

Performance of this kind slips back and forth between "a firm declaration of identity" and parody of the social clichés that haunt that identity, insisting upon "an experience of the sacred *despite* the historical corruption and compromise of identities."[75]

In an even more complex "comic turn," Schneider suggests that Spiderwoman also utilizes what she calls "countermimicry." In the "Indian Love Call" sequence of *Sun, Moon, Feather* (1981), for example, the native American actresses:[76]

> don't act out the Indian parts—the virulent near-naked, dancing brave or the dark Indian Princess—they fight over who gets to be beringleted, vaseline-over-the-lens Jeannette MacDonald and who has to play stalwart, straight-backed Canadian Mounty Nelson Eddy. They are not re-playing, re-membering, or re-claiming native images but appropriating the appropriate.

Countermimicry and cultural representation

Some of the most complex and challenging recent ethnic performances have utilized mimic or countermimic strategies to deal directly with the process of cultural stagings or representations of ethnicity. James Luna's

Bessie-award winning performance/installation *The Artifact Piece* (1987) was created in San Diego's Museum of Man, and provided ironic commentary on its own ethnographic surroundings and their cultural functions. Luna placed himself on display, his body laid out in one case labelled with tags identifying scars inflicted during drunken fights. Another case showed his college degree, photos of his children, his arrest record, and his divorce papers, along with objects used in contemporary Indian ceremonies. Explanatory panels described with mock ethnographic objectivity a modern Indian life in which AA meetings have taken the place of traditional ritual ceremonies.[77]

A similar but even more complex display was one of the key examples of cultural performance art of the 1990s, the well-known *Two Undiscovered Amerindians Visit* (1992) of Guillermo Gómez-Peña and Coco Fusco, first offered in Madrid and London, then in Australia and the United States, and finally the subject of a fascinating video documentary.[78] Drawing upon the once popular European and North American practice of exhibiting indigenous people from Africa, Asia, and the Americas in fairs, shows, and circuses, Gómez-Peña and Fusco displayed themselves for three days in a golden cage as recently discovered Amerindians from an island in the Gulf of Mexico. They performed such "traditional tasks" as sewing voodoo dolls, lifting weights, and watching TV, were fed sandwiches and fruit, and were taken to the bathroom on leashes by guards. As with the Luna display, explanatory panels provided mock scientific information on the "Indians" and their "native culture." To the surprise of the performers, many viewers took their exhibition seriously, playing out a rich variety of accommodations or resistances to the display process itself and raising more complex questions about the cultural interpretation of this display than they had anticipated. What began in *Undiscovered Amerindians* as an ironic commentary on appropriation, representation, and colonial imaging through the playful reconstruction of a once popular and symbolically charged intercultural performance became a far more complicated and interesting phenomenon as the performers gradually realized that all of these concerns had to be freshly negotiated, often in surprising and unexpected ways, in every new encounter.

Cultural performance from the 1990s onward has been so varied and complex that no "typical" example of it could be cited, but the *Undiscovered Amerindians*, aside from being one of its best-known examples, also clearly demonstrates one of its central concerns. This is the dynamic involved when a specific performer encounters a specific culturally and historically situated audience. In earlier politically engaged performance art, the activity of the performer remained central in explorations of appropriation, display, and representation. The movement of performance art outward into more heterogeneous reception situations and the development of more nuanced theoretical concern about cultural contact has focused attention more on the interplay of performer and public in particular historical situations. As Jill Dolan has noted, the modern performer must recognize and

Figure 8.4 Coco Fusco and Guillermo Gómez-Peña in *Two Undiscovered Amerindians*.
Source: Nancy Lytle.

interact with a range of "spectatorial communities, separated and differenti-
ated by class, race, and ideology."[79]

Coco Fusco and Latin American performance

While Gómez-Peña has been involved in performance work from the beginning, Coco Fusco was an independent writer and curator in New York
whose Cuban background gave her a parallel interest in border crossings
and post-colonial performance and art. After her work with Gómez-Peña,
Fusco turned to performance themes that foregrounded the experience of
women in Latin American countries. The widespread social confinement
and control of women's bodies, and in some cases their literal imprison-
ment and even execution, is suggested in the portrayals of death and burial
found in many of these pieces. In *Better Yet When Dead* (1997) she was displayed unmoving in an ornate coffin; in *Votos* (*Vows*, 1999) she appeared as
a cataleptic female mystic; and in her first performances in Cuba, in *El
Ultimo Deseo* (*The Last Wish*, 1997) she was again laid out as a corpse in the
name of those dying in exile, and in *El Evento Suspendido* (*The Suspended
Event*, 2000) she represented the forgotten and oppressed by writing letters
of hope while buried in a vertical position up to her chest.[80]

In addition to appearing as a performance artist, Coco Fusco has
developed international awareness of the rich performance tradition in
modern Latin America as well as the related traditions in Africa and the
Eurocentric world in general by means of interviews with leading artists,
reports on performances, and thoughtful critical essays. The two collected

volumes of her own writings on Latin performance[81] and the 2000 *Corpus Delecti*, a collection of essays she edited in relation to a program of Latina performance she curated in London in 1996,[82] have made her one of the leading interpreters in both theory and practice of contemporary intercultural performance.

Another important contribution to the growing international interest in and documentation of Latino and Latin American performance has been the work of Diana Taylor, a Professor of Performance Studies at New York University. With Juan Villegas she edited in 1994 a major collection of essays on this subject, *Negotiating Performance*, important not only in its geographical range (from Argentina to North America) but also in the range of activities that the protean term "performance" allowed its contributors to address: public art, such as billboards and living installations; indigenous performances, such as the rituals of the contemporary Mayas; carnival; drag shows; and demonstrations of political resistance, such as the Argentinian Madres de la Plaza de Mayo.[83] At New York University Taylor founded the Institute for Hemispheric Research for Performance and Politics, which maintains a digital archive, organizes seminars, and provides internet connections between researchers, artists, and political activists across the Americas.[84]

In addition to New York University, the Institute involves Ohio State University and Trinity College in the United States; the School of Drama at the University of Rio de Janeiro, Brazil; the Department of Communications at Pontificia Universidad Católica del Perú in Lima; and the Centro Regional de Investigaciones Multidisciplinarias at the Universidad Nacional Autonoma de Mexico. The range of interests announced by the Institute suggests something of the scope of contemporary performance studies: performance and politics; conquest and colonialism; memory, atrocity, and resistance; globalization, migration, and the public sphere; and spectacles of religiosities.[85]

Guillermo Gómez-Peña's border crossings

It is quite appropriate that *Undiscovered Amerindians* is probably the best-known performance piece of the 1990s, not only because it touched upon so many of the central concerns of performance in that decade—including spectatorship and display, the touristic gaze and cultural appropriation, colonialism, racism, and the dynamics of cultural interaction—but also because it featured two of the best-known and most influential performance artists of the decade. The interests and performance work of Gómez-Peña and Coco Fusco touch upon many of the central concerns of performance at the end of the century, and are often among the most significant examples of those concerns.

Gómez-Peña had no idea he was doing "performance art" when, as a student at the University of Mexico in the 1970s, he simulated assaults on the metro, disrupted public meetings with absurdist questions, and showed up at public places nude or in disguise,[86] but he already clearly recognized the power of such activity to challenge existing structures. In Los Angeles in 1981, inspired by ASCO performances and such ritualized observances as Day of the Dead parades, he founded a performance group, Poyesis Genética, which, very much in the spirit of the 1980s, sought "to create an intercultural space in which to fuse and juxtapose the various artistic and performing traditions brought by the members."[87] During the mid-1980s Poyesis evolved into the Border Arts Workshop, with performances focusing on the physical and cultural border between Mexico and the United States—which would echo through all of Gómez-Peña's subsequent work. In addition to group performances at or crossing the border, in 1988 Gómez-Peña created his solo persona, Border Bruho, who toured throughout North America and Europe exploring border crossings "between cultures, communities, institutions, and territories of thought and action."[88] Border Bruho was succeeded in 1990 by "the Warrior for Gringostroika," himself a hybrid character who expresses the complex multicultural heritage of the Americas using high-tech and pop culture materials. Though each of these characters bears a single name, they, like Gómez-Peña himself, host a variety of different personalities, not so much imaginative extensions of the artist's own complex personality as his sensitive projections of cultural types and stereotypes reflecting current cross-cultural politics. "Depending on the context," he has observed, "I am Chicano, Mexican, Latin American, or American in the wider sense of the term. The Mexican Other and the Chicano Other are constantly fighting to appropriate me or reject me. But I think my work might be useful to both sides because I'm a interpreter. An intercultural interpreter."[89]

Between 1990 and 1995 Gómez-Peña collaborated with Coco Fusco on a series of projects, the best known of which was the *Undiscovered Amerindians*. Other major performances commented upon the museum showcasing of cultural artefacts (*Year of the White Bear*, 1992) and the multinational corporations' exploitation of ethnic talent (*Mexarcane International*, 1994–5). During these same years, Gómez-Peña also began to collaborate with Chicano performance artist Roberto Sifuentes. With Roberto and other collaborators, Gómez-Peña turned in the mid-1990s to a series of projects combining the earlier interest in ethnographic display and public cultural images with digital technology. Internet users were encouraged to help construct the "new mythical Mexican and Chicano of the '90s," and with the aid of thousands of respondents Gómez-Peña and his collaborators created a series of "ethno-cyborgs," beginning with *El Mexterminator* in 1995.[90] In 1998 computer-processed voices were added to the various ethno-cyborgs so far created, in a piece called *BORDERscape 2000*. The ethno-cyborgs have also appeared in film and video and are being studied by performance theorist Lisa Wolford for a projected book on Ethno-Techno Art, which is planned to be "a new, multi-centric way of writing about performance,"[91] just as Gómez-Peña and his collaborators have provided new, multi-centric ways of creating performance. By combining digital and live work they are crossing another performative border—one which, as the world crosses the temporal border into the new century, seems certain to play an increasingly important role in future performance.

Intercultural performance in a global context

The growing interest in intercultural performance between North and South America is only part of a growing attention to performative border crossings around the world. A major area of such interest is Southeast Asia, where the contact and mixing of cultures is particularly striking and complex. Significantly, the first conferences of Performance Studies International to be held outside of North America or Europe are scheduled to take place in New Zealand in 2003 and Singapore in 2004. Something of the range of modern intercultural studies is suggested by the 2002 book *Women's Intercultural Performance*, written by two Australian scholars, Julie Holledge and Joanne Tompkins. Among its wide-ranging considerations are performances of Ibsen's *A Doll's House* in modern Japan, China and Iran and *Antigone* in Latin American protest theatre; the ritual performances in 1994 of Kim Kum Hwa, a Korean mystic, on tour in Australia; dramas dealing with the intercultural space created by the African diaspora, and the censorship controversies aroused at international performance festivals by the appearance of bare-breasted Aboriginal women or by the sexually explicit work of Annie Sprinkle.[92] The range of this study, involving performance work in North and South America, Europe, Asia, Africa, and the Middle East, and some of the many areas of contemporary performance contact, such as international touring and festivals, suggests something of the complexity, challenge, and excitement of contemporary work in cultural performance.

Whether, as some theorists have suggested, social, cultural, and political concerns became central to performance in the 1990s or not, there is no question that the extent of such interest vastly increased in those years in both amount and range, addressing an enormous variety of ecological, social, economic and political concerns with an equally wide variety of performance strategies. As the twentieth century drew to its close, certain other cultural and theoretical terms at one time closely associated with the modern concept of performance, such as postmodernism or poststructuralism, were beginning to seem dated, but performance continued to renew itself, accommodating with equal ease to such new areas of interest as cultural studies and post-colonialism. Once United States and European centered, it expanded its investigations to performance in other cultures and, perhaps most productively, to performance in those border areas where cultures meet—possibly the most significant area of cultural study in the plurivocal contemporary world.

What is performance?

The term "performance" has become extremely popular in recent years in a wide range of activities in the arts, in literature, and in the social sciences. As its popularity and usage have grown so has a complex body of writing about performance, attempting to analyze and understand just what sort of human activity it is. For the person with an interest in studying performance, this body of analysis and commentary may at first seem more of an obstacle than an aid. So much has been written by experts in such a wide range of disciplines, and such a complex web of specialized critical vocabulary has been developed in the course of this analysis, that a newcomer seeking a way into the discussion may feel confused and overwhelmed.

Drawing to a close

The blurring of boundaries

As the attentive reader may note, the above are the words that opened the Introduction to this study. Between writing those words and rewriting them, I have completed most of the material in this study, and I assume that between reading and re-reading them the reader has also considered much if not all of that material. This experience has caused me, as it may perhaps also cause the reader, to consider what sort of performance was involved in this process of writing about performance. Throughout this study I have felt some uneasiness with attempting to capture in descriptive or historical terms so complex, conflicted, and protean a phenomenon as performance, and have been troubled, even more than in most writing, with material from one discrete "chapter" constantly slipping away to bond with material in others. By a web of stylistic pointers in the nature of "as we have seen," "as we shall see in a later chapter," "this will be later developed in more detail," and so on, the rather porous borders have been maintained in the interest of presenting a series of more or less internally coherent mappings of the fluid territory of performance. Even while carrying out this project, however, I recognized that in a fundamental way it ran contrary to the nature of the subject. Trinh T. Minh-ha, a Vietnamese-American who has written movingly and perceptively of the search of the modern exile and refugee to find an identity and a voice, tellingly articulates a key insight of performance and of postmodernism: "Despite our desperate, eternal attempt to separate, contain, and mend, categories always leak."[1]

As Geertz's classic 1983 essay "Blurred Genres"[2] suggested, traditional anthropological concerns with continuous traditions, singular and stable cultures, coherent structures, and stable identities has been largely replaced by a concept of identity and culture as constructed, relational, and in constant flux, with the porous or contested borders replacing centers as the focus of interest, because it is at these borders that meaning is continually being created and negotiated. This concept clearly reflects the shifting reality of the post-colonial world, with its new patterns of global communication, multinational corporations, and the continual movement and displacement of peoples. Cultural analyst Renato Rosaldo has written: "All of us inhabit an interdependent late-twentieth-century world marked by borrowing and lending across porous national and cultural boundaries that are saturated with inequality, power, and domination."[3] The "classic norms" of social analysis are inadequate to deal with the questions of "conflict, change, and inequality" characteristic of this new social world. As a result, social analysts "no longer seek out harmony and consensus to the exclusion of difference and inconsistency" and "cultural borderlands have moved from a marginal to a central place."[4] The increasing fluidity and porousness of social and cultural structures is being reflected more and more at the personal level, giving rise to a new sense of self—what Robert Jay Lifton has called "the protean self," reflective of the flux of the postmodern world. This new sort of self may retain "corners of stability," but it is primarily engaged "in continuous exploration and personal experiment."[5] Lifton in fact cites performance art as one of the tools of such experimentation.

One reader of an early draft of this study complained that I had not made it clear whether I considered performance to be a new discipline or an interdisciplinary field. I sought reactions to this question from the directors of the two leading performance studies programs in America, Joseph Roach, then at New York University, and Dwight Conquergood at Northwestern, and found their responses almost identical—that it was neither. "It is of course an antidiscipline," said Roach, "and we're about to witness its staging of the world's first antidisciplinary conference [in May, 1994]." In the opening address of that conference Conquergood spoke in almost identical terms, calling the trickster the "guru" of this new antidiscipline.

Resisting conclusions

Now, coming to that part of the study where some sort of "conclusion" is normally expected, I feel a new uneasiness. Performance by its nature resists conclusions, just as it resists the sort of definitions, boundaries, and limits so useful to traditional academic writing and academic structures. It may be helpful, then, to consider these observations as a sort of anticonclusion to a study of this antidiscipline, framed in the mode of self-reflexivity—a mode that characterizes much modern (or postmodern) performative consciousness, whether one is speaking of theatrical performance, social performance, ethnographic or anthropological performance, linguistic performance or, as in the present case, the performance of writing a scholarly study. James Clifford, in *The Predicament of Culture* (1988), speaks of ethnography's growing awareness that the field is "from beginning to end, enmeshed in writing," and that writing, like any form of representation, is never innocent, but is always involved "in specific historical relations of dominance and dialogue."[6] In his study of Julia Kristeva, John Lechte devotes an interesting section to Felman's analysis of Austin's *How to Do Things with Words*, noting Austin's humor and conscious ambiguity and calling his writing "an instance of *doing* philosophy which is as much performative as it is constative." Lechte gives this analysis another turn by considering what sort of "performance" is being carried out in Felman's own writing, in her utilization of the French analytic mode with its structural/poststructural interests and emphases.[7]

Looking back with such a reflexive consciousness to the opening paragraph both of this study and of this Conclusion, and considering what sort of performance it seems to be carrying out, I now see operating in it a clear and familiar performative strategy—the establishing of a mediating "authorial" as well as "authoritative" voice, posing itself as a useful interpreter between the "experts in a wide range of disciplines" and their "complex web of specialized critical vocabulary," and the "confused and overwhelmed" newcomer to the field (who is or is in part the implied reader) who will profit by such informed interpretation to further an "interest in studying performance." Attempting to engage the illocutionary and performative operations of my own writing brings home how similar the operations of this sort of scholarly discourse are to the traditional operations of other scholarly discourses, where what used to be regarded as academic objectivity and neutrality becomes something very different when it is regarded performatively by cultural critics like Clifford, Geertz, or Conquergood. From this perspective, such discourse is seen as being fundamentally governed less by objective reality than by rhetorical strategies. As Geertz has observed: "The capacity to persuade readers ... that what they are reading is an authentic account by someone personally acquainted with how life proceeds in some place, at some time, among some group, is the basis upon which anything else ethnography seeks to do ... finally rests."[8]

This recognition that the performance of scholarly research and writing is by no means the innocent or transparent process it may seem has not led to ethnographers abandoning such activity, any more than it has prevented me from writing this book, but what it has done is alert them (and me) to the illocutionary and perlocutionary implications of their discourse, to consider how knowledge is created, shared, and legitimized, how fields of study are created, developed, and their boundaries protected, how social, cultural, and personal identity is involved in every sort of performative behavior. The Introduction to a recent collection of essays, *Creative Anthropology* (1993), notes "the acceptance of one's own role in producing ethnographic writing," as "the object of analysis also becomes an analyzing subject, and vice versa."[9] Performance here becomes not only a subject for study but also an interpretive grid laid upon the process of study itself, and indeed upon almost any sort of human activity, collective or individual. As Stephen Tyler has observed in his analysis of "Post-modern Ethnography," the aim of its research is "not to foster the growth of knowledge, but to restructure experience," and its scholarly writing seeks "not to reveal purposes, but to make purposes possible"[10]—that is, to demonstrate how interpretive strategies and performative practices are themselves called into being. So the present study of performance, which I began (and which the reader may well have begun) as a project devoted to the "growth of knowledge," has perhaps better served the purposes of an introduction to modern performance if it has also restructured experience and perceptions, and increased an awareness of how performance operates "to make purposes possible."

Some overviews

Conquergood's survey of the field

I began this study with a discussion of how this concern with performance has changed the fields of anthropology and ethnography, and it seems appropriate that these summary remarks have also begun there, since theorists with backgrounds in these fields continue to provide some of the most stimulating and perceptive analyses of how performance operates in the activities of individuals, societies, and cultures. I know of no better general summary of the current issues and themes in this fecund area than Conquergood's 1991 survey article "Rethinking Ethnography: Towards a Critical Cultural Politics."[11] Conquergood argues that a "radical rethinking" of ethnography is indeed under way, developing from four intersecting concerns, which might be advanced also as central concerns of current performance theory. Much of what I have already said in this section about writing and performance is based on two of these concerns—an awareness of the constructedness of much human activity and of its implication in rhetoric and in social and cultural encodings, and a particular interest in liminal territory—in boundaries and borders. As Bakhtin observed: "the most intense and productive life of culture takes place on the boundaries."[12]

A third concern discussed by Conquergood refers even more directly to one of the fundamental concerns of modern performance: "the return of the body." Conquergood opposes ethnography, an "embodied practice" which "privileges the body as a site of knowing," to most academic disciplines, which follow a mind/body hierarchy favoring abstractions and rational thought over sensual experience.[13] After establishing itself as a "respectable" academic discipline by following the rationalist model, modern ethnography is at last returning to its proper concern with the total sensual experience of a culture. The postmodern ethnographic text, says Tyler, "will be a text of the physical, the spoken and the performed."[14]

In his 1989 survey of current questions in ethnography, *Paths Toward a Clearing*, Michael Jackson advocates a return to what William James called "radical empiricism," which rejects the boundary between observer and observed of traditional empiricism in order to gain a sense of the immediate, active, ambiguous "plenum of existence," studying "the *experience* of objects and actions *in which the self is a participant.*"[15] Radical empiricism, says Jackson, requires a focus on "lived experience," which is concerned not with identity and closure but with interplay and interaction, and with that peculiar doubleness that we have elsewhere noted in performance theory and performative consciousness that "encompasses *both* the 'rage for order' *and* the impulse that drives us to unsettle or confound the fixed order of things," that "accommodates our shifting sense of ourselves as subjects and as objects, as acting upon and being acted upon by the world, of living with and without certainty, of belonging and being estranged."[16]

Most significantly, for our purposes of this study, Conquergood's fourth concern of contemporary ethnography is "the rise of performance," involving a shift from viewing "the world as text" to "the world as performance." This shift, suggests Conquergood, opened up a number of new areas of questioning, which he groups under five headings. The first two of these have particularly engaged ethnographic researchers, and are in fact those closest to the traditional concerns of that field. First comes the question of cultural process: what are the consequences of thinking about culture as "an unfolding performative invention instead of reified system"? Second is a question of research praxis: what are the implications of viewing fieldwork as "an enabling fiction between observer and observed"?

The other three areas, less developed so far by the writers Conquergood cites, are also those areas of more general performative concern, where much work in theory and practice has been done by people not involved in and indeed not necessarily familiar with the performative emphasis of modern social science as represented by Conquergood's examples. These other three areas deal with hermeneutics ("what kinds of knowledge are privileged or displaced when performed experience becomes a way of knowing, a method of critical inquiry, a mode of understanding?"), scholarly representation ("what are the rhetorical [or institutional] problematics of performance as a complementary or alternative form of 'publishing' research?"), and politics ("how does performance reproduce, enable, sustain, challenge, subvert, critique, and naturalize ideology?")[17]

I know of no other summary of the orientations, concerns, and challenges of contemporary performance studies so comprehensive and sharply focused as Conquergood's essay, and this seems appropriate, since the convergence of the concerns and of the rhetoric of theatre-oriented and of cultural-oriented theorists like Turner was particularly important in the development of modern performance study, and anthropological and especially ethnographic writing remains highly influential in this field.

Performance Studies International

In my conclusion to the first edition of this work, written in the spring of 1995 I looked to the First Annual Performance Studies Conference, held in March of that year at New York University with the theme "The Future of the Field," for an indication of how this recently established field was then being currently configured and negotiated. The conference brought together representatives from all over America (though primarily from the New York area, Chicago, and California), as well as from England, Canada, France, Israel, Serbia, and Slovenia. Only a handful of papers at this conference dealt with material that was clearly anthropological or ethnographic in nature (indeed, one of the criticisms voiced at the final "wrap up" session was that such research had been under-represented). What might be considered more traditional "theatre" and/or dance subjects were distinctly more common (Brecht, Grotowski, Beijing Opera, experimental theatre, minstrel shows, classical opera and dance), although these were naturally oriented toward the performance aspect of such work. Conquergood's three questions dealing with hermeneutics, scholarly representation, and politics were all extensively represented at this conference, with politics of gender, of class, and of culture, being especially prominent. Two sessions of papers considered the implications for performance of the emerging world of cybertechnology.

As I write this new conclusion, at the beginning of 2003, the annual Performance Studies conference is looking toward its ninth year, and its shifting concerns and locations over this period provide one of the clearest indications of the growing importance and diversity of the field. The first four conferences of the new organization were held in the United States, three of them general conferences following the model of the inaugural conference and the fourth a smaller conference focused more specifically upon death and performance. In 1999, Performance Studies reorganized itself as Performance Studies International, holding its first conference outside the United States at the Centre for Performance Research in Aberystwyth, Wales.

The Aberystwyth conference, with the engaging title "Here Be Dragons," focused upon extending the boundaries of performance studies, exploring its interrelationship with such cognate fields as cultural studies, human geography, history, archeology, anthropology, and theatre studies. After a return to the United States in 2000 for a conference on "the visceral and the virtual" at the University of Arizona, the organization met in Mainz, Germany in 2001. For this first conference outside the anglophone world the focus was appropriately upon the issue of language and cultural exchange, addressing the operations of performance in such areas as interculturalism, multilingualism, and translation (although there were very few non-English papers). After a return to New York University, its first location, for the conference of 2002, Performance Studies International continued to develop its global network by planning for conferences in 2003 for New Zealand and 2004 for Singapore. As the organization expanded internationally it also sought new ways to understand and discuss performance in addition to the finished products of conventional conference panels and presentations. The New Zealand conference plans demonstrate this clearly, providing three days of fieldwork by research teams instead of conventional paper presentations, with a final two days of talks and performances developed from this field experience.

The spread of performance study

Although Performance Studies International and its conferences are the largest and most ambitious gatherings in this field, performance has become so attractive a field of study that there are countless smaller conferences on the subject constantly being held. Almost simultaneously with the New Zealand conference, Columbia University is holding a conference with the theme "Bodies in Space: Performance in the Middle Ages." The preliminary call for papers provides an excellent indication of the current range of possible performance investigation:[18]

> We invite proposals for papers exploring performance, in its broadest sense, in the Middle Ages. Papers may address performance in dramatic, literary, political, ecclesiastical, courtly, domestic, and civic spaces; representations of bodies and space in manuscript illustrations, hagiographies, dramatic productions, feasts, processions, markets, torture, and liturgies; the performance of race, class, and gender; the role of music, art, and architecture in ritual and ceremony; questions of methodology; local vs macaronic, historicism, dramaturgy; or examination of modern productions of medieval drama.

Clearly the general themes and questions associated with performance can be and are being productively applied to an almost unlimited range of human activities, as the impressive variety of these conference themes and locales clearly indicates. The emphasis upon "theatrical" performance and that sort of contemporary activity generally designated as "performance" or "performance art" which characterized performance studies conferences and collections of essays in the early 1970s has clearly given way, a decade later, to a bewildering variety of studies, covering almost every aspect of human activity. As Elin Diamond rightly observed in the introduction to her 1996 collection *Performance and Cultural Politics*: "performance discourse, and its new theoretical partner, 'performativity,' are dominating critical discourse almost to the point of stupefaction."[19]

There are many reasons for the great popularity of "performance" as a metaphor or analytical tool for current practitioners of so wide a range of cultural studies. One is the major shift in many cultural fields from the what of culture to the how, from the accumulation of social, cultural, psychological, political or linguistic data to a consideration of how this material is created, valorized, and changed, to how it lives and operates within the culture, by its actions. Its real meaning is now sought in its praxis, its performance. The fact that performance is associated not just with doing but with re-doing is also important—its embodiment of the tension between a given form or content from the past and the inevitable adjustments of an everchanging present make it an operation of particular interest at a time of widespread interest in cultural negotiations—how human patterns of activity are reinforced or changed within a culture, and how they are adjusted when various different cultures interact. Finally, performance implies not just doing or even re-doing, but a self-consciousness about doing and re-doing, on the part of both performers and spectators.

All of these concerns are reflected in such statements as MacAloon's distinctly "theatricalized" model of "cultural performances" as a kind of crucible for cultural self-examination: "more than entertainment, more than didactic or persuasive formulations, and more than cathartic indulgences. They are occasions in which as a culture or society we reflect upon and define ourselves, dramatize our collective myths and histories, present ourselves with alternatives."[20] The theatrical metaphor has become so significant here that if one did not know the source of this quotation, one might likely assume that the subject was traditional theatre.

Jon McKenzie's Perform or Else

In the Conclusion to the first edition of this book I cited Elin Diamond's 1995 collection *Writing Performances*, noting the already wide diversity of performance study it represented, with essays on dance, performance art, cultural performance, the performance of identity and of sexual roles, the performance of writing, and performative aspects of photography.[21] The critical use of performance and performativity as critical tools to discuss a huge range of cultural activity has generated since the mid-1960s many major books and collections, a number of them already discussed in this introduction to the field. Even with this almost overwhelming abundance of work, however, when I cast about, for this second edition, for a single book that would provide the best overview of performance at this moment, I had little difficulty in selecting Jon McKenzie's stimulating and ambitious *Perform or Else*. Upon its appearance in 2001, McKenzie's book immediately established itself as a seminal text in the field. Indeed, an entire panel was dedicated to it at the 2002 Conference of ATHE in San Diego.

McKenzie's dense study might be said to open up the field of performance substantially in two directions; horizontally and vertically. Horizontally, after a useful overview of modern work in performance as "the embodied enactment of cultural forces" (essentially the concern of the present book),[22] McKenzie then turns to extended parallel analyses of how the concept of performance has been developed in modern organizational structures and theory and in technological discourse and practice. The emergence of performance as a central concern in these three major intellectual communities, McKenzie argues, places performance at "the power matrix of the New World Order, an order in which disorder is put to work, where bodies perform both physically and digitally, where new and multiple agents are maintained by audiovisual archives and transformed by liminautic power circuits."[23] The potential repressiveness and normalization of this power matrix presents new challenges to resistant performance, which McKenzie develops by opening a vertical dimension to his analysis, which he calls "perfumance." Following Butler and Derrida, McKenzie locates "perfumance" (a coinage emphasizing its bodily element) in the citationality and thus inevitable slippage of performance. In McKenzie's words, perfumance arises from the "citational mist" of all performance, its "incessant dis(emodying)-(mis)naming," the "becoming-mutational of normative forces" and the "becoming-normative of mutant forces."[24]

Thus McKenzie's book, while sharply expanding awareness of how pervasive and central a concept performance has become in the contemporary intellectual world, even that far removed from the cultural surroundings within which the concept was developed, suggests that along with the migration of this powerfully symbolic term has migrated a whole cluster of cultural operations which provide potential insights into the workings of performance across disciplines, as well as its strengths, its limitations, and its challenges.

Coda: an apologia for theatre

The introduction to McKenzie's book makes the bold "speculative forecast" that "performance will be to the twentieth and twenty-first centuries what discipline was to the eighteenth and nineteenth centuries, that is, an onto-historical formation of power and knowledge."[25] His book indeed makes a strong case for the possibility that this era may well come eventually to be remembered as the "age of performance," as the late seventeenth and early eighteenth centuries became known as the "age of reason" after the dominating intellectual trope of the period.

As performance moves on its triumphal path through the discourses of cultural, social, organizational, and technological study, theatrical performance, scarcely mentioned by McKenzie (or by many of his sources) seems to recede more and more into the background of this evolving world-view. I would like to close this study, therefore, not with McKenzie's epic vision of a New World Order playing out the tensions between performance and "perfumance," but with a defense of the importance and uniqueness of theatrical performance (including traditional "theatre" but also, and perhaps particularly, that contemporary "performance" which is most closely related culturally to theatre). The importance of praxis in the definition of selves and of societies can hardly be denied; nor the importance of such specific cultural occasions as ritual ceremonies or the celebration of cultural myths or history; nor the grounding in praxis of both organizational and technological interest in performance. What is generally missing in all such concerns, however, is the specific blending of occasion and reflexivity that characterizes "theatrical" performance. Cultural performance may indeed function as a kind of metacommentary on its society, and may be best studied in that function by ethnographers, but neither performers nor spectators can be primarily characterized as consciously seeking out cultural performance as metacommentary on their culture. This is yet less true in the case of organizational or technological performance, even when performance disrupts and deconstructs this performance. In "theatrical" performance, however, such activity is constantly foregrounded. Performers and audience alike accept that a primary function of this activity is precisely cultural and social metacommentary, the exploration of self and other, of the world as experienced, and of alternative possibilities. Margaret Wilkerson's comments on this function of theatre are rhetorically very close to those of MacAloon on cultural performance: "Theatre provides an opportunity for a community to come together and reflect upon itself," serving not only as a "mirror though which a society can reflect upon itself" but also as an aid to shaping "the perceptions of that culture through the power of its imaging."[26] I would argue further that this mirror and shaping function has always been more specifically associated with theatre than with most other cultural performance, and moreover that this aspect of traditional theatre has become even more prominent in the development of modern performance art.

This makes "theatrical" performance, whether it takes the form of "traditional" theatre or of performance art, a special (if not unique) laboratory for cultural negotiations, a function of paramount importance in the plurivocal and rapidly changing contemporary world. Jill Dolan has perhaps most clearly articulated this mission in her 1993 survey article "Geographies of Learning: Theatre Studies, Performance, and the 'Performative.'"[27]

> Theatre studies' distinct contribution across disciplines can be a place to experiment with the production of cultural meanings, on bodies willing to try a range of different significations for spectators willing to read them. Theatre studies becomes a material location, organized by technologies of design and embodiment (through artisanry and actor training), a pedagogically inflected field of play at which culture is liminal or liminoid and available for intervention.

Near the end of this article Dolan notes that even though poststructuralist theorists have raised legitimate concerns about theatre's capacity to generate an untheorized "communitas," theatre (and performance art) "remains a site to which people travel to view and/or experience something together," to "engage with the social in physically, materially embodied circumstances."[28] The conscious choice to gather for this particular kind of embodied activity, and the expectation of what kind of experience this will be, are equally important. Dolan's use of "engage in" rather than "observe" or "contemplate" points to a key concern. Even when "theatrical" performance serves only as metacommentary on social and cultural circumstances, the particular consciousness in the framing of this activity sets it apart from much other unreflective cultural activity. As theatre moves more in the direction of performance art, a further elaboration of this consciousness often occurs. The audience's expected "role" changes from a passive hermeneutic activity of decoding the performer's articulation, embodiment, or challenge of particular cultural material, to become a much more active entering into a praxis, a context in which meanings are not so much communicated as created, questioned, or negotiated. The "audience" is invited and expected to operate as a co-creator of whatever meanings and experience the event generates.

Many sorts of activity—political rallies, sporting events, public presentations, costume balls, religious rites—are clearly performative and are widely and rightly recognized as such. Many other activities, among them writing, everyday social interactions, and indeed almost any social or cultural activity, can surely be considered performative even if they are not normally thought of in that way. McKenzie has challenged us to recognize that performance has also moved to a central position in modern thinking about business organization and technology. Clearly the concept of performance has been extremely useful in the analysis and understanding of all of these operations, but I would argue that one can still also usefully distinguish "theatrical" performance from its many recently discovered close relations and find in it not only a particular orientation but also a particular utility.

A variety of attempts have been made to define the special quality of this sort of performance. Some commentators have stressed its corporality, speaking of "embodied" performance, and contrasting it, for example, with film or the plastic arts, but not of course with the vast array of social and cultural performance. Others have somewhat similarly stressed the importance of "presence," an emphasis which, as we have seen, has been seriously qualified by the postmodern aesthetics of absence and by postmodern performance theory's own growing attention to citation.

Without denying the importance either of the physical body or of presence, two other related concerns seem to me even more important in defining the particular quality and power of "theatrical" performance. One is that such performance is experienced by an individual who is also part of a group, so that social relations are built into the experience itself. Alan Read lays stress upon this quality in his study of the ethics of performance. In religious experience, ritual, and therapy, Read suggests (and, he might have added, in the plastic arts and writing), the operations involve yourself and the performer, whereas the act of theatre is a tripartite one, involving yourself, the performer, and the rest of the audience, and bringing the experience inevitably into the realm of the political and the social.[29]

Closely related to this is another concern; that of the particular way we become involved in this sort of performance. It is a specific event with its liminoid nature foregrounded, almost invariably clearly separated from the rest of life, presented by performers and attended by audiences, both of whom regard the experience as made up of material to be interpreted, to be reflected upon, to be engaged in—emotionally, mentally, and perhaps even physically. This particular sense of occasion and focus, as well as the over-arching social envelope, combine with the physicality of theatrical perform-ance to make it one of the most powerful and efficacious procedures that human society has developed for the endlessly fascinating process of cul-tural and personal self-reflexion and experimentation.

Glossary

The following are technical terms that have appeared in this book with definitions suggesting their most common use within performance theory. When a term has been first used in this sense by a particular person or is most closely associated with a particular person, that name is given as well.

actionism (Valerie Export) a kind of **guerrilla theatre**, inspired by the work of the Vienna Aktionist painters, that directly challenges specific cultural assumptions and structures, particularly those involving gender roles.

actual (Richard Schechner) a certain kind of event that stresses its involvement in the present instant even while often invoking material from elsewhere.

agon (Roger Caillois) one of the fundamental activities in human play, from the Greek word for "contest" or "conflict," thus the working out of the encounter of two opposing forces or concepts.

alea (Roger Caillois) or "chance," referring to the spontaneous, improvised quality of play.

attitudes an eighteenth-century solo entertainment which suggested emotions and evocations of classical art by the artist's poses and movements. See **tableaux vivants**.

behavior rehearsal (David Kipper) also called **behaviorodrama** and **replication therapy** a strategy of psychoanalytic therapy which uses theatrical rehearsal as a model for improving social/psychological skills. See **psychodrama**.

biomechanics (Vsevolod Meyerhold) a system of actor training, inspired by the study of efficient movements in work by Frederick Winslow Taylor, which seeks the most efficient and total physical control of the body as a machine.

body art art in which the body of the artist is both the subject and object of the work.

bricolage French term for the process of improvising solutions to problems by putting together whatever materials happen to be at hand. Applied by some **social constructionists** to the improvising of social behavior.

bruitism (Richard Huelsenbeck) an exploration of the expressive qualities of non-musical sound treated as music, one of the concerns of **Dada** and of futurism.

camp (Susan Sontag) exaggerated, consciously parodic role-playing, particularly associated with homosexual performance.

carnivalization (Mikhail Bakhtin) the process of providing a time and place within a culture when normal rules and accepted patterns of behavior are suspended in order to experiment with alternative possibilities.

citation (John Austin) the reference in language to previous use of the same linguistic material in a different specific context. See **iterability**.

comic turn (Homi Bhabha) the tendency within colonialism's system of representation to undermine presentations of dominated outsiders because of the destabilizing processes in mimicry. See **mimicry, countermimicry, carnivalization**.

communitas (Johan Huizinga) the feeling a spirit of totality or togetherness in a cultural group.

competence (Noam Chomsky) in linguistic theory, the general knowledge of the structure of a language, as opposed to "performance," the actual individual application of this knowledge.

conceptual art (Marcel Duchamp) art which directs special attention to the process of its creation, often stressing the use of unconventional materials.

constative (John Austin). See **speech-act**.

contextual folklore (Richard M. Dorson) folklore studies that are concerned less with specific texts than with the functions that text performs in a particular cultural situation.

conversational implicature (H.P. Grice) the unspoken contract between a speaker and hearer in a speech situation which allows communication to take place.

Cooperative Principle see **conversational implicature**

countermimicry (Rebecca Schneider) the imitation of the performance cliches of a dominant group by those dominated as a form of cultural resistance. See **mimicry, comic turn**.

creolization (James Clifford) the process of mixing and layering a variety of different cultures together.

cross-dressing see **drag**.

cultural performance (Milton Singer) particular organized units of activity or events within a society that involve a set of performers and an audience, including theatre and dance but also such social rituals as weddings and religious celebrations.

Dada (Tristan Tzara and others) nihilistic movement in the arts that flourished chiefly in France, Germany and Switzerland during and after the First World War.

deconstruction (Jacques Derrida) the critical process of revealing the contradictions and counter-movements within any intellectual construct or system which have been hidden in order to give that construct the appearance of unity and totality.

deep play and **shallow play** (Clifford Geertz) performative activity in which the participants reflect upon the assumptions of their own culture—in a more distanced and less serious manner in **shallow play**, and in a manner that may lead to serious challenge to those assumptions and perhaps to a change in them in **deep play**. See **social drama**.

dialogism (Mikhail Bakhtin) the characteristic of structures or texts that contain multiple messages and are open to change according to context, as opposed to **monologism**.

différance (Jacques Derrida) a term combining "difference" and "deferring," suggesting that feature in signs which prevents them from ever settling into a final, fixed meaning.

discourse (Jean-François Lyotard) the general structure in a narrative which allows it to communicate a meaning. Similar to Saussure's **langue** in language analysis.

double-coding (Charles Jencks) the combining in postmodern architecture of disparate elements, some of which will appeal to experts in the field and others to a more general public.

drag performance involving cross-dressing, or assuming the clothing and attitudes associated by one's culture with the other sex.

dramatism (Kenneth Burke) the analytical study of the strategies by which individuals attempt to influence by their actions the opinions or actions of others.

énoncé the structure which governs the way an act of speaking is articulated. See **langue**.

énonciation a particular act of speaking in a particular situation. See **parole**.

essentialist the position, in feminist theory, which argues that women's expression is biologically determined and thus essentially different from that of men, as opposed to **materialist**.

ethnography descriptive anthropology.

ethnomethodology (Harold Garfinkel) a study of the methods by which people create their individual patterns of social action. See **social constructionism**.

eurythmics (Emile Jaques-Dalcroze) a system of body control achieved by a combination of gymnastic exercises and music.

fabrication (Erving Goffman) the situation in which one of more individual consciously manipulate a **strip of experience** in order to mislead others.

figure (Jean-François Lyotard) a specific example of narration, similar to Saussure's **parole** in language analysis.

flow (Mihaly Csikszentmihalyi) the sensation felt in creative, playful, or religious experience when the normal process of intellectual reflection is suspended in the pleasure of the present moment.

frame, framing (Gregory Bateson and Erving Goffman) any device or convention which allows certain messages or symbols to be set apart and considered to have a special relationship to everyday reality.

front (Erving Goffman) the various elements such as setting, costume, voice, gesture, and so on that support the performance of a social role.

futurism (Filippo Marinetti) avant-garde artistic movement of the early twentieth century which emphasized change, speed, technical progress, and the rejection of traditional art forms.

ghosting (Marvin Carlson) the external associations evoked by the reappearance in the theatre of elements previously experienced in other contexts, such as a known actor in a new role.

guerrilla theatre (R.G. Davis) popular theatre performed in public spaces to bring political messages to its audiences.

habitus (Pierre Bourdieu) the embodied rituals of everyday life through which a culture sustains belief in its own structure and operation.

happening (Allen Kaprow) a performance event stressing physical, decontextualized activity.

hegemony the tendency of dominant cultural structures to suppress alternative voices within their domain in an attempt to enforce an impression of unity.

identity-thinking (Theodor Adorno) the culturally generated attempt to keep human activity consistent and predictable. See **negative dialectic**.

ilinx (Roger Caillois) or "vertigo," referring to the tendency of play to destabilize the normal structures of perception.

illocutionary acts (John Austin) acts of speaking that inform, assert, or in other ways act upon the speech situation, distinguished from **locutionary acts**, which simply refer to something, or **perlocutionary acts**, which seek some particular effect upon the hearer. See **speech-acts**.

index (Charles Pierce) a particular kind of sign which is closely related to what it represents. See **semiotics**.

interpretive communities see **speech-act communities**.

iterability (Jacques Derrida) the characteristic of language acts that allows them, while each occurring in a unique situation, still to echo similar previous language acts and thus be understood.

keying (Erving Goffman) the process in which a **strip of experience** is placed in a new context which gives it a different meaning.

langue (Ferdinand de Saussure) the general organizing principles of a language (see **competence**), as opposed to **parole**, the use of these principles in individual acts of speaking.

life art art presenting fragments of everyday experience for the contemplation of an audience.

liminal (Arnold Van Gennep) situated in a transitional state between two established positions or social configurations, the characteristic of the middle position in a **social drama**. See **liminoid**, **social dramas**.

liminoid (Victor Turner) a more restricted and individual form of the **liminal**, more characteristic of modern industrialized societies, with less clear and widely accepted cultural practices than traditional societies. Theatre, play, and recreation are **liminoid** activities. See **liminal**.

locutionary acts (John Austin)   See **illocutionary acts**.

masquerade (Mary Ann Doane)   the process of revealing the arbitrariness or constructed quality of some accepted cultural product, such as gender roles, by imitating it in an exaggerated fashion. See **mimicry**, **camp**.

materialist   the position, in feminist theory, which argues that women's expression is culturally determined and thus open to modification, as opposed to **essentialist**.

Merzbühne (Karl Schwitters)   an early twentieth-century experiment with total theatre, mixing objects and human actions, sound and lighting effects.

metacommunication   information provided to a reader or viewer that is not primarily concerned with communicating content but with calling attention to the medium which carries that content. See **framing**, **ostentation**.

metanarratives (Jean-François Lyotard)   large structures of meaning which provide cultures with general organizing principles.

mimicry (Luce Irigaray)   in response to Plato's concept of **mimesis**, or imitation, an excessive multiplication of similar alternatives in order to undermine the concept of a single, monolithic Truth.

miming (Herbert Rapaport)   the strategy of certain contemporary artists like Laurie Anderson to undermine presumably monolithic cultural patterns of belief by expressing hidden alternative variations within them. See **mimicry**.

minstrelsy   American popular entertainment of the nineteenth century in which White actors in blackface performed songs, dances, and comic routines, usually parodying supposed actions of Blacks.

monologism (Mikhail Bakhtin)   the characteristic of structures or texts that emphasizes a singular message unaffected by context, as opposed to **dialogism**.

montage (Sergei Eisenstein)   the effect achieved in theatre or film by the cumulative juxtaposition of images.

negative dialectic (Theodor Adorno)   a pattern of thinking that recognizes the continual resistance in human activity to set patterns. See **identity-thinking**.

non-matrixed performance (Michael Kirby)   performance lacking the traditional orienting features of drama, such as a specific represented time, place, character role, and so on. See **non-semiotic**.

non-semiotic performance (Michael Kirby)   performance that by the presenting of open-ended material without a specific meaning encourages attention to the meaning-making process itself.

ostentation (Umberto Eco)   the process of displaying an object or message in such a way as to call attention to it as a bearer of meaning.

parole (Ferdinand de Saussure)   individual and unique acts of speaking, as opposed to **langue**, the general principles governing these acts. See **utterance**.

performant function (Jean Alter) that aspect of performance which seeks to impress the spectator with a display of skill.

performative (John Austin) see **speech-act**.

performativity (Judith Butler) the quality of being created and sustained by repeated performance, particularly in relation to gender roles.

perlocutionary acts (John Austin) see **illocutionary acts**.

persona performance the presentation of alternative selves to audiences.

phenomenology the study of the operations of awareness and of the perception of the physical world.

pragmatics (Charles Morris) in linguistics, the study of the specific social dynamics of particular uses of language.

psychodrama (Jean Moreno) a strategy of psychoanalytic therapy which uses role-playing and staging of scenes in order to provide patients with new psychological insights. See **behavior rehearsal**.

psychosemiotics (Sue-Ellen Case) the male-oriented system of performance reception which offers the female figure as a sign to be interpreted according to the desire of a male spectator.

recipe knowledge (Alfred Schutz) an improvised provisional collection of guides to social action assembled by individuals, as opposed to the sort of established and consistent patterns Eric Berne called **scripts**. See also **social constructionism**, **bricolage**.

referential function (Jean Alter) that aspect of performance which communicates a message to the spectator. See **performant function**.

restored behavior (Richard Schechner) activity consciously separated from the person doing it, most commonly a **strip of experience** offered as if it is being quoted from elsewhere, as in ritual, theatre and other role-playing. See **keying**.

script (Eric Berne) a normative pattern of social activity repeated, possibly with variations, by individual members of a culture.

semiotic (Julia Kristeva) the poetic and physical language of the mother, emphasizing the flow of experience over discursive meaning, as opposed to **symbolic**.

semiotics (Ferdinand de Saussure) the study of signs, culturally generated units of meaning, and how they operate in society.

shallow play see **deep play**.

sign a word, object, or movement that stands for something else. See **semiotics**.

site-specific theatre performances created to be performed in, and often inspired by, a single specific location with particular historical, cultural, or spatial associations.

social constructionism (P.L. Berger and T. Luckman) the theory of social action which argues that people behave in society not according to established patterns of actions (see **scripts**) but by improvising behavior by assembling fragments of discontinuous material. See **recipe knowledge**.

social dramas (Victor Turner) repeated structures of action by which societies react to challenges to the established order. Faced with such a challenge the society enters a **liminal** (or transitional) state in which ordinary rules and practices are relaxed, and emerges from this into reintegrated state in which the challenge is absorbed or rejected. See **liminal**.

sociolinguistics the scientific study of language in its social or cultural context.

speech-act (John Austin) a speaking situation in which the words spoken do not simply assert, but perform some action. A speech of this kind Austin called **performative**, as opposed to the tradition idea of speech as assertion, which he called **constative**. See also **illocutionary acts**.

speech-act communities (Stanley Fish) groups of people who interpret the meaning of speech-acts in essentially the same way. Also called **interpretive communities**.

strategies (Michel de Certeau) institutionalized **scripts** or patterns of action that serve as general guides to social behavior.

strip of behavior (Richard Schechner) a sequence of human activity selected as raw material for another purpose, such as a performance.

strip of experience (Erving Goffman) a sequence of human activity set apart for analysis.

surrealism (André Breton) early twentieth-century artistic movement, strongly influenced by Freud, which looked to the unconscious as the grounding of imaginative work.

symbolic (Julia Kristeva) the logical and discursive language of the father, the traditional operations of language, as opposed to **semiotic**.

tableaux vivants "living pictures," posed scenes suggesting paintings or classic statuary, a popular form of entertainment during the nineteenth century. See also **attitudes**.

tactics (Michel de Certeau) the specific instances of behavior improvised by individuals in particular social situations. See **social constructionism**.

Tanztheater movement in modern German dance that draws more upon theatrical gesture and the movements of everyday life than upon the traditional vocabulary of dance in its compositions.

tellable (William Labov) referring to speech material that represents states of affairs that are considered unusual or contrary to expectations.

theatre of images (Bonnie Marrenca) theatre emphasizing visual perception over narration, such as the work of Robert Wilson.

theatre of mixed means (Richard Kostelanetz) theatre emphasizing the use of various media, such as taped sound, films, and video.

utterance (Mikhail Bakhtin) a specific and unique act of speaking set in its unique context. See **parole**.

walkabout a form of British performance in which a costumed performer improvises relationships with the general public.

Notes

Introduction

1 W.B. Gallie, *Philosophy and the Historical Understanding*, New York, Schocken Books, 1964, pp. 187–8.
2 Mary S. Strine, Beverly Whitaker Long, Mary Frances Hopkins, "Research in Interpretation and Performance Studies: Trends, Issues, Priorities," in Gerald Phillips and Julia Wood (eds), *Speech Communication: Essays to Commemorate the Seventy-Fifth Anniversary of the Speech Communication Association*, Carbondale, Ill., Southern Illinois University Press, 1990, p. 183.
3 Erik MacDonald, *Theater at the Margins: Text and the Post-Structured Stage*, Ann Arbor, Mich., University of Michigan Press, 1993, p. 175.
4 Diane Spencer Pritchard, "Fort Ross: From Russia with Love," in Jan Anderson (ed.), *A Living History Reader*, vol. 1, Nashville, Tenn., American Association for State and Local History, 1991, p. 53.
5 Like most uses of performance, this one has been challenged, particularly by the noted semiotician of circus, Paul Bouissac. Bouissac argues that what seems to be performance is actually an invariable natural response to a stimulus provided by a trainer, who "frames" it as performance. In Bouissac's words, the animal does not "perform," but "negotiates social situations by relying on the repertory of ritualized behavior that characterizes its species." ("Behavior in Context: In What Sense Is a Circus Animal Performing?" in Thomas Sebeok and Robert Rosenthal (eds), *The Clever Hans Phenomenon: Communication with Horses, Whales, Apes, and People*, New York, New York Academy of Sciences, 1981, p. 24). This hardly settles the matter. As we shall see, many theorists of human performance could generally accept Bouissac's alternate statement, and moreover anyone who has trained horses or dogs knows that, even accounting for an anthropomorphic bias, these animals are not simply "negotiating social situations" but are knowingly repeating certain actions for physical or emotional rewards—a process that, to me at least, seems to have important features in common with human performance.
6 Richard Schechner, *Between Theater and Anthropology*, Philadelphia, Pa., University of Pennsylvania Press, 1985, pp. 35–116.
7 David Román, *Acts of Intervention: Performance, Gay Culture, and AIDS*, Bloomington, Ind., Indiana University Press, 1998, xvii.

I The performance of culture

1 Richard Schechner, "Performance and the Social Sciences," *The Drama Review* 1973, vol. 17, p. 3.
2 Georges Gurvitch, "Sociologie du théâtre," *Les lettres nouvelles*, 1956, vols 34–6, p. 197.
3 Dell Hymes, "Breakthrough into Performance," in Dan Ben-Amos and Kenneth

S. Goldstein (eds), *Folklore: Performance and Communication*, The Hague, The Netherlands, Mouton, 1975, p. 13.

4 Richard Schechner, *Between Theater and Anthropology*, Philadelphia, Pa., University of Pennsylvania Press, 1985, p. 35.

5 John J. MacAloon, "Introduction: Cultural Performances, Culture Theory," in John J. MacAloon (ed.), *Rite, Drama, Festival, Spectacle*, Philadelphia, Pa., Institute for the Study of Human Issues, 1984, p. 9.

6 William H. Jansen, "Classifying Performance in the Study of Verbal Folklore," in *Studies in Folklore in Honor of Distinguished Service Professor Stith Thompson*, Bloomington, Ind., Indiana University Press, 1957, p. 110.

7 Milton Singer (ed.), *Traditional India: Structure and Change*, Philadelphia, Pa., 1959, p. xii.

8 Ibid., p. xiii.

9 Richard M. Dorson (ed.), *Folklore and Folklife, An Introduction*, Chicago, Ill., 1972, p. 45.

10 Hymes has developed this idea in a number of writings of the 1960s and 1970s, but see especially his "Introduction Toward Ethnographies of Communication" in *American Anthropologist*, 1964, vol. 66, pp. 1–34.

11 Ben-Amos and Goldstein, "Introduction," *Folklore: Performance and Communication*, p. 4.

12 Roger D. Abrahams, "Introductory Remarks to a Rhetorical Theory of Folklore," *Journal of American Folklore*, 1968, vol. 81, p. 145.

13 Kenneth Burke, *The Philosophy of Literary Form*, New York, Vintage Books, 1957, pp. 3, 93.

14 Richard Bauman, *Story, Performance, and Event: Contextual Studies in Oral Narrative*, New York, Cambridge University Press, 1986, p. 3.

15 Bauman, *Verbal Art as Performance*, Rowley, Mass., Newbury House, 1977, p. 11.

16 Gregory Bateson, *Steps to an Ecology of Mind*, San Francisco, Calif., Chandler, 1972, p. 179.

17 Ibid., p. 188.

18 Dwight Conquergood, "The Institutional Future of the Field," address given at the First Annual Performance Studies Conference: The Future of the Field, New York City, 24 Mar. 1995.

19 Arnold van Gennep, *The Rites of Passage*, trans. M.B. Vizedon and G.L. Caffee, Chicago, Ill., 1960, p. 21.

20 Victor Turner, *Dramas, Fields, and Metaphors*, Ithaca, NY, Cornell University Press, 1974, p. 33.

21 Richard Schechner, "Approaches to Theory/Criticism," *Tulane Drama Review*, 1966, vol. 10.

22 Turner, *From Ritual to Theatre*, New York, 1982, pp. 90–1.

23 Richard Schechner, *Essays on Performance Theory 1970–76*, New York, Drama Books, 1977, p. 144.

24 Turner, *From Ritual to Theatre*, New York, Performing Arts Journal Publications, p. 74.

25 Turner, *The Ritual Process: Structure and Anti-Structure*, Chicago, Ill., Aldine Publishing Co., 1969, p. 22.

26 Brian Sutton-Smith, "Games of Order and Disorder." Paper presented to the Symposium "Forms of Symbolic Inversion" at the American Anthropological Association, Toronto, 1 Dec. 1972, pp. 17–19. Quoted in Turner, *From Ritual*, p. 28.

27 Turner, *From Ritual*, pp. 20–60.

28 Ibid., p. 28.

29 Clifford Geertz, "Deep Play: Notes on the Balinese Cockfight," *Daedalus*, 1972, vol. 101, pp. 1–37.

30 Bruce Kapferer, "The Ritual Process and the Problem of Reflexivity in Sinhalese Demon Exorcisms," in MacAloon, *Rite, Drama*, p. 204.

31 MacAloon, *Rite, Drama*, p.1.
32 Roger Caillois, *Man, Play, and Games*, trans. Meyer Barash, New York, Free Press, 1961, p.13.
33 Ibid., pp.9–10.
34 Johann Huizenga, *Homo Ludens*, New York, Beacon, 1950, p.8.
35 Caillois, *Man, Play*, p.23.
36 Huizenga, *Homo Ludens*, p.10.
37 Ibid., p.14.
38 Ibid., pp.12–13.
39 Mikhail Bakhtin, *Rabelais and His World*, trans. Helen Iswolsky, Cambridge, Mass., MIT Press, 1965.
40 Ibid., pp.122–3.
41 Ibid., p.131.
42 See, for example, Michael D. Bristol, *Carnival and Theatre*, New York, Methuen, 1985.
43 See, for example, Mary Russo, "Female Grotesques: Carnival and Theory," in Teresa de Lauretis (ed.), *Feminist Studies/Critical Studies*, Milwaukee, Wis., University of Wisconsin Press, 1986, pp.213–29.
44 Jacques Ehrmann, "Homo Ludens Revisited," trans. Cathy and Phil Lewis, in Jacques Ehrmann (ed.), *Game, Play, Literature*, Boston, Mass., Beacon Press, 1968, p.33.
45 Huizenga, *Homo Ludens*, p.35.
46 Ehrmann, "Homo Ludens," p.46.
47 Marshall Sahlins, *Islands of History*, Chicago, Ill., University of Chicago Press, 1985, pp.xi-xiii.
48 Colin Turnbull, "Liminality: a synthesis of subjective and objective experience," in Richard Schechner and Willa Appel (eds), *By Means of Performance*, Cambridge, Mass., Cambridge University Press, 1990, p.50.
49 Ibid., p.76.
50 Dwight Conquergood, "Performing as a Moral Act: Ethical Dimensions of the Ethnography of Performance," *Literature in Performance*, 1985, vol.5, p.9.
51 Michael Taussig, *The Nervous System*, New York, Routledge, 1992, p.4.
52 Taussig, *The Magic of the State*, New York, Routledge, 1997, p.79.
53 Stephanie Kane, *The Phantom Gringo Boat*, Washington, DC, Smithsonian Institution Press, 1994, p.20.
54 Katherine Pratt Ewing, *Arguing Sainthood*, Durham, NC, Duke University Press, 1997, p.106.
55 Corinne Dempsey, "Religion and Representation in Recent Ethnograpies," *Religious Studies Review*, 2000, vol.26:1, 38.
56 Stefania Pandolfo, *Impass of the Angels*, Chicago, Ill., University of Chicago Press, 1997, p.5.
57 Johannes Fabian, *Power and Performance*, Madison, Wis., University of Wisconsin Press, 1990, p.19, quoted in Kirsten Hastrup, *A Passage to Anthropology*, London, Routledge, 1995, p.82.
58 Hastrup, pp.82–3.
59 Eugenio Barba, "Introduction," *The Secret Art of the Performer*, trans. Richard Fowler, London, Routledge, 1991, p.8.
60 Barba, "Introduction," p.10.
61 Barba, "Pre-expressivity," *The Secret Art*, p.203.
62 Ibid., pp.187–8.
63 Hastrup, p.90.
64 Hastrup's report first appeared as an article in *Cultural Anthropology*, "Out of Anthropology: The Anthropologist as an Object of Dramatic Representation," (1992). A reframed and edited version appears as Chapter 7 in the book *A Passage to Anthropology*, pp.123–45.

65 James Clifford, *The Predicament of Culture: Twentieth-Century Ethnography, Literature, and Art*, Cambridge, Mass., Harvard University Press, 1988, pp. 15, 230.

66 It should be noted, however, that certain theorists and practitioners have resisted the argument that all intercultural performance involves such mixing. Peter Brook has sought a theatre which transcends particular cultures in an appeal to universal human conditions beyond any divisions of race, culture, or class, a type of project Patrice Pavis calls "transcultural," while Eugenio Barba, as we have seen, attempts to achieve universality in quite the opposite way, through a "pre-expressive" appeal to some common ground of all humanity before it is individualized into specific culture traditions. This approach Pavis calls "precultural." Patrice Pavis, *Theatre at the Crossroads of Culture*, trans. Loren Kruger, Routledge, London, 1992, p. 20.

2 Performance in society

1 J.L. Moreno, *Psychodrama*, New York, Beacon House, 1946.

2 See the special issue of *Tulane Drama Review* on Theatre and the Social Sciences, Summer, 1966, and articles by and about the work of Berne in the Summer 1967 issue.

3 Patrick Campbell and Adrian Kear, *Psychoanalysis and Performance*, London and New York, Routledge, 2001.

4 Nicolas Evreinoff, *The Theatre in Life*, trans. Alexander Nazaroff, New York, Brentano's, 1927, p. 24.

5 Ibid., p. 30.

6 Ibid., pp. 49, 99–100.

7 Kenneth Burke, *A Grammar of Motives*, Cleveland, OH, Meridian, 1962, p. xvii.

8 Barbara Kirshenblatt-Gimblett, "A Parable in Context: A Social Interactional Analysis of Storytelling Performance," in Dan Ben-Amos and Kenneth S. Goldstein (eds), *Folklore: Performance and Communication*, The Hague, The Netherlands, Mouton, 1975, pp. 105–30.

9 Erving Goffman, "On Facework: An Analysis of Ritual Elements in Social Interaction," *Psychiatry*, 1955, vol. 18, pp. 213–31.

10 Goffman, *The Presentation of Self in Everyday Life*, Garden City, NY, Doubleday, 1959, p. 22.

11 Gregory Bateson, *Steps to an Ecology of Mind*, San Francisco, Calif., Chandler, 1972, p. 183.

12 Goffman, *Frame Analysis*, Garden City, NY, Doubleday, 1974, p. 157.

13 Ibid., pp. 124–5.

14 Quoted in Umberto Eco, "Semiotics of Theatrical Performance," *The Drama Review*, 1977, vol. 21, p. 112.

15 Bert O. States, *Great Reckonings in Little Rooms: On the Phenomenology of Theater*, Berkeley, Calif., University of California Press, 1985, pp. 35–6.

16 Goffman, *Presentation*, p. 208.

17 Ibid., p. 65.

18 Dell Hymes, "Breakthrough into Performance," in Ben-Amos and Goldstein, *Folklore*, p. 18.

19 Friedrich Nietzsche, *Human, All Too Human*, trans. Marion Faber, Lincoln, Nebr., University of Nebraska Press, 1984, p. 51.

20 George Santayana, *Soliloquies in England and Later Soliloquies*, New York, Charles Scribner's Sons, 1922, pp. 133–4.

21 Jean-Paul Sartre, *Being and Nothingness*, trans. Hazel E. Barnes, New York, Philosophical Library, 1956, pp. 59–60.

22 Bruce Wilshire, *Role Playing and Identity*, Bloomington, Ind., Indiana University Press, 1982, pp. 280–1.

23 Wilshire, "The Concept of the Paratheatrical," *The Drama Review*, 1990, vol. 34, pp. 177–8.

24 Robert Ezra Park, "Behind Our Masks," *Survey Graphic*, 1926, vol. 56, reprinted in *Race and Culture*, Glencoe, Ill., Free Press, 1950, pp. 249–50.

25 William James, *The Philosophy of William James*, New York, Random House, 1925, p. 128.

26 Ibid., pp. 133, 152.

27 J.L. Moreno, *Psychodrama*, New York, Beacon House, 1946, vol. 1, pp. 13–15.

28 Ibid., pp. 153, 174.

29 T. Sarbin and V. Allen, "Role Theory" in G. Lindzey and E. Aronson (eds), *The Handbook of Social Psychology*, Reading, Ma., Addison-Wesley, 1968, vol. 1, p. 548. For a more extended development of this parallel, see M.R. Goldfried and G.C. Davison, *Clinical Behavior Therapy*, New York, Holt, Reinhart & Winston, 1976.

30 See David A. Kipper, *Psychotherapy through Clinical Role Playing*, New York, Brunner/Mazel, 1986, pp. 20, 22.

31 Eric Berne, *Games People Play*, New York, Grove Press, 1964, p. 61.

32 Berne, *Transactional Analysis in Psychotherapy*, New York, Grove, 1961, p. 116.

33 Talcott Parsons, *The Structure of Social Action*, New York, McGraw-Hill, 1937, p. 733.

34 Alfred Schutz, "The Problem of Rationality in the Social World," in *Collected Papers*, The Hague, The Netherlands, Marinus Nijhoff, 1964, vol. 2, pp. 72–3.

35 See, for example, Harold Garfinkel, "Common Sense Knowledge of Social Structure: The Documentary Method of Interpretation," in J. Sher (ed.), *Theories of the Mind*, New York, Free Press, 1962, pp. 689–713.

36 Michel de Certeau, *The Practice of Everyday Life*, trans. Steven F. Rendall, Berkeley, Calif., University of California Press, 1984, p. xix.

37 Ibid.

38 Wlad Godzich, "The Further Possibility of Knowledge," in Michel de Certeau, *Heterologies*, Minneapolis, Minn., University of Minnesota, 1988, p. viii.

39 Alan Read, *Theatre and Everyday Life: An Ethics of Performance*, London, Routledge, 1993, p. 1.

40 Goffman, *Frame Analysis*, p. 10.

41 Richard Bauman, *Verbal Art as Performance*, Rowley, Mass., Newbury House, 1977, p. 22.

42 Hymes, "Breakthrough," p. 18.

43 Richard Schechner, *Between Theater and Anthropology*, Philadelphia, Pa., University of Pennsylvania Press, 1985, p. 35.

44 Ibid., p. 137.

45 D.W. Winnicott, *Playing and Reality*, London, Tavistock, 1971, p. 12, quoted in Schechner, *Between Theater*, p. 110.

46 Marvin Carlson, "Invisible Presences: Performance Intertextuality," *Theatre Research International*, 1994, vol. 19, pp. 111–17.

47 Michael Quinn, "Celebrity and the Semiotics of Acting," *New Theatre Quarterly*, 1990, vol. 4, pp. 155–6.

48 Ibid., p. 46.

49 Ibid., pp. 110–11.

50 Derived in turn from Mircea Eliade's "reactualization," utilized in Schechner's 1965 *Rites and Symbols of Initiation* as a term to characterize the operations of regularly repeated tribal ceremonies in which each repetition was seen as possessing all of the power of an originary act.

51 Schechner, *Essays in Performance Theory*, New York, Drama Book Specialists, 1977, p. 18.

52 Alan Read, "The Placebo of Performance," in Patrick Campbell and Adrian Kear (eds), *Psychoanalysis and Performance*, London, Routledge, 2001, p. 147.

53 Sigmund Freud, "An Autobiographical Study," in J. Strachey (ed.), *Complete Works*, London, Hogarth Press, 1959, vol. 20, p. 28.

54 Sue-Ellen Case, *Feminism and Theatre*, New York, Methuen, 1988, p. 114.
55 Case, *Performing Feminisms*, "Introduction," Baltimore, Md., Johns Hopkins, 1990, pp. 1, 8.
56 Elin Diamond, "Refusing the Romanticism of Identity: Narrative Interventions in Churchill, Benmussa, Duras," in *Performing Feminisms*, p. 93.
57 In addition to "Refusing the Romanticism of Identity," these include "Mimesis, Mimicry, and the 'True-Real,'" *Modern Drama*, 1989, vol. 32, pp. 58–72; "Realism and Hysteria: Notes Toward a Feminist Mimesis," *Discourse* 1990–1, vol. 31(1), pp. 59–92; and "The Violence of 'We': Politicizing Identification" in Janelle Reinelt and Joseph Roach (eds), *Critical Theory and Performance*, Ann Arbor, Mich., University of Michigan, 1992, pp. 390–8.
58 See especially Freud's *The Ego and The Id* (1923), pp. 12–66 in *Complete Works*, vol. 19.
59 Diamond, "The Violence of 'We'," p. 396.
60 Diamond, "The Violence of 'We'," p. 397.
61 Ann Pelligrini, *Performance Anxieties*, London, Routledge, 1997, p. 69.
62 Freud, *The Interpretation of Dreams* in *Complete Works*, vol. 4, p. 149.
63 Translated into English as *The Newly Born Woman* by Betsy Wing, Minneapolis, Minn., University of Minnesota, 1986.
64 Translated into English as *The Enigma of Woman: Woman in Freud's Writings* by Catherine Porter, Ithaca, NY, Cornell University, 1985.
65 Diamond, *Unmaking Mimesis*, London, Routledge, 1997, esp. pp. 4–39.
66 Lynda Hart, *Between the Body and the Flesh: Performing Sadomasochism*, New York, Columbia, 1998, p. 127.
67 Hart, *Body and the Flesh*, p. 27.
68 Hart, *Body and the Flesh*, p. 76.
69 Freud, *The Ego and the Id*, in *Complete Works*, vol. 19, pp. 28–9.
70 Jacques Lacan, *Speech and Language in Psychoanalysis*, trans. Anthony Wilden, Baltimore, Md., Johns Hopkins, 1981, pp. 83–5.
71 Peggy Phelan, *Mourning Sex*, London, Routledge, 1997, pp. 4–5.
72 Cathy Caruth, ed., *Trauma: Explorations in Memory*, Baltimore, Md., Johns Hopkins, 1994.
73 Caruth, "Traumatic Awakenings," in Andrew Parker and Eve Kosovsky Sedgwick (eds), *Performativity and Performance*, London, Routledge, 1995, pp. 106–7. On Levinas and trauma, see especially Elisabeth Wever, *Verfolgung und Trauma*, Vienna, 1990.
74 Diane Taylor, "Staging Social Memory: Yuyachkani," in Patrick Campbell and Adrian Kear (eds), *Psychoanalysis and Performance*, London, Routledge, 2001, p. 231.
75 Judith Butler, *The Psychic Life of Power: Theories in Subjection*, Stanford, Calif., Stanford University, 1997, 170–1.
76 Butler, *Psychic Life*, 146.

3 The performance of language

1 Ferdinand de Saussure, *Course in General Linguistics*, trans. Wade Baskin, London, Fontana, 1974, p. 15.
2 Sue-Ellen Case, *Feminism and Theatre*, New York, Methuen, 1988, p. 115.
3 Jean-François Lyotard, *Les dispositifs pulsionnels*, Union generale d'éditions Paris, 1973, p. 96.
4 Josette Féral, "Performance and Theatricality," *Modern Drama* , vol. 25(1), p. 178.
5 An approach introduced in Habermas' "On systematically distorted communication," *Inquiry*, 1970, vol. 13, pp. 205–18, and much more fully developed in the two volume *The Theory of Communicative Action*, Boston, Beacon Press, 1984, 1987.
6 A critique of the transcendentalism and privileging of competence in Habermas

from the point of view of ethnography of communication may be found in Michael Huspek, "Taking Aim on Habermas's Critical Theory," *Communication Monographs*, 1991, vol. 58, pp. 225–33.

7 Dell Hymes, *Foundations in Sociolinguistics: An Ethnographic Approach*, Philadelphia, Pa., University of Pennsylvania Press, 1974, p. 79.

8 John Dore and R.P. McDermott, "Linguistic Indeterminacy and Social Context in Utterance Interpretation," *Language*, 1982, vol. 58, p. 396.

9 Mikhail M. Bakhtin, *Speech Genres and Other Late Essays*, trans. Vern W. McGee, Austin, Tex., University of Texas Press, 1986, pp. 88–9.

10 Ibid., p. 93.

11 Julia Kristeva, "Le mot, le dialogue et le roman," *Critique*, 1967, vol. 239, pp. 438–65.

12 Julia Kristeva, *Desire in Language*, Leon Roudiez (ed.), trans. T. Gora, A. Jardine, and L. Roudiez, New York, Columbia University Press, 1980, p. 79.

13 Ibid., p. 79.

14 John Austin, *How to Do Things with Words*, Cambridge, Mass., Harvard University Press, 1975, pp. 5–6.

15 Austin, "Performative utterances," in J.O. Urmson and G.L. Warnock (eds), *Philosophical Papers*, Oxford, Oxford University Press, 1979, p. 249.

16 Austin, *How to*, p. 109.

17 John R. Searle, *Speech Acts: An Essay in the Philosophy of Language*, Cambridge, Cambridge University Press, 1969, p. 16.

18 Ibid., p. 17.

19 Ibid., pp. 24–5.

20 Charles W. Morris, *Foundations of the Theory of Signs*, in the *International Encyclopedia of Unified Science*, vol. 1, no. 2, Chicago, Ill., University of Chicago Press, 1938, p. 30.

21 R.C. Stalnaker, "Pramatics," in D. Davidson and G. Harman (eds), *Semantics of Natural Language*, Dordrecht, D. Reidel, 1972, p. 35.

22 Julia Kristeva, *La révolution du langage poetique*, Paris, Seuil, 1974, p. 340.

23 Emile Benveniste, "Analytical Philosophy and Language," in *Problems of General Linguistics*, vol. 1, trans. M.E. Meeks, Coral Gables, Fla., University of Miami Press, 1971, pp. 236–8.

24 Jerrold J. Katz, *Propositional Structure and Illocutionary Force*, Hassocks, Sussex, Harvester Press, 1977, p. xii.

25 Ibid., p. 177.

26 Shoshana Felman, *The Literary Speech Act: Don Juan with Austin, or Seduction in Two Languages*, trans. Catherine Porter, Ithaca, NY, Cornell University Press, 1983, p. 35.

27 Ibid., p. 143.

28 Monique Schneider, "The Promise of Truth—The Promise of Love," *Diacritics*, 1981, vol. 11, p. 32.

29 John Lechte, *Julia Kristeva*, London, Routledge, 1990, p. 28.

30 Felman, *Literary Speech Act*, p. 94.

31 Austin, *How to*, pp. 71, 104.

32 Andrew Parker and Eve Kosofsky Sedgwick, "Introduction" to *Performativity and Performance*, London, Routledge, 1995, p. 4.

33 Parker and Sedgwick, "Introduction," p. 5.

34 Richard Ohmann, "Speech Acts and the Definition of Literature," *Philosophy and Rhetoric*, 1971, vol. 4, pp. 13–15.

35 Ohmann, "Literature as Act," in Seymour Chatman (ed.), *Approaches to Poetics*, New York, Columbia University Press, 1973, p. 104.

36 Stanley Fish, *Is There a Text in This Class?*, Cambridge, Mass., Harvard University Press, 1980, p. 218.

37 Fish, *Is There a Text*, p. 243.

38 Mary Louise Pratt, *Toward a Speech Act Theory of Literary Discourse*, Bloomington, Ind., Indiana University Press, 1977, p. viii.

39 Ibid., p. 136.

40 Ibid., p. 115.

41 Kristeva, *Desire in Language*, p. 75.

42 Ibid., p. 46.

43 Sandy Petrey, *Speech Acts and Literary Theory*, London, Routledge, 1990, p. 79.

44 Austin, *How to*, p. 9.

45 Teun A. van Dijk, *Text and Context*, London, Longmans, 1977, p. 182.

46 Ibid., p. 177.

47 Ross Chambers, "Le masque et le miroir: Vers une théorie relationnelle du théâtre," *Études littéraires*, 1980, vol. 13, p. 104.

48 Eco, "Semiotics," p. 115.

49 Chambers, "Le masque," p. 398.

50 Ibid., pp. 401–2.

51 Timothy Gould, "The Unhappy Performative," in Parker and Sedgwick (eds), *Performativity and Performance*, London, Routledge, 1995, pp. 19–44.

52 Joseph A. Porter, *The Drama of Speech Acts: Shakespeare's Lancastrian Tetralogy*, Berkeley, Calif., University of California Press, 1979, p. 161.

53 Ohmann, "Literature as Act," p. 83.

54 Branislav Jakovljevic, "Shattered Back Wall: Performative Utterance of *A Doll's House*," *Theatre Journal*, 2002, vol. 54, pp. 431–48.

55 Keir Elam, *The Semiotics of Theatre and Drama*, London, Methuen, 1980, p. 159.

56 Eli Rozik, "Categorization of Speech Acts in Play and Performance Analysis," *Journal of Dramatic Theory and Criticism*, 1993, pp. 117–32. "Plot Analysis and Speech Act Theory," in Gérard Deledalle (ed.), *Signs of Humanity: L'homme et ses signes*, Berlin, Mouton de Gruyter, 1992, vol. 2, pp. 1183–91. "Speech Acts and the Theory of Theatrical Communication," *Kodikas/Code*, 1989, vol. 12, pp. 1–2, 41–55.

57 Quoted in Rozik, "Plot Analysis," p. 1191.

58 Geoffrey N. Leech, *Principles of Pragmatics*, London, Longmans, 1983. Stephen C. Levinson, *Pragmatics*, Cambridge, Cambridge University Press, 1983. Teun A. Van Dijk, *Text and Context*, London, Longmans, 1977.

59 Rozik, "Theatrical Speech Acts," pp. 44–5.

60 Rozik, "Plot Analysis", p. 1187.

61 Rozik, "Theatrical Conventions: A Semiotic Approach," *Semiotica*. 1992, vol. 89, p. 12.

62 Herbert H. Clark and Thomas B. Carlson, "Hearers and Speech Acts," *Language*, 1982, vol. 58, p. 332.

63 Elias Rivers, *Quixotic Scriptures: Essays on the Textuality of Spanish Literature*, Bloomington, Ind., Indiana University Press, 1983.

64 Rivers, *Things Done with Words: Speech Acts in Hispanic Drama*, Newark, NJ, Juan de la Cuesta, 1986.

65 Among the recent examples: Jack Halstead, "Peter Handke's *Sprechstücke* and Speech Act Theory," *Text and Performance Quarterly*, 1990, vol. 10, pp. 183–93; Kathleen O'Gorman, "The Performativity of the Utterance in *Deirdre* and *The Player Queen*, in Leonard Orr (ed.), *Yeats and Postmodernism*, Syracuse, NY, Syracuse University Press, 1991, pp. 90–104; Stephen H. Fleck, "Barthes on Racine: A Different Speech Act Theory," *Seventeenth Century French Studies*, 1992, vol. 14, pp. 143–55; Günter Graf, "Sprechakt und Dialoganalyse—Methodenansatz zur externen Dramainterpretation" [on Lessing's *Emilia Galotti*], *Wirkendes Wort*, 1992, vol. 41, pp. 315–38.

66 Beverly Whitaker Long, "Editorial Statement," *Literature in Performance*. 1980, vol. 1, p. v.

67 James W. Chesebro, "Text, Narration and Media," *TPQ*, 1989, vol. 9, pp. 2–4.

68 Andrew Parker and Eve Kosofsky Sedgwick, "Introduction" to *Performativity and Performance*, London: Routledge, 1995, pp.1–2.
69 For those who wish to review the major documents in this controversy, Derrida's "Signature Event Context" first appeared in English in *Glyph*, 1977, vol.1, which also contained J.R. Searle's "Reiterating the Differences: A Reply to Derrida." Derrida's reply in *Glyph*, "Limited Inc abc..." and an "Afterword" were published together with his original article as *Limited Inc.*, Evanston, Northwestern University Press, 1988. Searle refused to give permission for his reply to be printed in this collection, but he continued the debate, most notably in his review of Jonathan Culler's *On Deconstruction* in the *New York Review of Books*, 27 Oct. 1983, pp.74–9.
70 Derrida, "Signature Event Context," in *Limited Inc.*, p.18.
71 Ibid., p.79.
72 Pierre Bourdieu, *Language and Symbolic Power*, ed. John B. Thompson, trans. Gino Raymond and Matthew Adamson, Cambridge, Mass., Harvard University Press, 1991, p.190.
73 Judith Butler provides a thoughtful and detailed discussion of the differences between Bourdieu and Derrida on this issue in her *Excitable Speech*, London, Routledge, 1997, pp.142–59.
74 Judith Butler, *Gender Trouble*, London, Routledge, 1990, p.25.
75 Judith Butler, *Bodies that Matter*, London, Routledge, 1993, p.95.
76 Butler, *Gender Trouble*, "Preface," 2nd edn, London, Routledge, 1999, pp.xiv–xv.
77 Butler, *Bodies*, p.10.
78 Butler, *Bodies*, p.244.
79 Judith Butler, *The Psychic Life of Power: Theories in Subjection*, Stanford, Calif., Stanford University, 1997, pp.170–1.
80 Butler, *Excitable Speech*, p.62.
81 Quoted in Linda Greenhouse, "An Intense Attack by Justice Thomas on Cross-Burning," *New York Times*, Dec. 12, 2002, p.1. See also Adam Liptak, "Symbols and Free Speech," *New York Times*, Dec. 15, 2002, p.5.
82 Butler, *Excitable Speech*, p.147.
83 Pierre Bourdieu, *The Logic of Practice*, Stanford, Calif., Stanford University Press, 1990, see especially pp.66–79.
84 Butler, *Excitable Speech*, p.155.

4 Performance in its historical context

1 RoseLee Goldberg, *Performance: Live Art 1909 to the Present*, New York, Harry N. Abrams, 1979.
2 Goldberg, *Performance Art: From Futurism to the Present*, New York, Harry N. Abrams, 1988.
3 Ibid., p.9.
4 Carol Simpson Stern and Bruce Henderson, *Performance: Texts and Contexts*, White Plains, NY, Longmans, 1993, pp.382–405.
5 Ibid., pp.382–3.
6 Ibid., p.6.
7 Goldberg, *Performance Art*, p.8.
8 Jean Alter, *A Socio-Semiotic Theory of Theatre*, Philadelphia, Pa., University of Pennsylvania Press, 1990, p.32.
9 Posturers, like later contortionists, could place their limbs and other parts of their bodies in unusual and grotesque positions. The famous Joseph Clark (d. 1690), according to the Transactions of the Royal Philosophical Society, "could disjoint almost his whole body," and specialized in the imitation of all sorts of physical deformity. A "Grimacing Spaniard" in London in 1698 worked entirely with facial changes, turning his mouth, nose, and eyes into various shapes, con-

tracting and expanding his features, and licking his nose with his tongue. Thomas Frost, *The Old Showmen and the London Fairs*, London, Tinsley Brothers, 1875, pp. 59, 61.

10 Ibid., p. 19.

11 Joseph Strutt, *The Sports and Pastimes of the People of England*, London: Thomas Tegg, 1845, pp. 180–1.

12 Ibid., p. 185.

13 M.C. Bradbrook, *The Rise of the Common Player*, Cambridge, Mass., Harvard University Press, 1962, p. 97.

14 John Evelyn, *The Diary of John Evelyn*, William Bray (ed.), London, Dent, 1966, vol. 1, p. 325.

15 John Gay, *Poetry and Prose*, Vinton A. Dearing (ed.), Oxford, Oxford University Press, 1974, vol. 1, p. 121.

16 A lively description of the many performative activities in this famous venue may be found in Henry Morley, *Memoires of Bartholomew Fair*, London, Chatto & Windus, 1880.

17 John S. Clarke, *Circus Parade*, London, B.T. Batsford, 1936, p. 7.

18 The close relationship between these various forms of popular performance and the world of scientific and cultural display in late nineteenth-century Europe and America is engagingly studied in Jane R. Goodall's *Performance and Evolution in the Age of Darwin*, London, Routledge, 2002.

19 See, for example, Johann Goethe, *Italienische Reise*, Gedenkausgabe, Zurich, 1948, vol. 11, pp. 228.

20 Kirsten Gram Holmström, *Monodrama, Attitudes, Tableaux Vivants*, Uppsala, Almqvist and Wiksells, 1967, p. 143.

21 Flora Fraser, *Emma, Lady Hamilton*, New York, Alfred A. Knopf, 1987, p. 107.

22 Carl Wittke, *Tambo and Bones*, Durham, NC, Duke University Press, 1930, p. 9–19.

23 Peter Jelavich, *Munich and Theatrical Modernism*, Cambridge, Mass., Harvard University Press, 1985, p. 160.

24 Richard Kostelanetz, *On Innovative Performance(s): Three Decades of Recollections on Alternative Theater*, Jefferson, NC, McFarland, 1994, pp. 50, 56. Concerning performance in writing, it might be noted that Kostelanetz, unlike the author of this book, makes a point of spelling theatre with an "er," a choice which he feels marks a necessary American separation from the European tradition (p. 54).

25 Robert C. Toll, *On With the Show! The First Century of Show Business in America*, New York, Oxford University Press, 1976, pp. 267–9.

26 John S. Gentile, *Cast of One: One-Person Shows from the Chautauqua Platform to the Broadway Stage*, Urbana, Ill., University of Illinois Press, 1989.

27 Laurence Senelick, *Cabaret Performance 1890–1920*, New York, PAJ Publications, 1989, p. 9.

28 Edward Braun (ed.), *Meyerhold on Theatre*, New York, Hill and Wang, 1969, p. 136.

29 Konstantin Rudnitsky, *Russian and Soviet Theater 1905–1932*, trans. Roxane Permar, New York, Harry N. Abrams, 1988, p. 57.

30 Ibid., p. 97.

31 Spencer Golub, *Evreinov: The Theatre of Paradox and Transformation*, Ann Arbor, Mich., UMI Research Press, 1984, p. 9.

32 Rudnitsky, *Russian and Soviet Theater*, p. 17.

33 Braun, *Meyerhold*, pp. 148–9.

34 See N. Prevots, *American Pageantry*, Ann Arbor, Mich., University of Michigan Press, 1990.

35 Frantisek Deák, "Russian Mass Spectacles," *The Drama Review*, 1975, vol. 19, p. 22.

36 F.T. Marinetti, "The Pleasure of Being Booed" in R.W. Flint (ed.), *Let's Murder the Moonshire: Selected Writings*, trans. R.W. Flint and A.A. Coppotelli, Los Angeles, Calif., Sun and Moon, 1991, p. 122.

37 Marinetti, "The Variety Theater," in *Let's Murder*, pp. 125, 128.

38 Tristan Tzara, "Zurich Chronicle 1915–1919" in Hans Richter, *Dada: Art and Anti-Art*, New York, n.d., pp. 223–4.
39 Richard Huelsenbeck, *En Avant Dada: Eine Geschichte des Dadaismus*, trans. in Robert Motherwell, *The Dada Painters and Poets*, Wittenborn, NY, Schultz, 1951, p. 26.
40 André Breton, "First Manifesto," trans. Herbert S. Gershman in *The Surrealist Revolution in France*, Ann Arbor, Mich., University of Michigan Press, 1974, p. 35.
41 William A. Camfield, *Francis Picabia: His Life and Times*, Princeton, NJ, Princeton University Press, 1979, pp. 210–11.
42 Fernand Léger, "Vive Rélâche," *Paris-Midi*, 17 Dec. 1924, p. 4.
43 Antonin Artaud, "The Theater of Cruelty (First Manifesto)" in *The Theater and Its Double*, trans. Mary Caroline Richards, New York, Grove Press, 1958, p. 93.
44 Lazlo Moholy-Nagy, "Theater, Circus, Variety," in Walter Gropius (ed.), *The Theater of the Bauhaus*, trans. Arthur S. Wensinger, Middletown, Conn., Wesleyan University Press, 1961, p. 58.
45 Karl Schwitters, "Merzbühne" 1919, p. 3, quoted in John Elderfield, *Karl Schwitters*, London: Thames & Hudson, 1985, pp. 109–10.
46 Thomas Leabhart, *Modern and Post-Modern Mime*, New York: St Martin's Press, 1989, p. 135.
47 R.G. Davis, "Politics, Art, and the San Francisco Mime Troupe," *Theatre Quarterly*, 1975, vol. 5(18), p. 26.
48 Natalie Crohn Schmitt, *Actors and Onlookers: Theater and Twentieth Century Scientific Views of Nature*, Evanston, Ill., Northwestern University Press, 1990, p. 8.
49 John Cage, "The Future of Music: Credo" in Richard Kostelanetz (ed.), *John Cage*, New York, Praeger, 1970, p. 54.
50 Goldberg, *Performance Art*, p. 140.
51 "Woks," *Art News*, Mar. 1959, p. 62.
52 Goldberg, *Performance Art*, pp. 130–1.
53 Quoted in Michael Kirby, *Happenings: An Illustrated Anthology*, New York, Oxford University Press, 1965, p. 47.
54 Kirby, *Happenings*, p. 21.
55 Allan Kaprow, *Assemblages, Environments, and Happenings*, New York, H.N. Abrams, 1966, p. 185.
56 Ibid., p. 188.
57 Ibid., pp. 188–96.
58 Kostelanetz, "Mixed-Means Theater," first published in *Contemporary Dramatists*, New York, St James Press, 1977, reprinted in *Innovative Performance(s)*, p. 3.
59 A good survey of this development is provided by Michael Rush in his *New Media in Late 20th-Century Art*, New York, Thames & Hudson, 1999.
60 Kostelanetz, *Innovative Performance(s)*, pp. 5–7.
61 Timothy J. Wiles, *The Theater Event: Modern Theories of Performance*, Chicago, Ill., University of Chicago Press, 1980, p. 117.
62 James D. Bigley, "Living History and Battle Reenactment, "*History News*, 1988, vol. 42, p. 16.
63 James Deetz, "The Link from Object to Person to Concept," in Zipporah W. Collins (ed.), *Museums, Adults and the Humanities*, Washington, DC, American Association of Museums, 1981, p. 8.

5 Performance art

1 Willowby Sharp, "Body Works: A Pre-Critical, Non-Definitive Survey of Very Recent Works Using the Human Body or Parts Thereof," *Avalanche*, 1970, vol. 1, p. 17.
2 Cindy Nemser, "Subject–Object: Body Art," *Arts Magazine*, 1971. vol. 46, p. 42.

3 For example, see ibid., p. 38.

4 Christine Tamblyn, "Hybridized Art," *Artweek*, 1990, vol. 21, p. 27.

5 Robin White, Interview with Chris Burden, *View*, 1979, quoted in Carl E. Loeffler and Darlene Tong (eds), *Performance Anthology*, San Francisco, Calif., Last Gasp Press, 1989, p. 399.

6 Willowby Sharp and Liza Bear, Interview with Chris Burden, *Avalanche*, 1973, vol. 8, p. 61.

7 Quoted in RoseLee Goldberg, *Performance Art: From Futurism to the Present*, New York, Harry N. Abrams, 1988, p. 156.

8 Vito Acconci, *Steps into Performance (And Out)*, quoted in Michael Rush, *New Media in Late 20th-Century Art*, New York, Thames & Hudson, 1999, p. 50.

9 Andree Hayum, "Notes on Performance and the Arts," *Art Journal*, 1975, vol. 34, p. 339.

10 Quoted by Michael Rush, *New Media*, p. 42.

11 The first critic, I believe, to gather such artists as Robert Wilson, Richard Foreman, and the Wooster Group under the rubric "performance theatre" was Timothy Wiles in his 1980 *The Theatre Event*.

12 Richard Kostelanetz, "Mixed-Means Theater," first published in *Contemporary Dramatists*, New York, St. James Press, 1977, reprinted in *Innovative Performance(s)*, p. 3.

13 Bonnie Marranca, *The Theatre of Images*, New York, Drama Book Specialists, 1977, p. xv.

14 Sandy Craig, *Dreams and Deconstructions: Alternative Theatre in Britain*, Ambergate, Amber Lane Press, 1980, p. 97.

15 Toby Coult and Baz Kershaw, *Engineers of the Imagination: The Welfare State Handbook*, London, Methuen, 1983, p. 217.

16 Anthony Howell and Fiona Templeton, *Elements of Performance Art*, The Ting, The Theatre of Mistakes, 1977, p. 17.

17 Bettina Knapp, "Sounding the Drum: An Interview with Jerome Savary," *Tulane Drama Review*, 1970, vol. 15, p. 94.

18 Quoted in Bim Mason, *Street Theatre and Other Outdoor Performance*, London, Routledge, 1992, p. 84.

19 Jacki Apple, "The Life and Times of Lin Hixson," *The Drama Review*, 1991, vol. 35(4), p. 28.

20 *The Drama Review* presented a special issue on the works of Abdoh in Fall, 1995 (39:4). See also the collection *Reza Abdoh*, Daniel Mufson (ed.), Baltimore, Md., Johns Hopkins, 1999.

21 Jacki Apple, "Art at the Barricades," *Artweek*, 1990, vol. 21, p. 21.

22 Richard Foreman, "The Life and Times of Sigmund Freud," *Village Voice*, 1 Jan., 1970.

23 Quoted in Laurence Shyer, *Robert Wilson and His Collaborators*, New York, Theatre Communications Group, 1989, p. xv.

24 Ernest Albrecht, *The New American Circus*, Gainesville, Fla., University Press of Florida, 1995, pp. 15–17.

25 Albrecht, *New American Circus*, pp. 29–31.

26 Phillip Dennis Cate, "The Cult of the Circus," in Barbara Stern Shapiro (ed.), *Pleasures of Paris: Daumier to Picasso*, Boston, Mass., Godine, p. 38.

27 Albrecht, *New American Circus*, p. 100.

28 Albrecht, *New American Circus*, p. 86.

29 Thomas Leabhart, *Modern and Post-Modern Mime*, New York, St Martin's Press, 1989, p. 123.

30 Published by Theatre Communications Group, New York.

31 Douglas Martin, "Old-Time Vaudeville Looks Young Again," the *New York Times*, 24 Nov. 2002, Arts, p. 5.

32 Quoted in Burnham, "Performance Art," p. 416.

33 Eleanor Munro, *Originals: American Women Artists*, New York, Simon, 1979, p. 427.
34 These walkabout examples are drawn from Mason, *Street Theatre*, especially the section "Walkabout," pp. 166–77.
35 Samuel G. Freedman, "Echoes of Lenny Bruce, via Bogosian and Reddin," *New York Times*, 19 Jan. 1986, sec. 2, p. 5.
36 Janice Arkatoy, "Bogosian's One-Man Bunch: Bouncing Ideas off *Funhouse* Walls," *Los Angeles Times*, 5 Apr. 1985, sec. 6, p. 2.
37 M. Walsh, "Post-Punk Apocalypse," *Time*, 1983, vol. 121, p. 68.
38 M. Small, "Laurie Anderson's whizzbang techno-vaudeville mirrors life in these United States," *People Weekly*, 1983, vol. 19, p. 107.
39 John Howell, *Laurie Anderson*, New York, Thunder's Mouth Press, 1992, p. 75.
40 Barbara Smith, "Ordinary Life," *High Performance*, 1978a, vol. 1, p. 40.
41 Jacki Apple, "Art at the Barricades," *Artweek*, 1990, vol. 21, p. 21.
42 Henry Louis Gates Jr, "Sudden Def," *The New Yorker*, 19 Jun. 1995, p. 42.
43 Jon Pareles, "A New Platform for New Poets," *New York Times*, 10 Nov. 2002, sec. 2, pp. 1, 25.
44 Goat Island, "Letter to a Young Practitioner," in Maria M. Delgado and Caridad Svich (eds), *Theatre in Crisis? Performance Manifestos for a New Century*, New York, Palgrave, 2002.
45 Tim Etchells, *Certain Fragments: Contemporary Performance and Forced Entertainment*, London, Routledge, 1999.
46 Peggy Phelan, "Performing Questions, Producing Witnesses," Foreword to Etchells, *Certain Fragments*, p. 10.
47 Etchells, *Certain Fragments*, p. 51.
48 Richard Schechner, "Guerrilla Theatre: May 1970," *Tulane Drama Review*, 1970, vol. 14, p. 163.
49 Françoise Kourilsky, *Le Bread and Puppet Theatre*, Lausanne, Le Cité, 1971, p. 26.
50 Steven Durland, "Witness, The Guerrilla Theater of Greenpeace," *High Performance*, 1987, vol. 10, pp. 30–5.
51 Jorge-Uwe Albig, "Heiliger Krieg um Bäume und Steine," *Art*, 1987, vol. 6, pp. 64–9.
52 Regina Vater, "Ecology Art is Alive and Well in Latin America," *High Performance*, 1987, vol. 10, p. 37.
53 Helen Spackman, "Minding the Matter of Representation: Staging the Body (Politic)," in Patrick Campbell (ed.), *The Body in Performance*, Singapore, Harwood Academic Publishers, 2000, p. 10.
54 Johannis Birringer, *Theatre, Theory, Postmodernism*, Bloomington, Ind., Indiana University Press, 1993, pp. 220–1.
55 Philip Auslander, *Liveness*, London: Routledge, 1999, p. 158.
56 The program was first aired on February 15, 1994 in Channel 4's *Without Walls* season.
57 Birringer, "Contemporary Technology/Performance," *Theatre Journal*, 1999, vol. 51(4), p. 366.
58 Birringer, "Contemporary Technology," pp. 367–8.

6 Performance and the postmodern

1 Anne Kisselgoff, "Not Quite/New York," *New York Times* 27 Sep. 1981.
2 Frank Rich, "The Regard of Flight," *New York Times*, 10 May 1985.
3 Nick Kaye, *Postmodernism and Performance*, New York, St Martin's Press, 1994, pp. 22–3.
4 Michel Benamou, "Presence as Play," in M. Benamou and C. Caramello, *Performance in Postmodern Culture*, Milwaukee, Wis., Center for Twentieth Century Studies, 1977, p. 3.

5 Ihab Hassan, "The Question of Postmodernism," in Harry R. Garvin (ed.), *Romanticism, Modernism, Postmodernism, Bucknell Review*, 1980, vol. 25, pp. 123, 125.

6 Thomas Leabhart, *Modern and Post-Modern Mime*, New York, St Martin's Press, 1989, pp. 128–9.

7 Clement Greenberg, "After Abstract Expressionism," *Art International*, 1962, vol. 6, p. 30.

8 Michael Fried, "Art and Objecthood," in Gregory Battcock (ed.), *Minimal Art*, New York, Dutton, 1968, p. 127.

9 Ibid., pp. 139, 145.

10 Michael Kirby, "Nonsemiotic Performance," *Modern Drama*, 1982, vol. 25, p. 110.

11 Bonnie Marranca, *The Theatre of Images*, New York, Drama Book Specialists, 1977, p. 3.

12 Richard Foreman, *Plays and Manifestos*, Kate Davy (ed.), New York, New York University Press, 1976, p. 145.

13 Xerxes Mehta, "Some Versions of Performance Art," *Theatre Journal*, 1984, vol. 36, p. 165.

14 Louis Horst and Carroll Russell, *Modern Dance Forms*, San Francisco, Calif., Dance Horizons, 1961, pp. 16, 24.

15 Sally Banes, *Democracy's Body: Judson Dance Theater, 1962–1964*, Ann Arbor, Mich., University of Michigan Press, 1983, p. 3.

16 Sally Banes, *Terpsichore in Sneakers: Post-Modern Dance*, 2nd edn, Middletown, Conn., Wesleyan University Press, 1987, p. xv.

17 Kaye, *Postmodernism*, pp. 76–7.

18 Banes, *Terpsichore*, p. xiv.

19 Susan Manning, "Modernist Dogma and Post-modern Rhetoric," *The Drama Review*, 1988, vol. 32, p. 34.

20 Michael Kirby, "Post-Modern Dance," *The Drama Review*, 1975, vol. 19, pp. 3–4.

21 Kisselgoff, "Not Quite/New York."

22 Sally Banes, "Is It All Postmodern?" *The Drama Review*, 1992, vol. 36, pp. 59–62.

23 Linda Hutcheon, *A Poetics of Postmodernism*, London, Routledge, 1988, p. 92.

24 John Barth, "The Literature of Replenishment: Postmodern Fiction," *Atlantic Monthly*, 1980, vol. 245, pp. 68, 70.

25 Banes, "Is It All Postmodern?" pp. 59–62.

26 Roger Copeland, "Postmodern Dance/ Postmodern Architecture/ Postmodernism," *Performing Arts Journal*, 1983, vol. 7, p. 39.

27 A title like Jon Whitmore's *Directing Postmodern Theater*, Ann Arbor, Mich., University of Michigan Press, 1994, might suggest a clear body of material being addressed, but this is not really so. Whitmore lists a group of artists, including Richard Foreman, Peter Brook, Robert Wilson, Martha Clarke, and JoAnne Akalaitis, who "have contributed to the development of the postmodern theatre" but not all of whom are "hard-core postmodernists." These "hard-core postmodernists" are not identified, though postmodern performance Whitmore generally defines as "primarily nonlinear, non-literary, nonrealistic, nondiscursive and nonclosure oriented" (pp. 3–4). In fact Whitmore's approach is heavily semiotic, as is indicated by his opening assertion: "The reason for creating and presenting theater is to communicate meanings" (p. 1). The rest of the book is devoted to the analysis, with much insight and intelligence, of the various semiotic systems in theatre and how they communicate, but those theorists and practitioners who relate postmodernism with poststructuralism would surely reject this orientation toward so structuralist an approach as semiotics, and the communication of meanings would equally surely be specifically rejected as a goal by many if not most "hard-core postmodernists." This is not to condemn Whitmore's book, which is useful and thorough in its project, but only to suggest how far theatre studies is from a consensus as to what postmodern theatre might be.

28 Hal Foster, "(Post)Modern Polemics," *New German Critique*, 1984, vol. 33, reprinted in *Recodings: Art, Spectacle, Cultural Politics*, Seattle, Wash., Bay Press, 1985, p. 121.
29 Ibid., p. 125.
30 Ibid., p. 128.
31 Ibid., p. 129.
32 Fredric Jameson, *Fables of Aggression*, Berkeley, Calif., University of California Press, 1979, p. 20.
33 Henry M. Sayre, "The Object of Performance: Aesthetics in the Seventies," *The Georgia Review*, 1983, vol. 37, p. 174.
34 Ibid., p. 182.
35 Josette Féral, "Performance and Theatricality: the Subject Demystified," *Modern Drama*, 1982, vol. 25, p. 175.
36 Jacques Derrida, *Writing and Differance*, trans. Alan Bass. Chicago, Il., University of Chicago Press, 1978, p. 249–50.
37 Herbert Blau, "Universals of Performance: or, Amortizing Play," *Sub-Stance*, 1983, vols 37–8, pp. 143, 148.
38 Chantal Pontbriand, "The Eye Finds No Fixed Point..." trans. C.R. Parsons, *Modern Drama*, 1982, vol. 25, p. 157.
39 Ibid., pp. 155, 158.
40 Kaye, *Postmodernism*, pp. 22–3.
41 Féral, "Performance and Theatricality," p. 179.
42 Fredric Jameson, "Foreword" to Jean-François Lyotard, *The Postmodern Condition: A Report on Knowledge*, Minneapolis, Minn., University of Minnesota Press, 1984, p. vii.
43 Ibid., pp. xxiv, xxvii.
44 Bill Readings, *Introducing Lyotard: Art and Politics*, London, Routledge, 1991, p. 69.
45 David George, "On Ambiguity: Towards a Post-Modern Performance Theory," *Theatre Research International*, 1989, vol. 14, p. 83.
46 Joel C. Weinsheimer, *Gadamer's Hermeneutics: A Reading of "Truth and Method"*, New Haven, Conn., Yale University Press, 1985, pp. 109–10.
47 Eve Sonneman, "Situation Esthetics: Impermanent Art and the Seventies Audience," *Artforum*, 1980, vol. 18, pp. 22–9.
48 Barbara Freedman, *Staging the Gaze*, Ithaca, NY, Cornell University Press, 1991, p. 74.
49 Jon Erickson, "Appropriation and Transgression in Contemporary American Performance," *Theatre Journal*, 1990, vol. 42, p. 235.
50 Randy Martin, *Performance as Political Act: The Embodied Self*, New York, Bergin and Garvey, 1990, pp. 175–6.
51 Jean-François Lyotard, "Notes on the Critical Function of the Work of Art," trans. Susan Hanson, *Driftworks*, New York, Semiotext(e), 1984, p. 78.
52 Philip Auslander, *Presence and Resistance: Postmodernism and Cultural Politics in Contemporary American Performance*, Ann Arbor, Mich., University of Michigan Press, 1994, p. 31.
53 Alan Read, *Theatre and Everyday Life: An Ethics of Performance*, London, Routledge, 1993, p. 90.
54 Barbara Adams and Stuart Allan, "Theorizing Culture: An Introduction," in *Theorizing Culture: An Interdisciplinary Critique after Postmodernism*, New York, New York University Press, 1995, p. xiii. Of course, one must also recognize that most "isms" have a limited shelf life, and postmodernism had perhaps exhausted most of its cultural capital by the end of the century. As James Taylor, editor of the popular culture magazine *Shocked and Amazed*, observed, "Postmodern is so last century" (quoted in Douglas Martin, "Old-Time Vaudeville Looks Young Again," the *New York Times*, 24 Nov. 2002, Arts, p. 5.
55 Ibid., p. xv.

56 Ibid., p.xvi.
57 Barbara Adams, "The Temporal Landscape of Global/izing Culture and the Paradox of Postmodern Futures," in Adams and Allen, *Theorizing Culture*, p.259.

7 Performance and identity

1 Jill Dolan, *The Feminist Spectator as Critic*, Ann Arbor, Mich., University of Michigan Research Press, 1988, p.3.
2 Michelene Wandor, *Carry On, Understudies*, New York, Routledge & Kegan Paul, 1986, p.131.
3 Linda Walsh Jenkins, "Locating the Language of Gender Experience," *Women and Performance Journal*, 1984, vol.2, pp.6–8.
4 Rosemary K. Curb, "Re/cognition, Re/presentation, Re/creation in Woman-Conscious Drama: The Seer, The Seen, The Scene, The Obscene," *Theatre Journal*, 1985, vol.37, p.304.
5 Dolan, *Feminist Spectator*, p.10.
6 Sue-Ellen Case, *Feminism and Theatre*, New York, Methuen, 1988, p.82.
7 Yvonne Rainer, "The Performer as a Persona," *Avalanche*, 1972, Summer, p.50.
8 Ibid., p.125.
9 Carolee Schneemann, *More Than Meat Joy*, New Paltz, NY, Domentext, 1979, p.52.
10 Quoted in Leo Rubinflen, "Through Western Eyes," *Art in America*, 1978, vol.66, p.76.
11 Jacki Apple, "The Life and Times of Lin Hixson," *The Drama Review*, 1991, vol.35(4), p.30.
12 Quoted in Moira Roth, "Autobiography, Theater, Mysticism and Politics: Women's Performance Art in Southern California," in Carl Loeffler and Darlene Tong (eds), *Performance Anthology*, San Francisco, Calif., Last Gasp Press, p.466. See also Faith Wilding, "The Feminist Art Program at Fesno and Cal Arts, 1970–75" in Norma Broude and Mary D. Garrard (eds), *The Power of Feminist Art: The American Art Movement of the 1970s, History and Impact*, New York: Harry N. Abrams, 1996, pp.32–47.
13 A point stressed by Elizabeth Zimmer in "Has Performance Art Lost Its Edge?" *Ms.*, 1995, vol.5, p.78.
14 Martha Rosler, "The Private and the Public: Feminist Art in California," *Artforum*, 1977, vol.16, p.69.
15 Linda Frye Burnham, "*High Performance*, Performance Art, and Me," *The Drama Review*, 1986, vol.30, p.40.
16 Barbara T. Smith, "Ordinary Life," *High Performance*, 1978, vol.1, p.47.
17 Mary Beth Edelson, "Pilgrimage/See for Yourself," *Heresies*, Spring, 1978, pp.96–9.
18 Sally Banes, *Terpsichore in Sneakers*, Boston, Houghton Mifflin, 1980, p.156.
19 Linda Montano, "Mitchell's Death," *High Performance*, 1978, vol.1, p.35; Barbara T. Smith, "The Vigil," *High Performance*, 1978, vol.1, p.49.
20 Schneemann, *Meat Joy*, p.238.
21 Quoted in Rubinflen, "Through Western Eyes," p.76.
22 See Linda Montano, *Art in Everyday Life*, Los Angeles, Calif., Astro Artz, 1981, unpaginated.
23 Moira Roth, *The Amazing Decade*, Los Angeles, Calif., Astro Artz, 1983, p.124. See also Yvonne Rainer, *The Films of Yvonne Rainer*, Bloomington, Ind., Indiana University Press, 1989.
24 Josette Féral, "What is Left of Performance Art? Autopsy of a Function, Birth of a Genre," *Discourse*, 1992, vol.14, pp.148–9.
25 Roth, *Amazing Decade*, pp.17, 20, 102.
26 Marilyn Nix, "Eleanor Antin's Traditional Art," *Artweek*, 1972, vol.3, p.3.

27 Quoted in Linda Frye Burnham, "Performance Art in Southern California: An Overview," in Loeffler and Tong, *Performance Anthology*, p. 406.

28 Eleanor Munro, *Originals: American Women Artists*, New York, Simon, 1979, p. 427.

29 Marcia Traylor, "Catalog: Autobiographical Fantasies," *Laica Journal*, 1976, vol. 10.

30 Catherine Elwes, "Floating Femininity: A Look at Performance Art by Women" in Sarah Kent and Jacqueline Morreau (eds), *Women's Images of Men*, London, Writers and Readers Publishing, 1985, p. 162.

31 Erving Goffman, *Stigma: Notes on the Management of Spoiled Identity*, Englewood Cliffs, NJ, Prentice-Hall, 1963, pp. 94, 101.

32 Esther Newton, *Mother Camp: Female Impersonators in America*, Chicago, Ill., University of Chicago Press, 1972, p. 108.

33 Wilde's life "performance" is analyzed in Ed Cohen's "Posing the Question: Wilde, Wit, and the Ways of Men," in Elin Diamond, *Writing Performances*, London, Routledge, 1995.

34 Quoted in John S. Gentile, *Cast of One: One-Peson Shows from the Chautauqua Platform to the Broadway Stage*, Urbana, Ill., University of Illinois Press.

35 Susan Sontag, "Notes on 'Camp,'" in *Against Interpretation*, New York, Farrar Straus & Giroux, 1966, pp. 280, 286.

36 Newton, *Mother Camp*, p. 107.

37 This of course does not mean that cross-dressing cannot provide a site of social and cultural tension and identity exploration in traditional theatre as well, as many recent theorists of English Renaissance culture have argued. See, for example, Jonathan Dollimore, *Sexual Dissidence*, Oxford, Oxford University Press, 1991, especially Ch. 18; Rudolf Dekker and Lotte van De Pol, *The Tradition of Female Transvestism in Early Modern Europe*, New York, St Martin's Press, 1989; Stephan Orgel, "Nobody's Perfect," *South Atlantic Quarterly*, 1989, vol. 88, pp. 7–29.

38 Occasionally performance artists like Split Britches have utilized performance to explore different gender possibilities within themselves in the same piece. In his *I Got the He-Be-She-Be's* (1986), John Fleck, stripped naked, played his own female and male halves, caressing, cajoling, battering, and having sex with himself.

39 See John Lahr, "Playing Possum," *New Yorker*, 1 Jul. 1991, pp. 38–66.

40 Mark Gevisser, "Gay Theater Today," *Theater*, 1990, vol. 21, p. 46.

41 Laurence Senelick, "Boys and Girls Together," in Lesley Ferris (ed.), *Crossing the Stage*, Routledge, London, 1993, pp. 82, 93. Senelick's monumental *The Changing Room*, Routledge, London, 2000, offers an encyclopedic study of drag and cross dressing from around the world, and from tribal rituals to current performance art.

42 Joe Laurie Jr, *Vaudeville*, New York, n.d., p. 92.

43 Gevisser, "Gay Theater," p. 48.

44 David Drake, "Gay Activist or Beauty Queen?" *Theater Week*, 5 Aug., 1991, p. 19.

45 Quoted in Burnham, "Performance Art," p. 416.

46 Alisa Solomon, "It's Never too Late to Switch," in Ferris, *Crossing the Stage*, p. 145.

47 It is important also to note that although recent theory, much interested in the implications of performance in identity formation and political placement, has traced these implications in earlier performance work, such work (drag in particular) rarely aroused any speculation in performers or audiences at the time of its creation. A clear example of the shift was Ron Vawter's re-creation of a 1981 Jack Smith performance in 1992. The original production, like all of Smith's work, was concerned primarily with flamboyant and excessive display, akin to the Aristophanic exuberance of the early Theatre of the Ridiculous. Ten years later, in a more reflexive performative context, Vawter saw this piece (and a

companion enactment of Roy Cohn) in a quite different light, as statements "about repression and how the homosexual deals with repression" ("Two Strangers Meet Through an Actor." interview with Stephen Holden, *New York Times*, 3 May, sec. 2, p. 8). Even *New York Times* reviewer Frank Rich was sufficiently aware of the theoretical placement of Vawter's re-enactment to characterize it as "an heroic act of minority cultural anthropology" ("Diversities of America in One-Person Shows, *New York Times*, 15 May, sec. C, p. 1).

48 Peggy Phelan provides an excellent analysis of the NEA funding controversy in her "Money Talks, Again," *The Drama Review*, 1991, vol. 35, 131–42.
49 Proceedings of the United States Supreme Court, no. 97–371, National Endowment for the Arts et al. v. Karen Finley et al., 25 Jun. 1998.
50 Elinor Fuchs, "Staging the Obscene Body," *The Drama Review*, 1989, vol. 33(1), p. 33.
51 C. Carr, "Unspeakable Practices, Unnatural Acts: The Taboo Art of Karen Finley," *The Village Voice*, 1986, 24 Jun., 17.
52 "Hallelujah! Ron Athey: A Story of Delivery," directed by Catherine Gund Saalfield.
53 Directed by Kirby Dick.
54 Barbara Rose, "Is It Art? Orlan and the Transgressive Act," *Art in America*, 1993, Feb., pp. 82–7.
55 And in performance theory. See, for example, Philip Auslander, "Orlan's Theatre of Operations," *Theatre Forum*, 1995, vol. 7, pp. 25–31; Tanya Augsburg, "Orlan's Performative Transformations of Subjectivity" in Phelan and Lane, *The Ends of Performance*, pp. 285–314.
56 Arlene Croce, "Discussing the Undiscussable," *New Yorker*, 2 Jan. 1995, pp. 54–60.
57 Ibid., 58.
58 Dale Harris, "The Patron Saint of Suffering," *Wall Street Journal*, 16 Jan. 1995.
59 Grace Glueck, "In a Roguish Gallery," *New York Times*, 12 May 1989, sec. C, p. 3.
60 C. Carr, "Revisions of Excess," *Village Voice*, May, 1989, reprinted in Carr, *On Edge: Performance at the End of the Twentieth Century*, Middletown, Conn., Wesleyan University Press, 1994, p. 179.
61 Moira Roth, "Vision and Re-visions: A Conversation with Suzanne Lacy," *Artforum*, 1980, pp. 39–40. See also Jeff Kelley, "The Body Politics of Suzanne Lacy," in Nina Felshin (ed.), *But Is It Art?: The Spirit of Art as Activism*, Oxford, Oxford University Press, 2001.
62 For example by Barbara Christian, in "The Race for Theory," *Feminist Studies*, 1988, vol. 14.
63 From a company press flyer quoted by Rebecca Schneider, in "See the Big Show: Spiderwomen Theater Doubling Back," in Lynda Hart and Peggy Phelan (eds), *Acting Out: Feminist Performances*, Ann Arbor, Mich., University of Michigan Press, 1993, p. 241.
64 Quoted in Lenora Champagne (ed.) *Out from Under: Texts by Women Performance Artists*, New York, Theatre Communications Group, 1990, pp. 92–3.
65 See Raewyn Whyte, "Robbie McCauley: Speaking History Other-Wise," in Hart and Phelan, *Acting Out*, pp. 277–93.
66 See Linda Frye Burnham and Steven Durland (eds), *The Citizen Artist: An Anthology from High Performance Magazine 1978–1998*, New York, Critical Press, 1998.
67 Quoted in Margot Mifflin, "Performance Art: What is it and where is it going? *Art News*, 1992, vol. 91, p. 87.
68 Tim Miller, "Tim Miller" in Thomas Leabhart (ed.), *California Performance*, vol. 2, *Los Angeles Area, 1991/1992*, Claremont, Calif., Pomona College, Mime Journal, 1991.
69 Quoted in Elizabeth Zimmer, "Out of Left Field," *Dance Magazine,* 1989, Sep., p. 52.
70 "Beau Sia," interview by A.D. Amorosi, *Philadelphia City Paper*, 22–29 Oct. 1998.

71 Jon Pareles, "A New Platform for New Poets," *New York Times*, 10 Nov. 2002, sec. 2, p. 25.
72 Jacki Apple, "Art at the Barricades," *Artweek*, 1990, vol. 21, p. 21.
73 Quoted in Mifflin, "Performance Art," p. 89.

8 Cultural performance

1 Phillip Zarilli, "For Whom Is the King a King? Issues of Intercultural Production, Perception and Reception in a Kathikali *King Lear*," in Joseph Roach and Janelle Reinelt, *Critical Theory and Performance*, Ann Arbor, Mich., University of Michigan Press, 1992, p. 16.
2 Richard Schechner, "Guerrilla Theatre: May 1970," *Tulane Drama Review*, 1970, vol. 14, p. 163.
3 R.G. Davis, "Guerrilla Theatre," *Tulane Drama Review*, 1966, vol. 10, pp. 130–6.
4 Robin Morgan, *Going Too Far*, New York, Random House, 1977, pp. 65, 72, 75.
5 See Cynthia Freeland, "Gender, Genius, and Guerrilla Girls," in Nina Felshin (ed.), *But is it Art? An Introduction to Art Theory*, Oxford, Oxford University Press, 2001, pp. 122–47.
6 See Suzi Gablik, "A Conversation with the Guerrilla Girls," *Art in America*, 1994, Jan., pp. 43–7. The gorilla masks and programmatic anonymity of the Guerrilla Girls suggest how far their work is from the performance of personal identity which was the basis of the preceding chapter.
7 See Harry Gamboa Jr, *Urban Exile: Collected Writings*, ed. Chon A. Noriega, Minneapolis, Minn., University of Minnesota Press, 1998.
8 Quoted in Coco Fusco, *The Bodies that Were Not Ours*, London, Routledge, 2001, p. 54.
9 C. Ondine Chavoya, "Orphans of Modernism: The Performance Art of Asco," in Coco Fusco (ed.), *Corpus Delecti: Performance Art of the Americas*, London, Routledge, 2000, pp. 240–64.
10 See Aldo Damian Menendez, "Art Attack: The Work of ARTECALLE," trans. by Coco Fusco, in Coco Fusco (ed.), *Corpus Delecti*, pp. 75–80.
11 *Ibid.*, 50.
12 Jeanie Forte, "Women's Performance Art: Feminism and Postmodernism," in Sue-Ellen Case (ed.), *Performing Feminisms: Feminist Critical Theory and Theatre*, Baltimore, Md., Johns Hopkins, 1990, p. 253.
13 Valie Export, "Persona, Proto-Performance, Politics: A Preface," trans. Jamie Daniel, *Discourse*, 1992, vol. 14, p. 33. See also Export's essay "Feminist Actionism" in Nabakowski, et al. (eds), *Frauen in der Kunst*, Frankfurt, Suhrkamp, 1980.
14 Valie Export, 1991 Interview by Andrea Juno and V. Vale, in Andrea Juno and V. Vale (eds), *Angry Women*, San Francisco, Calif., Re/Search Publications, 1993, p. 193.
15 Michelene Wandor, *Carry On, Understudies: Theatre and Sexual Politics*, London, Routledge & Kegan Paul, 1981, p. 87.
16 Sue-Ellen Case, *Feminism and Theatre*, New York, Methuen, 1988, p. 120.
17 *Ibid.*, p. 17.
18 See "Sonia Knox" in Lorne Falk (ed.), *Agit Prop: Performance in Banff*, Banff, Banff Centre Press, 1982, p. 30.
19 Jill Dolan, "The Dynamics of Desire: Sexuality and Gender in Pornography and Performance," *Theatre Journal*, 1987, vol. 39(2), pp. 162–3.
20 Quoted in Elinor Fuchs, "Staging the Obscene Body," *The Drama Review*, 1989, 33(1), p. 44.
21 See Angelika Czekay, "Distance and Empathy: Constructing the Spectator of Annie Sprinkle's Post-POST PORN MODERNIST—Still in Search of the Ultimate Sexual Experience," *Journal of Dramatic Theory and Criticism*, 1993, vol. 7(2), pp. 177–92.

22 Forte, "Women's Performance Art," p. 268.

23 Jeannette Laillou Savona, "French Feminism and Theatre: An Introduction," *Modern Drama*, 1984, vol. 27, p. 540.

24 Marcia K. Moen, "Peirce's Pragmatism as Resource for Feminism," *Transactions of the Charles S. Peirce Society*, Amherst, Mass., University of Massachusettes Press, 1991, p. 439.

25 Forte, "Women's Performance Art," p. 260.

26 *About Time* Catalogue, ICA, London, Sep. 1980, quoted in Catherine Elwes "Floating Femininity: A Look at Performance Art by Women," in Sarah Kent and Jacqueline Morreau (eds), *Women's Images of Men*, London, Writers and Readers Publishing, 1985, p. 170.

27 Rachel Bowlby, "The Feminine Female," *Social Text*, 1983, p. 62, quoted in Forte, "Women's Performance Art," p. 261.

28 Jill Dolan, "The Dynamics of Desire: Sexuality and Gender in Pornography and Performance," *Theatre Journal*, 1987, vol. 39, p. 159.

29 Jacques Derrida, "The Ends of Man," *Margins of Philosophy*, trans. Alan Bass, Chicago, Ill., University of Chicago Press, 1982, p. 135.

30 Audre Lorde, *Sister/Outsider: Essays and Speeches*, Freedom, Calif., Cross Press, 1984, p. 223.

31 Peggy Phelan, *Unmarked*, London, Routledge, 1993, p. 148.

32 Ibid., pp. 152–3.

33 Elwes, "Floating Femininity," p. 173.

34 Judith Butler, *Gender Trouble*, London, Routledge, 1990, p. 145.

35 Michel de Certeau, *The Practice of Everday Life*, trans. Steven F. Rendall, Berkeley, Calif., University of California Press, 1984, p. xix.

36 Philip Auslander, *Presence and Resistance: Postmodernism and Cultural Politics in Contemporary American Performance*, Ann Arbor, Mich., University of Michigan Press, 1994, p. 31.

37 Theodore W. Adorno, *Negative Dialectics*, trans. E.B. Ashton, New York, Seabury Press, 1973, p. 5.

38 S. Buck-Morss, *The Origin of Negative Dialectics: Theodore W. Adorno, Walter Benjamin, and the Frankfurt Institute*, Hassocks, Sussex, Harvester Press, 1977, p. 54.

39 Judith Butler, *Bodies that Matter*, New York, Routledge, 1993, p. 94.

40 Elin Diamond, "Mimesis, Mimicry, and the 'True-Real,'" *Modern Drama*, 1989, vol. 32, pp. 59–60.

41 Luce Irigaray, "The Power of Discourse," in *This Sex Which is Not One*, trans. Catherine Porter with Carolyn Burke, Ithaca, NY, Cornell University Press, 1985, p. 76.

42 Herman Rapaport, "'Can You Say Hello?' Laurie Anderson's *United States*," *Theatre Journal*, 1986, vol. 38, p. 384.

43 Mary Ann Doane, "Film and the Masquerade: Theorizing the Female Spectator," *Screen*, 1982, vol. 23, p. 81.

44 Mary Russo, "Female Grotesques: Carnival and Theory," in Teresa de Lauretis (ed.), *Feminist Studies/Critical Studies*, Bloomington, Ind., Indiana University Press, 1986, p. 85.

45 Quoted in Wandor, *Carry On*, p. 72.

46 Elwes, "Floating Femininity," p. 172.

47 Jon Erickson, "Appropriation and Transgression in Contemporary American Performance," *Theatre Journal*, 1990, vol. 42, p. 235.

48 Sue-Ellen Case and Jeanie K. Forte, "From Formalism to Feminism," *Theater*, 1985, vol. 16, p. 65.

49 Elwes, "Floating Femininity," p. 154.

50 Kate Davy, "Constructing the Spectator: Reception, Context, and Address in Lesbian Performance," *Performing Arts Journal*, 1986, vol. 10, p. 47.

51 Sue-Ellen Case, "Toward a Butch-Femme Aesthetic," in Lynda Hart (ed.), *Making*

a Spectacle: Feminist Essay on Contemporary Women's Theatre, Ann Arbor, Mich., University of Michigan Press, 1989, pp. 283, 296.

52 Stefan Brecht, *Queer Theatre*, London, Methuen, 1986, pp. 31–2.

53 Butler, *Gender Trouble*, p. 31.

54 Earl Jackson Jr, "Kabuki Narratives of Male Homoerotic Desire in Saikuku and Mishima," *Theatre Journal*, 1989, vol. 41(4), p. 459.

55 Kate Davy, "Fe/male Impersonation: The Discourse of Camp," in Reinelt and Roach, *Critical Theory*, p. 244.

56 Teresa de Lauretis, "Sexual Indifference and Lesbian Representation," *Theatre Journal*, 1988, vol. 40, p. 169–71.

57 David Román, "Performing All Our Lives: AIDS, Performance, Community," in Reinelt and Roach, *Critical Theory*, p. 215.

58 Ibid., p. 218.

59 Evan MacColl, "Grass Roots of Theatre Workshop," *Theatre Quarterly*, 1973, vol. 3, pp. 58–68.

60 See Armand Gatti, "Armand Gatti on Time, Place and the Theatrical Event," trans. Nancy Oakes, *Modern Drama*, 1982, vol. 25, pp. 70–6.

61 Augusto Boal, *The Theatre of the Oppressed*, trans. Charles A. and Marie-Odilia McBride, New York, Theatre Communications Group, 1979. See also the special issue on Boal published by *The Drama Review*, 1990, vol. 34.

62 Toby Coult and Baz Kershaw, *Engineers of the Imagination: The Welfare State Handbook*, London, Methuen, 1983, p. 219.

63 The 1981 version of this work is described in Bim Mason, *Street Theatre and Other Outdoor Performance*, London, Routledge, 1992, pp. 134–5.

64 Lance Carlson, "Performance Art as Political Activism," *Artweek*, 3 May, 1990, p. 24.

65 See Rena Fraden, *Imagining Medea: Rhodessa Jones and Theater for Incarcerated Women*, Chapel Hill, NC, University of North Carolina Press, 2001.

66 Josette Féral, "What is Left of Performance Art? Autopsy of a Function, Birth of a Genre," *Discourse*, 1992, vol. 14, pp. 148–9.

67 Una Chaudhuri, "Introduction: Instant Rachel," in Rachel Rosenthal, *Rachel's Brain and Other Storms*, London, Continuum, 2001, p. 7.

68 Tim Miller, *Body Blows*, Madison, Wis., University of Wisconsin Press, 2002, p. xxviii.

69 Judith Butler, "The Force of Fantasy: Feminism, Mapplethorpe, and Discursive Excess," *Differences*, 1990, vol. 2, p. 121.

70 Homi Bhabha, *The Location of Culture*, London, Routledge, 1994. See especially the essays "Of Mimicry and Man: The Ambivalence of Colonial Discourse," and "The Other Question: Stereotype, Discrimination and the Discourse of Colonialism."

71 Homi Bhabha, "Of Mimicry and Man: The Ambivalence of Colonial Discourse," *October*, 1984, vol. 28, p. 126.

72 See, for example, Robert Young, "The Ambivalence of Bhabha," in *White Mythologies: Writing, History and the West*, London, Routledge, 1990, pp. 141–56; Benita Parry, "Signs of Our Times: Discussions of Homi Bhabha's *The Location of Culture*, in *Third Text*, 1994, vols 28/29, pp. 5–24.

73 Paul Gilroy, *The Black Atlantic: Modernity and Double Consciousness*, London, Verso, 1997.

74 Rebecca Schneider, "See the Big Show: Spiderwoman Theater Doubling Back," in Hart and Phelan, *Acting Out*, p. 237.

75 Ibid., p. 251.

76 Ibid., p. 246.

77 Margot Mifflin, "Performance Art: What Is It and Where Is It Going?" *Art News*, 1992, vol. 91(4), p. 88.

78 See Coco Fusco, "The Other History of Intercultural Performance," *The Drama Review*, 1994, vol. 38, pp. 143–67.

79 "Epilogue" to "Desire Cloaked in a Trenchcoat" in Lynda Hart and Peggy Phelan (eds), *Acting Out: Feminist Performances*, Ann Arbor, Mich., University of Michigan Press, 1993, p.113.
80 Each of these performances is described and illustrated in Coco Fusco, *The Bodies that Were Not Ours*, London, Routledge, 2001.
81 Coco Fusco, *English is Broken Here*, New York, The New Press, 1995, and *The Bodies*.
82 Coco Fusco, *Corpus Delecti: Performance Art of the Americas*, London: Routledge, 2000.
83 Diana Taylor and Juan Villegas (eds), *Negotiating Performance: Gender, Sexuality, and Theatricality in Latin/o America*, Durham, NC, Duke University Press, 1994.
84 The website of the Institute is http//hemi.ps.tsoa.nyu.edu.
85 Ibid.
86 Guillermo Gómez-Peña, *Warrior for Gringostroika*, Saint Paul, Greywolf Press, 1993, pp.19–20.
87 Ibid., p.22.
88 Ibid., p.29.
89 Quoted in Carr, "Rediscovering America," *Village Voice*, Oct. 1991, reprinted in Carr, *On Edge: Performance at the End of the Twentieth Century*, Middletown, Conn., Wesleyan University Press, 1994, p.196.
90 Gómez-Peña, *Dangerous Border Crossings*, London, Routledge, 2000, p.49.
91 Ibid., p.57.
92 Julie Holledge and Joanne Tompkins, *Women's Intercultural Performance*, London, Routledge, 2000.

Conclusion

1 Thi Minh-Ha Trinh, *Women, Native, Other: Writing Postcoloniality and Feminism*, Bloomington, Ind., Indiana University Press, 1989, p.94.
2 Clifford Geertz, "Blurred Genres," in *Local Knowledge: Further Essays in Interpretive Anthropology*, Stanford, Calif., Stanford University Press, 1983, pp.19–35.
3 Renato Rosaldo, *Culture and Truth: The Remaking of Social Analysis*, Boston, Mass., Beacon, 1989, p.45.
4 Ibid., p.28.
5 Robert Jay Lifton, *The Protean Self*, New York, Basic Books, 1993, p.1.
6 James Clifford, *Predicament of Culture*, Cambridge, Mass., Harvard University Press, 1988, pp.23, 25.
7 John Lechte, *Julia Kristeva*, London, Routledge, 1990, 27.
8 Clifford Geertz, *Works and Lives: The Anthropologist as Author*, Stanford, Calif., Stanford University Press, 1988, p.143.
9 "Introduction," to Smadar Lavie, Kirin Narayan, and Renato Rosaldo (eds), *Creativity/Anthropology*, Ithaca, NY, Cornell University Press, 1993, p.6. This collection is dedicated to Turner, whose work is the focus of the introduction. The close relationship between creativity, play, carnival is also stressed, with references to Huizinga and Bakhtin.
10 Stephen Tyler, *The Unspeakable: Discourse, Dialogue, and Rhetoric in the Postmodern World*, Madison, Wis., University of Wisconsin Press, 1987, pp.212, 218.
11 Dwight Conquergood, "Rethinking Ethnography: Towards a Critical Cultural Politics," *Communication Monographs*, 1991, vol.58, pp.179–94.
12 Mikhail Bakhtin, *Speech Genres*, Austin, Tex., University of Texas Press, 1986, p.2.
13 Conquergood, "Rethinking Ethnography," p.180.
14 Tyler, *The Unspeakable*, p.225.
15 James M. Edie, "Notes on the Philosophical Anthropology of William James," in J.M. Edie (ed.), *An Invitation to Phenomenology: Studies in the Philosophy of Experience*, Chicago, Ill., Quadrangle Books, 1965, p.119.

16 Michael Jackson, *Paths Toward a Clearing: Radical Empiricism and Ethnographic Inquiry*, Bloomington, Ind., Indiana University Press, 1989, p.2.
17 Conquergood, "Rethinking Ethnography," p.190.
18 Columbia University Medieval Guild, Call for Papers, circulated by email, 20 Dec. 2002.
19 Elin Diamond, "Introduction" to *Performance and Cultural Politics*, London, Routledge, 1966, p.2.
20 John J. MacAloon (ed.), *Rite, Drama, Festival, Spectacle: Rehearsals Toward a Theory of Cultural Performance*, Philadephia, Pa., Institute for the Study of Human Issues, 1984, p.1.
21 Marvin Carlson, *Performance: A Critical Introduction*, London, Routledge, 1996, p.194.
22 Jon McKenzie, *Perform or Else: From Discipline to Performance*, London, Routledge, 2001, p.8. In this context, McKenzie cites the first edition of the present work as the "first book-length study to examine this development."
23 Ibid., p.189.
24 Ibid., p.203.
25 Ibid., p.18.
26 Margaret Wilkerson, "Demographics and the Academy," in Janelle Reinelt and Joseph Roach (eds), *Critical Theory and Performance*, Ann Arbor, Mich., University of Michigan Press, 1992, p.239.
27 Jill Dolan, "Geographies of Learning: Theatre Studies, Performance, and the 'Performative,'" *Theatre Journal*, 1993, vol.45, p.432.
28 Ibid., p.441.
29 Alan Read, *Theatre and Everyday Life: An Ethics of Performance*, London, Routledge, 1993, p.90.

Bibliography

Abrahams, Roger D. (1968) "Introductory Remarks to a Rhetorical Theory of Folklore," *Journal of American Folklore*, vol. 81, pp. 143–58.

Adams, Barbara (1995) "The Temporal Landscape of Global/izing Culture and the Paradox of Postmodern Futures," in Adams and Allen, *Theorizing Culture*, pp. 249–62.

Adams, Barbara and Stuart Allan (1995) *Theorizing Culture: An Interdisciplinary Critique after Postmodernism*, New York: New York University Press.

Adorno, Theodor W. (1973) *Negative Dialectics*, trans. E.B. Ashton, New York: Seabury Press.

Albig, Jorge-Uwe (1987) "Heiliger Kreig um Bäume und Stein," *Art*, vol. 6, pp. 64–9.

Albrecht, Ernest (1995) *The New American Circus*, Gainesville, Fla.: University of Florida Press.

Alter, Jean (1990) *A Sociosemiotic Theory of Theatre*, Philadelphia, Pa.: University of Pennsylvania Press.

Amorosi, A.D. (1998) "Beau Sia," *Philadelphia City Paper*, 22–9 Oct., 1998.

Anderson, Jay (ed.) (1991) *A Living History Reader*, vol. 1, Nashville, Tenn.: American Association for State and Local History.

Apple, Jacki (1990) "Art at the Barricades," *Artweek*, vol. 21.

—— (1991) "The Life and Times of Lin Hixson," *The Drama Review*, vol. 35(4).

Arkatoy, Janice (1985) "Bogosian's One-Man Bunch: Bouncing Ideas Off *Funhouse* Walls," *Los Angeles Times*, 5 Apr., sec. 6, p. 2.

Artaud, Antonin (1958) *The Theatre and Its Double*, trans. Mary Caroline Richards, New York: Grove Press.

Augsburg, Tanya (1998) "Orlan's Performative Transformations of Subjectivity," in Phelan and Lane, *The Ends of Performance*, pp. 285–314.

Auslander, Philip (1994) *Presence and Resistance: Postmodernism and Cultural Politics in Contemporary American Performance*, Ann Arbor, Mich.: University of Michigan Press.

—— (1995) "Orlan's Theatre of Operations," *Theatre Forum* vol. 7, pp. 25–31.

—— (1997) *From Acting to Performance: Essays on Modernism and Postmodernism*. London: Routledge.

—— (1999) *Liveness*, London: Routledge.

Austin, J.L. (1975) *How to Do Things with Words*, Cambridge, Mass.: Harvard University Press.

—— (1979) *Philosophical Papers*, J.O. Urmson and G.L. Warnock (eds), Oxford: Oxford University Press.

Bakhtin, Mikhail (1965) *Rabelais and His World*, trans. Helen Iswolsky, Cambridge, Mass.: MIT Press.

—— (1986) *Speech Genres and Other Late Essays*, trans. Vern W. McGee, Austin, Tex.: University of Texas Press.

Banes, Sally (1980) *Terpsichore in Sneakers: Post-Modern Dance*, Boston, Mass.: Houghton Mifflin.

—— (1983) *Democracy's Body: Judson Dance Theater, 1962–1964*, Ann Arbor, Mich.: University of Michigan Press.

—— (1987) *Terpsichore in Sneakers: Post-Modern Dance*, 2nd edn, Middletown, Conn.: Wesleyan University Press.

—— (1992) "Is It All Postmodern?" *The Drama Review*, vol. 36, pp. 59–62.

Barba, Eugenio (1991) "Introduction," in Eugenio Barba and Nicola Savarese (eds), *The Secret Art of the Performer*, trans. Richard Fowler, London: Routledge.

Barnouw, Erik (ed.) (1989)*International Encyclopedia of Communications*, New York: Oxford University Press.

Barrett, Amanda and José Esteban Muñoz (eds) (1996) *Queer Acts*, special edition of *Women and Performance*, vol. 8(2), p. 16.

Barth, John (1980) "The Literature of Replenishment: Postmodern Fiction," *Atlantic Monthly*, vol. 245, pp. 65–71.

Bateson, Gregory (1972) *Steps to an Ecology of Mind*, San Francisco, Calif.: Chandler.

Battcock, Gregory (ed.) (1966) *Minimal Art*, New York: Dutton.

Battcock, Gregory and R. Nikas (eds) (1984) *The Art of Performance: A Critical Anthology*, New York: Dutton.

Bauman, Richard (1977) *Verbal Art as Performance*, Rowley, Mass.: Newbury House.

—— (1986) *Story, Performance, and Event: Contextual Studies in Oral Narrative*, New York: Cambridge University Press.

—— (1989) "Performance," in Barnouw, *International Encyclopedia of Communications*.

Belghazi, Taieb (1995) "Cultural Studies, the University and the Question of Borders," in Adams and Allen, *Theorizing Culture*, pp. 165–73.

Ben-Amos, Dan and Kenneth S. Goldstein (eds) (1975) *Folklore: Performance and Communication*, The Hague: Mouton.

Benamou, Michel and Charles Caramello (1977) *Performance in Postmodern Culture*, Milwaukee, Wis.: Center for Twentieth Century Studies.

Benveniste, Emile (1971) "Analytical Philosophy and Language," in *Problems of General Linguistics*, vol. 1, trans. M.E. Meeks, Coral Gables, Fla.: University of Miami Press.

Berger, P.L. and T. Luckman (1967) *The Social Construction of Reality*, Garden City, NY: Doubleday.

Berne, Eric (1961) *Transactional Analysis in Psychotherapy*, New York: Grove Press.

—— (1964) *Games People Play*, New York: Grove Press.

—— (1967) "Notes on Games and Theatre," *Tulane Drama Review*, vol. 11(4), pp. 89–91.

Bhabha, Homi (1984) "Of Mimicry and Man: The Ambivalence of Colonial Discourse," *October*, vol. 28, pp. 125–33.

—— (1994) *The Location of Culture*, London: Routledge.

Bharucha, Rustom (1993) *Theatre and the World: Performance and the Politics of Culture*, London: Routledge.

Bigley, James D. (1988) "Living History and Battle Reenactment," *History News*, vol. 42, p. 16.

Birringer, Johannes (1993) *Theatre, Theory, Postmodernism*, Bloomington, Ind.: Indiana University Press.

—— (1998) *Media and Performance: Along the Border*, Baltimore, Md.: Johns Hopkins University Press.

—— (1999) "Contemporary Technology/Performance," *Theatre Journal*, vol.51(4), pp.361–81.

Blau, Herbert (1982) *Blooded Thought: Occasions of Theatre*, New York: Performing Arts Journal Publications.

—— (1983) "Universals of Performance: Or, Amortizing Play," *Sub-Stance*, vols 37–8, pp.140–61.

—— (1987) *The Eye of Prey*, Bloomington, Ind.: Indiana University Press.

—— (1990) *The Audience*, Baltimore, Md.: Johns Hopkins University Press.

—— (1992) *To All Appearances: Ideology and Performance*, London: Routledge.

Boal, Augusto (1979) *The Theatre of the Oppressed*, trans. Charles A. and Marie-Odilia McBride, New York: Theatre Communications Group, 1979.

Bouissac, Paul (1981) "Behavior in Context: In What Sense is a Circus Animal Performing?" in Sebeok and Rosenthal, *Clever Hans*, pp.18–25.

Bourdieu, Pierre (1990) *The Logic of Practice*, Stanford, Calif.: Stanford University Press.

—— (1991) *Language and Symbolic Power*, ed. John B. Thompson, trans. Gino Raymond and Matthew Adamson, Cambridge, Mass.: Harvard University Press.

Bowlby, Rachel (1983) "The Feminine Female," *Social Text*, 1983, p. 62.

Bradbrook, M.C. (1962) *The Rise of the Common Player*, Cambridge, Mass.: Harvard University Press.

Braun, Edward (ed.) (1969) *Meyerhold on Theatre*, New York: Hill & Wang.

Brecht, Stefan (1986) *Queer Theatre*, London: Methuen.

Bret, Philip, Sue-Ellen Case and Susan Leigh Foster (eds) (1995) *Cruising the Performative*, Bloomington, Ind.: Indiana University Press.

Breton, André (1974) "First Manifesto," trans. Herbert S. Gershman, in Gershman, *The Surrealist Revolution*.

Brewer, Mária Minich (1985) "Performing Theory," *Theatre Journal*, vol. 37, pp.13–30.

Bristol, Michael D. (1985) *Carnival and Theatre*, New York: Methuen.

Bronson, A. and Peggy Gale (eds) (1979) *Performance by Artists*, Toronto: Art Metropole.

Broude, Norma and Mary D. Garrard (eds) (1996) *The Power of Feminist Art: The American Art Movement of the 1970s, History and Impact*, New York: Harvey N. Abrams.

Buck-Morss, S. (1977) *The Origin of Negative Dialectics: Theodore W. Adorno, Walter Benjamin, and the Frankfurt Institute*, Hassocks, Sussex: Harvester Press.

Burke, Kenneth (1945) *A Grammar of Motives*, Cleveland, OH: Meridian.

—— (1957) *The Philosophy of Literary Form*, New York: Vintage Books.

Burnham, Linda Frye (1986) "*High Performance*, Performance Art, and Me," *The Drama Review*, vol.30, pp.15–51.

—— (1989) "Performance Art in Southern California: An Overview," pp.390–438 in Loeffler and Tong, *Performance Anthology*.

Burnham, Linda Frye and Steven Durland (eds) (1998) *The Citizen Artist: An Anthology from High Performance Magazine 1978–1998*, New York: Critical Press.

Butler, Judith (1988) "Performative Acts and Gender Constitution: An Essay in Phenomenology and Feminist Theory," *Theatre Journal*, vol.40, pp.519–31.

—— (1990) *Gender Trouble*, London: Routledge.

—— (1990) " The Force of Fantasy: Feminism, Mapplethorpe, and Discursive Excess," *Differences*, vol.2, p.121.

—— (1993) *Bodies that Matter*, New York: Routledge.

—— (1997) *The Psychic Life of Power: Theories in Subjection*, Stanford, Calif.: Stanford University.

—— (1997) *Excitable Speech*, London: Routledge.

Cage, John (1970) "The Future of Music: Credo," in Richard Kostelanetz, *John Cage*, p. 54.

Caillois, Roger (1954) *Man, Play, and Games*, trans. Meyer Barash, New York: Free Press.

Camfield, William A. (1979) *Francis Picaba: His Life and Times*, Princeton, NJ: Princeton University Press.

Campbell, Patrick (ed.) (1996) *Analysing Performance*, Manchester, Manchester University Press.

—— (ed.) (2000) *The Body in Performance*. Singapore: Harwood Academic Publishers.

Campbell, Patrick and Adrain Kear (2001) *Psychoanalysis and Performance*. London: Routledge.

Carlson, Lance (1990) "Performance Art as Political Activism," *Artweek*, vol. 22, pp. 23–4.

Carlson, Marvin (1994) "Invisible Presences: Performance Intertextuality," *Theatre Research International*, vol. 19, pp. 111–17.

—— (1996) *Performance: A Critical Introduction*, London: Routledge.

Carr, C. (1986) "Unspeakable Practices, Unnatural Acts: The Taboo Art of Karen Finley," *The Village Voice*, 24 Jun., 17 ff.

—— (1994) *On Edge: Performance at the End of the Twentieth Century*, Middletown, Conn.: Wesleyan University Press.

Caruth, Cathy (ed.) (1994) *Trauma: Explorations in Memory*, Baltimore, Md.: Johns Hopkins.

—— (1995) "Traumatic Awakenings," in Parker and Sedgwick (eds) *Performativity and Performance*, pp. 89–107.

Case, Sue-Ellen (1988) *Feminism and Theatre*, New York: Methuen.

—— (1989) "Toward a Butch-Femme Aesthetic," in Hart, *Making a Spectacle*, pp. 282–9.

—— (ed.) (1990) *Performing Feminisms: Feminist Critical Theory and Theatre*, Baltimore, Md.: Johns Hopkins University Press.

Case, Sue-Ellen and Janelle Reinelt (eds) (1991) *The Performance of Power*, Iowa City, Ia.: University of Iowa Press.

Case, Sue-Ellen and Jeanie K. Forte (1985) "From Formalism to Feminism," *Theater*, vol. 16, pp. 62–5.

Cate, Phillip Dennis (1991) "The Cult of the Circus," in Barbara Stern Shapiro (ed.), *Pleasures of Paris: Daumier to Picasso*, Boston, Mass.: Godine, pp. 36–48.

Causey, Matthew (1999) "The Screen Test of the Double: The Uncanny Performer in the Space of Technology," *Theatre Journal*, vol. 51(4), pp. 383–94.

Chambers, Ross (1980) "Le masque et le miroir: vers une théorie relationelle du théâtre," *Études littéraires*, vol. 13.

Champagne, Lenora (ed.) (1990) *Out from Under: Texts by Women Performance Artists*, New York: Theatre Communications Group.

Chatman, Seymour (ed.) (1973) *Approaches to Poetics*, New York: Columbia University Press.

Chaudhuri, Una (2001) "Introduction: Instant Rachel," in Rachel Rosenthal, *Rachel's Brain and Other Storms*, London: Continuum.

Chavoya, C. Ondine (2001) "Orphans of Modernism: The Performance Art of Asco," in Fusco, *Corpus Delecti*, pp. 240–64.

Cheng, Meileng (2002) *In Other Los Angeleses: Multicentric Performance Art*, Berkeley, Calif.: University of California.

Chesebro, James W. (1989) "Text, Narration, and Media," *Text and Performance Quarterly*, vol. 9, pp. 2–4.

Chomsky, Noam (1965) *Aspects of the Theory of Syntax*, Cambridge, Mass.: MIT Press.

Christian, Barbara (1988) "The Race for Theory," *Feminist Studies*, vol. 14, pp. 67–79.

Cixous, Hélène (n.d.) "Le Rire de la Méduse," *L'Arc*, vol. 61, pp. 45–7.

Cixous, Hélène and Catherine Clément (1986) *The Newly Born Woman*, trans. Betsy Wing, Minneapolis, Minn.: University of Minnesota.

Clark, Herbert H. and Thomas B. Carlson (1982) "Hearers and Speech Acts," *Language*, vol. 58, pp. 332–73.

Clarke, John S. (1936) *Circus Parade*, London: B.T. Batsford.

Clifford, James (1988) *The Predicament of Culture: Twentieth-Century Ethnography, Literature, and Art*, Cambridge, Mass.: Harvard University Press.

Cohen, Ed (1995) "Posing the Question: Wilde, Wit, and the Ways of Men," in Diamond, *Writing Performances*.

Conquergood, Dwight (1985) "Performing as a Moral Act: Ethical Dimensions of the Ethnography of Performance," *Literature in Performance*, vol. 5, pp. 1–13.

—— (1991) "Rethinking Ethnography: Towards a Critical Cultural Politics," *Communication Monographs*, vol. 58, pp. 179–94.

—— (1992) "Ethnography, Rhetoric, and Performance," *Quarterly Journal of Speech*, vol. 78, pp. 80–97.

—— (1995) "Of Caravans and Carnivals: Performance Studies in Motion," *The Drama Review*, vol. 39(4), pp. 137–41.

Copeland, Roger (1983) "Postmodern Dance/ Postmodern Architecture/ Postmodernism," *Performing Arts Journal*, vol. 7, pp. 27–43.

Coult, Toby and Baz Kershaw (1983) *Engineers of the Imagination: The Welfare State Handbook*, London: Methuen.

Counsell, Colin (1996) *Signs of Performance: An Introduction to Twentieth Century Theatre*, London: Routledge.

Craig, Sandy (1980) *Dramas and Deconstructions: Alternative Theatre in Britain*, Ambergate: Amber Lane Press.

Croce, Arlene (1995) "Discussing the Undiscussable," *New Yorker*, 2 Jan., pp. 54–60.

Curb, Rosemary K. (1985) "Re/cognition, Re/presentation, Re/creation in Woman-Conscious Drama: The Seer, The Seen, The Scene, The Obscene," *Theatre Journal*, vol. 37, pp. 302–16.

Czekay, Angelika (1993) "Distance and Empathy: Constructing the Spectator of Annie Sprinkle's Post-POST PORN MODERNIST—Still in Search of the Ultimate Sexual Experience," *Journal of Dramatic Theory and Criticism*, vol. 7(2), pp. 177–92.

Danet, Brenda (1997) "Speech, Writing and Performativity: An Evolutionary View of the History of Constitutive Ritual," in Louise Gunnarsson-Britt (ed.), *The Construction of Professional Discourse*, London: Longman.

Davidson, Donald and Gilbert Harman (eds) (1972) *Semantics of Natural Language*, Dordrecht: D. Reidel.

Davis, R.G. (1966) "Guerrilla Theatre," *Tulane Drama Review*, vol. 10, pp. 130–6.

—— (1975) "Politics, Art, and the San Francisco Mime Troupe," *Theatre Quarterly*, vol. 5(18), p. 26.

Davy, Kate (1986) "Constructing the Spectator: Reception, Context, and Address in Lesbian Performance," *Performing Arts Journal*, vol. 10, pp. 43–54.

—— (1992) "Fe/male Impersonation: The Discourse of Camp," in Reinelt and Roach, *Critical Theory*, p. 224.

Deák, Frantisek (1975) "Russian Mass Spectacles," *The Drama Review*, vol. 19, p. 22.

Debord, Guy (1967) *The Society of the Spectacle*, Detroit, Mich.: Black and Red.

de Certeau, Michel (1984) *The Practice of Everyday Life*, trans. Steven F. Rendall, Berkeley, Calif.: University of California Press.

Deetz, James (1981) "The Link from Object to Person to Concept," in Zipporah W. Collins (ed.), *Museums, Adults and the Humanities*, Washington, DC: American Association of Museums, p. 8.

Dekker, Rudolph and Lotte van De Pol (1989) *The Tradition of Female Transvestism in Early Modern Europe*, New York: St Martin's Press.

de Lauretis, Teresa (1986) *Feminist Studies/Critical Studies*, Milwaukee, Wis.: University of Wisconsin Press.

—— (1988) "Sexual Indifference and Lesbian Representation", *Theatre Journal*, vol. 40, pp. 169–71.

Deledalle, Gérard (ed.) (1992) *Signs of Humanity: L'homme et ses signes*, Berlin: Mouton de Gruyter, vol. 2, pp. 1183–91.

Delgado, Maria M. and Caridad Svich (eds) (2002) *Theatre in Crisis? Performance Manifestos for a New Century*, New York: Palgrave.

Dempsey, Corinne Dempsey (2000) "Religion and Representation in Recent Ethnographies," *Religious Studies Review*, vol. 26(1).

Derrida, Jacques (1977) "Signature Event Context," *Glyph*, 1977, vol. 1.

—— (1978) *Writing and Difference*, trans. Alan Bass, Chicago, Ill.: University of Chicago Press.

—— (1982) "The Ends of Man," *Margins of Philosophy*, trans. Alan Bass, Chicago, Ill.: University of Chicago Press.

—— (1988) *Limited Inc.*, Evanston, Ill.: Northwestern University Press.

De Saussare, Ferdinand (1974) *Course in General Linguistics*, trans. Wade Baskin, London: Fontana.

Diamond, Elin (1989) "Mimesis, Mimicry, and the 'True-Real,'" *Modern Drama*, vol. 32, pp. 58–72.

—— (1990) "Refusing the Romanticism of Identity: Narrative Interventions in Churchill, Benmussa, Duras," in Case, *Performing Feminisms*.

——(1990–1) "Realism and Hysteria: Notes Toward a Feminist Mimesis," *Discourse*, vol. 31, pp. 59–92.

—— (1992) "The Violence of "We:' Politicizing Identification," in Reinelt and Roach, *Critical Theory*, pp. 390–8.

—— (ed.) (1995) *Writing Performances*, London: Routledge.

—— (ed.) (1996) *Performance and Cultural Politics*, London: Routledge.

—— (1997) *Unmaking Mimesis*, London: Routledge.

Doane, Mary Ann (1982) "Film and the Masquerade: Theorizing the Female Spectator," *Screen*, vol. 23.

Dolan, Jill (1987) "The Dynamics of Desire: Sexuality and Gender in Pornography and Performance," *Theatre Journal*, vol. 39(2), pp. 156–74.

—— (1988) *The Feminist Spectator as Critic*, Ann Arbor, Mich.: University of Michigan Research Press.

—— (1989) "In Defense of the Discourse: Materialist Feminism, Postmodernism, Poststructuralism . . . and Theory," *The Drama Review*, vol. 33(3), pp. 58–71.

—— (1993) "Geographies of Learning: Theatre Studies, Performance, and the 'Performative,'" *Theatre Journal*, vol. 45(4), pp. 417–42.

Dollimore, Jonathan (1991) *Sexual Dissidence*, Oxford: Oxford University Press.

Dore, John and R.P. McDermott (1982) "Linguistic Indeterminacy and Social Context in Utterance Interpretation," *Language*, vol. 58, pp. 374–98.

Dorson, Richard M. (ed.) (1972) *Folklore and Folklife: An Introduction*, Chicago, Ill.: University of Chicago Press.

Drake, David (1991) "Gay Activist or Beauty Queen?" *Theater Week*, 5 Aug., p. 19.

Durland, Steven (1987) "Witness, the Guerrilla Theater of Greenpeace," *High Performance*, vol. 10, pp. 30–5.

Eco, Umberto (1977) "Semiotics of Theatrical Performance," *The Drama Review*, vol. 21, pp. 107–17.

Edelson, Mary Beth (1978) "Pilgrimage/See for Yourself," *Heresies*, Spring, pp. 96–9.

Edie, James M. (1965) *An Invitation to Phenomenology: Studies in the Philosophy of Experience*, Chicago, Ill.: Quadrangle Books.

Ehrmann, Jacques (ed.) (1968) *Game, Play, Literature*, trans. Cathy and Phil Lewis, Boston, Mass.: Beacon Press.

Elam, Keir (1980) *The Semiotics of Theatre and Drama*, London: Methuen.

Elderfield, John (1985) *Karl Schwitters*, London: Thames & Hudson.

Elwes, Catherine (1985) "Floating Femininity: A Look at Performance Art by Women," in Kent and Moreau, *Women's Images*, pp. 63–94.

Enslin, Elizabeth (1994) "Beyond Writing: Feminist Practice and the Limitations of Ethnography," *Cultural Anthropology*, vol. 9(4), pp. 537–58.

Erickson, Jon (1990) "Appropriation and Transgression in Contemporary American Performance," *Theatre Journal*, vol. 42(2), pp. 225–36.

Etchells, Tim (1999) *Certain Fragments: Contemporary Performance and Forced Entertainment*, London: Routledge.

Evelyn, John (1966) *The Diary of John Evelyn*, ed. William Bray, vol. 1. London: Dent.

Evreinoff, Nikolas (1927) *The Theatre in Life*, trans. Alexander Nazaroff, New York: Brentano's.

Ewing, Katherine Pratt (1997) *Arguing Sainthood*, Durham, NC: Duke University Press.

Export, Valie (1991) Interview by Andrea Juno and V. Vale, in Juno and Vale (eds), *Angry Women*, San Francisco, Calif.: Re/Search Publications, pp. 186–93.

—— (1992) "Persona, Proto-Performance, Politics: A Preface," trans. Jamie Daniel, *Discourse*, vol. 14.

Fabian, Johannes (1990) *Power and Performance*, Madison, Wis.: University of Wisconsin Press.

Falk, Lorne (ed.) (1982) *Agit Prop: Performance in Banff*, Banff: Banff Centre Press.

Felman, Shoshana (1993) *The Literary Speech Act: Don Juan with Austin, or Seduction in Two Languages*, Ithaca, NY: Cornell University Press.

Felshin, Nina (ed.) (2001) *But is it Art? An Introduction to Art Theory*, Oxford: Oxford University Press, 2001

Féral, Josette (1982) "Performance and Theatricality: The Subject Demystified," *Modern Drama*, vol. 25, pp. 170–81.

—— (1992) "What is Left of Performance Art? Autopsy of a Function, Birth of a Genre," *Discourse*, vol. 14, pp. 142–62.

—— (ed.) (2002) *Theatricality*, special issue of *SubStance*, vols 31(2), 31(3).

Fernandez, J. (1986) *Persuasions and Performances: The Play of Tropes in Cultures*, Bloomington, Ind.: Indiana University Press.

Ferris, Lesley (1993) *Crossing the Stage*, London: Routledge.

Fine, Elizabeth (1984) *The Folklore Text: From Performance to Print*, Bloomington, Ind.: Indiana University Press.

Fish, Stanley (1980) *Is There a Text in This Class?*, Cambridge, Mass.: Harvard University Press.

Fischer, Jean (2001) "Witness for the Prosecution: The Writings of Coco Fusco," in Fusco, *The Bodies that Were Not Ours*, pp. 223–30.

Fleck, Stephen H. (1992) "Barthes on Racine: A Different Speech Act Theory, *Seventeenth Century French Studies*, vol. 14, pp. 143–55.

Fluxus (1963) *Fluxus I: An Anthology*, ed. George Maciunas, New York: ReFlux Editions.

Foreman, Richard (1970) "The Life and Times of Sigmund Freud," *Village Voice*, 1 Jan.

—— (1976) *Plays and Manifestos*, ed. Kate Davy, New York: New York University Press.

Forte, Jeanie (1990) "Women's Performance Art: Feminism and Postmodernism," in Case, *Performing Feminisms*, pp. 251–69 .

Foster, Hal (1985) *Recodings: Art, Spectacle, Cultural Politics*, Seattle, Wash.: Bay Press.

Fraden, Rena (2001) *Imagining Medea: Rhodessa Jones and Theater for Incarcerated Women*, Chapel Hill, NC: University of North Carolina Press.

Fraser, Flora (1987) *Emma, Lady Hamilton*, New York: Alfred A. Knopf.

Freedman, Barbara (1991) "Echoes of Lenny Bruce, via Bogosian and Reddin," *New York Times*, 19 Jan., sec. 2, p. 5.

—— (1991) *Staging the Gaze*, Ithaca, NY: Cornell University Press.

Freeland, Cynthia (2001) "Gender, Genius, and Guerrilla Girls," in Felshin, *But is it Art?*, pp. 122–47.

Freud, Sigmund (1923) *The Ego and The Id*, in J. Strachey (trans. and ed.), *The Standard Edition of the Complete Psychological Works of Sigmund Freud*, London: Hogarth Press, vol. 19, pp. 12–66.

—— (1955) *The Interpretation of Dreams*, in J. Strachey (trans. and ed.), *The Standard Edition of the Complete Psychological Works of Sigmund Freud*, London: Hogarth Press, vol. 4.

—— (1959) "An Autobiographical Study," in J. Strachey (trans. and ed.), *The Standard Edition of the Complete Psychological Works of Sigmund Freud*, London: Hogarth Press, vol. 20.

Fried, Michael (1968) "Art and Objecthood," in Battcock, *Minimal Art*.

Frost, Thomas (1875) *The Old Showmen and the London Fairs*, London: Tinsley Brothers.

Fuchs, Elinor (1989) "Staging the Obscene Body," *The Drama Review*, vol. 33(1), pp. 33–58.

Fusco, Coco (1994) "The Other History of Intercultural Performance," *The Drama Review*, vol. 38, pp. 143–67.

—— (1995) *English is Broken Here*, New York: The New Press.

—— (1995) *Let's Get it On: The Politics of Black Performance*, ed. Catherine Ugwu, London, The Institute for Contemporary Arts.

—— (ed.) (2000) *Corpus Delecti: Performance Art of the Americas*, London: Routledge.

—— (2001) *The Bodies that Were Not Ours*, London, Routledge.

Gablik, Suzi (1994) "A Conversation with the Guerrilla Girls," *Art in America*, Jan., pp. 43–7.

Gallie, W.B. (1964) *Philosophy and the Historical Understanding*, New York: Schocken Books.

Gamboa, Harry, Jr (1998) *Urban Exile: Collected Writings*, ed. Chon A. Noriega, Minneapolis, Minn.: University of Minnesota Press.

Garfinkel, Harold (1962) "Common Sense Knowledge of Social Structure: The Documentary Method of Interpretation," in J. Sher (ed.), *Theories of the Mind*, vol. 1, pp. 689–712.

Garner, Stanton B., Jr (1994) *Bodied Spaces: Phenomenology and Performance in Contemporary Drama*, Ithaca, NY: Cornell University Press.

Garvin, Harry R. (ed.) (1980) *Romanticism, Modernism, Postmodernism, Bucknell Review*, special issue, vol. 25.

Gates, Henry Louis, Jr (1995) "Sudden Def," *The New Yorker*, 19 Jun., pp. 34–42.

Gatti, Armand (1982) "Armand Gatti on Time, Place and the Theatrical Event," trans. Nancy Oakes, *Modern Drama*, vol. 25, pp. 70–6.

Gay, John (1974) *Poetry and Prose*, ed. Vinton A. Dearing, Oxford: Oxford University Press.

Geertz, Clifford (1972) "Deep Play: Notes on the Balinese Cockfight," *Daedalus*, vol. 101, pp. 1–37.

—— (1983) *Local Knowledge: Further Essays in Interpretive Anthropology*, Stanford, Calif.: Stanford University Press.

—— (1988) *Works and Lives: The Anthropologist as Author*, Stanford, Calif.: Stanford University Press.

Gentile, John S. (1989) *Cast of One: One-Person Shows from the Chautauqua Platform to the Broadway Stage*, Urbana, Ill.: University of Illinois Press.

George, David (1989) "On Ambiguity: Towards a Post-Modern Performance Theory," *Theatre Research International*, vol. 14.

Gershman, Herbert S. (1974) *The Surrealist Revolution in France*, Ann Arbor, Mich.: The University of Michigan Press.

Gevisser, Mark (1990) "Gay Theater Today," *Theater*, vol. 21, pp. 46–51.

Gilroy, Paul (1997) *The Black Atlantic: Modernity and Double Consciousness*, London: Verso.

Glueck, Grace (1989) "In a Rougish Gallery," *New York Times*, 12 May, sec. C, p. 3.

Goat Island (2002) "Letter to a Young Practitioner," in Maria M. Delgado and Caridad Svich (eds), *Theatre in Crisis? Performance Manifestos for a New Century*, New York: Palgrave, 2002.

Godzich, Wlad (1988) "The Further Possibility of Knowledge," in Michel de Certeau, *Heterologies*, Minneapolis, Minn.: University of Minnesota.

Goethe, Johann (1948) *Italianische Reise. Gedenkausgabe*, vol. 11, Zurich: Artemis.

Goffman, Erving (1955) "On Facework: An Analysis of Ritual Elements in Social Interaction," *Psychiatry*, vol. 18, pp. 213–31.

—— (1959) *The Presentation of Self in Everyday Life*, Garden City, NY: Doubleday.

—— (1963) *Stigma: Notes on the Management of Spoiled Identity*, Englewood Cliffs, NJ: Prentice-Hall.

—— (1974) *Frame Analysis*, Garden City, NY: Doubleday.

Goldberg, RoseLee (1979) *Performance: Life Art 1909 to the Present*, New York: Harry N. Abrams.

—— (1988) *Performance Art: From Futurism to the Present*, New York: Harry N. Abrams.

Goldfried, M.R. and G.C. Davison (1976) *Clinical Behavior Therapy*, New York: Holt, Reinhart & Winston.

Golub, Spencer (1984) *Evreinov: The Theatre of Paradox and Transformation*, Ann Arbor, Mich.: University of Michigan Research Press.

Gómez-Peña, Guillermo (1993) *Warrior for Gringostroika*, St Paul, Minn.: Greywolf Press.

—— (1996) *The New World Border*, San Francisco, Calif.: City Lights.

—— (2000) *Dangerous Border Crossings*, London, Routledge.

Goodall, Jane R. Goodall (2002) *Performance and Evolution in the Age of Darwin*, London: Routledge.

Goodman, Lizbeth (1993) *Contemporary Feminist Theatres*, London: Routledge.

Gould, Timothy (1995) "The Unhappy Performative," in Parker and Sedgwick (eds), *Performativity and Performance*, London: Routledge, pp. 19–44.

Goulish, Matthew (2000) *39 Microlectures in Proximity of Performance*, London: Routledge.

Graf, Günter (1992) "Sprechakt und Dialoganalyse—Methodenansatz zur externen Dramainterpretation," *Werkendes Wort*, vol. 41, pp. 315–38.

Graver, David (1995) "Violent Theatricality: Displayed Enactments of Aggression and Pain," *Theatre Journal*, vol. 47, pp. 43–64.

Greenberg, Clement (1962) "After Abstract Expressionism," *Art International*, vol. 6.

—— (1965) "Recentness of Sculpture," *Arts*, vol. 39, pp. 22–5.

Greenhouse, Linda (2002) "An Intense Attack by Justice Thomas on Cross-Burning." *New York Times*, 12 Dec., p. 1.

Grindal, Bruce T. and William H. Shephard (1987/88) "Redneck Girl: From Performance to Experience," *Journal of the Steward Anthropology Society*, vol. 17, pp. 193–218.

Gropius, Walter (ed.) (1981) *The Theater of the Bauhaus*, trans. Arthur S. Wensinger, Middletown, Conn.: Wesleyan University Press.

Gurvitch, Georges (1956) "Sociologie du théâtre," *Les Lettres nouvelles*, vol. 34–6.

Habermas, Jürgen (1970) "On Systematically Distorted Communication," *Inquiry*, vol. 13, pp. 205–18.

—— (1984, 1987) *The Theory of Communicative Action*, Boston, Mass.: Beacon Press.

Haedicke, Susan C. and Tobin Nellhaus, eds. (2001) *Performing Democracy*, Ann Arbor, Mich.: University of Michigan.

Halstead, Jack (1990) "Peter Handke's *Sprechstücke* and Speech Act Theory," *Text and Communication Quarterly*, vol. 10, pp. 183–93.

Harris, Dale (1995) "The Patron Saint of Suffering," *Wall Street Journal*, 16 Jan.

Harris, William (1994) "Demonized and Struggling with his Demons," *New York Times*, 23 Oct., sec. H, p. 31.

Hart, Lynda (ed.) (1989) *Making a Spectacle: Feminist Essays on Contemporary Women's Theatre*, Ann Arbor, Mich.: University of Michigan Press.

—— (1998) *Between the Body and the Flesh: Performing Sadomasochism*, New York: Columbia.

Hart, Lynda and Peggy Phelan (eds) (1993) *Acting Out: Feminist Performances*, Ann Arbor, Mich.: University of Michigan Press.

Hassan, Ihab (1971) *The Dismemberment of Orpheus: Towards a Postmodern Literature*, Madison, Wis.: University of Wisconsin Press.

Hastrup, Kirsten (1995) *A Passage to Anthropology*, London: Routledge.

Hayum, Andree (1975) "Notes on Performance and the Arts," *Art Journal*, vol. 34, pp. 337–40.

Heathfield, A., F. Templeton and A. Quick (1998) *Shattered Anatomies: Traces of the Body in Performance*, Bristol: Arnolfini Live Publication.

Hill, Leslie and Helen Paris (2001) *Guerrilla Performance and Multimedia*, London: Continuum.

Holden, Stephen (1992) "Two Strangers Meet Through an Actor," New York Times, 3 May, sec. 2, p. 8.

Holledge, Julie, and Joanne Tompkins (2000) Women's Intercultural Performance, London: Routledge.

Holmstöm, Kirsten Gram (1967) Monodrama, Attitudes, Tableaux Vivants, Uppsala: Almqvist & Wiksells.

Horst, Louis and Carroll Russell (1961) Modern Dance Forms, San Francisco, Calif.: Dance Horizons.

Howell, Anthony and Fiona Templeton (1977) Elements of Performance Art, London: Ting Books.

Howell, John (1992) Laurie Anderson, New York: Thunder's Mouth Press.

Huelsenbeck, Richard (1951) En Avant Dada: Eine Geschichte des Dadaismus, trans. in Motherwell, The Dada Painters.

Hughes-Freeland, Felicia (1998) Ritual, Performance, Media, London: Routledge.

Huizinga, Johan (1950) Homo Ludens, New York: Beacon Press.

Huspek, Michael (1991) "Taking Aim on Habermas' Critical Theory," Communication Monographs, vol. 58, pp. 225–33.

Hutcheon, Linda (1988) A Poetics of Postmodernism, London: Routledge.

Hymes, Dell (1964) "Introduction Toward Ethnographies of Communication," American Anthropologist, vol. 66, pp. 1–34.

—— (1974) Foundations in Sociolinguistics: An Ethnographic Approach, Philadelphia, Pa.: University of Pennsylvania Press.

—— (1975) "Breakthrough into Performance," in Ben-Amos and Goldstein, Folklore.

Irigaray, Luce (1985) This Sex Which Is Not One, trans. Catherine Porter with Carolyn Burke, Ithaca, NY: Cornell University Press.

Issacharoff, Michael and Robin F. Jones (1988) Performing Texts, Philadelphia, Pa.: University of Pennsylvania Press.

—— (1989) Discourse as Performance, Stanford, Calif.: Stanford University Press.

Jackson, Earl, Jr (1989) "Kabuki Narratives of Male Homoerotic Desire in Saikuku and Mishima," Theatre Journal, vol. 41(4), pp. 459–77.

Jackson, Michael (1989) Paths Toward a Clearing: Radical Empiricism and Ethnographic Inquiry, Bloomington, Ind.: Indiana University Press.

Jackson, Shannon (1993) "Ethnography and the Audition: Performance as Ideological Critique," Text and Performance Quarterly, vol. 13, pp. 21–43.

Jaggar, Alison (1983) Feminist Politics and Human Nature, Totowa, NJ: Rowan & Allanheld.

Jakovljevic, Branislav (2002) "Shattered Back Wall: Performative Utterance of A Doll's House," Theatre Journal, vol. 54, pp. 431–48.

James, William (1925) The Philosophy of William James, New York: Random House.

Jameson, Fredric (1979) Fables of Aggression, Berkeley, Calif.: University of California Press.

—— (1984) "Foreword," to Lyotard, The Postmodern Condition.

Jansen, William H. (1957) "Classifying Performance in the Study of Verbal Folklore," in Studies in Honor of Distinguished Service Professor Stith Thompson, Bloomington, Ind.: Indiana University Press.

Jelavich, Peter (1985) Munich and Theatrical Modernism, Cambridge, Mass.: Harvard University Press.

Jencks, Charles (1977) The Language of Postmodern Architecture, New York: Rizzoli.

Jenkins, Linda Walsh (1984) "Locating the Language of Gender Experience," Women and Performance Journal, vol. 2, pp. 6–8.

Jones, Amelia (1998) *Body Art: Performing the Subject*, Minneapolis, Minn.: University of Minnesota Press.

Jones, Amelia and Andrew Stephenson (eds) (1999) *Performing the Body: Performing the Text*, London: Routledge.

Juno, Andrea and V. Vale, eds. (1993) *Angry Women*, San Francisco, Calif.: Re/Search Publications.

Kane, Stephanie (1994) *The Phantom Gringo Boat*, Washington, DC: Smithsonian Institution Press.

Kapferer, Bruce (1984) "The Ritual Process and the Problem of Reflexivity in Sinhalese Demon Exorcisms," in MacAloon, *Rite, Drama*, pp. 179–207.

Kaprow, Allan (1966) *Assemblages, Environments, and Happenings*, New York: Harry N. Abrams.

Katz, Jerrold J. (1977) *Propositional Structure and Illocutionary Force*, Hassocks, Sussex: Harvester Press.

Kaye, Nick (1994) *Postmodernism and Performance*, New York: St Martin's Press.

—— (1996) *Art into Theatre: Performance Interviews and Documents*, Amsterdam: Harwood Academic Publishers.

Kelley, Jeff (2001) "The Body Politics of Suzanne Lacy," in Nina Felshin (ed.), *But Is It Art?*

Kent, Sarah and Jacqueline Morreau (eds) (1985) *Women's Images of Men*, London: Writers and Readers Publishing.

Kipper, David A. (1965) *Psychotherapy through Clinical Role Playing*, New York: Brunner/Mazel.

Kirby, Michael (1965) *Happenings. An Illustrated Anthology*, New York: Oxford University Press.

—— (1975) "Post-Modern Dance," *The Drama Review*, vol. 19, pp. 3–4.

—— (1982) "Nonsemiotic Performance," *Modern Drama*, vol. 25, pp. 105–11.

Kirschenblatt-Gimblett, Barbara (1975) "A Parable in Context: A Social Interactional Analysis of Storytelling Performance," in Ben-Amos and Goldstein, *Folklore*, pp. 105–30.

Kisselgoff, Anne (1981) "Not Quite/New York," *New York Times*, 27 Sep.

Knapp, Bettina (1970) "Sounding the Drum: An Interview with Jerome Savary," *Tulane Drama Review*, vol. 15, pp. 92–9.

Kofman, Sarah (1985) *The Enigma of Woman: Woman in Freud's Writings*, trans. Catherine Porter, Ithaca, NY: Cornell University Press.

Kostelanetz, Richard (1968) *The Theater of Mixed Means*, New York: Dial.

—— (1970) *John Cage*, New York: Praeger.

—— (1994) *On Innovative Performance(s): Three Decades of Recollections on Alternative Theater*, Jefferson, NC: McFarland.

Kourilsky, Françoise (1971) *The Bread and Puppet Theatre*, Lausanne: Le Cité, p. 26.

Kristeva, Julia (1967) "Le mot, le dialogue, et le roman," *Critique*, no. 239, pp. 438–65.

—— (1974) *La révolution de la langue poétique*, Paris: Seuil.

—— (1980) *Desire in Language*, ed. Leon Roudiez, trans. T. Gora, A. Jardine, and L. Roudiez, New York: Columbia University Press.

Lacan, Jacques (1981) *Speech and Language in Psychoanalysis*, trans. Anthony Wilden, Baltimore, Md.: Johns Hopkins.

Lahr, John (1991) "Playing Possum," *The New Yorker*, 1 Jul., pp. 38–66.

Laurie, Joe, Jr (n.d.) *Vaudeville*, New York.

Lavie, Smadar, Kirin Narayan and Renato Rosaldo (eds) (1993) *Creativity/Anthropology*, Ithaca, NY: Cornell University Press.

Leabhart, Thomas (1989) *Modern and Post-Modern Mime*, New York: St Martin's Press.

—— (ed.) (1991) *California Performance*, vol. 2, *Los Angeles Area, 1991/1992*, Claremont, Calif.: Pomona College, Mime Journal.

Lechte, John (1990) *Julia Kristeva*, London: Routledge.

Leech, Geoffey N. (1983) *Principles of Pragmatics*, London: Longmans.

Léger, Fernand (1924) "Vive Relâche," *Paris-Midi*, 17 Dec.

Levinson, Stephen C. (1983) *Pragmatics*, Cambridge: Cambridge University Press.

Lewin, Kurt (1936) *The Principles of Topological Psychology*, New York: McGraw-Hill.

Lifton, Robert Jay (1993) *The Protean Self*, New York: Basic Books.

Lindzey, G. and E. Aronson (eds) (1968) *The Handbook of Social Psychology*, Reading, Mass.: Addison-Wesley.

Liptak, Adam (2002) "Symbols and Free Speech," *New York Times*, 15 Dec., p. 5.

Loeffler, Carl E. and Darlene Tong (eds) (1989) *Performance Anthology*, San Francisco, Calif.: Last Gasp Press.

Long, Beverly Whitaker (1980) "Editorial Statement," *Literature in Performance*, vol. 1, pp. i–v.

Lorde, Audre (1984) *Sister/Outsider: Essays and Speeches*, Freedom, Calif.: Cross Press.

Lyotard, Jean-François (1973) *Les dispostifis pulsionnels*, Paris: Union generale d'editions.

—— (1984) *The Postmodern Condition: A Report on Knowledge*, Minneapolis, Minn.: University of Minnesota Press.

—— (1984) "Notes on the Critical Function of the Work of Art," trans. Susan Hanson, in *Driftworks*, New York: Semiotext(e).

MacAloon, John J. (ed.) (1984) *Rite, Drama, Festival, Spectacle: Rehearsals Toward a Theory of Cultural Performance*, Philadelphia, Pa.: Institute for the Study of Human Issues.

MacColl, Evan (1973) "Grass Roots of Theatre Workshop," *Theatre Quarterly*, vol. 3, pp. 58–68.

MacDonald, Erik (1993) *Theater at the Margins: Text and the Post-Structured Stage*, Ann Arbor, Mich.: University of Michigan Press.

Mannheim, Karl (1936) *Ideology and Utopia*, New York: Harcourt, Brace.

Manning, Susan (1988) "Modernist Dogma and Post-Modern Rhetoric," *The Drama Review*, vol. 32, pp. 32–9.

Marinetti, F.T. (1991) *Let's Murder the Moonshine: Selected Writings*, ed. R.W. Flint, trans. R.W. Flint and A.A. Coppotelli: Los Angeles, Calif.: Sun and Moon.

Marranca, Bonnie (1977) *The Theatre of Images*, New York: Drama Book Specialists.

Martin, Douglas (2002) "Old-Time Vaudeville Looks Young Again," *New York Times*, 24 Nov., Arts, pp. 5, 7.

Martin, Randy (1990) *Performance as Political Act: The Embodied Self*, New York: Bergin & Garvey.

Mason, Bim (1992) *Street Theatre and Other Outdoor Performance*, London: Routledge.

McCall, M.M. and Howard Becker (1990) "Performance Science," *Social Problems*, vol. 37, pp. 117–32.

McKenzie, Jon (2001) *Perform or Else: From Discipline to Performance*, London: Routledge.

Mehta, Xerxes (1984) "Some Versions of Performance Art," *Theatre Journal*, vol. 36, pp. 164–98.

Menendez, Aldo Damian (2000) "Art Attack: The Work of ARTECALLE," trans. Coco Fusco, in Fusco (ed.), *Corpus Delecti*, pp. 275–80.

Mifflin, Margot (1992) "Performance Art: What Is It and Where Is It Going?" *Art News*, vol. 91(4), pp. 84–9.

Miller, Tim (1991) "Tim Miller" in Thomas Leabhart (ed.), *California Performance*, Claremont, Calif.: Pomona College, Mime Journal, vol. 2, pp. 122–7.

—— (2002) *Body Blows*, Madison, Wis: University of Wisconsin Press.

Moen, Marcia K. (1991) "Peirce's Pragmatism as a Resource for Feminism," *Transactions of the Charles S. Peirce Society*, Amherst, Mass.: University of Massachusetts Press.

Moholy-Nagy, Lazlo (1961) "Theater, Circus, Variety," in Gropius, *The Theater of the Bauhaus*.

Montano, Linda (1978) "Mitchell's Death," *High Performance*, vol. 1, p. 35

—— (1981) *Art in Everyday Life*, Los Angeles, Calif.: Astro Artz.

Moreno, J.L. (1946) *Psychodrama*, vol. 1, New York: Beacon Press.

Morgan, Robin (1977) *Going Too Far*, New York: Random House.

Morley, Henry (1880) *Memoires of Bartholomew Fair*, London: Chatto & Windus.

Morris, Charles W. (1938) "Foundations of the Theory of Signs," in *The International Encyclopedia of Unified Science*, vol. 1(2), Chicago, Ill.: University of Chicago Press.

Motherwell, Robert (1951) *The Dada Painters and Poets*, Wittenborn, NY: Schultz.

Mufson, Daniel (ed.) (1999) *Reza Abdoh*, Baltimore, Md.: Johns Hopkins.

Munro, Eleanor (1979) *Originals: American Women Artists*, New York: Simon.

Nemser, Cindy (1971) "Subject-Object: Body Art," *Arts Magazine*, vol. 46, pp. 38–42.

Newton, Esther (1972) *Mother Camp: Female Impersonators in America*, Chicago, Ill.: University of Chicago Press.

Nietzsche, Friedrich (1984) *Human, All Too Human*, trans. Marion Faber, Lincoln, Nebr.: University of Nebraska Press.

Nix, Marilyn (1972) "Eleanor Antin's Traditional Art," *Artweek*, vol. 3, p. 3.

O'Gorman, Kathleen (1991) "The Performativity of the Utterance in *Deirdre* and *The Player Queen*," in Orr, *Yeats*, pp. 90–104.

Ohmann, Richard (1971) "Speech Acts and the Definition of Literature," *Philosophy and Rhetoric*, vol. 4, pp. 10–15.

Orgel, Stephan (1989) "Nobody's Perfect," *South Atlantic Quarterly*, vol. 88, pp. 7–29.

Orr, Leonard (ed.) (1991) *Yeats and Postmodernism*, Syracuse, NY: Syracuse University Press.

Paget, Marianne (1990) "Performing the Text," *Journal of Contemporary Ethnography*, vol. 19, pp. 136–55.

Pandolfo, Stefania (1997) *Impass of the Angels*, Chicago, Ill.: University of Chicago Press.

Pareles, Jon (2002) "A New Platform for New Poets," *New York Times*, 10 Nov., sec. 2, pp. 1, 25.

Park, Robert Ezra (1950) *Race and Culture*, Glencoe, Ill.: Free Press.

Parker, Andrew and Eve Kosovsky Sedgwick (eds) (1995) *Performativity and Performance*, London: Routledge.

Parry, Benita (1994) "Signs of Our Times: Discussions of Homi Bhabha's *The Location of Culture*, in *Third Text*, vols 28/29, pp. 5–24.

Parsons, Talcott (1937) *The Structure of Social Action*, New York: McGraw-Hill.

Pavis, Patrice (1992) *Theatre at the Crossroads of Culture*, trans. Loren Kruger, London: Routledge.

Pelligrini, Ann (1997) *Performance Anxieties*, London: Routledge.

Petrey, Sandy (1990) *Speech Acts and Literary Theory*, London: Routledge.

Phelan, Peggy (1991) "Money Talks, Again," *The Drama Review*, vol. 35, pp. 131–42.

—— (1993) *Unmarked*, London: Routledge.

—— (1997) *Mourning Sex*, London: Routledge.

—— (1999) "Performing Questions, Producing Witnesses," Foreword to Tim Etchells, *Certain Fragments*, pp. 9–14.

Phelan, Peggy and Jill Lane (eds) (1998) *The Ends of Performance*. New York: New York University Press.

Phillips, Gerald and Julia Woods (eds) (1990) *Speech Communication: Essays to Commemorate the Seventy-fifth Anniversary of the Speech Communications Association*. Carbondale, Ill.: Southern Illinois University Press.

Pontbriand, Chantal (1982) "The Eye Finds No Fixed Point on Which to Rest..." trans. C.R. Parsons, *Modern Drama*, vol. 25, pp. 154–62.

Porter, Joseph A. (1979) *The Drama of Speech Acts: Shakespeare's Lancastrian Tetrology*, Berkeley, Calif.: University of California Press.

Pratt, Mary Louise (1977) *Toward a Speech-Act Theory of Literary Discourse*, Bloomington, Ind.: Indiana University Press.

Prevots, N. (1990) *American Pageantry*, Ann Arbor, Mich.: University of Michigan Press.

Pritchard, Diane Spencer (1991) "Fort Ross: From Russia With Love," in Anderson, *A Living History Reader*, p. 53.

Proceedings of the United States Supreme Count (1998), no. 97–371, "National Endowment for the Arts et al. V. Karen Finley et al.," 25 Jun.

Quinn, Michael (1990) "Celebrity and the Semiotics of Acting," *New Theatre Quarterly*, vol. 4, pp. 154–61.

Rainer, Yvonne (1972) "The Performer as a Persona," *Avalanche*, Summer, pp. 50–2.

—— (1989) *The Films of Yvonne Rainer*, Bloomington, Ind.: Indiana University Press.

Rapaport, Herman (1986) " 'Can You Say Hello?' Laurie Anderson's *United States*," *Theatre Journal*, vol. 38, pp. 339–54.

Read, Alan (1993) *Theatre and Everyday Life: An Ethics of Performance*, London: Routledge.

—— (2001) "The Placebo of Performance," in Patrick Campbell and Adrian Kear (eds), *Psychoanalysis and Performance*, London: Routledge, pp. 147–66.

Readings, Bill (1991) *Introducing Lyotard: Art and Politics*, London: Routledge.

Reinelt, Janelle and Joseph Roach (eds) *Critical Theory and Performance*, Ann Arbor, Mich.: University of Michigan Press.

Rich, Frank (1985) "The Regard of Flight," *New York Times*, 10 May.

—— (1992) "Diversities of America in One-Person Shows," *New York Times*, 15 May, sec. C, p. 1.

Richter, Hans (n.d.) *Dada: Art and Anti-Art*, New York.

Rivers, Elias (1983) *Quixotic Scriptures: Essays on the Textuality of Spanish Literature*, Bloomington, Ind.: Indiana University Press.

—— (1986) *Things Done with Words: Speech Acts in Hispanic Drama*, Newark, NJ: Juan de la Cuesta.

Riviere, Joan (1929) "Womanliness as a Masquerade," *International Journal of Psycho-Analysis*, vol. 10, pp. 303–13.

Roach, Joseph (1996) *Cities of the Dead*. New York: Columbia University.

Román, David (1992) "Performing All Our Lives: AIDS, Performance, Community," in Reinelt and Roach, *Critical Theory*, pp. 208–22.

—— (1998) *Acts of Intervention: Performance, Gay Culture, and AIDS*, Bloomington, Ind.: Indiana University Press.

Rosaldo, Renato (1989) *Culture and Truth: The Remaking of Social Analysis*, Boston, Mass.: Beacon Press.

Rose, Barbara (1993) "Is It Art? Orlan and the Transgressive Act, " *Art in America*, Feb., pp. 82–7.

Rosenthal, Rachel (2001) *Rachel's Brain and Other Storms*, London: Continuum.

Rosler, Martha (1977) "The Private and the Public: Feminist Art in California," *Artforum*, vol. 16, pp. 66–77.

Roth, Moira (1980) "Vision and Re-visions: A Conversation with Suzanne Lacy," *Artforum*, vol. 19(3), pp. 39–45.

—— (1983) *The Amazing Decade*, Los Angeles, Calif.: Astro Artz.

—— (1989) "Autobiography, Theater, Mysticism and Politics: Women's Performance Art in Southern California," in Loeffler and Tong, *Performance Anthology*, p. 466.

Rozik, Eli (1989) "Speech Acts and the Theory of Theatrical Communication," *Kodikas/Code*, vol. 12.

—— (1992) "Plot Analysis and Speech Act Theory" in Deledalle, *Signs of Humanity*, pp. 1183–91.

—— (1992) "Theatrical Conventions: A Semiotic Approach," *Semiotica*, vol. 89, p. 12.

—— (1993) "Categorization of Speech Acts in Play and Performance Analysis," *Journal of Dramatic Theory and Criticism*, vol. 8, pp. 117–32.

Rubinflen, Leo (1978) "Through Western Eyes," *Art in America*, vol. 66, pp. 75–83.

Rudnitsky, Konstantin (1988) *Russian and Soviet Theater 1905–1932*, trans. Roxane Permar, New York: Harry N. Abrams.

Rush, Michael (1999) *New Media in Late 20th-Century Art*, New York: Thames & Hudson.

Russo, Mary (1986) "Female Grotesques: Carnival and Theory," in de Lauretis, *Feminist Studies*, pp. 213–29.

Sahlins, Marshall (1985) *Islands of History*, Chicago, Ill.: University of Chicago Press.

Saivetz, Deborah (1997) "Releasing the 'Profound' Physicality of Performance," *New Theatre Quarterly*, vol. 13(52), pp. 329–38.

Sandford, M. (1995) *Happenings and Other Acts*, London: Routledge.

Santayana, George (1922) *Soliloquies in England and Later Soliloquies*, New York: Charles Scribner's Sons.

Sarbin, T. and V. Allen (1968) "Role Theory," in Lindzey and Aronson, *The Handbook of Social Psychology*, pp. 488–567.

Sartre, Jean-Paul (1956) *Being and Nothingness*, trans. Hazel E. Barnes, New York: Philosophical Library.

Savona, Jeanette Laillou (1984) "French Feminism and Theatre: An Introduction," *Modern Drama*, vol. 27, pp. 540–3.

Sawyer, Robert Keith (ed.) (1997) *Creativity in Performance*, Greenwich, NY: Ablex.

Sayre, Henry M. (1983) "The Object of Performance: Aesthetics in the Seventies," *The Georgia Review*, vol. 37.

Scarry, Elaine (1995) *The Body in Pain: The Making and Unmaking of the World*, New York, Oxford University Press.

Schechner, Richard (1965) *Rites and Symbols of Initiation*, New York: Harper.

—— (1966) "Approaches to Theory/Criticism," *Tulane Drama Review*, vol. 10, pp. 20–53.

—— (1970) "Guerrilla Theatre: May 1970," *Tulane Drama Review*, vol. 14, pp. 163–8.

—— (1973) "Performance and the Social Sciences," *The Drama Review*, vol. 17, pp. 5–36.

—— (1977) *Essays on Performance Theory 1970–76*, New York: Drama Book Specialists.

—— (1983) *The End of Humanism: Writings on Performance*, New York, PAJ Publications.

—— (1985) *Between Theater and Anthropology*, Philadelphia, Pa.: University of Pennsylvania Press.

Schechner, Richard and Willa Appel (eds) (1990) *By Means of Performance*, Cambridge, Mass.: Cambridge University Press.

Schmitt, Natalie Crohn (1990) *Actors and Onlookers: Theater and Twentieth Century Scientific Views of Nature*, Evanston, Ill.: Northwestern University Press.

Schneemann, Carolee (1979) *More than Meat Joy*, New Paltz, NY: Domentext.

Schneider, Monique (1981) "The Promise of Truth—The Promise of Love," *Diacritics*, vol. 11.

Schneider, Rebecca (1993) "See the Big Show: Spiderwoman Theater Doubling Back," in Hart and Phelan, *Acting Out*, pp. 227–56.

—— (1997) *The Explicit Body in Performance*. London: Routledge.

Schutz, Alfred (1964) *Collected Papers*, vol. 2, The Hague: Martinus Nijhoff.

Searle, John R. (1969) *Speech Acts: An Essay in the Philosophy of Language*, Cambridge: Cambridge University Press.

—— (1977) "Reiterating the Differences: A Reply to Derrida," *Glyph*, vol. 1.

—— (1983) *On Deconstruction* (review), *New York Review of Books*, 27 Oct., pp. 74–9.

Sebeok, Thomas and Robert Rosenthal (eds) (1981) *The Clever Hans Phenomenon: Communication with Horses, Whales, Apes, and People*, New York: New York Academy of Sciences.

Senelick, Laurence (1989) *Cabaret Performance 1890–1920*, New York: Performing Arts Journal Publications.

—— (1993) "Boys and Girls Together," in Ferris, *Crossing the Stage*, pp. 80–95.

—— (2000) *The Changing Room*, London: Routledge.

Sharp, Willowby (1970) "Body Works: A Pre-Critical, Non-Definitive Survey of Very Recent Works Using the Human Body or Parts Thereof," *Avalanche*, vol. 1, pp. 14–17.

Sharp, Willowby and Liza Bear (1973) "Chris Burden: The Church of Human Energy," *Avalanche*, vol. 8, pp. 54–61.

Sher, J. (ed.) (1962) *Theories of the Mind*, New York: Free Press.

Shyer, Laurence (1989) *Robert Wilson and His Collaborators*, New York: Theatre Communications Group.

Singer, Milton (ed.) (1959) *Traditional India: Structure and Change*, Philadelphia, Pa.: American Folklore Society.

Small, M. (1983) "Laurie Anderson's Whizzbang Techno-Vaudeville Mirrors Life in these United States," *People Weekly*, vol. 19, p. 107.

Smith, Barbara T. (1978) "Ordinary Life," *High Performance*, vol. 1, pp. 45–7.

—— (1978) "The Vigil," *High Performance*, 1978, vol. 1, p. 49.

Solomon, Alisa (1993) "It's Never Too Late to Switch," in Ferris, *Crossing the Stage*, pp. 144–54.

—— (1997) *Redressing the Canon*, London, Routledge.

Sonneman, Eve (1980) "Situation Esthetics: Impermanent Art and the Seventies Audience," *Artforum*, vol. 18, pp. 22–9.

Sontag, Susan (1966) *Against Interpretation*, New York: Farrar, Straus & Girous.

Spackman, Helen (2000) "Minding the Matter of Representation: Staging the Body (Politic)" in Patrick Campbell (ed.), *The Body in Performance*, Singapore: Harwood Academic Publishers, pp. 5–22.

Spackman, Helen and Patrick Campbell (1998) "Re-presenting the Body in Performance: Without Anaesthetic: The Terrible Beauty of Franko B," *The Drama Review*, vol. 42(4), pp. 56–74.

Stalnaker, R.C. (1972) "Pragmatics," in Davidson and Harman (eds), *Semantics of Natural Language*.

States, Bert O. (1985) *Great Reckonings in Little Rooms: On the Phenomenology of Theater*, Berkeley, Calif.: University of California Press.

Stern, Carol Simpson and Bruce Henderson (1993) *Performance: Texts and Contexts*, White Plains, NY: Longmans.

Strachey, J. (ed.) (1953–74) *The Standard Edition of the Complete Works of Sigmund Freud*, London: Hogarth Press.

Strine, Mary S., Beverly Whitaker Long and Mary Frances Hopkins (1990) "Research in Interpretation and Performance Studies: Trends, Issues, Priorities," in Phillips and Woods, *Speech Communication*, pp. 181–93.

Strutt, Joseph (1845) *The Sports and Pastimes of the People of England*, London: Thomas Tegg.

Tamblyn, Christine (1990) "Hybridized Art," *Artweek*, vol. 21, pp. 18–19.

Taussig, Michael (1992) *The Nervous System*, New York: Routledge.

—— (1997) *The Magic of the State*, New York: Routledge.

Taylor, Diane (2001) "Staging Social Memory: Yuyachkani," in Campbell and Kear (eds) *Psychoanalysis and Performance*, pp. 218–36.

Taylor, Diane and Juan Villegas Morales (eds) (1994) *Negotiating Performance: Gender, Sexuality and Theatricality in Latin/o America*, Durham, NC: Duke University.

Toll, Robert C. (1976) *On With the Show! The First Century of Show Business in America*, New York: Oxford University Press.

Traylor, Marcia (1976) "Catalog: Autobiographical Fantasies," *Laica Journal*, vol. 10.

Trinh, Thi Minh-Ha (1989) *Women, Native, Other: Writing Postcoloniality and Feminism*, Bloomington, Ind.: Indiana University Press.

—— (1991) *When the Moon Waxes Red: Representation, Gender and Cultural Politics*, London: Routledge.

Trippi, Laura (1994) "Visiting Hours," New York: Program of the New Museum.

Turnbull, Colin (1990) "Liminality: A Synthesis of Subjective and Objective Experience," in Schechner and Appel, *By Means of Performance*, pp. 50–81.

Turner, Victor (1957) *Schism and Continuity*, Manchester: Manchester University Press.

—— (1969) *The Ritual Process: Structure and Anti-Structure*, Chicago, Ill.: Aldine Publishing Co.

—— (1974) *Dramas, Fields, and Metaphors*, Ithaca, NY: Cornell University Press.

—— (1982) *From Ritual to Theatre*, New York: Performing Arts Journal Publications.

—— (1984) "Liminality and the Performative Genres," in MacAloon, *Rite, Drama*, pp. 19–41.

Turner, Victor and Edith Turner (1982) "Performing Ethnography," *The Drama Review*, vol. 26, pp. 33–50.

Tyler, Stephen (1987) *The Unspeakable: Discourse, Dialogue, and Rhetoric in the Postmodern World*, Madison, Wis.: University of Wisconsin Press.

Tzara, Tristan (n.d.) "Zurich Chronicle 1915–1919," in Richter, *Dada*.

van den Heuvel, Michael (1991) *Performing Drama/Dramatizing Performance: Alternative Theater and the Dramatic Text*, Ann Arbor, Mich.: University of Michigan Press.

van Dijk, Teun A. (1977) *Text and Context*, London: Longmans.

van Gennep, Arnold (1908, 1960) *The Rites of Passage*, trans. M.B. Vizedon and G.L. Caffee, Chicago, Ill.: Chicago University Press.

Vater, Regina (1987) "Ecology Art is Alive and Well in Latin America," *High Performance*, vol. 10, pp. 30–5.

Vercoe, Caroline (2001) "Agency and Ambivalence: A Reading of Works by Coco Fusco," in Fusco, *The Bodies that Were Not Ours*, pp. 231–46.

Wagner, Arthur (1967) "Transactional Analysis and Acting," *Tulane Drama Review*, vol. 11(4), pp. 81–8.

Walsh, M. (1983) "Post-Punk Apocalypse," *Time*, vol. 121, p. 68.

Wandor, Michelene (1986) *Carry On, Understudies: Theatre and Sexual Politics*, London: Routledge & Kegan Paul.

Weber, Elisabeth (1990) *Verfolgung und Trauma*, Vienna: Passagen.

Weimann, Robert (1992) "(Post)Modernity and Representation: Issues of Authority, Power, Performativity," *New Literary History*, vol. 23(4), pp. 955–81.

Weinsheimer, Joel C. (1985) *Gadamer's Hermeneutics: A Reading of "Truth and Method,"* New Haven, Conn.: Yale University Press.

Whitmore, Jon (1994) *Directing Postmodern Theater*, Ann Arbor, Mich.: University of Michigan Press.

Whyte, Raewyn (1993) "Robbie McCauley: Speaking History Other-Wise," in Hart and Phelan, *Acting Out*, pp. 277–94.

Wilding, Faith (1996) "The Feminist Art Program at Fesno and Cal Arts, 1970–75," in Broude and Garrard, *The Power of Feminist Art*, pp. 32–47.

Wiles, Timothy (1980) *The Theater Event: Modern Theories of Performance*, Chicago, Ill.: University of Chicago Press.

Wilkerson, Margaret (1991) "Demographics and the Academy," in Case and Reinelt, *The Performance of Power*, pp. 238–41.

Wilshire, Bruce (1982) *Role Playing and Identity*, Bloomington, Ind.: Indiana University Press.

—— (1990) "The Concept of the Paratheatrical," *The Drama Review*, vol. 34, pp. 177–8.

Winnicott, D.W. (1971) *Playing and Reality*, London: Tavistock.

Wittke, Carl (1930) *Tambo and Bones*, Durham, NC: Duke University Press.

Worthen, William (1995) "Disciplines of the Text, Sites of Performance," *The Drama Review*, vol. 39, pp. 13–28.

—— (1998) "Drama, Performativity and Performance," *PMLA*, vol. 113(5), pp. 1093–107.

Yarbro-Bejarano, Yvonne (1993) "Cherrie Moraga's 'Shadow of a Man,'" in Hart and Phelan, *Acting Out*, pp. 85–104.

Young, Robert (1990) "The Ambivalence of Bhabha," in *White Mythologies: Writing, History and the West*, London: Routledge, pp. 141–56.

Zarrilli, Phillip (1992) "For Whom Is the King a King? Issues of Intercultural Production, Perception and Reception in a Kathikali *King Lear*," in Roach and Reinelt, *Critical Theory*.

Zimmer, Elizabeth (1989) "Out of Left Field," *Dance Magazine*, Sep., pp. 52–3.

—— (1995) "Has Perfomance Art Lost Its Edge?" *Ms*, vol. 5(5), pp. 78–83.

Name index

Subject index